Arab Spring
in Egypt

Arab Spring
in Egypt

Revolution and Beyond

Edited by
Bahgat Korany
Rabab El-Mahdi

An AUC Forum for International Affairs Edition
The American University in Cairo Press
Cairo New York

Dar el Kutub No. 11528/11
ISBN 978 977 416 536 8

Dar el Kutub Cataloging-in-Publication Data

Korany, Bahgat
    Arab Spring in Egypt: Revolution and Beyond/ Bahgat Korany and Rabab El-Mahdi/. —Cairo:
The American University in Cairo Press, 2012
        p.   cm.
        ISBN 978 977 416 536 8
        1. Egypt—History   2. Revolutions   I. Title

1 2 3 4 5   16 15 14 13 12

Designed by Jon W. Stoy
Printed in Egypt

To those who lost their lives for the sake of a better life for others

Contents

Acknowledgments

This is the third volume to emerge from the AUC Forum since it launched its collaboration with the American University in Cairo Press. Our thanks go first and foremost to our colleagues from Al-Ahram Center for Political and Strategic Studies, UCLA, and especially the Political Science Department at the American University in Cairo, our home institution. They all took on the challenge set by this project despite their busy schedules and produced chapters in record time. Thanks also to Randi Danforth of the American University in Cairo Press, whose marked enthusiasm from the start of the project spurred us to move quickly. We thank Hossam El-Hamalawy, an AUC graduate and now an internationally recognized blogger, for allowing us to use one of his photographs on the jacket of this book. Karim Hamdy helped in collecting data for the tables in chapters ten and thirteen. Shaima Ragab, the efficient manager of the AUC Forum, has been instrumental in keeping our plans on track and making them fall into place. Miriam William has continued this effort. Our enthusiasm to produce this book would have had little result without the committed collaboration of these colleagues and friends.

Contributors

Holger Albrecht is an assistant professor at the American University in Cairo. He has published numerous articles on authoritarianism and regime change, state–society relations, political opposition, and Islamist movements. His main focus in recent years has been the relationship between authoritarian regimes and political opposition in Egypt and elsewhere in the Middle East and North Africa.

Dina Bishara is a PhD candidate at George Washington University. Her dissertation focuses on the politics of labor organization in Egypt. Her research interests also include authoritarianism, state corporatism, and the formation of class and cross-sectoral identities among workers.

Sheila Carapico is a professor of political science and international studies at the University of Richmond, as well as a visiting professor at the American University in Cairo (AUC). Many years ago she spent a junior year abroad at AUC. Later she was a fellow at the American Research Center in Egypt. More recently she served as Visiting Chairperson at the Political Science Department at AUC during 2010 and the spring semester of 2011. She was fascinated by the Egyptian Revolution and the Tahrir Square protests. Author of *Civil Society in Yemen: The Political Economy of Activism in Modern Arabia* (1998) and numerous articles and book chapters on Yemen, she held a Fulbright fellowship in San'a in 1993–94. A contributing editor to *Middle East Report*, she has written and been interviewed about both the Egyptian and the Yemeni revolutions-in-progress. Her forthcoming book is entitled *Promoting Arab Democratization: International Political Aid in Practice*.

Ibrahim Al-Houdaiby is a political researcher and columnist focusing on Islamic movements, democratization, and the political economy of the Middle East.

Hazem Kandil is the Cambridge University Lecturer of Political Sociology and Fellow of St. Catharine's College. His work examines military-security institutions and revolutionary movements. He has taught at the American University in Cairo and the University of California, Los Angeles, and has published on revolutions, warfare, the sociology of intellectuals, and Islamism.

Bahgat Korany is a professor of international relations and political economy at the American University in Cairo, director of the AUC Forum, and research professor at the University of Montreal. He has been an elected member of Canada's Royal Society since 1994. In addition to about seventy book chapters and articles in specialized periodicals from *Revue Française de Sciences Politiques* to *World Politics*, Korany has published nine books in English or French. He is at present the lead author of the tenth-anniversary volume of the UNDP's Arab Human Development Report. He is the editor of *The Foreign Policies of Arab States* (AUC Press, 2008) and *The Changing Middle East* (AUC Press, 2010).

Ann Lesch is a professor of political science and associate provost for international programs at the American University in Cairo. She has been president of the Middle East Studies Association and the Sudan Studies Association, director of the Palestinian American Research Center, and dean of AUC's School of Humanities and Social Sciences. She is the author of numerous books and articles on Sudanese, Egyptian, and Palestinian politics.

Rabab El-Mahdi is an associate professor of political science at the American University in Cairo and co-editor of *Egypt: The Moment of Change* (2009). She is also the author of a number of publications including, most recently, *Empowered Participation or Political Manipulation? Civil Society and the State in Egypt and Bolivia* (2011), "Orientalizing the Egyptian Revolution" (*Jadaliyya*, April 2011), "Labor Protests in Egypt: Causes and Meanings" (*Review of African Political Economy*, September 2011), and "Women in the Revolution," co-authored with Lila Abu-Lughod (*Feminist Studies*, January 2012).

Javed Maswood specializes in political economy and comparative politics. He is the author of several books on Japanese politics and foreign policy, and on international political economy. He is currently working on a research monograph on globalization and development.

Usha Natarajan (PhD, MA, LLB, BA) is an assistant professor in the Department of Law, American University in Cairo. She is an international lawyer and has worked with UNDP, UNESCO, and the World Bank with law reform initiatives in Asia, including Indonesia.

Dina Shehata is a senior researcher at Al-Ahram Center for Political and Strategic Studies.

Hania Sholkamy is an Egyptian anthropologist. She holds a PhD from the London School of Economics and Political Sciences. She is an associate research professor at the Social Research Center and coordinator of the Pathways to Women's Empowerment Research Consortium in partnership with the Institute of Development Studies at Sussex, U.K.

Nadine Sika earned her PhD degree from Cairo University in comparative politics. She is currently an assistant professor of political science at the American University in Cairo. She has published a book and a number of journal articles on education reform and Middle East politics.

Samer Soliman is an assistant professor of political science at the American University in Cairo. His latest book on Egypt is *The Autumn of Dictatorship*. Soliman is one of the founders of the new Egyptian Social Democratic Party.

Introduction

Bahgat Korany and Rabab El-Mahdi

The term 'Arab Spring,' while controversial, has come to represent the events that have rocked this region since the beginning of 2011. At the time of writing, the Arab Spring has seen the collapse of four heads of the region's authoritarian regimes: Ben Ali's in Tunisia on 17 January, Mubarak's in Egypt on 11 February, Qadhafi's in Libya on 23 August, and Saleh in Yemen. In snowball fashion, contentious politics and protest movements have spread to the rest of the Arab world from Yemen to Syria, Morocco to Bahrain. Three main patterns have emerged so far:

1. Some regimes have fallen, creating the Arab world's first presidents removed from office by popular will; they have even been put on trial.

2. Other regimes, like those in Syria and Yemen, remain in place, but are fighting so fiercely for their survival that they have plunged their countries into bloody and savage civil war. Bahrain was 'saved' from this pattern by the intervention of the Gulf Cooperation Council (GCC)—principally Saudi forces—which changed the domestic balance in favor of the incumbent regime.

3. Finally, there are regimes that may not feel they are fighting for their lives, but do see the writing on the wall. They have tried to pacify their populations by responding at last to longstanding demands: King Abdullah of Jordan and King Mohammed VI of Morocco have pushed through constitutional amendments or created employment opportunities; King Abdullah of rentier state Saudi Arabia, on his return from medical treatment in the United States in April 2011, offered his people $36 billion.

The common denominator underlying these patterns is the broad contentious politics sweeping the region. By 'contentious politics' we mean "episodic, public, collective interaction among makers of claims and their objects when (a) at least one government is a claimant, an object of claims, or a party to the claims and (b) the claims would, if realized, affect the interests of at least one of the claimants" (McAdam, Tarrow, and Tilly 2001, 5).

The current protests, while not explicitly coordinated, are not isolated phenomena like the bread riots that took place in the Maghreb in the 1980s or Egypt in 1977. They have two major consequences. First, whatever the outcome of these efforts to bring about democratic change, the region will never be the same. The mass protests of 2011 are a milestone separating 'before' from 'after.' Second, although they were not predicted, these events were predictable: the cracks were there to see if one looked through the right conceptual lens. During the media frenzy that followed the protests, many of us were asked, as scholars of the modern Middle East, whether we had foreseen these events. We had not, at least not their magnitude or their capacity to bring down the heads of longstanding authoritarian regimes in such a short time. Some analyses had, however, drawn attention to the fault lines and the possibility of an earthquake that would shatter the myth of 'Arab exceptionalism' (see chapter one).

For these and other reasons, the protest movements of 2011 therefore raise crucial questions about the way we see, analyze, and understand the Middle East. They suggest that it is time to reconsider systematically the relevance of our conceptual frameworks, much as students of Eastern Europe and the 'socialist bloc' were obliged to do following the collapse of the Soviet Union in 1991.

The challenge for Middle East scholars is not quite as extreme as that which confronted Kremlinologists when the USSR crumbled and vanished in the space of months. The Arab Middle East is still there, and its states are still (dys)functional. But the events of 2011 compel us to look at politics from below instead of primarily from above. Authoritarian political leadership might be 'persistent' or 'resilient,' and the president/king might be a pharaoh, the Custodian of the Holy Places, Amir al-Mu'minin, or the Great Man of history. But a reductionist focus on the leader and his coterie does little to illuminate the complex web of state–society relations that is an integral aspect of politics in this region.

By zooming in on the events in Egypt's Tahrir Square, the chapters in this book analyze group dynamics and state–society relations through the lens of contentious politics. The analysis is centered on Egypt because of this country's demographic, cultural, and political centrality in the region.

Egypt is not, however, viewed as unique, but as representative of regional trends, or as a comparative case study. For instance, many aspects of the Egyptian protests have been echoed across the region: the slogans, youthful element, and use of social media reflected and inspired protest tactics in other countries from Morocco to Yemen. While Tunisia was the spark to these uprisings, Egypt, because of historical, political, and demographic reasons, turned this spark into a full-fledged fire.

Chapter one, by the book's editors, takes the present moment of turbulence and change as a starting point from which to raise conceptual and empirical questions about our understanding of Egypt and the region. Contentious politics is explored as a conceptual framework through which to study the current regional dynamics. The rest of the book is organized into four parts that focus on different aspects of contentious politics. Part One explores the resilience of authoritarianism—still rampant in the region—with an anatomy of Egypt's fallen regime. Ann Lesch, in chapter two, paints a sweeping portrait of the period from 25 January to the regime's collapse, considering the basic prerequisite questions of 'why' and 'how.' In chapter three, Samer Soliman adopts a political economy focus ('follow the money') to examine how Egypt's fiscal crisis and economic liberalization led to system fragmentation. The singular place occupied by religious discourse both before and after the regime's collapse prompts Nadine Sika to address this issue head-on in chapter four. She analyzes the interaction between state, Church, al-Azhar, and religious groups to show how religious discourse is evolving into new social movements, bypassing official religious institutions. Indeed, both al-Azhar and the Church have been working hard since 25 January to recover lost ground, suddenly aware that they risk being marginalized.

The six chapters in Part Two form the heart of the book, considering Tahrir Square as a microcosm of Egypt to examine group dynamics. Both politically and symbolically, Tahrir Square has become the embodiment of a protest regime in its own right, a sort of street parliament in Egypt and beyond. In chapter five, Dina Bishara looks at labor groups and seeks to answer three main questions: Why and how did workers participate in the 2011 mass contention? What explains the timing of workers' participation? And what impact did workers' participation have on the outcome of the revolution? In chapter six, Dina Shehata turns her attention to the youth movements that are usually perceived as the bulwark of the revolution, giving a detailed overview of their mobilization and a description of their various movements and tracing the fate of these movements since the fall of the regime. Ibrahim El Houdaiby in chapter seven turns to the much-discussed but little-understood Islamist participation in Tahrir Square and beyond. He offers insight into the diversity within these groups, who range from Salafis to the Muslim Brotherhood, and looks at the variables and milestones that will determine how these groups evolve and affect post-revolution Egypt. Although women were very present in Tahrir Square, even camping there overnight in tents, their role is often overlooked in much the same way that women are marginalized in society. In chapter eight, Hania Sholkamy sheds light on women's participation in the revolution. She analyzes the benign agenda of the old regime toward women and traces the emergence, since its collapse, of a nascent factionalism that is dividing women along religious and political lines. She concludes by identifying five key challenges for women's action in the post-revolution period. The section closes with Hazem Kandil's examination of present-day Egypt's central institution—the military—before, during, and after the revolution. Across the Arab world, the military's behavior has largely decided the fate of the regime, either contributing to the regime's immediate collapse, as in Tunisia and Egypt, or propping up its resistance, as in Syria and Libya. Yet despite the singular cohesiveness of the military as an institution, Kandil demonstrates that it has been surprisingly under-analyzed and so gives it some much-deserved attention by comparing the 1952 coup to the 2011 revolution.

The three chapters of Part Three look beyond the Tahrir Square experience in both time and place, exploring the way Egypt's relationships with other states have shaped its internal dynamics. In chapter ten, Sheila Carapico looks closely at the western programs of democracy brokers prior to 25 January. Both while Mubarak was in power and after he fell, the question of 'foreign money' had been used to put pressure on civil society organizations (CSOs). This was true even before the new U.S. ambassador to Egypt confirmed that in the first six months of 2011, $40 million had been donated to Egyptian CSOs to promote democracy. Carapico points to key events to demonstrate that this revolution was "home-grown and organic."

In chapter eleven, Javed Maswood and Usha Natarajan consider the transition in Egypt through comparison with Indonesia. They maintain that democratization in Indonesia has largely been hailed as successful despite being "accompanied by large-scale violence and instability."

Maswood and Natarajan avoid stale comparisons with Iran and Turkey to bring fresh insight through a rare cross-regional analysis. They highlight the central role of the military in both countries, in a thought-provoking echo of Kandil's study in chapter nine.

Part Three concludes with Holger Albrecht's discussion of 'the day after': the post-Mubarak transition. Albrecht reminds us of Samuel Huntington's seminal three global waves of democratization and wonders whether the Arab Spring marks the beginning of a fourth wave. He thinks not, at least in the short term. Indeed, a common expression on the streets of Cairo today is: "Mubarak is gone, but Mubarakism will take much longer to go."

In chapter thirteen, Korany goes farther down the same path with a critical look at the transition literature, drawing particular attention to the challenges of transition. This concluding chapter attempts to pull the threads together and looks at the regional impact of the protest movement in Egypt and across the Arab world. Are we really witnessing a new Middle East? If so, in what specific respects? Can the change really be traced to social media? What are the challenges for Middle East restructuring and the general transition to democracy? Could new social processes like social media lead to a new grassroots pan-Arabism? Could a critical look at the transition literature and the experiences of others, especially from the global South, help to understand the challenges brought by the Arab Spring?

The appendices situate Egypt on the scale of global development, from education and health indicators to poverty, inequality, and corruption. These sociopolitical ills underlie the tensions that triggered protests, inspired mobilization, and finally brought down an aging and ailing regime that was out of touch with its base. Mubarak's speeches during the crisis offered too little too late and were clearly out of touch with the mood on the street. The most popular protest slogans reflected this widening gap between the governing elite 'above' and the street politics 'below.'

It is certainly worth mentioning that all the contributing authors have based their analysis on close contact with—and even participation in—the contentious politics about which they write. They were all in Tahrir Square bearing witness to these events; some even spent the nights in tents on the square. Their methodology is therefore similar to the anthropologist's 'participant observation.' We have all been privileged to be, so to speak, in the front seat watching history being made.

The authors' principal frame of reference is the contentious politics that empirically binds our analyses and even our personal experiences. The basic elements of this framework are outlined in chapter one to bring out the thread running through the rest of the book. While we do not pretend to offer a unified theory of contentious politics in the Middle East, the field data presented and analyzed here are a necessary prerequisite to such a theory. We hope that with this unifying perspective, we have succeeded in creating a coherent volume despite the diversity of authors and analysis.

1

The Protesting Middle East

Bahgat Korany and Rabab El-Mahdi

At the time of writing, the Arab Spring has already brought down four heads of state, in Tunisia, Egypt, Libya, and Yemen. Others, as in Syria and perhaps Bahrain, are fighting for survival. And from Morocco to Jordan, opposition to the government is growing. It appears then that the hallmark of the Arab world in 2011 is the rise of protest movements: a dissension driven from below.[1] What distinguishes the Arab Spring from protest movements elsewhere is the intensity and density of the 2011 protests—a peak in contentious politics, or a phase of heightened conflict, both organized and unorganized, across the social and political system to challenge authorities (Tarrow 1998, 142). The final result of how politics is being reshaped is far from known, but it is definitely undergoing major changes.

It is not only the behavior of political actors, however, that must change in line with the shifting terrain, but also the lens through which politics is viewed (Fish 2011). Analysts must be able to comprehend the current shift and recognize that it may reflect the end of 'Arab exceptionalism' or 'resilient authoritarianism' in the region. A deeper change in thinking is required than the one debated by (traditional) area specialists and (emerging) social science applications, which has already been decided in favor of more sophisticated conceptual and methodological approaches. While a generation of Middle East scholars has advanced the field by borrowing analytical tools from political economy, political sociology, and institutional approaches, a gap remains between our conceptual frameworks and the changing politics on the ground.

The Arab Spring revealed that most of the new scholarly approaches remain deficient in fundamental, and indeed epistemological, ways. The flaws run deeper than those of earlier conceptual and methodological models, going to the very heart of the fundamental assumptions and intellectual mindset used to decode present state–society relations in the region. Put simply, this epistemological deficiency is a firm conviction in the absolute primacy of 'politics from above,' 'formal politics,' and institutions at the expense—and even the exclusion—of 'politics from below,' 'informal politics,' and extra-institutional dynamics.

It should be noted that being concerned with 'politics from above' is not wrong in itself. It can often be justified in this region where top political authority is over-present and domineering. But when interest in the top of the political pyramid pretends to tell the full story while excluding other approaches, it becomes partial in both senses of the word: incomplete and biased. The bias is glaring, and indeed becomes damaging, when formerly excluded and marginalized sectors assume the lead role, as they have done during the Arab Spring. In this context, a 'politics from above' approach becomes misleading because 'real politics' does not emanate from the regime or the work of formal institutions, but from grassroots protest movements. This goes some way to explain why most of us, despite being specialists on the region, were surprised by what happened at the beginning of 2011 (Gausse 2011).

Although the events of the Arab Spring could not be precisely predicted, there were indicators of some forthcoming change if analysts had looked at things from a different perspective (Bayat 2009; El-Mahdi 2009b; Hopkins 2009). The lenses through which we viewed the region acted as blinders; had we looked differently, our attention might have been drawn to the fault lines that undermine the prevalent belief in 'Arab exceptionalism' (Korany 2010, 1–4, 197–203).

Arab exceptionalism stems from the assumption of a static Arab politics, whose authoritarianism is both persistent and resilient. In its most extreme form, à la Bernard Lewis, this authoritarianism is quasi-genetic, arising from some cultural or Islamic foundation (Anderson 1995; Lockman 2005, for a critique of the political-culture and orientalist approach to Arab politics). A less biased political economy approach links authoritarianism to the type of state: in particular, the rentier state and its sources of revenue (Luciani 1995 and 2008; Korany 2008 and 2010). But even then, and despite the focus on state–society relations, the analysis is skewed in favor of the state as the possessor of resources. Similarly, the institutional approach focusing on elections and change within Arab regimes, despite having provided a nuanced analysis on understanding authoritarian dynamics, still missed the crux of changing politics in the Middle East (Brownlee 2007a). The result is too much emphasis on the top of the political system, at the expense of its base: on politics from above to the exclusion of the dynamics of politics from below.

It is not our intention here to go to the other extreme and simply replace the dominant top-down approach to Middle East Studies with an equally facile bottom-up analysis. The objective is rather to bring the two into some balance, but even this requires some adjustment. The 'politics from below' approach is a relative newcomer to the region (Bayat 2009; Clark 1995 for an early attempt; El-Mahdi and Marfleet 2009b; Wiktorowicz 2004). It has been applied much more extensively in Europe and Latin America than in the Middle East. A period of trial and error may be necessary, but a good start would be a synthesis of what is known in the sociological literature on social movements as 'contentious politics' (Snow and Benford 1992; Tarrow 1996a; Tilly, Tilly, and Tilly 1975), with its emphasis on social protest processes.

Protest movements are, in the Middle East as elsewhere, prime manifestations of 'contentious politics,' and it would be wrong to assume that their first appearance in Egypt was in 2011. Their history in the region is outlined in the different chapters of the present volume. The current uprisings can be traced back to the turn of the millennium, specifically the second Palestinian Intifada, which reclaimed the Arab street for politics and mobilization (Bayat 2007; Sadiki 2007; El-Mahdi 2009b).

In Egypt, various forms of mobilization over the past decade have cumulatively paved the way for the revolution/uprising: the protest movements against the wars on Iraq in 2003 and Gaza in 2008; the rise of the pro-democracy movement, with Kefaya and in support of judiciary independence in 2004–2005; the labor protests that began in Mahalla in 2006 and spread throughout Egypt, eventually counting more than 1.7 million demonstrators; and finally, the anti-sectarian protests that peaked after the church bombing in Alexandria in early 2011.

Each of those movements brought 25 January closer by bringing people together to break the fear barrier, politicizing them over the specific issues that they cared most about, reinstating the dynamics of collective resistance and active expression against different forms of abuse (social, political, or economic), and exposing the regime's exploitive policies on multiple fronts. Indeed, it could be said that the 2011 uprising had even deeper roots, since labor protests had been taking place, with various highs and lows, even before 2000 (Beinin and Lockman 1984).[2]

By analyzing the protests from multiple perspectives—thematically in Part One, and exploring different group dynamics in Part Two—this book attempts to illuminate the uprising as a milestone in contemporary Egyptian politics. The objective is to capture and anatomize this key moment of history in the making, rather than presenting our own 'theory' at this early stage of the Arab Spring. As such, and without underestimating the specificities of each state involved, we are using Egypt as a microcosm for understanding the 'silenced' dynamics within the region—that is, the dynamics that had not previously received enough attention and documentation.

Indeed, this kind of detailed analysis from the field could be a prerequisite for developing a theory of contentious politics in the Middle East. Two approaches and bodies of literature offer a good starting point: social movement theory, and the theory of covert/everyday resistance put forward by James Scott and later developed into what Bayat calls 'quiet encroachment.'

From the vast literature that comprises social movement theory, with its distinct North American and European schools (the first focusing on resource mobilization and the political process model, the second on new social movements), three concepts are particularly useful for understanding the current events: 'mobilizing structures' and resource mobilization; the 'Political Opportunity Structure' (POS); and framing.

Mobilizing structures and resource mobilization deal with collective action, the essence of contentious politics. Mancur Olson's pioneering work in this neo-institutionalist approach is grounded in market-based reasoning and the 'free rider' model. The present contentious politics is very different—even directly contrasting—because it emphasizes the pooling of resources—political, financial, and cultural—and the ways in which different structures can be more or less useful in mobilizing resources for the purpose of dissent (Tarrow 1996b).

For instance, during the January 2011 protests it was very clear how activists used their networks and existing relationships, with each other and with the media, to spread their messages. Bloggers used social media and connections with local and international broadcasters and newspapers. Labor activists capitalized on their networks in factories and workplaces and within the labor movement at large. Human rights activists mobilized the support of global civil society. Most importantly, the football fan groups known as 'Ultras' used their existing organizational structures and police-combat tactics as invaluable resources to capture the space for protest in Cairo (Tahrir Square) and to protect other protesters from police brutality.

When on 28 January the Mubarak government authorities cut off cell phone and Internet facilities, many parents had no choice but to go out into the streets to get news about their sons and daughters. As a result, they saw at first hand vivid instances of police brutality. Provoked and shocked by this brutality, they spontaneously pulled together to defend themselves and their children. Food chains were improvised, tents and blankets were brought to Tahrir Square, and doctors established emergency clinics on the spot.

In this way, the severing of communication channels was transformed from a constraint into an opportunity, which brings us to the second conceptual pillar of the contentious politics approach: 'Political Opportunity Structure' (POS). The emphasis here is on the process itself: why people participate in contention and why their numbers increase at a particular time. POS is thus a "consistent—but not necessarily formal, permanent or natural—dimension of the political struggle" (Tarrow 1998, 19–20). The POS model is useful for understanding the evolution of a dispute, as well as its political process, by bringing together the various elements that combine to create the political opportunity for collective dissent. A vital strand of the POS of the 25 January uprising is the fact that 2011 was the year of scheduled presidential elections in which the only likely candidates were the ailing president (Mubarak) and his groomed, ambitious son (Gamal). Another is that the uprising took place not long after the most heavily rigged parliamentary elections Egypt had seen in decades, which seem to have frustrated hopes that change could be wrought through existing institutions.

The POS was strengthened by police brutality and heavy-handedness, which increased the volume of protesters to such an extent that police forces were overpowered and routed. It was bolstered again by the hesitation and division within the political elite, even at the highest levels. The president's position was undermined by the rift that grew between him and his minister of interior, Habib al-Adli. It was further eroded when Mubarak ordered the armed forces into the streets, but they refused to fire on the people. Indeed, photographs taken in the streets of Cairo, Alexandria, and other cities show scenes of camaraderie between the armed forces and the protesters. Fragmentation within the governing elite continued and intensified as leading figures were sacked or jumped ship. The regime seemed to be on the run, and protesters could smell that victory was close. The political opportunity was there.

Thus POS acts like an open door that protesters realize they can pass through—or a door they realize they are strong enough to push open. In this, POS plays a double role: It is a process factor that accounts for the chances of a protest's success. Just as importantly, it addresses the nagging problem of agency versus structure and acts like a bridge between the two to emphasize the impact of the protesters' role in influencing the political results of the struggle. The POS model emphasizes the organic interaction between agency and structure.

Framing is the third important concept for understanding contentious politics. Frames help people to define their interaction in similar terms, to give it 'similar meaning,' and by doing so, to come together. Drawing attention to similarities in this way creates a frame of alignment, ideological or cultural, which offers people "interpretative schemes . . . to make sense of events [in a consensual way, and thus] . . . guide collective action" (Snow and Benford 1992). Framing creates the necessary resonance to transform individual subjectivity into shared inter-subjectivity, and thereby to transform dispersed, disgruntled individuals into an organized protest movement, with shared objectives and even a shared identity. Civil society is thus redefined (more on this in chapter thirteen).

This organic interaction could be concretized in the street through the media, both old and new. Satellite broadcasters such as Al Jazeera and Al Arabiya are now bolstered by Facebook and Twitter. When photographs of massive protests and the camaraderie between armed forces and demonstrators were widely diffused, the media—both old and new— helped to increase the strength of the existing opportunity. While the media fueled the protest, it must be noted that they did not cause it (see chapter thirteen). 'Communication action' is essential to collective action: it helps to create for people far from the physical action—in other cities and villages, and sympathizers abroad—the picture of a common cause, a joint frame of action.

These three concepts taken together create a system, or an interactive whole, with tremendous power to explain how and why the uprising took place. For instance, the rate and effectiveness of public mobilization depend very much on the balance sheet of the costs and benefits, constraints and opportunities—in other words, the POS—and whether these are acted upon collectively rather than as dispersed groups—depending on the degree of framing.

Another body of literature that is beneficial to our analysis is Asef Bayat's approach of 'quiet encroachment' or 'non-movement' (Bayat 2007, 2009). Building on James Scott's pioneering approach of "everyday forms of resistance"—how survival mechanisms of the subaltern and popular classes can constitute elements of resistance to the system of power—Bayat focuses on urban collective movements of resistance: the way that people in large urban communities create pressure on the dominant institutions and hegemonic classes even without structured resistance, simply through their daily lives. In Egypt, the mushrooming shantytowns and slums and the large informal economy were prime examples of Bayat's 'quiet encroachment.' These groups, without being organized, played a clear and decisive role in the January protests. In Suez governorate it was Arbin Square, with its high concentration of popular classes and popular neighborhoods, that bore the brunt of the protests. In Cairo, it was residents of the impoverished 'Umraniya neighborhood who broke the security siege of Tahrir Square on 28 January. It seemed that the 'quiet encroachment' of these sectors for years finally turned into a very loud one.

While both social movement theory and quiet encroachment have their limitations, they promise valuable insight when used in tandem with classical approaches of institutional politics to understand and contextualize the Arab Spring.

Conclusion

We have tried to go beyond the impasse of choosing between agency and structure to emphasize their interaction and codetermination. Structure clearly sets the parameters, but these parameters are not irreversible. Indeed, it is because so many analysts assumed that they *were* irreversible that they believed so strongly in the durability of political authoritarianism.

Although contentious politics seems to be a useful approach for decoding the Arab Spring, it is important to reflect on how it can be adapted to make it more widely applicable to Middle East studies, now and in the future. For despite its wealth, its increasingly proven relevance, and its growing interdisciplinary credentials, the vast literature on contentious politics needs better theoretical integration and more empirical applications in regions like the Middle East.[3] This should facilitate the epistemological shift that Middle East studies needs in order to cope with milestone events such as the Arab Spring.

The problem we face now is not only that many political scientists studying the Middle East could not detect the nascent changes, but that they seem not to be conceiving the unfolding events in their totality. Three key misconceptions result from the persistent overemphasis on 'politics of the elite' that this volume attempts to overcome. The first is that the current mobilization was abrupt and completely unexpected—hence often named the 'Arab Awakening,' which implies a previous state of dormancy. The second is that these uprisings are 'Facebook' revolutions—sometimes even called 'Revolution 2.0'—which implies that social media were the main mobilizing force. The third is that this is a 'youth' revolution, where the term is used to refer specifically to middle-class youth who have used social media for communication.

This volume analyzes recent events from a historical–structural perspective to deconstruct such myths. As has already been noted, the current uprisings have roots in local and regional protests, including the second Palestinian Intifada and Egyptian labor protests. Consequently, the actors and mobilization tools behind the Egyptian Revolution are broader than those to which current accounts draw attention. They include labor protests and strikes, pro-democracy groups, peasant protests, sit-ins, and an erosion of the corporatist social pact that sustained authoritarianism.

By expanding the horizons through which we analyze and understand the Egyptian Revolution, we are trying to reinvigorate the study of politics in connection with the lives of 'ordinary people' and with economic changes. While this approach has been used by many within Middle East Studies (Beinin and Lockman 1984; Beinin 2009b; Bayat 2007, 2009; Ayubi 1995; Mitchell 1991), it is not the usual model used in the study of Middle East politics.

By providing a brief historiography of the revolution as an example of contentious politics, we attempt to draw the attention of other students of the region to the multiplicity of elements that underlie such milestone events. In tandem, the analyses of our different chapters point to the equal weights of history, structure, and agency in deciding the path and consequently the outcome of this turning point. Similarly, it would be a mistake to underestimate the impact of the Egyptian Revolution by seeing it through the reductivist, mainstream lens of 'democratic transition' without considering the history of contention in the country and the uprising's specific societal context. While there are methodological and conceptual justifications for comparing the Egyptian Revolution to its classic precursors and the literature on revolutions (Skocpol 1979; Tilly, Tilly, and Tilly 1975; Tilly 1978), ignoring major differences among these events would be analytically and normatively misleading.

Our study therefore aims to supplement current mainstream Middle East studies with new conceptual frameworks that can serve not only to understand the Arab Spring, but also to change how we study the region. The last great paradigm shift in Middle East studies was Edward Said's groundbreaking *Orientalism*, published more than thirty years ago. An epistemological shift is long overdue and sorely needed.

Notes

1   As a number of the book's chapters show, many protests erupted before 2011, and they were long in the making. For an Egyptian social psychologist looking at the ordeal of his society, see Fadhel 2008. Other 'indigenous' social analyses attracted attention to contention and protests before their mass eruption in 2011. A notable example is one of the contributors to this volume, Dina Shehata, who edited a collection of essays on new protest movements in Egypt (2010). All of these essays are to the point concerning contentious politics and mass protests, but see especially Sameh Fawzi, Manar Shorbagy, Rabab El-Mahdi, and Amr Shobaky. Similarly, thanks to a very insightful editorial board, the American University in Cairo's series Cairo Papers in Social Science has paid special attention to the issue of contentious politics/mass protests/social movements. See for instance, Hopkins 2009.
2   See also Joel Beinin and Hossam El-Hamalawy, "Egyptian Textile Workers Confront the New Economic Order," *Middle East Report Online*, 25 March 2007, http://www.merip.org/mero/mero032507.html
3   For recent contributions in this respect, see Algerian sociologist AbdelNasser Gabi, "al-Harakat al-ihtijajiya fi al-Jazai'r" (Doha: Arab Center for Research and Policy Studies online), http://www.dohainstitute.org/Home/Details/5d045bf3-2df9-46cf-90a0-d92cbb5dd3e4/e62cf0d7-b405-4d61-92d3-5bddcd207e50

2

Concentrated Power Breeds Corruption, Repression, and Resistance

Ann M. Lesch

On 25 January 2011, thousands poured into Tahrir Square, the symbolic heart of Cairo. Many streamed past the iconic statue of Saad Zaghlul (leader of Egypt's 1919 revolution) and followed his outstretched arm across the venerable Qasr al-Nil bridge. Others broke through security barriers as they raced through downtown streets or marched in long lines along the Nile Corniche from the south and north. Chanting and waving placards, they denounced the security forces and the hated minister of interior and called for *'aish* (bread), *karama* (dignity), and *hurriya* (freedom). Simultaneously, thousands crowded into the port city of Alexandria and confronted the heavily armed security forces in gritty working-class Suez City.

The huge outpouring astonished the youthful organizers, whose previous attempts to demonstrate had resulted in a hundred or so people assembling in Tahrir Square—and those few were quickly surrounded and detained by riot police.[1] This time the activists went into the streets to appeal directly for support. For example, thousands responded to those appeals in Bulaq al-Dakrur, a sprawling district in Giza governorate that had suffered intense police repression and heavy unemployment, and joined up with thousands more chanting outside Mustafa Mahmud Mosque in middle-class Mohandiseen before they all headed to Tahrir Square. Thousands of other people marched from districts throughout Cairo and Giza to reach the square.

Once in the square, protesters outnumbered the heavily armed riot police. Even though trucks with powerful water cannons charged into the crowds and police shot tear gas and rubber bullets, demonstrators held their ground, chanting *"Silmiya! Silmiya!"* (Peaceful! Peaceful!). They pushed back against the barricades, seeking to reach the nearby parliament, council of ministers, and Ministry of Interior. A protest seeking limited reforms swiftly transformed into a revolutionary uprising. By evening, people were calling not only to end police brutality and remove the minister of interior, but also for President Hosni Mubarak to leave *(irhal)*.

Anger at Mubarak's rule had built up gradually. An accidental president who came to power after Anwar Sadat's assassination on 6 October 1981, Mubarak initially calmed the public, released political prisoners, and encouraged parliamentary elections. However, as soon as he began his second term in 1987, he refused to reform the constitution, extended the state of emergency, excluded opposition parties from local councils, and tightened the grip of the ruling National Democratic Party (NDP) over parliament. His May Day speech in 1988 threatened, "I am in charge, and I have the authority to adopt measures. . . . I have all the pieces of the puzzle, while you do not" (Lesch 1989, 100).

Concentrated Power

The political system concentrated power in the executive branch (Lesch 2004, 591–93, 601, 606). The candidate for president was selected by the People's Assembly (the lower house of parliament) and ratified by public referendum, where the choice was 'yes' or 'no.' The president served a six-year term, renewable indefinitely. He appointed—and removed—the prime minister and council of ministers, dissolved the bicameral parliament, vetoed bills, and bypassed the legislature by putting issues to vote in referenda. The NDP controlled around three-quarters of the seats in the People's Assembly, except in 1995 and 2010, when the NDP-linked candidates won 94 and 97 percent of the seats, respectively. Moreover, the president appointed all the governors, mayors, and deputy mayors, a third of the members of the Majlis al-Shura (Consultative Assembly), and ten members of the lower house.

Local councils were elected according to a winner-take-all system that guaranteed the NDP's monopoly (Lesch 2004, 599, 606). This monopoly encouraged widespread corruption among local government officials—documented by the Central Auditing Organization—which included embezzling public funds and receiving substantial bribes to ignore infractions of building codes and let villagers build on agricultural lands.[2]

Violence by the security forces

The state of emergency consolidated the absolute power of the president by empowering him—and, by delegation, the prime minister and minister of interior—to restrain the movement of individuals, search persons or places without warrants, tap telephones, monitor and ban publications, forbid meetings, and intern suspects without trial (Lesch 2004, 597–99; International Federation for Human Rights [FIDH] 2001). Gatherings of more than five people were illegal. The state often referred civilians to Emergency State Security courts and draconian military courts, where officers served as judges and there was no judicial appeals process.

Security forces were unleashed in the 1990s against violent Islamist groups that sought to destabilize Egypt by assassinating government officials, targeting police and security officers, harassing Christians, and attacking foreign tourists.[3] Islamist groups renounced violence in 1997 after a bloody attack on tourists near Luxor, but even so, emergency and military courts continued to operate. They prosecuted civilians charged with non-violent infractions, such as politicians' meetings and journalists' criticism of regime figures and government policies. Police increasingly harassed people on the street, demanding bribes from shop owners and minivan drivers and free food from street vendors and restaurants. A vendor who could not pay the bribe risked disappearing into a police station for a few days. Police seized and beat people in order to coerce false confessions or pressure them to become informers. A case reported by Human Rights Watch demonstrated that even public figures were not exempt from torture: Actress Habiba Muhammad Said was tortured until she 'confessed' to killing her Qatari husband in 1999. By the time the actual killers confessed and she was released, she had spent five years in prison.[4]

Police harassed people who came to the police station to get IDs or other routine documents and nabbed those who 'talked back' to them. For example, police entered a café where Ahmed Abdeen Said was sitting, frisked him, took his mobile telephone, and told him he wouldn't have any problems if he left the café. However, when Ahmed asked them to return his mobile, they seized him, took him to Muski police station, beat him with sticks, and subjected him to electric shocks.[5] In other cases, police routinely picked up workers while they stood in the street waiting to be hired and took them to the police station, where they were forced to 'select' the crime with which they would be charged.[6] Amnesty International concluded that torture was "systematic in police stations, prisons and SSI [State Security Investigations] detention centers and, for the most part, committed with impunity. . . . [Security and plainclothes police assault people] openly and in public as if unconcerned about possible consequences."[7] Even the government-appointed National Council on Human Rights, in its first annual report in 2004, expressed deep concern about that year's seventy-four cases of "blatant" torture and the thirty-four persons who had died in police or SSI detention.[8] And a U.S. diplomat cabled in 2009 that Omar Suleiman, director of the General Intelligence Directorate, and Interior Minister Habib al-Adli "keep the domestic beasts at bay, and Mubarak is not one to lose sleep over their tactics."[9]

Gamal Mubarak's neoliberal government

During the 2000s, a new set of politicians led by the president's youthful son, Gamal, assumed leading positions in the government and the NDP. Gamal returned to Cairo in the late 1990s, after a six-year stint in London as an investment banker with the Bank of America.[10] His father appointed him to the NDP general secretariat in February 2000. That June, while commenting on Orbit satellite during the funeral for Syrian president Hafez al-Assad, the outspoken sociologist Saad Eddin Ibrahim opined that the Mubaraks were grooming Gamal to succeed his father, just as Bashar al-Assad was doing in Syria. Ibrahim paid for that remark with months in prison.

But Ibrahim's observation was prescient. At the NDP congress in September 2002, convened under the slogan "A New Style of Thinking," Gamal created the party's Policies Secretariat. He proclaimed, "We need audacious leaders who are able to prepare their country for the future and implement some reforms even when they are unpopular" (Mubarak 2009).

In July 2004 a cabinet reshuffle elevated Ahmed Nazif from minister of communications and information technology to prime minister. Lauded as 'modernizers,' the new ministers claimed that they would reduce the bureaucratic stranglehold and reinvigorate economic growth. They combined obsequiousness, as they knew that they owed their positions to the Mubaraks, with arrogance, as they believed that they could act with impunity, with no accountability to the public (Al Aswany 2011, 13–14). Businessmen and U.S.-trained technocrats controlled the economic portfolios, led by Youssef Boutros Ghali, who moved from the Ministry of Economics to the Ministry of Finance. An economic analyst with the International Monetary Fund (IMF) from 1981 to 1986, he negotiated Egypt's agreements with the World Trade Organization and the U.S. government, including the U.S.–Israel–Egypt Qualifying Industrial Zones (QIZ) agreement in 2004. Rachid Mohamed Rachid, who owned Fine Foods and presided over the Middle East branch of Unilever, succeeded Boutros Ghali as minister of economics, tasked with privatizing industry and international trade. Ahmad al-Maghrabi, chair of the board of Accor Hotels, became minister of housing, and Gamal persuaded al-Maghrabi's business-partner cousin Muhammad Mansour to become minister of transport. Soon after, another Maghrabi cousin, Zuhair Garana, became minister of tourism. Garana Travel was "one of the largest companies of hotels, floating hotels and travel companies," according to the State Information Service (SIS) website. Amin Abaza, founder of Nile Cotton Trade—the largest cotton trading company in Egypt—and chair of the Egyptian Association of Cotton, became minister of agriculture. Even the minister of health, Dr. Hatem al-Gabali, was primarily a businessman in the field of medical management, who owned the private Dar Al Fouad Hospital and served on the boards of banks and industrial firms. Holdovers from the previous cabinet included minister of petroleum Sameh Fahmi, who fostered private-sector investment in the oil and gas sectors and managed the natural-gas sales to Israel and Jordan.[11]

These appointments were a recipe for corruption, as the ministers ignored the public interest in favor of their and their friends' private interest. Amr Hashim Rabi', researcher at Al-Ahram Center for Political and Strategic Studies, commented: "The obvious coupling of wealth and authority hurt the party's image as the guardian of public welfare. Egyptians saw rich businessmen within the NDP receiving unfair advantages from their close associations with the party, including market monopolies and tax exemptions for their projects."[12]

The 2005 elections
The concentration of power accelerated in 2005, even though a competitive presidential election was held for the first time and opposition politicians won 23 percent of the seats in the People's Assembly. Although the first round of polling was calm, Central Security clamped down on subsequent rounds in order to prevent Muslim Brotherhood candidates from winning. Judges

were present in the polling stations in the 2000 and 2005 elections, but this only served to strengthen NDP efforts to ensure that their candidates would win. NDP operatives bussed public-sector workers to the polling stations, gave voters pre-marked ballots, provided tangible favors and bribes, deployed the police to prevent people from entering the polling stations, closed polling stations where Brotherhood candidates had strong support, and even employed thugs to attack voters with machetes and swords. As the Brotherhood candidates won many seats in the first two rounds of elections, riot police were deployed in the third and final round to prevent people from reaching the polling stations. Thus, the judges—sitting inside—could not stop the fraud. The Judges' Club refused to certify the elections results, which had resulted in the NDP obtaining three-quarters of the seats and opposition parties being excluded from all but twelve seats. The signal victory for the opposition came with the Brotherhood candidates, who won eighty-eight seats by running as independents. The Brotherhood's victory scared the regime, stoking its determination to prevent a similar outcome in the future (El-Mahdi 2009a, 99; Marfleet 2009, 16, 25; Kassem 2004, 41, 63–67; Boutaleb 2004, 14–15, on the 2000 elections).[13]

In the presidential election, Nu'man Gum'a of al-Wafd opposition party won a mere 2.7 percent of the votes (according to the official count). Ayman Nour, arrested briefly on charges that he had forged signatures on petitions to found al-Ghad Party, gained 7.6 percent of the votes, but was rearrested and sentenced to five years in prison. Afterward, the government engineered splits within both parties. Evidently the regime would not tolerate the slightest challenge.

Amendments to the constitution (authored by Gamal's NDP Policies Secretariat) ensured that only the NDP could run for the presidency in the future. The amendments provided that, in order to nominate a presidential candidate, a party must have operated for five years and must hold at least 5 percent of the seats in both houses—a provision that effectively ruled out all the opposition parties. An individual could stand for president, but only with the support of 250 elected officials from the two houses of parliament and from local councils—a provision that ruled out any independent figure and, especially, the Muslim Brotherhood (Sullivan and Jones 2007, 4).

When the Judges' Club subsequently lobbied to uphold judicial independence and voting transparency, the government retaliated by referring two senior judges to a disciplinary tribunal and removing judges entirely from the polling stations. The government even withdrew the authority of the Higher Judiciary Council to appoint judges, handing that over to the executive branch (El-Mahdi 2009a, 99; Sullivan and Jones 2007, 7, 8, 16).

Meanwhile, the president appointed Gamal a deputy secretary general of the NDP in February 2006. Gamal's Policies Secretariat drafted the above-mentioned constitutional amendments, which cleared the barriers to his own succession. At the NDP's annual congress in September 2008, Gamal launched and headed a forty-six-member Higher Policies Council. In 2008, the NDP won 99 percent of seats in the local council elections.[14]

The 2010 elections

The power plays culminated in the rigged June 2010 Consultative Council and November 2010 People's Assembly elections, orchestrated by NDP Secretary General of Organizational Affairs Ahmed Ezz. The NDP won eighty of the eighty-eight seats contested in June, leaving four seats to opposition parties, four for independents, and completely shutting out the Brotherhood.[15] Then the NDP (including allied independent candidates) won 97 percent of the seats in the People's Assembly election. Eight seats were set aside for opposition parties: five for Tagammu', one for al-Ghad, and one each for two small parties. Despite prior election deals, Brotherhood and al-Wafd candidates were relegated to one and six seats, respectively, in the first round of voting. Angered, they boycotted the runoff elections. No opposition party obtained 5 percent of the seats—the threshold for nominating a presidential candidate the following September.

As usual, arrests of candidates, crackdowns on campaigning, and blocking access to polling stations were combined with the distribution of pre-filled ballots, faked voting cards, and vote buying. Government employees, manning the polls and freed from judicial supervision, obsequiously acquiesced to this falsification. As usual, cabinet ministers who ran for parliament used their official positions to pay for campaign literature, promise services, coerce employees to vote, and bribe others to support them. Fewer thugs may have been employed than in 2000 and 2005, however, as few people bothered to vote. Moreover, the government had arrested hundreds of Muslim Brothers during the previous year, leading influential member Abdel Moneim Aboul Fotouh to conclude, "The elections are completely in the hands of the Interior Minister now. He decides who wins and who loses and who can run."[16]

Despite the arrests and fraud, Gamal and Ezz arrogantly proclaimed that the NDP's "crushing victory" validated their plans for a new wave of neoliberal economic policies.[17] Coming months before the presidential elections and in the wake of the president's serious medical crisis in spring 2010, this deepened expectations that Gamal was the anointed successor. An (unnamed) NDP member of parliament commented in retrospect that Ahmed Ezz went too far: "The stupid part is, we had the opposition inside the parliament under a covered roof. He took the opposition into the street."[18]

Limits on public expression

The exclusion of opposition forces from the political arena in autumn 2010 was accompanied by systematic crackdowns on the media, cultural expression, and university life. The government closed down nineteen TV and satellite channels, hacked or blocked websites, and pressured private businessmen to stop using outspoken critics as editors, opinion writers, and talk-show hosts. The new head of al-Wafd Party bought the independent *al-Dustur* newspaper and sacked its iconoclastic editor, Ibrahim Eissa, allegedly at the government's behest. Eissa, who had faced dozens of trials for outspoken criticism of government officials, was sacked for publishing an interview with former International Atomic Energy Agency director Mohamed ElBaradei (who himself was banned from the official newspapers and TV) and for opposing Gamal's succession (Al Aswany 2011, 59, 190–92). Naguib Sawiris's ONTV channel canceled Eissa's talk show and Orbit cancelled Amr Adib's "Cairo Today" talk show, under pressure from government-run Nilesat. The Association for Freedom of Thought and Expression (AFTE) concluded, "The Ministry of Mass Media and Communication has tightened its fist over all media channels to markedly reduce the space for freedom of expression."[19]

There had been a partial opening of the press and television in the early 2000s: several independent (and outspoken) newspapers appeared, and satellite TV offered new options for free expression. Nonetheless, the government controlled and limited press and cultural output through censorship and Ministry of Information directives. And most Egyptians accessed only the government-controlled radio and television channels and the official newspapers. Journalists were beaten, jailed, and/or fined when they investigated corruption or police brutality and were charged with incitement or libel when they criticized government policies or political leaders. Legislation passed in 2006 made thirty-five offenses punishable by prison sentences of up to five years, such as publishing 'fake' news, undermining 'national security,' and defaming a domestic or international figure, public servant, or head of state. Those indicted included prominent journalist Hamdi Qandil, for insulting the foreign minister in *al-Shuruq*; the chief editor of *Sawt al-umma*, charged multiple times with publishing 'misinformation,' inciting public opinion, and defaming police officers; and a journalist for Al Jazeera, for false reporting and harming Egypt's national interest when he documented cases of torture (Sullivan and Jones 2007, 9–10). The government also clamped down on the Internet: State Security required Internet cafés and mobile phone companies to register each customer so that it could track Internet and phone use.[20]

The State Security presence was pervasive throughout government offices, schools, churches, mosques, and cafés. For example, as many as twenty-six State Security officers monitored conversations and activities in the Asyut governorate building.[21] State Security vetted—and vetoed—job applicants and candidates for all elections. The crackdown was particularly fierce against universities, accelerating in 2007 after the 1979 student charter was amended to give administrative bodies—and, behind them, State Security—the right to bar students from running in university elections. State Security approved the appointment of presidents and deans, vetoed teaching-staff employment and promotions, vetted graduate teaching assistants, determined the eligibility of students to live in dormitories, and interfered in scientific research, the choice of textbooks, and faculty travel abroad for conferences.[22] The State Security presence was overtly threatening, as guards stood at the gates and at each building. Plainclothes officers quelled demonstrations and threatened and arrested student activists. The climax came in autumn 2010, when the government refused to implement the Supreme Administrative Court's ruling that banned these guards from campuses. It also blocked all anti-regime candidates from contesting seats in the student-union elections.[23]

Control over non-governmental organizations (NGOs) was similarly tight. They were regulated under laws promulgated in 1964 and 2002 by the Ministry of Social Affairs, later renamed (without irony) the Ministry of Social Solidarity. NGOs operated under enormous constraints. The ministry approved their bylaws, boards of directors, and budgets; regulated fundraising and approved activity programs; replaced members of the governing boards and transferred funds to other NGOs; and could close them, at will. Thus, the government could strangle the operation of any NGO whose leadership or activities it questioned.

The Privatization/Corruption Nexus

In contrast to the tightening control over political and social life, the government claimed to celebrate economic privatization. In 1991, Egypt signed an Economic Reform and Structural Adjustment Program with the IMF and the World Bank. The government canceled progressive income taxes, exempted stocks and bonds from taxes, made more than 50 percent cuts in corporate tax, and privatized nearly two hundred firms during the 1990s (Marfleet 2009, 17; El-Naggar 2009, 38). Many public services were privatized, such as electricity production and distribution, waste treatment, parking garages, the subway system, roads, and tunnels (Denis 2006, 58). Privatization benefited ministers and members of parliament, opening the door to corruption on an unprecedented scale. They sold significant portions of the public sector for their personal benefit and decreased public investment in agriculture, land reclamation, housing, education, and health. They promoted private investment in export-oriented agriculture, the construction of gated communities for the elite (Denis 2006, 60), and the establishment of for-profit private universities and hospitals. The drive reached its apex with the autumn 2010 elections, which consolidated this nexus of government, party, parliament, and crony capitalism. Abd al-Halim Qandil, the outspoken editor of *al-'Arabi*, opined, "A seat in Parliament is the best investment in Egypt: One million spent on a campaign will generate ten million after the election of the candidate, who will use his position to make corrupt gains."[24]

The governing elite tightly controlled the labor force. Ever since the late 1950s, public-sector workers had been required to join a union under the authority of the government-controlled Egyptian Trade Unions Federation (ETUF) and were banned from striking (Lesch 2004, 616, 620; Posusney 1997; Bianchi 1986). After the labor law was modified in 2003, many workers were hired on short-term contracts under which they had no medical or social insurance benefits. The monthly minimum wage had not been raised since 1984 (Law No. 53), when it was set at the 2011 equivalent of $6; it had risen only via cost-of-living increases to about $25.[25] The ETUF enforced government policy rather than representing its millions of members.

Private-sector workers suffered even more, as the 2003 Labor Law failed to protect the length of contract, salary level, hours at work, overtime compensation, vacation, or lunch breaks. Workers often lacked health and injury insurance. In addition, many private-sector firms forced new hires to sign, along with the contract, form number 6, which allowed the employer to fire them without warning, cause, or severance pay.[26]

In rural areas, legislation enforced in 1997 ended four decades of land reform. Tenant farmers, whose tenancies had been permanent (and inherited), abruptly lost all their rights. Landowners could seize their land-holdings and forcibly displace the tenants—or impose whatever rental rate they desired. Rents increased tenfold or more, which tenants often found impossible to pay. Moreover, tenants could only lease land for a year or less, which destroyed their incentive to invest in long-term improvements.

When the government closed agricultural cooperatives and stopped subsidizing fertilizers and pesticides, small landowners resorted to high-interest loans from the Bank of Development and Agricultural Credit in order to purchase necessities. (Tenant farmers were not eligible for these loans.) When they could not pay back loans whose annual interest rate might reach 17 percent, the bank seized the property and sometimes threw them in jail. In addition, living expenses rose when the government privatized water, electricity, and phone services and stopped cleaning irrigation canals. In some villages, water was so scarce that farmers irrigated with sewage, even though they knew its risk to human health. To survive, whole families resorted to daily wage labor on landowners' estates (Bush 2005, 17–18).

Not surprisingly, primary-school enrollment in rural areas dropped markedly after 1997, exacerbating the vicious cycle of poverty, illiteracy, and landlessness. The Land Center for Human Rights, which undertook longitudinal assessments of many villages, reported—as one of many examples—that primary-school enrollment in one village's sole school was 84 percent in 1995, but dropped to 62 percent in 1999, only two years after tenants began to lose their holdings. As of 2001, 24 percent of children living in rural areas had never entered school and another 21 percent dropped out during elementary school. With the countryside already suffering from 47 percent illiteracy—as against 26.6 percent in urban areas—the urban/rural social divide increased markedly (LCHR 2001).

Concentrated wealth

Impoverishment of the rural and urban labor force contrasted with the concentration of wealth in the small elite. Indeed, in December 2007, Nader Fergany, the lead author of the *Arab Human Development Report*, wrote in *The Financial Times* that "one percent controls almost all the wealth of the country" (quoted in Marfleet 2009, 18). The Central Auditing Organization, which reported directly to the president, unveiled numerous scandals that occasionally resulted in prison sentences and fines against low- or middle-level officials. But the president himself decided whether senior officials' infractions would be punished (Al Aswany 2011, 35). Many agencies—the Illicit Gains Authority (affiliated with the Ministry of Justice), the Public Funds Investigative Unit, and others attached to ministries and banks—filed reports concerning the budgets of ministries and state agencies and their associated companies and banks. They detailed instances of squandering funds, selling or purchasing by direct order rather than tender, and failing to follow legal processes, among other infractions. Conscientious officials became frustrated by the inaction. Indeed, Mohamed Ghanan, head of an investigative unit within the Ministry of Interior, fled to Zurich in 2005, where he proclaimed: "The Mubarak era will be known . . . as the era of thieves. His official business is the looting of public money, and we find that the super-corrupt, ultradelinquents have attained state posts."[27]

Some ministers and governors distributed state lands to favored persons or sold land at suspiciously low prices. For example, in the 1990s, Ibrahim Suleiman, minister of housing and new urban communities, provided eight thousand acres free to the Talaat Moustafa Group to build the luxurious Madinaty gated community, a deal that the judiciary voided in autumn 2010; sold land cheaply for the Marina resort and along the Fayoum desert road; and razed 129 blocks of low-income housing in Qattamiya because they adjoined an upscale golf course and villa complex. Hisham Talaat Moustafa (jailed for the contract killing of his Lebanese diva girlfriend) confessed that he had sold housing units in Madinaty well below market prices to Gamal and Alaa Mubarak.[28] The Mubarak brothers received land by 'direct order' from housing ministers Suleiman and al-Maghrabi and benefited from tourism projects licensed by tourism minister Garana, such as the Pyramisa Isis Island Hotel in Aswan, which consumes twenty-eight acres of a formerly pristine nature preserve. They held shares in Dream properties (owned by Ahmed Bahgat), Mövenpick hotels (Hussein Salem), and City Stars Mall (Sharbatly family).[29] Other special deals involved the president himself, his business buddy Hussein Salem, and Alaa's father-in-law, Magdy Rasekh, who chaired the SODIC real estate company, the third largest property developer in Egypt. These deals have been under investigation since the 25 January Revolution.

The Maghrabi–Mansour–Garana trio epitomized this concentration of wealth and corruption. Transport minister Mansour's brother Yassin chaired Palm Hills Urban Development, the second-largest land holding company in Egypt, which Mansour & Maghrabi Investment and Development (MMID) founded. MMID's interests encompassed almost everything, from tobacco and computer sales to vehicles, food distribution, and Crédit Agricole Bank (CAB).[30] MMID owned 25 percent of CAB, a bank that was formed after the government sold the Egyptian American Bank at a huge loss. In the pungent words of economic analyst Ahmad El-Sayed El-Naggar, this deal represented the "unholy marriage between the state and business" (2009, 46).

Housing Minister al-Maghrabi not only favored the Mubaraks in land deals, but also gave state land and flats intended for low-income tenants to public figures and employees. For example, he sold land in New Cairo at below-market prices to Akhbar al-Youm Investment Company, which that company resold to MMID's Palm Hills. Using a middleman meant that he had not sold the land to himself, which would have been blatantly illegal.[31]

Commissions on business deals were easy ways to gain wealth, sometimes legally but often illegally. The most shocking deal—still under investigation—involved Gamal allegedly obtaining 5 percent and Alaa and Oil Minister Sameh Fahmi 2.5 percent each on the $1.5 billion deal to sell natural gas to Israel, clinched in 2005 by Hussein Salem's East Mediterranean Gas Company.[32]

In addition, the Mubarak brothers are said to have held free or discounted shares (sometimes as many as 50 percent) in the largest trade and investment companies operating in Egypt. They also used their investment agencies to leverage business for themselves and their business partners. Gamal Mubarak's MED Invest Partners received substantial fees for advising western investors on the purchase of stocks and entire companies in Egypt. In 1997 Gamal purchased an 18 percent stake in EFG Private Equity, the largest investment bank in Egypt and a subsidiary of EFG-Hermes. This reaped LE37 million (about $6.25 million) in profits for him in the first nine months of 2010 alone.[33] It was not coincidental that the government designated EFG-Hermes to create a LE2.5 million fund (about $425,000) to manage public–private investment in transport, energy, education, healthcare, and infrastructure under the Public–Private Partnership Central Unit established in May 2010 and headed by the prime minister.

Ahmed Ezz provides a prime example of leveraging connections to grab economic and political power. After opening a small steel factory in Sadat City in 1995 (with help from his iron-trading father), Ezz bought several public-sector steel companies in rapid succession, drained them of their resources, and absorbed them into his private-sector Ezz Steel. By 2006 he was the billionaire owner of 70 percent of Egypt's steel and iron production and had diversified into construction-related fields, such as ceramic products for the bathroom and kitchen.[34] He controlled (and arbitrarily raised) the price of steel and thereby manipulated the cost of construction. His special relationship with Gamal Mubarak enabled him to get unsecured bank loans and pay back old loans by taking out new ones.

Ezz's political star rose along with his economic power, reflecting his close ties to Gamal. Ezz became the secretary of the Organizational Affairs Committee of the NDP and a member of parliament in 2000, joined Gamal's new Policy Committee in 2002, and was re-elected to the People's Assembly in 2005. As chair of its planning and budget committee and a member of the committee for legislation, he made sure that the 2006 Law on Protection of Competition and Prohibition of Monopolistic Practices was too weak to affect his interests. At his request, the ceiling for penalties was reduced from LE50 million ($8.4 million) to LE10 million ($1.7 million), and the provision that the first wrongdoer to report a violation would be exempted from 50 to 70 percent of the penalty was dropped entirely. Given Ezz's power, it was not surprising that the court that fined twenty cement industry executives for price fixing ruled that Ezz Steel was not a monopoly, but instead competed in a free market environment. Most notoriously, Ezz orchestrated the NDP election 'victory' in November 2010. His economic clout had enabled him to ignore the label "the consumer's number one enemy," levied by the group "Consumers against Increasing Prices,"[35] and he thought his political clout similarly enabled him to ignore popular anger at his political machinations. However, U.S. ambassador Francis J. Ricciardoni, in an unguarded moment, called Ezz the most "reviled" of the corrupt politico-businessmen. It was no surprise that protesters torched Ezz Steel's Cairo headquarters on 28 January 2011—the only corporate office attacked during the revolution.[36]

The rich/poor divide

The divide between rich and poor became acute not only in the rural areas but also in the cities. The rich constructed gated communities while urban infrastructure decayed and informal housing burgeoned. Two-thirds of the residents of Greater Cairo lived in unplanned areas that generally lacked basic utilities and public services (Sims 2010, 83, 95, 106). It took appalling incidents such as the Duweiqa rockslide in 2008 that killed eighteen people and displaced thousands to call attention to the desperate conditions. Even then, the government failed to provide appropriate housing for the displaced families.[37] The informal sector comprises 60 percent of the work force—a sector that has continued to grow as thousands of blue-collar workers lost their jobs, more than a million farmers lost their land, and unemployment soared among young people. By 2008, youth unemployment (ages 15–29) was three times the 26 percent overall rate of unemployment (El-Naggar 2009, 42). And the World Bank estimated that a third of Egyptians subsisted on less than two dollars a day.

Deteriorating public health and education systems and escalating food prices meant that the vast majority could not access the glittering high-tech industries and costly private hospitals and schools. Only two percent of the budget was allocated for the health sector (Darwish 2007, 10). Public-sector doctors received such low wages that they had to work in several hospitals, as well as in private clinics, to make ends meet. Ninety-two percent of all students crowded into poorly serviced public schools. A study of public preparatory-level (junior high) schools in 2000 showed that at least 30 percent lacked medical clinics or medical staff, had classes of forty-five or more students (well above the legal limit of thirty-six), and operated in double shifts, which made sports and extracurricular activities impossible (El-Tawila et al. 2000, xvii–xix). Five years later, a UNDP report found that 40 percent of public schools crammed more than forty children into each classroom, and that some classrooms held eighty students, a situation that "makes learning of any kind impossible" (Handoussa 2005, 69). The Ministry of Education had no budget for curriculum development and no strategic plan to train and enhance teachers' performance (Handoussa 2005, 56–57, 70).

These problems were symptomatic of the government's lack of strategic thinking, with ministers focused on showing loyalty to the president, not on public service. For example, no coherent policies were developed to counter the bird flu epidemic and then the H1N1 swine flu, other than abruptly closing schools and killing poultry and pigs. There was no plan to cope with the resulting hardships to producers, disruptions to the school year, and increases in poultry and meat prices. Moreover, garbage collectors, who fed edible garbage to their pigs, suddenly had no way to dispose of that refuse. Garbage piled up in the streets, creating additional health risks. Moreover, when Egyptians of international stature offered assistance—notably Nobel laureate Ahmed Zewail's proposed scientific research complex and civil engineer Mamdouh Hamza's effort to construct housing for families displaced by floods in Aswan governorate—the government blocked their implementation (Al Aswany 2011, 24–25, 139–42).

Mounting Opposition

Given the overwhelming power of the state, the severe restrictions imposed on public gatherings as a result of the state of emergency, and the unchecked violence by police and security forces, Egyptians were afraid to protest. Nonetheless, individuals and groups tried to expose the conditions and challenge government actions. Often these actions took indirect form, as in the novels and films that managed to pass the censor. Alaa Al Aswany's *The Yacoubian Building*, Youssef Chahine and Khaled Youssef's *Hiya fawda* (This is Chaos) on police corruption, Youssef's *Hina maysara* (When Things Get Better) on urban poverty, and Mohamed Diab's *678* on the sexual harassment of women are outstanding examples.

Whereas there were few human rights groups even in the 1990s, by 2010 there were dozens of organizations that reported on rural and urban poverty, deteriorating environmental conditions, harassment of women and activists, restrictions on the press, police coercion, and thuggery during elections. As the government would not register them as NGOs—and as they sought to avoid the draconian controls wielded by the Ministry of Social Solidarity—they often registered as non-profit companies. Initially, they printed their reports in limited editions, but access to the Internet enabled them to disseminate their findings widely.

In the early 2000s, politically oriented groups emerged that embarked on direct action in public space. In 2000–2002, the Palestinian Intifada and Israeli re-invasion of the West Bank rekindled political activism that culminated in demonstrations in 2003 in Tahrir Square against the U.S. invasion of Iraq—the largest protests since the bread riots of 1977.[38] Founders of the Egyptian Movement for Change (Kefaya/Enough), the 9 March movement, and the April 6 youth movement were inspired by those demonstrations.

Street protests sometimes merged economic concerns with political demands. Thus, doctors protested against the neglect of public-sector hospitals, grossly inadequate equipment, and the need for patients to pay for bandages and even anesthetics. Journalists and lawyers protested on the steps of their syndicate headquarters. Even judges demonstrated in front of the syndicate and at the High Court when the government took legal action against two senior judges who refused to certify the 2005 elections—joined by crowds who chanted "Judges, judges, save us from the tyrants" (El-Mahdi 2009a, 99). Nonetheless, these demonstrations usually attracted too few people to break out of the constraints imposed by the security forces. They also remained focused on specific grievances.

The 9 March movement, formed in 2004 to call for university and academic independence, took its name from the date in 1932 when the first president of Fuad University (now Cairo University), Lutfi al-Sayyid, resigned to protest the firing of the noted intellectual Taha Hussein as dean of arts. The 9 March movement held annual demonstrations and publicized infringements of the freedom of faculty and students in the classroom, but fewer than seven hundred professors joined as others feared punishment and dismissal.

Kefaya was founded in 2004 by intellectuals and community activists from across the political spectrum, who were encouraged by the anti-war and university-based street mobilization and concerned about the upcoming presidential and parliamentary elections. They linked the issues of corruption, the state of emergency, Mubarak's fifth term, and dynastic succession. Three hundred people joined Kefaya's first protest in December 2004 outside the High Court. Kefaya held symbolic protests at the Cairo International Book Fair, national universities, and Tahrir Square, and simultaneous demonstrations in fourteen cities in April 2005. These protests brought together activists from across the political spectrum with the core message: *Enough!* As the first movement to expose the pervasive corruption and call directly for regime change, Kefaya "breathed life into Egyptian politics" (El-Mahdi 2009a, 92). But police attacks on demonstrators—including stick-wielding assaults on female protesters—prevented the street protests from swelling. Moreover, activists found it difficult to sustain a broad coalition that combined secularists and Islamists.[39]

The April 6 movement was formed in 2008 to support strikes in the textile city of al-Mahalla al-Kubra (discussed below). Its call for a one-day general strike resonated with the public, but could not succeed in the face of a draconian security crackdown. Central Security mauled the demonstrations mounted by April 6 movement activists in Cairo, but the movement organized effectively through online media. Through blogs, Flickr, Twitter, and Facebook they amassed seventy thousand online members by 2009 and fostered heated debates on sensitive issues. *Democracy Digest* editor Michael Allen reported that "to coincide with the NDP['s annual] conference [in November 2008], young activists launched a parallel cyber-conference to highlight and satirize the government's failures. As the regime has stifled freedom of criticism, harassing journalists and seeking to curb satellite TV, the web has become a vital outlet for expressing grievances and criticism of the regime—and for confronting opposition elites, too" (2008).

Labor protests

Meanwhile, struggles rooted in labor grievances broke out in autumn 2004, as soon as Ahmed Nazif's new government renewed the drive to sell public-sector factories to Egyptian and foreign businessmen. Workers were angry at the loss of benefits, forced retirement with inadequate (or unpaid) compensation, and the shrinkage of job opportunities. With three million Egyptians employed on short-term contracts by 2010, this concern became widespread.[40] Workers had the coherence and strength to speak out, unlike farmers, who could not resist orders to hand over their land (see Bush 2009, 61–62, on the sporadic rural protests).

The first strike was emblematic of subsequent protests: a ten-day struggle in October 2004 by hundreds of workers at Qalyub Spinning Company, one of six mills operated by the ESCO conglomerate.[41] The mill had just been sold to a private investor, but the workers had not been consulted, even though they owned a 10 percent share. They also feared that they would be fired (and denied retirement packages) or paid lower wages and benefits. The strike resumed in February 2005; although repressed, workers did gain back pay, lump-sum payments, and partial enforcement of the labor law (Beinin 2009a, 78).

In December 2006, when workers in the giant textile factories in al-Mahalla al-Kubra protested against the government's failure to pay end-of-year bonuses and called for dismantling the ETUF, the government hastily reinstated the bonus.[42] Protests escalated as privatization accelerated and food prices skyrocketed. Whereas 2006 witnessed 222 labor protests, there were more than seven hundred protests of varying kinds in each of the subsequent years—despite ever fiercer security repression.[43] Thus, when workers in Mahalla's Misr Spinning and Weaving Company went on strike on 6 April 2008, demanding a monthly minimum wage of LE1,200 (about

$250 at that time), security forces not only attacked the strikers but sent thugs to create an image of chaos by burning public institutions.[44]

Wildcat strikes were also rife in the non-unionized private sector. These ranged from the November 2004 strike by 287 workers at Spanish–Egyptian-owned Ora Misr Asbestos Products Company in Tenth of Ramadan Industrial City,[45] where workers suffered serious illnesses due to unrestricted exposure to asbestos, to multiple strikes against the Turkish-owned Mega Textile Company in Sadat City over pay, benefits, and work conditions.[46]

Moreover, many workers were angry that challenges to the 2006 ETUF election results, although upheld in court, were not implemented. They began to form independent trade unions that represented, for example, municipal real estate tax collectors, teachers, health technicians, and pensioners. The municipal real estate tax collectors, who demonstrated in front of the Finance Ministry for eleven days in December 2007, were the most successful: all 55,000 tax collectors won a 300 percent salary increase and broke the ETUF's lock-hold by winning a court order that permitted them to establish the first independent union.[47]

Many strikers demanded an LE1,200 ($215) national monthly minimum wage—at a time when wages were typically a quarter or half that amount. Khaled Ali, the dynamic lawyer who founded the Egyptian Center for Economic and Social Rights in 2010, joined with the Center for Trade Union and Workers' Services in a court case that won the long-sought LE1,200 minimum wage. To underline their insistence on implementing the court ruling, workers rallied in Cairo on 3 April 2010. When the cabinet refused to meet with them and offered a meager LE280 ($47) minimum wage, hundreds demonstrated on 2 May and held their ground against the massive security deployment, chanting, "A fair minimum wage or let this government go home" and "Down with Mubarak and all those who raise prices." Unsettled by this Labor Day protest, Mubarak issued his standard warning about the risk of chaos. In the autumn, the government proposed a LE400 minimum wage ($67), still only a third of what the court had ordered.[48]

The widespread nature of worker protests was symbolized by sit-ins in front of the parliament that often continued for weeks. For example, despite a severe heat wave in May 2010, Amonsito workers held placards that called for back pay, alongside workers from the recently closed Nubaria Company for Agricultural Mechanism and the Telephone Equipment Company. They were joined by staff from the State Litigation Authority and farmers from Beheira governorate, who were voicing their own grievances.[49] By the summer of 2010, two million workers had participated in organized protests at 3,300 factories or before parliament over the past six years. Alaa Al Aswany reflected that, even though hundreds of workers and their families had slept for months in front of the parliament and cabinet buildings "because their lives are no longer tolerable," neither the president nor the prime minister had "taken the trouble to go out and listen . . . or to try to help them in any way" (Al Aswany 2011, 38, 44).

Political alternatives

Meanwhile, noted intellectuals sought ways to resolve the country's crisis. Salaheddin Hafez, a senior political analyst at *al-Ahram*, proposed in 2008, shortly before his death, that fifty public figures convene to find a way to bring about change. The doyen of journalists Muhammad Hassanein Heikal, decrying the "folly of power displayed by Egypt's dictators,"[50] suggested in 2009 the formation of a twelve-member "Board of Trustees of the State and the Constitution." State-run media vilified Heikal and the notables whom he proposed—in particular Amr Moussa, whom Mubarak had shifted from foreign minister to the League of Arab States in 2001 when Moussa's popularity became threatening; Mohamed ElBaradei, who had just stepped down as director of the International Atomic Energy Agency; and Ahmed Zewail, who had received the Nobel Prize for chemistry in 1999. In Al Aswany's frank words, "all of them [were] much more eligible than Gamal Mubarak to take on the presidency." A "Campaign against Succession" began at the same time, which aimed "to restore the natural right of Egyptians to choose who rules them" (Al Aswany 2011, 5, 6).

ElBaradei stepped up to the challenge and returned to Cairo in February 2010, declaring that he would run for president only if the constitution were altered and the state of emergency ended.[51] Many people rallied around his National Alliance for Change and signed its petition to abolish the emergency laws and the restrictions on candidacy for the president and to establish full judicial supervision of elections, independent election monitoring, equal access to the media for all candidates, voting with the national ID, and a system to enable expatriates to vote. Even the Muslim Brotherhood, after it was shut out of the Shura Council in June 2010, backed this drive.[52] By August the petition had garnered 88,000 handwritten and 341,000 online signatures.[53]

"We Are All Khaled Said"

Meanwhile, the April 6 movement, Kefaya, and the Know Your Rights Campaign were organizing around a potent issue: police torture. That campaign began to mobilize people who had been on the sidelines. The cyberworld that had emerged over the past decade had transformed the mode of communication for many people and enabled activists to heighten fellow Egyptians' awareness of state repression and corruption. Moreover, the growing concern about (and direct experience of) police brutality by Egyptians from all walks of life, and their enhanced willingness to risk speaking out, were crucial in preparing the ground for the 25 January Revolution.

Public outrage was sparked by the very public beating-to-death, just before midnight on 6 June 2010, of 28-year-old Khaled Said, seized as he entered an Internet café in Alexandria. According to relatives and eyewitnesses, State Security agents sought out Khaled after he posted a police video that showed police officers dividing up the spoils from a drug heist at the Sidi Gaber police station. Plainclothes agents banged his head against a marble shelf and then hit and kicked him in a nearby building, as he cried "I'm dying!" The agents took his body to the police station, but returned after ten minutes, left him on the ground, and called an ambulance. When Khaled's brother went to the hospital, he took photos of Khaled's fractured skull, broken nose, and dislocated jaw.[54]

Late that night, seventy young men and women gathered across from the police station, demanding justice. They received the usual response: they were beaten, dragged along the street, attacked by police dogs, and arrested. Protests continued throughout the summer: funeral prayers at Sidi Gaber mosque, attended by six hundred mourners who then spilled out into the street; vigils outside the Ministry of Interior headquarters in Cairo; silent protests along waterfronts and bridges throughout Egypt; and violently suppressed demonstrations in downtown areas whose participants included both well-known politicians and opposition groups and people who felt that they, their children, or their grandchildren could all have been Khaled Said. One teenager commented, "This is an extraordinary case. This guy was tortured and killed on the street. I did not know him but I cannot shut up forever."[55] "For the sake of Khaled! For the sake of Egypt!" *('Ashan Khalid! 'Ashan Masr!)* became a rallying cry, voiced in fear as well as in the determination to restore individual and collective dignity *(karama)*.

Dozens of Facebook groups supported the cause, of which 'We Are All Khaled Said' became the most famous. They not only raised awareness about Said's case and encouraged the vigils and protests, but also circulated reports about police brutality, many of which had been posted in the past but had not received such intense scrutiny. The most notorious video showed policemen using a broom handle to sodomize Emad al-Kabir, a 21-year-old minivan driver, in the Bulaq al-Dakrur police station in January 2006. The police posted the video to the cell phones of other van drivers in order to intimidate them. Instead, al-Kabir took them to court and the video went viral on the web.[56] At the time, Hafez Abu Saeda, head of the Egyptian Organization of Human Rights, warned, "Police brutality is systematic and widespread. . . . The humiliation of the simple citizen has become so widespread that people are fed up."[57]

Pushed to the Brink

The usually cautious and conservative *Economist* stated bluntly on 11 September 2008: "By damming up the normal flow of politics, Egypt's rulers risk bringing on the deluge" (quoted in Marfleet 2009, 17).

Indeed, by the end of 2010, Egyptians had been pushed to the brink by the sharply rising prices of basic foods, escalating unemployment, crackdowns on the media and universities, outrageous rigging of the parliamentary elections, an ever-lengthening list of corrupt actions by the elite, and fear that 82-year-old Mubarak might run for re-election in September 2011 or, even worse, hand power to his hated son. Nonetheless, protesters themselves agree that it took the swift removal of President Ben Ali to make them think: If dramatic change is possible in Tunisia, maybe we can do the same in Egypt.

The regime had kept itself in power by its hold over the security forces, its dominance of the political structures and economy, its control over the media, and the underlying authority of the armed forces. Its hold over the security apparatus remained secure, but the excessive force employed by the police and security forces deeply alienated the public and began to cause people to react overtly against it. Dominance of political and economic life also reached an extreme point, as did crackdowns on the media, coming after brief promises of widened political participation and the opening of new modes of expression. Even well-tamed opposition parties could not tolerate their exclusion from the parliamentary game in the final months of the regime. And military officers were disturbed by the boiling public discontent, as well as increasingly anxious that Gamal might succeed his father—a step that they strongly opposed.

The seemingly sudden transformation, triggered on 25 January, can therefore be seen as the culmination of a decade of first gradually, then rapidly increasing public disgust and overt opposition. As the campaigns—often focused on specific issues—merged with the overall call for dignity and social justice, the dispersed individuals transformed into an organized protest movement. Their agency overcame the factors that had been inhibiting collective action, creating a sustained momentum and deepening determination to achieve comprehensive change.

The key pillar collapsed when the government removed all the security forces from their positions on 28 January 2011. The Supreme Council of the Armed Forces, ordered to secure the streets that night, emphasized that their loyalty was to the nation, not the person of the president. They made it clear that they would not fire on the protesters. By then, Egyptians realized that to stop being subjects and to become citizens, they had to seize their rights. The struggle to seize and secure those rights and ensure social justice continues.

Notes

1 Rabab El-Mahdi, lecture in conference hosted by the Free University of Berlin and the American University in Cairo, Cairo, 8 May 2011; Moaaz Elzoughby, "The Dynamics of Egypt's Protest," *Arab Reform Brief* 45, Arab Reform Initiative, 23 February 2011, http://arab-reform.net; Heba Morayef, "The View from Liberation Square," *International Herald Tribune*, 28 January 2011, http://www.nytimes.com/2011/01/09/opinion/29iht-edmorayef29.html

2 Darwish 2007, 78; Kefaya, "Corruption in Egypt: The Black Cloud Is Not Disappearing," July 2006, www.irinnews.org and http://free.egyptians.4t.com/alfasad.htm

3 Fandy 1994; Lesch 2004, 619–20; Kim Murphy, *Los Angeles Times*, 27 November 1994.

4 Human Rights Watch, *Work on Him until He Confesses: Impunity for Torture in Egypt*, January 2011, 18–19; Al Aswany 2011, 151–52, 157–58, 166–67.

5 Human Rights Watch, *Work on Him*, 21–27.

6 Wendell Steavenson, "Cairo: The Word on the Street," *The New Yorker* blog, 25 May 2011, www.newyorker.com/online/blogs/wendell-steavenson/2011/05/the-word-on-the-street.html; Bradley 2008, 118–29.

7 Amnesty International, *Annual Report for 2010*, http://amnesty.org/en/region/egypt/report

8 Human Rights Watch, *Work on Him*, 34.

9   "Cables: Israel Favored Egypt's VP Suleiman," Wikileaks, cited by ABC News, 7
     February 2011, http://abcnews.go.com/blotter
10   Gamal Essam El-Din, "How Gamal Brought the Whole Mubarak House Down,"
     Ahram Online, 15 April 2011, http://english.ahram.org.eg/News/9988.aspx
11   Egypt State Information Service: www.sis.gov.eg/en
12   Michael Allen, "Egypt: Clinically Dead Regime Fumbles Reform, Harasses Cyber-
     activists," *Democracy Digest* (blog), 3 November 2008, http://www.demdigest.net/
     blog/2008/11/egypt-clinically-dead-regime-fumbles-reform
13   See also Issandr El Amrani, "Controlled Reform in Egypt: Neither Reformist nor
     Controlled," *Middle East Report (MER)* online, 15 December 2005, www.merip.org/
     mero/mero121505
14   Amr Hamzawy and Mohammed Herzallah, "Egypt's Local Elections Farce: Causes
     and Consequences," *Policy Outlook* 10, Carnegie Endowment for
     International Peace, 2008, http://carnegieendowment.org/2008/04/14/
     egypt-s-local-elections-farce-causes-and-consequences/7in
15   Issander El Amrani, "Egypt's Shura Council Elections, and Its Future," 3 June
     2010, http://www.arabist.net.blog/2010/6/3egypts-shura-council-elections-and-
     its-future
16   *Al-Masry Al-Youm*, 23 March 2010.
17   Essam El-Din, "How Gamal Brought the Whole Mubarak House Down."
18   Kareem Fahim, Michael Slackman, and David Rohde, "Egypt's Ire Turns to
     Confidant of Mubarak's Son," *New York Times*, 7 February 2011, http://www.
     wichaar.com/news/296/ARTICLE/24010/2011-02-07.html
19   Association for Freedom of Thought and Expression (AFTE), Semi-annual
     Report, July–December 2010, www.en.afteegypt.org
20   Allen, "Egypt: Clinically Dead Regime."
21   Wendell Steavenson, "Big Fish on the Nile," *The New Yorker* blog, 31 May 2011,
     www.newyorker.com/online/blogs/wendell-steavenson/2011/05/big-fish-on-the-
     nile.html
22   Human Rights Watch, *Reading between the "Red Lines": The Repression of Academic
     Freedom in Egypt*, June 2005, http://hrw.org/reports/2005/egypt0605; florian
     Kohstall, "A New Window for Academic Freedom in Egypt," *OpenDemocracy*, 14
     March 2011, www.opendemocracy.net/author/florian-kohstall
23   Marwa Al-A'sar, "Court Bans Police Presence on Egypt's University Campuses,"
     Daily News Egypt, 25 October 2010, http://www.thedailynewsegypt.com/education/
     court-bans-police-presence-on-egypts-university-campuses
24   El Amrani, "Controlled Reform in Egypt."
25   Hesham Sallam, "Striking Back at Egyptian Workers," *Middle East Report (MER)*
     259, June 2011, www.merip.org/mer/mer259; U.S. Commercial Service, "Doing
     Business in Egypt: 2010 Country Commercial Guide for U.S. Companies," http://
     export.gov/egypt/doingbusinessinegypt/eg_eg_031951.asp
26   New Women Foundation, "The State of Egyptian Female Workers in the
     Industrial Sector," 2009, http://nwrcegypt.org; al-Boraie 2011.
27   Marcus Baram, "How the Mubarak Family Made Its Billions,"
     Huffington Post, 11 February 2011, www.huffingtonpost.com/2011/02/11/
     how-the-mubarak-family-made-its-billions
28   "Mubarak Regime Stalwarts Confess to Corrupt Business Dealings," *Al-Masry
     Al-Youm*, 6 June 2011, http://www.almasryalyoum.com/en/node/465460

29 Baram, "How the Mubarak Family Made Its Billions"; Kefaya, "Corruption in Egypt."

30 Ibtessam Zayed and Salma Hussein, "Mohamed Mansour: A Tarnished Captain of Industry," *Ahram Online*, 10 March 2011, http://english.ahram.org.eg/News/6724. aspx; Mansour Group, www.mansourgroup.com; Kefaya, "Corruption in Egypt."

31 "Ex-ministers of Housing, Tourism to Answer Profiteering Charges Next Week," MENA Report, *Al-Masry Al-Youm*, 28 February 2011, http://www.almasryalyoum. com/en/news/ex-ministers-housing-tourism-answer-profiteering-charges-next-week; "Palm Hills Plans to Appeal Court Land Sale Verdict," Reuters Report, *Ahram Online*, 27 April 2011, http://english/ahram.org/eg/News/10878.aspx; Bassem Aboul El-Abass, "Palm Hills," *Ahram Online*, 11 May 2011, http://english.ahram.org/ eg/News/11521.aspx

32 "Former Petroleum Minister Investigated for Israel-gas Deal," *Al-Masry Al-Youm*, 2 March 2011, http://www.almasryalyoum.com/en/node/336993; "Mubarak's Sons Got More Than US $187 mln from Israeli Gas Deal, Says Paper," AFP Report, *Al-Masry Al-Youm*, 6 March 2011, http://www.almasryalyoum/com/en/node/341409

33 EFG-Hermes data in Abdel Rahman Shalaby, "Presidential Scion Gamal Mubarak Took LE189.45 Million in Profits from EFP Hermes," *Al-Masry Al-Youm*, 15 February 2011, http://www.almasryalyoum.com/en/news/presidential-scion-gamal-mubarak-took-le18945-million-in-profits-from-efg-hermes

34 Vignal and Denis 2006, 70; "Court Resumes in Ezz Trial," *Ahram Online*, 7 May 2011, http://english.ahram.org.eg/News/11599.aspx

35 "Court Resumes in Ezz Trial."

36 Kareem Fahim, Michael Slackman, and David Rohde, "Egypt's Ire Turns to Confidant of Mubarak's Son," *New York Times*, 7 February 2011, http://www. wichaar.com/news/296/ARTICLE/24010/2011-02-07.html

37 Land Center for Human Rights, *Conditions of Human Rights*, 2004, www.lchr-eg. org; Amnesty International, *Annual Report for 2010*.

38 Human Rights Watch, *Work on Him*, 11; El-Mahdi 2009a, 89, 93–94.

39 Carnegie Endowment, "Constitutional and Legal Framework," 1 September 2010, http://egyptelections.carnegieendowment.org/2010/09/01/constitutional-and-legal-framework

40 Sallam, "Striking Back."

41 Joel Beinin, "Popular Social Movements and the Future of Egyptian Politics," *MERIP* online, 10 March 2005, www.merip.org/mero/mero031006

42 Philip Rizk, "Egypt and the Global Economic Order," *Al Jazeera*, 15 February 2011, http://english.aljazeera.net/indepth/opinion/2011/02/20112148356117884.htm; Beinin, "Popular Social Movements"; Beinin 2009a, 79–80.

43 Sallam, "Striking Back."

44 Rizk, "Egypt and the Global Economic Order"; Joel Beinin, "Egyptian Workers Demand a Living Wage," *Foreign Policy* online, 12 May 2010, http://mideast. foreignpolicy.com/posts/2010/05/12; Beinin 2009a, 83–84.

45 Beinin, "Popular Social Movements"; Beinin 2009a, 77.

46 Marwa Hussein, "Mega Textile Workers' Strike in El Sadat City Shows No Sign of Ending," *Ahram Online*, 12 May 2011, http://english.ahram.org.eg/News/11975.aspx

47 Beinin, "Egyptian Workers Demand a Living Wage"; Beinin 2009a, 79.

48 "Labor Leaders Reject New Minimum Wage," *Al-Masry Al-Youm*, 5 May 2010, http://www.egyptindependent.com/node/39324

49 Hesham Omar Abdel Halim, "Protesters in Front of Parliament Threaten to Escalate Protests," *Al-Masry Al-Youm*, 14 May 2010, http://www.egyptindependent. com/node/41453; "Protests Continue Outside Parliament," *Al-Masry Al-Youm*, 16 May 2010, http://www.egyptindependent.com/node/41895

50 Robert Fisk, "Mohamed Heikal: 'I Was Sure My Country Would Explode. But the Young Are Wiser than Us,'" *The Independent*, 15 February 2011, www.independent. co.uk/news/world/africa/mohamed-heikal-i-was-sure-my-country-would-explode-but-the-young-are-wiser-than-us-2215070.html

51 Jack Shenker, "Supporters Give Mohamed ElBaradei Hero's Welcome at Cairo Airport," *The Guardian*, 19 February 2010, http://www.guardian.co.uk/world/2010/feb/19/mohamed-elbaradei-egypt-heavy-security; Al Aswany 2011, 15–17, 31–33, 135.

52 Issandr El Amrani, "Egypt's Shura Council Elections, and Its Future," 3 June 2010, http://www.arabist.net/blog/2010/6/3/egypts-shura-council-elections-and-its-future.html

53 Mohsen Semeika, "6 April, MB Obtain Signatures for ElBaradei's Reform Demands," *Al-Masry Al-Youm*, 1 August 2010, http://www.egyptindependent.com/node/60504

54 Human Rights Watch, *Work on Him*, 20–21, 53, 61, 67, www.hrw.org/reports/2011/01/30-work-him-until-he-confesses-0; Nadeem Center for the Rehabilitation of Victims of Violence (NCRVV), Statement, 11 June 2010, www. alnadeem.org; Hamdi Kasem, "Lawyers: Police Forged Alex's Victim's Record," *Al-Masry Al-Youm*, 20 June 2010, http://www.egyptindependent.com/node/50620; Gamaa Hamdullah, "2 Alex Policemen Detained in Khaled Saeed Case," *Al-Masry Al-Youm*, 30 June 2010, http://www.egyptindependent.com/node/53178; Ahmed Shalaby and Mostafa El Marsfawy, "Khaled Saeed Case Investigation," *Al-Masry Al-Youm*, 12 July 2010, http://www.egyptindependent.com/node/55686; ABC News, 7 February 2010; Amnesty International, *Annual Report for 2010*

55 Noha El Hennawy, "Trial of Police in Khaled Saeed Case Begins," *Al-Masry Al-Youm*, 27 July 2010, http://www.egyptindependent.com/node/59185

56 Human Rights Watch, *Work on Him*, 21, 45, 81.

57 *Time*/CNN, 23 January 2007, www.time.com/time/printout/0,8816,1581608,00. html

3

The Political Economy of Mubarak's Fall

Samer Soliman

The long rule of President Hosni Mubarak can be explained by his manipulation of the distribution of economic resources, and his demise is related
to the dwindling of public revenues and its effects on Egyptian politics.

When Mubarak took office in 1981, state coffers enjoyed relatively
important flows of rentier revenues coming from oil, the Suez Canal, and
foreign aid. This was a legacy of President Anwar Sadat. Indeed, the end of
the military conflict with Israel had given Sadat the chance to reopen the
Suez Canal in 1975, recover oil reserves in Sinai, and receive significant foreign aid from the west. These rentier revenues restored the health of a fiscal
system weakened by low income from taxation. In the early 1980s, they
constituted about half of public income and raised that income enough for
the regime to maintain a level of public spending amounting to 55 percent
of GDP (Soliman 2011). These important flows of public money transformed Egypt into a semi-rentier state that depends to a great extent on
non-tax income. While it is true that Egypt does not depend as heavily on
rentier revenues as the Arab Gulf states, rent and its manipulation can go a
long way toward explaining political stability and change under Mubarak.

During the 1980s, Mubarak blocked the process of economic liberalization launched by his predecessor and restored a degree of the 'economic
planning' that had been common under Nasser. A five-year plan—a tradition that had stopped under Sadat—was launched in 1982. The official

discourse emphasized the importance of the public sector. Customs duties were increased so as to control imports. Mubarak also clipped the wings of powerful business magnates associated with the Sadat era, like Rashad Osman and Esmat al-Sadat (for more detail, see Soliman 1998).

The shift in economic policy stemmed from more than the exigencies of building the legitimacy of the new president. Mubarak would not have partially reverted to economic planning had it not been for the growth in state revenues, a trend that began in the mid-1970s. Indeed, the growth of the Egyptian state apparatus was the irony of the 1970s. While the official discourse emphasized the conversion to a market economy, the centrally steered economy was growing. Undoubtedly, the rise of a new and very conspicuous class of capitalist entrepreneurs and a very ostentatious nouveau riche gave the impression that the private sector was taking over an increasing share of public-sector resources. In fact this did not occur during the 1970s. As money flowed into the pockets of the rising entrepreneurial class and a segment of the middle and professional classes, state-controlled revenue sources poured even more into the coffers of the national treasury. Consequently, government control over the nation's resources increased. According to a World Bank study, public spending soared from 48 percent of the GDP in 1974 to 62 percent in 1981 (Ahmed 1984).

By the late 1980s, however, the important rentier revenues with which Mubarak started his rule were dwindling. Despite being one of the largest recipients of foreign aid in the third world, Egypt saw its funds shrinking both in absolute terms and in their ratio to GDP. This was the result, on the one hand, of the fiscal crisis in major industrial nations, which forced them to reduce levels of aid to third-world countries, and, on the other, to Eastern Europe's growing need for foreign aid in the 1990s. The collapse in oil prices played a key role in this process. Although Egypt as an oil-exporting nation does not match the stature of the Persian Gulf countries, oil is one of the most important determinants of its financial fluctuations. The prices of oil and energy in general do not only affect oil and natural gas exports; they also affect the yield from Suez Canal transit fees, which is heavily contingent on the oil trade. The population boom further reduced the importance and effect of rentier revenues coming from foreign aid, oil, and the Suez Canal.

By the late 1980s, public revenues had fallen to nearly half of what they had been at the beginning of the decade (Ministry of Finance 1981/82–1989/90). Logic suggests that lower income should lead to lower government spending. But while such an adjustment makes fiscal sense, it is a political tinderbox. Reducing government expenditures means reducing or even cutting off the flow of funds to persons and groups that have come to expect them. An authoritarian regime such as Egypt's, which depended on handouts to secure its control over society, has very little flexibility when it comes to tightening the purse strings. As a consequence, the national deficit began to soar, and Egypt soon had one of the highest deficits in the world (IMF 1991).

By the end of that decade, the Egyptian regime had become an international mendicant, so desperate was it for funding from any source. In 1990, the World Bank's International Development Association described the financial situation in Egypt as "precarious" (Lofgren 1993). When the Egyptian government stopped paying its debts, it was palpably evident that Egypt was on the verge of bankruptcy again. A Reuters report (17 July 1990) quoted an Egyptian economic expert as saying, "For twenty years we've been saying that Egypt is on the brink of bankruptcy, but some miracle would always intervene to save the economy. This time I see no way out of the crisis." But, perhaps to the embarrassment of the economic expert, heaven stepped in again. Less than two weeks after he issued the prognosis, Iraqi tanks rumbled into Kuwait. Washington began to mobilize an international coalition to free Kuwait. The war effort would depend heavily on the two most important regional powers—Egypt and Syria—and Washington would have to pay generously for their cooperation. The miracle was at hand.

Creditor nations quickly agreed to cancel half of Egypt's foreign debt. Before they actually wrote off the debt, however, Egypt had to implement the economic reform program that had been jointly formulated with the IMF and World Bank. This time, the government showed a spirit of enthusiasm and dedication that it had lacked three years earlier, when it failed to implement a structural adjustment agreement with the IMF. The regime had therefore to abandon its break from the economic liberalization initiated by President Sadat and to accept the economic reforms imposed by the international financial institutions.

Thanks to Egypt's strategic importance and Mubarak's skills in maneuvering, the regime was able to negotiate a structural adjustment program more lenient than those imposed on many other third-world countries. The privatization program did not lead to a layoff of public employees, and the regime was able to maintain some subsidies, especially those of basic foodstuffs like bread. Mubarak thereby managed during his long rule to avoid any sudden increase in prices or any rapid drop in the standard of living of the middle and lower classes. Impoverishment, when it took place, was gradual and slow. The riots of January 1977—which had brought the army into the streets to impose order—were not repeated.

The focus of Egypt's economic reform program was deficit reduction, and the deficit declined from 6 percent of the GDP in the year prior to the implementation of the program to 0.6 percent in 1993–94. International financial agencies could not praise this feat enough. To cite one of the many reports that extolled it, an IMF study of 1998 proclaimed that, in 1996–97, Egypt had achieved the highest level of fiscal balance in the Middle East and North Africa after Algeria (Handy et al. 1998). Egypt's economic future seemed promising. The regime had brought inflation under control, now that it had stopped turning to the mint to finance its deficit. The stock market, defunct since the nationalizations of the 1960s, had been resuscitated and was showing some vitality. The slogan "Egypt: the tiger on the Nile" reflected the government's confidence that Egypt would soon surge to the fore of emerging states.

The results of the economic reform program were a central subject of public debate in the 1990s. The government's claim that the program was an unmitigated success was corroborated by reports from international financial agencies. Critics, however, countered that this success was confined to fiscal performance (the shrinking budgetary deficit) and did not extend to the economy as a whole. Successful economic reform, they argued, would be manifested in many ways, most importantly in increased production and in higher per capita income levels.

While the debate homed in on such issues, little attempt was made to explain why fiscal reform had succeeded so well. Was the success in reducing the budget deficit the consequence of the reform measures themselves? Or did it have more to do with circumstances that coincided with the implementation of these measures? In fact it was the latter, because apart from the sales tax that was introduced in 1991, fiscal policy underwent no other significant change. In a letter to the World Bank in May 1991, Minister of International Cooperation Dr. Maurice Makramallah pledged that the Egyptian government would deregulate the economy (WB 1991). The aim of the letter was to obtain a loan from the bank, and with this in mind Makramallah stressed, in particular, the Egyptian government's commitment to reducing public spending. The president of the World Bank presented this letter to the bank's board of directors along with his recommendation to accept the pledge and grant the loan. Among the other documents he presented was a schedule listing the maximum levels of public spending that the Egyptian government had vowed not to exceed. But in reality, there was a huge gap between promised and actual levels of expenditure. Spending rose in relation to the GDP from 37.3 percent in 1989–90 (before the economic reform program) to 49.9 percent in 1991–92.[1] For many years after the economic reform program was put into effect, public spending continued to increase. Only in 1994–95 did it begin to decline. Clearly, then, it was not by fulfilling its pledges to the IMF that the Egyptian government managed to reduce the national deficit. So what did produce this achievement?

The answer is higher revenues. Several factors contributed to the growth in income. In addition to taking part in the coalition to drive Iraq out of Kuwait, which brought many financial perks, the government reduced the value of the Egyptian pound (whose official exchange rate was considerably higher than its worth on the black market). The effect was to raise the value of Egypt's oil exports and Suez Canal fees when calculated in Egyptian pounds. In addition, the government introduced a general sales tax, which also brought in several billions of pounds. These sources generated higher revenues, and correspondingly higher levels of public spending. The early 1990s was a grace period in the decline of state revenues. As of the middle of that decade, however, the downward trajectory of the 1980s resumed, primarily due to the fall in rentier incomes.

From a Semi-rentier State to a Predatory Tax State: Taxation without Representation

With the contraction of rentier revenues during the late 1980s and the intensification of the fiscal crisis, the regime had to work on two fronts: to increase public revenues and to reduce and reorganize public expenditures. Attempts to grow public revenues were managed by political/security logic. But the regime started with the measures that entailed the lowest possible political cost, even if they came at a high economic price, before proceeding to politically costlier measures like income tax. The regime therefore launched its program with the 'inflation tax,' which is to say that it issued new banknotes.

From the perspective of the regime, the inflation tax had the great advantage of relative secrecy. Unlike other taxes, which are imposed by the Ministry of Finance and must be made public, this tax is levied quietly by the central bank. Also, whereas other taxes require a parliamentary bill, all it takes to print new currency is a decision by the central bank's board of directors. Of course, sudden price spikes betray the issuance of new banknotes, but here the government has room for deniability: it can always blame inflation on imported goods, or it can lash out at greedy merchants.

In the second half of the 1980s, the Egyptian regime adopted an energetic policy of turning to the mint. According to a World Bank study, Egypt was among the third-world governments that did so most frequently (Dinh and Guigale 1991). The inflation rate of over 25 percent distorted the fundamental variables of the economy. The interest rate (about 10 percent) became negative, which encouraged consumption and discouraged saving. The collapse of their currency also drove Egyptians to real estate speculation, precipitating an expanding bubble in real estate prices. Meanwhile, many who had the means changed their savings into hard currency, a sensible choice for the individual, but one that generated an unprecedented wave of dollarization.

Although, as noted above, the political costs of the inflation tax were low in the short term, the impact ultimately hit civil servants, the main constituency of the regime. As inflation ate away at civil servants' salaries, the mid- and long-term political costs of the inflation tax grew increasingly great. Fortunately, the need for the government to commit itself to a program for economic reform in 1990 put an end to the spiral. Now the government had to stop financing its budgetary deficit by minting new currency and turn to more solid sources, such as government bonds and certificates.

During the 1990s, the government's expenditures continued to exceed its income, and it still had to borrow. What is unique about this period, though, is that the government turned to local instead of foreign sources to finance its deficit. Public debt climbed from LE100 billion in 1992/93 to LE549 billion in 2009/10. The absolute value of the domestic debt does not fully convey the nature of the problem, which becomes more apparent when we take into account the ratio of debt to GDP, which climbed to approximately 67.4 percent by 2009 (Ministry of Finance 2010a). The government said that this ratio was still within the safety range, but its claim may have rested on thin ice. The Maastricht Agreement, for example, states that the ratio of debt to GDP of EU member states should not exceed 60 percent. EU economists clearly felt that any higher ratio was worrisome. There is no clear reason why Egypt should be able to exceed the 60 percent threshold without courting danger.

To what institutions did the regime turn for loans? The government's largest creditor is the National Investment Bank, which furnished more than half its loans. The bank controls vast resources. Its assets come chiefly from insurance and pension funds, which accounted for two-thirds of the bank's assets at the end of the 1990s (Elias 2000, 75). It would appear, then, that the people were lending money to the state via the National Investment Bank. Insurance and pension funds are private property; they are deductions from people's income that are intended to be paid back to them in the event of retirement or disability. In fact, it would be more appropriate to describe the state's access to people's retirement and pension funds as a partial tax rather than a loan, because it lacked the free and voluntary approval of the donors. No one asked them whether their insurance and pension funds should be loaned to the state. They had no say in the matter. Another reason that these loans have more in common with a tax is the negative interest rate that the government was paying throughout the 1980s. At a time when the inflation rate was more than 20 percent, the government was paying 6 percent interest (Ministry of Economy). In other words, the government was appropriating a portion of the funds.

In the late 1990s, the government had little choice but to stop forcing the insurance and pension funds to grant subsidized loans. The funds were showing a disturbingly growing deficit that the government had to cover through allocations from the national budget. Clearly, the regime had to find a solution to this potentially explosive problem. In November 2003, former Prime Minister Atef Ebeid told *al-Ahram* that the Council of Ministers was studying a proposal from the Ministry of Finance to give shares in public-sector companies to the insurance and pension funds in exchange for the government's debt.[2] The idea aroused considerable anxiety, which prompted the People's Assembly to ask the prime minister for clarification. Ebeid allayed the mounting concerns, assuring his audience that the funds were perfectly safe and the government was still the chief guarantor of pensions.[3] That is, even if the funds went bankrupt, the government would issue payments to pensioners out of the national budget. The government ultimately had to reject the proposal.

During the 1990s, the insurance and pension funds were still controlled and administered by the Ministry of Social Solidarity. Increasingly, however, the management of these funds was the subject of a conflict between state institutions. In 1998, an open struggle erupted between Mervat al-Tellawi, minister of social solidarity, and Youssef Boutros Ghali, minister of economy, over the management of these funds, because Boutros Ghali was pressuring al-Tellawi to invest pension fund assets in the stock market. In 2006, Boutros Ghali—by then minister of finance—managed to gain control of the funds, an act that created suspicion and anger among opposition groups. In recent years, societal actors have become important players in this struggle. Many court claims were brought against Ghali for dissipation of public money. Even after the fall of Mubarak, these claims are still wending their way through Egyptian courts.

Theoretically, the government's growing indebtedness to the public should transform the nature of the relationship between state and society. If private agencies grant loans to the government, they inevitably want guarantees that they will get their money back at the highest possible interest rate. The government, in turn, must be able to convince the public that it is financially sound and capable of paying back the loans. This transformation naturally heightens public interest (concern) in fiscal policy. Some political economists regard the extent to which private agencies are willing to lend money to the government as a barometer of confidence in the fiscal performance of the government as well as in the regime and its stability (Ducros 1982, 77). That is, the greater the government's debt to the public, the more the public presses for government accountability. This is precisely what happened in Egypt.

As the government exhausted its ability to mobilize revenue using measures with relatively low political cost, like inflation and external and internal public debt, it was obliged to turn to the more transparent and politically costlier sales tax. The tax was introduced in two stages: the first, implemented in 1991, hit manufacturers and importers; the second covered retailers and was implemented in 2001. The opposition did not succeed in preventing the tax. In April 1991 it was approved by the People's Assembly—not surprising, since the assembly was dominated by the governing elite via the ruling National Democratic Party, whose parliamentary deputies had to vote with the government whatever their personal opinions were. Since 1991, the sales tax has been one of the chief sources of national income. Its share of the total government revenues increased from 13.1 percent in the year it went into effect to 14.4 percent in 1996–96, 16.7 percent in 2000–2001 (Ministry of Finance 1997–2003), and to 23 percent in 2007–2008 (Ministry of Finance 2008).

The government had originally planned to implement the second phase, covering retailers, in 1993, but postponed this change several times. That the government was aware of how difficult it would be to put phase two into effect was evidenced by the greater-than-seven-year interval between the time it announced its intention and the actual implementation thereof. When phase two of the general sales tax finally went into effect in April 2001, it encountered stiffer resistance from retailers than the government had had from businessmen prior to the implementation of the first phase. Protest took many forms, but the most curious and most powerful was the 'Muski Uprising.' Merchants in that famous popular market area in Old Cairo simply decided one day to shut their stores and sit outside them or, in some cases, to join protest marches against the tax. The riot police were brought in to disperse the demonstrators and to intimidate the merchants into reopening their shops. Although the strike was aborted with relative ease, this by no means diminishes its significance. To my knowledge, it was the first organized protest demonstration against a tax in modern Egyptian history.

One of the laws that most clearly proclaimed the rise of the predatory state in Egypt in the late 1980s was Law 228 of 1989, which imposed a tax on Egyptian civil servants working abroad. Their numbers had increased tremendously during that decade, and their remittances amounted to an average $3 billion per year (CBE 1991). In light of the budgetary deficit, it was only natural that these sums would make the authorities' mouths water. Law 228 set a remarkable precedent. Until then, taxation had followed the territorial principle: only people residing within the geographical boundaries of the state were taxable. This principle rests on the fact that citizens resident abroad do not benefit from the services provided by the state. The state justified the new tax on the grounds that the government safeguards all their rights, such as health insurance, until they return from abroad (Mohammed 1997).

Opposition to the new law eventually reached the Supreme Constitutional Court. In 1993, the court ruled that it was unconstitutional to impose a tax on workers abroad. The ruling was founded on fundamental considerations that the tax conflicted with the principle of equality, since it only applied to public-sector and not private-sector employees (Mohammed 1997). The government interpreted the ruling as applying only to the litigants who had filed the suit, so that only the parties to the claim would get their money back. It should be borne in mind that during the four years Law 228 was in effect, it had raked in LE240 million.

Following its defeat in the court, the government hastily pushed through a new law intended to avoid the previous pitfalls. Law 208 of 1994 expanded the tax to include private-sector workers abroad, thereby meeting the principle of equality. Even then, the new law did not escape litigation on the grounds of unconstitutionality, which, again, the Supreme Constitutional Court upheld in a 1998 ruling. Again, the court found that the law violated the principle of fairness, this time because the tax only applied to salaried employees and not to experts on special contracts (Mohammed 1997). The government did not try to come up with another version of the law, but it was quick to assert that the ruling only applied to those who had brought the suit.[4] In addition, the president, citing the need to safeguard the fundamental resources of the state, issued a decree in July 1998 stipulating that the rulings of the Supreme Constitutional Court could not be applied retrospectively in the area of taxation.[5]

As noted above, the regime pursued various means to resolve its fiscal difficulties throughout the 1980s and 1990s. It started with the inflation tax, then took on foreign debt, imposed a tax on Egyptians working abroad, took on domestic debt, and finally introduced the general sales tax. When these and other means failed to halt the deterioration of Egypt's finances, and two decades after coming into power, the Mubarak regime finally turned to the formidable challenge that it had long been avoiding: income tax reform.

In 2000, Medhat Hassanein was appointed minister of finance, and it was not long before he declared his intent to issue a new law for the comprehensive reform of the income tax system, which everyone felt had long since reached obsolescence. The government acknowledged that the system was incapable of collecting the revenues it needed. Many sectors of society felt that it was inefficient and unjust. Salaried employees, for example, felt that they were the only sector that was compelled to pay taxes because these were deducted at source. Businessmen regarded the system as cumbersome and the tax authority itself as medieval. More importantly, they felt the tax rates of 40 percent on commercial profits and 32 percent on manufactures and exports were outrageous. Each group had its own reasons for condemning the existing tax system, but all were unanimous in their conviction that it desperately needed a total overhaul.

The relative inequity of the Egyptian tax system is also reflected in the limited contribution by rich individuals and companies to the financial support of the state. This is most apparent in the very low revenues from capital and inheritance taxes, as well as in the fact that taxes on commercial and industrial profits account for only 4.4 percent of total tax revenue, even though there are about five million manufacturers, merchants, and businessmen who should be paying. The low revenues are all the more surprising when we consider that the tax authority invests the bulk of its energies in this area, with around sixty thousand employees. The largest single contribution from direct taxes comes from financial firms, which supply about 30 percent of total tax revenues. Nevertheless, at least half of this amount is derived from public-sector organizations, notably the General Petroleum Organization, the Suez Canal Company, and the Central Bank. Doctors, lawyers, consultants, and other practitioners of the liberal professions contribute a mere 0.2 percent of the total revenues, which is to say practically nothing at all, despite their relatively high incomes. Meanwhile, salaried employees contribute 4 percent to the total revenues, or nearly the same amount derived from the profits of commerce and industry (Ministry of Finance 2002).

Tax evasion remains a major characteristic of the Egyptian tax system. Estimates in late 1990s placed the cost between LE14 billion and LE20 billion (Mohammed 1997). A recent study by the Organization for Economic Cooperation and Development has shown Egypt to be among the countries with high levels of tax evasion (OECD 2010). The penalty for tax evasion is prison, but it has never been imposed. The tax authority would rather reach an understanding with tax evaders and collect fines equivalent to the amount of money they owe. Tax evasion thus makes sound business sense, especially for businessmen and merchants who feel that the taxes are excessive. If the tax evader is caught, then the cost is no more than he would have had to pay by being honest. If he is successful, which the odds seem to favor, then his bank account is all the more robust. At the same time, the authorities' reluctance to invoke the penalty of prison against tax evaders conveys weakness.

The minister of finance Medhat Hassanein affirmed in 2000 that the new tax law would address the problems of the taxation system. At its heart, the draft of the law had that neoclassicist magic formula: "To increase tax revenues you must lower taxes." The rationale was that lower taxes would encourage businessmen to obey the law and hand over what they owed to the government. The same logic was applied to the practitioners of the liberal professions. So it was that the new law reduced the maximum tax on business profits from 40 to 30 percent (Ministry of Finance n.d.).

The debate over the tax bill continued throughout Hassanein's term as finance minister, which ended in June 2004. His successor, Youssef Boutros Ghali, reintroduced the bill with some modifications. Perhaps the most important of these was the reduction of the maximum tax on business profits to 20 percent, half of the existing maximum rate. Hassanein's logic was reaffirmed: Businessmen had been evading taxes because the taxes were so high that evasion was worth the risk. Lowering taxes would therefore inspire them to abide by the tax laws. Unfortunately, there was a hole in the premise. The problem was much deeper and more complex. It was not only high taxes that encouraged businesses to evade tax, but also the ease with which they could do it as a result of the notorious corruption of Egypt's tax bureaucracy. There was also an important political factor. When a ruling regime lacks legitimacy and the prevalent conviction is that tax revenues are used to finance a corrupt bureaucracy, and when there is little transparency in how the government spends its money, the motivation for tax evasion remains high. These were the problems that the minister of finance could not remedy, because they were connected to the entire political order and affected every aspect of government.

The new tax law went into effect in June 2005. Two years later, the Ministry of Finance boasted that the new law had been highly successful; as proof it reported that revenues rose from 7.1 percent of the GDP in 2004–2005 to 9 percent in 2005–2006 and remained at 9 percent the following year. Sadly, the devil always lurks in the details. When we look at the small print, we find that the rise in income tax revenues was derived primarily from the gas tax and the Suez Canal Company. Meanwhile, tax revenues from private-sector companies (financial firms) actually fell in the first year from 1.7 percent to 1.4 percent of the GDP and then returned to 1.7 percent of the GDP the following year (Ministry of Finance, Closing Accounts, 2007–2008). Only in 2008–2009 did they actually increase to 2 percent of the GDP (Ministry of Finance, Closing Accounts, 2009–10). In other words, the new tax law has not so far been successful in generating any significant increase in tax revenues. The failure to reverse the decline in state revenues was one of the main problems that weakened the Mubarak regime, for decreasing revenues means contracting expenditures and hence more social discontent.

To sum up, the long process of turning the Egyptian state from a semi-rentier state to a tax state has introduced some important changes in the relationship between state and society. First, it contracted the controlling capacity of the political regime and limited the number of its supporters. Second, the drive to levy more tax income to cover the loss of rent created a conflict between state and society. The percentage of tax-related suits against the state rose from 32.2 percent in 1995 to 42 percent in 2000 (Ministry of Justice 2001).

In their study of the rentier state in the Arab world, Hazem Beblawi and Giacomo Luciani demonstrate a direct causal relationship between the nature of state revenues and the political character of the state (Beblawi and Luciani 1987). Rentier revenues generate an authoritarian state; tax revenues create a democratic one. Why? According to the theory, the rentier state is rich and does not have to depend on society for tax revenues. Instead, society depends on the state for just about everything: income, jobs, education, health care, and other social services. The enormous financial resources of such states, as of the Persian Gulf countries, place them in a position of strength with respect to their citizens, allowing them to dominate in an authoritarian manner. Conversely, where the state depends on society as a major source of funds, society is elevated to a position of partnership and insists upon forms of public supervision and control. The formula is straightforward: those who have the ability to give have power over those who take. It applies as much to the relationship between state and society as it does to that between individuals in society.

So what happens when the rentier state grows poor, its revenues dwindle, and its deficit climbs? Rentier theory tells us that government will have little choice but to levy taxes, and at this point society can insist that government listen to society, show society some respect, and account for how it plans to spend or has spent the funds it has collected from the public. In other words, this is when the public can force government to become democratic.

To suggest that the end of rent and the rise of the tax state should necessarily lead to democracy is reductionist. And indeed, the rentier state theory sometimes does have reductionist tones.[6] Formulated differently, the theory is plausible. True, rentier revenues are conducive to authoritarian government, but authoritarianism has causes other than money. Meanwhile, although the drying up of rentier revenues and the growth of taxation are conducive to democratization, the desire to control the public purse is in itself one of several potential sources of democracy.

My argument is that the turn to the tax state, the conflict between state and society over taxes, the failure of the regime to levy enough tax income, and the resistance of society against these taxes are important factors behind Mubarak's fall. In the last years of his rule, the term 'taxpayer' had become a political term, used to oppose Mubarak and advance claims for transparency and accountability. It is worth noting that 'taxpayer' is a term used not by state authorities, but rather by financiers.

Public Expenditures: The Decline of the Regime's 'Political Purchasing Power'

The contraction of public revenues as a percentage of GDP should sooner or later lead to a similar contraction in public expenditures. The tactic adopted by Mubarak was to reorganize public expenditure in order to limit the political dangers induced by its contraction. Internal security was prioritized, hence the drive to reduce expenditures on the army in exchange for its increased financial autonomy. In fact, the army was given the ability to develop a big economic empire of civil industries, construction companies, and service projects. At the same time, expenditures on internal security were rising at the expense of expenditures on development, including education and health. The extraordinary inflation of the police machine was one of the major features of Mubarak's rule. It was meant to compensate for the weakening of other mechanisms of control, such as money and ideology. But in Mubarak's last years in power, the inflation of the police became a burden on the regime. The machine that was designed to repress political dissidence worked with a logic that transcended politics. Excesses and crimes by policemen against ordinary non-politicized citizens became daily practice. As corruption and income inequality in the Ministry of Interior reached unprecedented levels, police in the lower ranks made their living by racketeering at the expense of the population. The people's rage against the police and the burning of many police stations during the revolution testify to the extent of the police brutality that Egyptians endured under Mubarak.

In tandem with the reprioritization of funding allocations to government agencies, there was a shift in the distribution of resources within the various agencies themselves that favored the upper echelons of the bureaucracy. Otherwise put, under the pressure of the fiscal crisis, remuneration of government employees became less equitable. Simultaneously, a blind eye to bribery, kickbacks, and other forms of increasingly widespread corruption enabled the employees to compensate for the shrinking of their official salaries. Thus corruption under Mubarak became the very mechanism by which state institutions were managed.

As the state's revenues declined, so did the regime's political purchasing power. The state could no longer afford to expand the government payroll, except by creating jobs with few responsibilities and even less pay, and it could not afford to purchase new supporters. The most it could do was to try to hold on to its existing support base: some five million state employees. The bulk of those supported the regime passively, which is to say by remaining submissive.

Meanwhile, the political purchasing power of the emerging bourgeoisie was rising as this class owned and managed more material and human resources. The regime succeeded in persuading members of this class to fill part of the growing gap in the provision of social services which resulted from the state's dwindling resources. The state, however, paid a high price for this tradeoff as centralized control over these services unraveled.

The People's Assembly elections in the last decade testify to this development. For the first time in its history, the ruling National Democratic Party (NDP) failed in 2000 to obtain at least two-thirds of the seats in the People's Assembly. It received less than 40 percent of the vote and could only secure a majority in the house by including independents in its ranks. But the NDP's poor showing did not work in favor of the official opposition parties. These together won only sixteen seats, barely 3.6 percent of the house. Most of the independents who won had originally been NDP members who succeeded in defeating the NDP's official candidates. This important transformation points to a certain fragmentation in the political system and to a decreasing capacity of the ruling group to impose discipline within its ranks. Many of these independents were businessmen, who garnered seventy-seven seats—more than double the thirty-seven they had won in the 1995 elections (Ben Néfissa and Arafât 2005). In 2000, money was lavished on the campaigns as never before: it had clearly made considerable inroads against government connections as a source of power.

The People's Assembly elections in 2005 confirmed the growing influence of big business in Egyptian politics. Businessmen reaped 22 percent of the parliamentary seats, up from 17 percent in 2000 and only 12 percent in 1995 (Soliman 2006). One of the most striking features of these elections was the remarkable increase in electoral bribes, as noted in the reports by the agencies that monitored the polls. While the number of businessmen in parliament increased, the representation of labor in the 2005 parliament shrank to 4 percent, down from 7.5 percent in the previous assembly (Soliman 2006). The same trend of increasing business representation persisted in 2010, when the percentage of businessmen reached 35 percent.[7]

The 'Bourgeoisification' of the Ruling Party

In the years immediately preceding the revolution, the NDP had undergone an important metamorphosis that we can call the 'bourgeoisification' of the party. The party's key figures used to be ex-officers and bureaucrats like Kamal al-Shazly and Safwat al-Sharif. Yet the old guard had increasingly been marginalized in favor of a rising business elite that included Gamal Mubarak, the president's son, and Ahmad Ezz, the steel magnate and the party strongman in charge of its organizational committee. The bourgeoisification of the ruling party reflected Egypt's changing political economy from bureaucratic to neoliberal authoritarianism. The shift was meant to strengthen the party by supporting it with the financial and human resources in the hands of businessmen. Instead, this metamorphosis of the party and its leadership had a destabilizing effect in the political sphere. It created resentment among other social groups, especially when the businessmen joining and leading the party were accused of monopolistic and corrupt practices.

The decline of the rentier/caretaker state has had the strongest impact on the salaried modern middle class (see Shawqi and Soliman 1998). This segment of society, according to some analysts, formed the social base of the Nasserist regime and was the hardest hit, economically and socially, by economic liberalization. The common impression is that the middle class has collapsed, an idea encapsulated in the title of the book by the eminent economist Ramzi Zaki, *Farewell to the Middle Class* (1997). The Egyptian Revolution in 2011, where the wealthy middle class played an important role, shattered this myth. Indeed, the Open Door policy of the 1970s and the economic reform of the 1990s affected different parts of the middle class in completely different ways. Some parts flourished; others declined. Some of its members had levels of education and the social and political connections that paved the way to new jobs in the private sector or in the civil service. Those who lacked these advantages had to accept lower-status and lower-paying jobs in either the private or public sector. Others, more unfortunate, were forced to join the ranks of the unemployed.

Our central premise here is that the shrinking state and the growing private sector have moved the middle class toward greater heterogeneity, with the fortunes of some portions rising while others have fallen, resulting in greater autonomy from the state of those who prospered, and marginalization of those in decline. A major indication of the autonomy of the well-to-do middle class is that it no longer uses or needs to use services provided by the state. Its members send their children to private schools, receive medical treatment in private hospitals, and travel in private modes of transportation. Most have satellite dishes and are hooked up to the Internet, which largely frees them from the state's ideological machinery. The public services that the well-to-do continue to depend on are still monopolized by the state, namely infrastructure and the justice and security services. On these matters, well-to-do middle-class people have little good to say.

The lower middle classes harbor a deep rancor against the regime. Those in government employ (apart from a fortunate few) have been angered by the decline in their standard of living and the deterioration in their working conditions. If they manage to draw a decent income, they probably do so through commissions (baksheesh) and kickbacks. Many have a vehement hatred for the private sector, but it is an instinctive hatred rather than one founded on belief in a possible alternative; it cannot, therefore, serve as an indicator of a sense of affiliation with or faith in the state. In addition to its material decline, this class also suffered deterioration in social status and moral stature, in part due to the lack of an ideology that accords any pivotal role to civil servants in the new era.

While the government has been offering fewer and fewer services to the middle classes, it is asking them for more and more taxes and fees. The liberal professions, in particular, will be expected to bear more of the brunt of funding the state. Fiscal authorities feel that this group currently contributes the lowest share.[8] This situation continues in the post-revolution period. In 2009, tax revenues from individual private professions were only LE292 million, compared to LE8 billion from wage earners (Ministry of Finance 2010b, 35). Therefore, the new tax law both reduces the tax rates for the liberal professions and toughens the penalty for evasion. The carrot-and-stick approach aims to break this sector's relative autonomy and draw it into a closer relationship with the state, in an enlarged role as financiers for the state. Presumably this development has encouraged the liberal professional class to take a greater interest in public affairs and to become more politically involved. People who pay out money are generally keen to follow up on the fruits it yields. It is sufficient to note that on 16 February 2009, for the first time in the history of the July 1952 order, pharmacists went on strike to protest a government-ordered tax hike: the General Syndicate of Egyptian Pharmacists called on all pharmacies to close shop until the Ministry of Finance backed down on its decision to place them in a higher tax bracket and apply this retroactively.[9] The pharmacists' strike indisputably marks a qualitative shift in political behavior within the liberal professions, which have long constituted one of the most important politically uninvolved segments of the middle class.

As for the workers, the Egyptian Revolution was preceded by some important changes in their sociopolitical conditions. By the middle of the first decade of the new millennium, labor activism had attained such an unprecedented level as to compel Joel Beinin, a prominent expert on the Egyptian labor movement, to observe, "This constitutes the largest and most sustained social movement in Egypt since the campaign to oust the British occupiers after World War II" (Beinin 2007). Labor activism was so inspiring to middle-class activists that one of the main groups that triggered the Egyptian Revolution, the April 6 movement, was named after an important strike organized in April 2006 by the workers of al-Mahalla al-Kubra, a city in the Delta. Public-sector workers played the biggest role in the protest activities at the outset of the new millennium, even though the majority of the working class is now employed in the private sector. It is an indication that the end of the rentier/caretaker state was a crucial factor behind the political mobilization that preceded the Egyptian Revolution.

The wave of strong workers' activism showed that the Federation of Trade Unions—controlled by the regime and designed to contain the workers—was exhausted. The creation of a new, independent trade union of real estate tax collectors in 2009 was an exceptionally important development. Until then, the idea of free and independent trade unions was a concept and a right defended primarily by the left. When the real estate tax collectors managed to conduct a successful strike and sit-in for about two weeks, they ended by declaring their own independent trade union.

Since the revolution, independent trade unions have proliferated in Egypt. Indeed the official Federation of Trade Unions was completely discredited after its leaders vigorously defended Mubarak during the revolution. The head of the federation was arrested on charges of incitement to murder some of the demonstrators. The Administrators' Board of the federation was dissolved under pressure from the new independent unions, and an interim committee was formed by the labor minister to run the federation.

Conclusion

Authoritarian regimes perpetuate themselves not only through repressive means; they also use money. With money, they can buy the loyalty of some segments of society and placate others. While this applies to authoritarian regimes in general, in rentier or quasi-rentier states the money factor becomes even more important. Consequently, it is impossible to understand the evolution of these types of regime without placing state revenues and expenditures at the heart of the analysis. The political economy perspective is, in short, greatly advantageous to our investigation of these governments.

The fall of the Mubarak regime reinforces the notion that there should be 'no taxation without representation.' Under Mubarak, the shift away from rent and the resulting drive of the Egyptian state to mobilize more resources from taxation created a conflict between state and society. This conflict can be inferred from numerous indicators, including the 'tax strikes' that took place during Mubarak's final years in power. The deterioration of state services and the decay of many state institutions, coupled with the predatory inclinations of the state, drove many in the middle class (including its upper echelons) to swell the ranks of the opposition. The Mubarak regime was thus brought down not only by the economic losers, but also by some of the winners. The strong participation in the revolution by youth from the educated and well-off upper middle class testifies to the fact that many in the middle class are determined to become full citizens and hold their government accountable.

Meanwhile, the last years of Mubarak's rule also saw the strongest wave of workers' protests Egypt had experienced since the 1940s, the bulk of which were led by public-sector workers. This discontent among the working classes and the poor was one result of the state's fiscal crisis, where dwindling state revenues had forced a contraction and reorganization of state expenditures. Resources were increasingly concentrated on security while social spending decreased, thereby contributing to public anger and limiting the regime's 'political purchasing power.'

The end of the rentier state and the contraction of the public sector opened the door to the rise of the Egyptian bourgeoisie. Economically, this class possesses growing material and human resources. In an attempt to empower itself and to contain the business class, the regime co-opted some business magnates within its ranks. Business elements thereby increased their power and influence over the ruling party and the cabinet. But this orientation created a discontent among the middle classes and intellectuals. The army's undermining of the Mubarak regime in January 2011 suggests that the military institution has also had reservations about the increasing political power of the business elites.

Post-Mubarak, the Egyptian state faces the same fiscal challenge. It must mobilize more money from taxation in order to meet its needs. The main difference between the Mubarak era and its successor lies in the potential transformation of the political regime. A democratically elected government should have greater legitimacy to levy more tax revenues and fight taxation fraud effectively. If it manages this, it will succeed where Mubarak failed. The mobilization of higher tax revenue is necessary to meet the mounting pressures on the state to increase spending on education, health, and social expenditures in general. The consolidation of a democratic system in Egypt rests partly on the capacity of the new government to meet the growing demands of its social role.

Notes

1 These figures are based on the author's calculations from statistics from the Ministry of Finance's closing accounts for the national budget for several years, and from the Egyptian Central Bank's annual reports, also for several years.
2 Mohamed Ali Hassan, "The Future of Pension Funds," al-Ahram, 4 March 2004.
3 Naglaa Zekri, "Ebeid Says: The Government Is the Guarantor of Pension Funds," al-Ahram, 15 March 2004.
4 al-Ahram, 4 January 1998.
5 Sherif Mansur, "The President Issues a Decree Concerning the Tax on Egyptians Abroad," al-Wafd, 13 July 1998.
6 For a critique of this theory see, for example, Herb 2003.
7 http://www.islamonline.net/i3/ContentServer?pagename=IslamOnline/i3LayoutA &c=OldArticle&cid=1172571455063 (21 November 2010).
8 Interview with former minister of finance Midhat Hassanein, 23 August 2002.
9 Akram al-Sayyad, "Pharmacists Declare Strike," Al-Masry Al-Youm, 18 February 2009.

4

Dynamics of a Stagnant Religious Discourse and the Rise of New Secular Movements in Egypt

Nadine Sika

Agents of political socialization have been adept at influencing Egyptians' religious consciousness over the past three decades, especially religious institutions and the media. However, the new social movements that played a key role in calling for the 25 January 2011 protests, which turned into a revolution, were predominantly secular. During the eighteen-day uprising, none of the revolutionaries' chanted slogans had religious connotations. Rather, ideas of human rights, social equity, freedom, and dignity prevailed. Religious symbolism was present in marches launched from mosques after Friday prayers toward major public squares in different Egyptian cities, but this symbolism did not transmute into religious slogans during the revolution. And since the fall of Mubarak, the newly forged social movements have retained their secular ideals even with the rising tide of new Islamist movements and leaders in the Egyptian public sphere.

During the first decade of the new millennium, the regime enacted a number of reforms to silence the growing national and international criticism of its authoritarian tendencies. For instance, article 76 of the constitution was amended so that the president would be elected directly by the people instead of through a plebiscite in the National Assembly. In 2007, amendments were made to thirty-four more articles in the constitution. These reforms were presented by the regime as a milestone on the road to democratic reform. But rather than expanding political participation and accountability, these reforms effectively institutionalized authoritarianism (see, for example, Kienle 2001; Lust-Okar 2005; Schlumberger 2007). Meanwhile, the Mubarak regime relied extensively on religious institutions to gain and maintain legitimacy within Egyptian society and thereby encroached increasingly on the public sphere, of which the religious institutions were an integral part. Superficial state reforms and growing cynicism germinated the seeds of the emerging social movements.

According to theorists, individuals who want either to retain or to re-create their lifestyles in the public sphere, which the state has occupied, turn to grassroots mobilization through new social movements (Melucci 1980; Habermas 1984, 1989). These have loose organizational structures, no hierarchy, and high mobilization capacities, and tend to rise and fall instantaneously (Howard 2003; Hannigan 1991). They play key roles in civil society organizations, yet they are more autonomous than professional and religious associations. They pose a challenge to the boundaries of institutional politics and place themselves between private and public life (Offe 1990; Bayat 1998). Their ability to mobilize through informal networking with the masses and other civil society organizations challenges state authorities and can be influential in changing politics in authoritarian regimes (Bayat 1998). They are mainly associated with the rise of a developing middle class consisting of young, educated individuals (Kreisi 1998).

In this chapter, I will argue that when the regime becomes entrenched in the public sphere, new social movements develop in contrast and opposition to prevailing social attitudes and reinforce new values that the political system has failed to introduce (Della Porta and Diani 2006). Here new social movements utilize the prevailing crisis, which is the inability of a regime to further develop its hegemony over society: "The [regime's] existing options of articulation can no longer hold society together, which will fall apart if a new agent (and model) of integration does not arise." To be successful, this new model needs to encompass moral leadership, authority, and unity among the different factions of society, especially civil society (Tugal 2004, 24).

The following analysis will shed light on how new social movements in Egypt were able to bypass the official stagnant religious discourse and gain legitimacy for their new human rights stance. It analyzes the dynamics of the interactions between the state, al-Azhar, the Coptic Orthodox Church, and the Islamist movements, as well as their religious discourse. This analysis will show how these four institutions helped to strengthen authoritarianism in Egypt, and how their stagnant discourse created a political opportunity for new social movements to grow in new public spheres, both on the street and online, through websites, Facebook, and Twitter. In these spaces, movements advocated for the end of authoritarianism without resorting to religious slogans. The study will also look at the socioeconomic problems encountered by Egyptian youth over the past decade and the inability of the state, religious institutions, and Islamist movements to address them. This gap precipitated the development of a new discourse that bypassed the official religious line and developed a new counter-political consciousness and identity based on global human rights standards.

The Co-opting of al-Azhar in the 1960s and Beyond

In 1961 the Nasser regime endorsed enormous transformation measures for al-Azhar. These measures were intended mainly to modernize and reform the religious institution, to transform the 'traditional' religious teachings into more modern approaches in step with modern society. Nasser contended that the clergy (ulama) were not able to change their institution alone because of their traditional thinking and analysis, but needed the state to guide them on the path to modernization. According to Nasser, "the shaykhs have become completely isolated from the modernizing segments of society, and their traditional views almost totally rejected" (Zaghal 1999, 374). In pursuit of this goal, the regime introduced new laws to embed the religious institution in the political sphere.

First, it introduced new subjects to the curriculum, mainly social sciences, alongside the already existing religious subjects. It also introduced modern faculties, such as engineering and medicine. Second, and more influential in subverting the power of al-Azhar, was the 1961 law that reorganized the institution, placing it under the jurisdiction of the Ministry of Endowments (*awqaf*). Thus, all of al-Azhar's finances were to be redirected through state institutions, which ensured the control of state officials over the functions of the institution (Moustafa 2000). This law also subsumed the Grand Sheikh's power to the Egyptian president, transforming al-Azhar into an integral part of the Egyptian state bureaucracy, and making the ulama economically dependent on the state—civil servants rather than independent clergy. Moreover, the president retained all power to appoint al-Azhar's Grand Sheikh, as well as the members of the Academy of Islamic Research (*Mujamma' al-Buhuth al-Islamiya*). Thus, al-Azhar became a modern institution with the same hierarchy as any modern university (Zaghal 1999). The state was also keen to control all mosques, traditionally outside its hegemony. Through the nationalization of endowment lands, the state was able to control the mosques associated with them and to take charge of their administration. The number of state-owned mosques increased tremendously from 1962 onward. These mosques were also given financial incentives (Moustafa 2000).

When Sadat came to power in 1970, he adopted a more religiously inclined public persona, becoming known as 'the pious president.' As a result, there were more religious ulama and sheikhs in the Egyptian public sphere than there had been during the Nasserite era (Zaghal 1999). Nevertheless, clashes took place between al-Azhar and Sadat's regime after the ulama pleaded that the legislation concerning al-Azhar be amended. Sadat did not want al-Azhar to be completely independent of the regime, and by 1974, the al-Azhar sheikhdom had lost all its power to the Ministry of Endowments. Conversely, the rise of radical Islamism toward the end of the 1970s compelled al-Azhar to submit to the state and abandon political intervention. The Sadat regime also developed a network of district offices across Egypt's governorates, which took charge of selecting and monitoring the imams who would preach in state mosques (Gaffney 1991). Candidates were screened by directors from al-Azhar University and the Ministry of Endowments to determine their political impartiality and their adherence to a moderate interpretation of Islam (Gaffney 1991; Moustafa 2000). According to the undersecretary for the Ministry of Endowments, Muhammad Abdel Azim, these candidates were obliged to have at least a bachelor's degree from either al-Azhar University (any of the departments in the Faculty of Theology) or Cairo University's Dar al-'Ulum.[1]

When Mubarak succeeded Sadat, he appointed Sheikh Jad al-Haq, a former minister of endowments, to the position of Grand Sheikh of al-Azhar. Under his leadership, the government nationalized more mosques, bringing them under state ownership and control, and curtailed the development of new private mosques (Moustafa 2000). Since the early 1990s the state was thereby able to control not just al-Azhar, but also the religious public sphere more broadly, by sporadically creating spaces in which the Muslim Brotherhood could voice their opinions as a counterpoint to more radical Islamist groups. The state security apparatus also influenced the Salafi movements by allowing them to express their own religious interpretations—*ijtihad*, concerning Islamic social issues—far from the political sphere. These movements are known to mobilize people through informal networking, based on their shared interpretation of Islam: "Social relations and activities form the organizational grid and matrix of the movement, connecting like-minded Muslims through common religious experiences and personal relationships" (Wiktorowicz 2000).

The phenomenon that saw the rise of new preachers was also encouraged by the state as a move toward de-politicizing citizens. In the 1980s, state-controlled television massively increased its Islamic discourse, and the number of imams increased more than threefold from the early 1980s to the 1990s. New preachers emerged with new and innovative Islamic programs, such as Islamic talk shows, which were aired by young, educated preachers like Amr Khaled and Moez Masoud (Moll 2010).

Al-Azhar also increased its educational institutions by opening new branches of the university and developing new primary schools. For its part, the ruling National Democratic Party (NDP) published its own magazines, like *al-Liwa al-islami* and *Aqidati*, to inculcate the 'correct' teachings of Islam (Bayat 1998).

The Islamization of society increased enormously with the rising popularity of Islamic books and television shows. By 1994, more than a quarter of the books published in Egypt were religious, a 25 percent rise from the 1980s. Islamist sentiments also increased, with Islamists becoming active civil society actors; professional syndicates, the mass media, formal education, and community services became increasingly Islamized. The majority of the followers of the Muslim Brotherhood during the 1980s and 1990s were young men and women from the modern middle class (Bayat 1998).

Islamist social welfare organizations were essential during the 1990s to fill the gap created by government non-intervention in the socioeconomic sphere, which had resulted from the economic liberalization process begun with Sadat's open door policy. They built their own associations with alternative mosques, schools, and women's organizations, solidifying the grassroots basis for Islamist movements like the Muslim Brotherhood. Although the state was lenient with the growing influence of the Muslim Brothers in society, it was fearful of their expanding political power. It felt compelled to develop its own Islamist sentiments and discourse both to legitimate its political power and to counter the Muslim Brotherhood's growing influence. As Bayat (1998) points out, "it was a peculiar kind of revivalism, in that the fusion of Islamic symbols into the people's everyday life contributed to the production of a somewhat secularized religion."

Religious discourse became hegemonic, increasing the general religiosity of society. Nevertheless, as will be discussed later, while these interactions between the state and the Islamist movements were influential in developing religiosity within society, they were not able to accommodate the rising social discontent within the socioeconomic structure. Neither al-Azhar nor the Islamist movements nor the state were able to create an alternative discourse to address the rising discontent of the middle class and the growing number of unemployed youth. Unlike in the 1990s, when the Islamists had played an essential role in mobilizing middle-class professionals and helping the poor, during the 2000s they effectively abandoned the middle class. They were more inclined to help the poor by offering health care services, education, and financial assistance, than to help the middle class find jobs or enjoy a better standard of living (Bayat 2009). Islamist movements were also busy trying to contain their own internal struggles and reconcile their position with the Egyptian authorities so as to attain political power through parliamentary elections, and so made little effort to mobilize the middle class against the regime.[2]

The Coptic Orthodox Church and the Egyptian Regime: Mutual Dependency

Egyptian Copts are the largest Christian Arab community in the Middle East and North Africa (MENA) region. Estimates based on the 2000 census report that 5.6 percent of the Egyptian population is Coptic; Coptic authorities put that figure higher: between 10 and 20 percent (Fargues 2001). In 1996, Egyptian sociologist and activist Saad Eddin Ibrahim proposed an international conference on minorities in the Arab world. He included Egyptian Copts among the minority groups. The Egyptian government banned the conference with the consent of the majority of prominent Coptic figures like Patriarch Shenouda, because they argued that Copts are not a 'minority' but rather part of the Egyptian nation (Fargues 2001). Nevertheless, over the past decade the Coptic Orthodox Church has helped to develop the Christian community's feelings of being a minority by building up Coptic Christianity as a counter-Islamic religious identity.

When Nasser introduced mandatory Islamic education to school curricula and brought the Christian missionary schools under state control, Egypt saw its first sectarian riots since the Crusades (Hassan 2003).

Sectarian differences continued to be an issue under Sadat, who Islamized the public sphere, and who regarded himself as 'the pious [Muslim] president.' Sadat's civil Islamization measures, coupled with his visit to Jerusalem, provoked criticism from many Egyptians as well as from the Coptic patriarch. Sadat responded in a public parliamentary address in 1980, remarking that "the pope must understand that I am the Muslim president of a Muslim country." This fueled Coptic resentment toward the president and provoked sectarian violence in 1981, when Copts and Muslims clashed in the Cairo middle-class district of al-Zawya al-Hamra (Hassan 2003). Sadat's response was to confine the patriarch in Wadi al-Natrun Monastery, further angering and alienating the Coptic community.

Mubarak recalled the patriarch in 1985, four years after he came to power, which briefly increased the Church's trust in the government. As noted above, however, the government's emphasis on Islam as the state religion only continued to grow. For example, as Herrera points out:

Implicit in the upbringing component of schooling is the attempt— by planners and educators—to transmit to students regardless of their religious affiliation, a sense of belonging to a Muslim society with a culture and history embedded in Islam. Islamic symbols are formally incorporated into the daily life of students among other means, rituals, religious passages in textbooks, religious signs and posters displayed throughout schools. (Herrera 2006, 28)

Meanwhile, the state largely excludes Copts from public office. Few Copts occupy posts in the Egyptian intelligence and police forces. Indeed, in 2005 there were only three Copts in the Egyptian parliament; there had been twenty-seven in 1942.[3] The state security apparatus dealt directly with the Church as the sole institution in charge of all Copts. When a sociopolitical issue arose within the Church or between the Church and another institution, State Security contacted the Church directly to instruct it how to proceed. This maneuvering increased the power of the Coptic Church as an institution in both public and political spheres and increased its domination over Copts in Egypt. Moreover, once-independent Coptic institutions (like the General Millet Council, for instance) have increasingly been incorporated into the structure of the Church. The elected members of the General Millet Council are overwhelmingly individuals with close ties to the Coptic Church, and are even chosen from a group of individuals known to have the 'blessing' of the patriarch, suggesting that the Millet Council is merely a puppet of the Church (Fattah 2009).

Feeling threatened by the rise of political Islamist groups, the Church consistently supported Mubarak. For instance, Coptic authorities declared their endorsement of Mubarak for the national plebiscite before the constitutional reforms of 2005 and continued to endorse him in the subsequent parliamentary elections. The Church also allowed the government to make diplomatic use of Coptic ties with other African nations, particularly Ethiopia (Fattah 2009). In turn, the regime supported the Church by providing churches with state security forces, sending a representative to all high-profile Coptic events, and helping to legitimize the authority of Church figures over their congregations. That is to say, both the Mubarak regime and the Church authorities enjoyed mutual benefits from the prevailing status quo. This dependency allowed the regime and the Church to restrain a common threat—the Islamist movements—and to maintain power within their own spheres.

The Islamic religious discourse: From hegemony to stagnation

The state's dominance over al-Azhar had important repercussions on its ability to develop an independent discourse. This is evident, for instance, in the fact that between 2000 and 2004 *Majallat al-Azhar* (Al-Azhar Institutions' Magazine) devoted a great deal of space to the Islamization of society in general, but did not discuss citizenship issues. The magazine emphasized the role of religion in an individual's life, through prayer, fasting, and justice writ large. The concept of justice, however, was addressed only as a matter between individuals—how people act toward one another—never in the deeper, societal sense of justice by the ruler or ruling class. And the cure it advocated for all the ills facing Egyptian society was that people should become more pious (Zayed 2007).

Al-Bayoumi argues in one opinion piece that modern Egyptian intellectuals—mainly social scientists and philosophers with bachelor's degrees from non-religious universities—should not teach Egyptian university students because their knowledge of Islam is minimal, superficial, and influenced by the west (Al-Bayoumi 2001b, 74). He contends that incorporating Islamic teachings in all school and university curricula is necessary to ensure that Egypt's youth benefit from Islamic upbringing and morality. By underlining the threat posed by the erosion of religion's role in society, the discourse turns its criticism on youth and liberal intellectuals. It confronts the apathetic behavior of youth and their tendency to imitate the 'secular' west, rather than returning to the true teachings of Islam. The magazine systematically criticizes the educational system, at both the primary and the university levels, for its lack of Islamic teachings. State university education and social scientists who teach in that system draw ire for neglecting to teach Islamic social sciences and focusing too narrowly on western secularism (Zayed 2007, 45, 50). The relationship between east and west is portrayed through criticism of western secularism and emphasis on the importance of Islamizing the social sciences to "return to true Islamic ethics" (Zayed 2007, 50).

The perspective offered by the magazine is largely conservative, especially on the subject of women's rights, including rights to employment, inheritance, and education. For instance, the magazine stresses the importance of women remaining at home to protect the morality of their families. It does allow that necessity may sometimes require women to take outside employment, but stresses that they should only be employed in certain sectors, like education and medicine. It insists on maintaining inequality between men and women and criticizes important feminist writers like Qassim Amin (Zayed 2007, 51).

Another common topic is to portray as atheists Egyptian scholars who teach 'secular literature' that supposedly undermines 'Egyptian culture.' Al-Bayoumi asserts, for instance, that secular intellectuals who advocate freedom of expression and liberty are in fact merely promoting immorality and atheism (2001a, 73). He contends that these scholars should reflect on the meaning of Islam to understand the true elements of Muslim culture.

Finally, although al-Azhar portrays itself as a 'centrist' religious institution, it undermines the freedom of expression of any critical analysis that interprets Islam from a perspective different from its own. In 2010, for instance, the Council on Islamic Research, which is part of al-Azhar Institution, banned several books by liberal authors because, the council said, these books taught liberalism, which contradicts Islamic teachings.[4]

The Muslim Brotherhood, meanwhile, has been struggling with its political and ideological thinking. Its members have been relentlessly trying to show the public that they support democratic rule by reiterating their argument that democracy is 'shura.'[5] Throughout the 2000s, the Muslim Brotherhood was influenced by the many reformist thinkers in its ranks who helped to develop a liberal interpretation of Islam. They have been primarily concerned with attaining political power, and with that goal in mind they developed a platform in 2007 in which they laid out their main ideas regarding Islam and politics. In this platform they advanced a proposal to ensure that all laws in the country would conform with shari'a. They proposed that a body of religious scholars be elected to judge the extent to which all Egyptian laws abide by shari'a. In the same platform, they also proposed that women and non-Muslims be excluded from the office of president.[6] In his inauguration speech in 2010, Muhammad Badie, the elected supreme general guide of the Muslim Brotherhood, took a step back from these controversial issues by showing a more tolerant attitude, especially to women and Copts, and recognizing their importance in Egyptian society. He addressed the issue of 'resisting' the rulers by arguing that the Muslim Brotherhood believes in incremental rather than radical change in society. Accordingly, he stressed the importance of constitutional reforms alongside dialogue between the Brotherhood and the government.[7] His speech did not display any confrontational attitude toward the authoritarian regime; on the contrary, he articulated ways to initiate incremental reforms through the parliament and by becoming assimilated in the political process. On international issues, Badie urged east–west cooperation, but highlighted the Palestinian problem as the most pertinent issue confronting Arab Muslims, and one that should be dealt with more radically than other international questions.[8] Thus, the Brotherhood's opposition to the government is discerned only on foreign policy issues; they barely touched on national justice, human rights, and socioeconomic problems.

Al-Azhar and the Brotherhood have primarily been concerned with general religious issues; they rarely addressed youth in a direct manner. In contrast, a new wave of preachers, preaching Islamic neoliberalism,[9] was a driving force in inspiring Egyptian youth to develop a religious identity. The preachers addressed them in colloquial language, and in their speeches they gave examples from their youthful, middle-class audience's everyday life. This tactic attracted many young people; in fact, these preachers had mass followings. They addressed social issues by focusing on individual, not collective, behavior; they were mainly concerned with young people's adherence to religion, and with criticizing youth behavior. Amr Khalid, for instance, one of the most prominent young preachers, was concerned with the question of why the west was more developed than the east. The main reason, he suggested, lay in the failure of the east to acquire a positive work ethic. He was critical of Arab youth for not working as hard as their western counterparts, for watching television, and for being too concerned with romantic relationships. The only way Arabs could attain western standards was, he said, through a revival based on the true teachings of Islam, including hard work (Zayed 2007, 80).

Islamic revivalism, Khalid suggested, should be inspired by the *sahaba* and their ability to revive the Islamic *umma*, and should imitate them in the hard work that furthered their research and advanced the sciences. Khalid posited that development in the Muslim world depended on individuals' deep understanding of their religion, which should be acquired by close and constant reading of the Qur'an. This, he said, would inspire Muslims to feel compassion for other believers, which would in turn fuel development in the true manner of Islam. To build up this community, he argued, youth needed to develop their religious identity through work and deeds in their everyday life, and be tolerant of their neighbors. Meanwhile, women should contribute to the Islamic revival by being pious and dressing appropriately (Zayed 2007, 82).

Even though Khalid's discourse is mostly critical of youth, he gained popularity because at the end of each show, he painted a picture of how much brighter their future would be if they would adhere to the 'true' meaning of Islam (Zayed 2007, 85). Khalid's harsh criticism of the Brotherhood for its statements against Copts and women brought his discourse closer to the hearts and minds of middle-class youth (al-Habaal 2010). Essentially, instead of blaming the ruling elite for inefficient economic development and planning, Khalid criticized youth for their lack of productivity, an attitude based on neoliberal economic ideals he had formed in the course of his career. In other words, he defended and legitimized social inequality and the international capitalist mode of production by blaming young people for their own unemployment and poor standards of living, and absolving the crony and nepotistic capitalist system in Egypt of its responsibility for these ills (Amin 2007).

The discourse of the Coptic Orthodox Church: Sectarian identity and submission to authoritarianism

According to Zayed, the discourse of the Coptic patriarch is based on idealism and spirituality, rather than on participation in society and the real world. Between 2000 and 2004, the majority of the patriarch's lectures were concerned with Orthodox faith and values; very few dealt with social issues (Zayed 2007, 127). He focused mostly on the importance of the family as an institution, and the importance of the Coptic Orthodox Church and its hierarchy within society. Within this context, he encouraged Copts to turn to their clergy for answers, but addressed political issues only vaguely: "Copts are responsible before their nation, before their church, and before their conscience about their political apathy" (127). This statement was addressed to individuals rather than to church leaders, and it dealt with Copts as believers rather than as citizens with an Egyptian identity.

The patriarch was vocally intolerant of other Christian sects. In one address, he forbade Coptic Orthodox Christians to attend the services of any other sect, even when unable to attend a Coptic Orthodox Church.[10] Predictably, this drew considerable criticism from the Evangelical and Catholic congregations of Egypt. This stance, which might be described as reactionary, was suggestive of the degree to which the patriarch wished to seclude the Coptic Church from other Egyptian institutions.

Bishop Moussa, the 'youth bishop,' has shown more interest in addressing social and political issues. His approach, however, concentrates heavily on the role of religious affiliation in an individual's political identity. In the 1990s, during his weekly speeches, he spoke mostly on feelings of affiliation and exclusion in society. By the new millennium, he had turned his attention to the problems of globalization (Zayed 2007, 128). In 1994, Bishop Moussa touched on national identity by saying, "patriotism enhances the feeling of love toward the nation and its institutions, . . . makes an individual understand his obligations toward the country, and opens an individual's heart to brothers and sisters who belong to different religious backgrounds" (129), but he never developed this idea in subsequent addresses.

The marked under-emphasis on national and political involvement indicates the extent to which Copts are expected to identify with the church rather than the nation. In fact, by encouraging Copts to address church rather than public figures with their concerns, the Coptic Church is incrementally becoming the intermediary between Coptic citizens and the state. This conflation of sacred with political space is dangerous because it condenses the political attitude of an entire minority into the views of a handful of religious authorities (Morcos 2009).

The majority of articles in the Coptic newspaper *Watani* focus on the Copts' sociopolitical problems, and almost a third of its articles are dedicated to Egyptian and Arab news (Zayed 2007). Youssef Sidhum, the editor in chief, often publishes pieces about the political issues pertaining to the construction of churches, discrimination against Copts in the social sphere, and inequality in news reporting (Zayed 2007, 140). His editorial piece before the 2010 parliamentary elections, for instance, concedes that the NDP is the major player in the political sphere, without questioning the Copts' own political legitimacy. Thus, at the height of social discontent with the general performance of the NDP in all aspects of Egyptian life, the Coptic Church and intellectuals associated with it were more concerned with sectarian issues than with corruption and authoritarianism per se.

Religious institutions: Out of touch, out of time

The previous sections dealt with the general discourses of the main religious institutions in Egypt and illustrated their increasing dominance in the public sphere. Nevertheless, they remained out of touch with regard to collective problems. Together, religious institutions and the authoritarian regime have effectively developed a 'secularized religion' (Bayat 1998) in which Egyptian society has grown increasingly pious and concerned with religious symbolism. This has increased the country's sectarian divide by polarizing public consciousness in terms of religious affiliations rather than national affinities. But while the discourses of religious institutions have increased general piety, they have not resulted in more than a superficial understanding of religion, nor have they tackled the prevailing socioeconomic or political problems of the day. Issues like social justice, for instance, which are pillars of both the Christian and the Muslim faiths, have scarcely been addressed at all.

Socioeconomic Difficulties and the Rise of New Secular Movements

The presence of new social movements in Egypt increased after the American invasion of Iraq. The 20 March Movement for Change was established in 2003 as a direct consequence of that invasion, but it also voiced slogans against the regime, thereby demonstrating its commitment to the struggle against dictatorship and despotism (Kheir 2011). The neoliberal economic reforms added to the social pressures on the middle and lower classes, which, beginning in 2006, were made manifest in a new wave of protest movements galvanized by workers and technocrats (Shehata 2010). The establishment of the April 6 movement, for instance, was directly related to its members' ability to mobilize collaboration with the al-Mahalla al-Kubra textile workers' strike against the government in 2008 (Shobaky 2009).

In the meantime, according to the 2004 Arab Human Development Report, youth have not been effectively integrated in governance of the region, despite their growing numbers (Rutherford 2008). Because education levels rose during the 1980s and 1990s, especially at the primary level, today's youth are more educated than earlier generations. One important result of this expansion in the education sectors is that adult literacy rates increased enormously from 1990 to 2010. Literacy rates in general during this period rose from 44.4 to 66.4 percent.[11] Although the overall quality of education in Egypt remains low, the prevalence of a literate citizenry with access to Internet and the ability to acquire information from different sources helped to fuel the new movements that drove the protests.

Growing inequalities in the standard of living and economic and social opportunities were and are the norm in Egypt. Income disparities in the industrial sector, for instance, have been growing incrementally since the 1960s, but took a dramatic leap between 1999 and 2002 (Henry and Springborg 2010). Corruption, nepotism, and cronyism are particularly widespread. According to Transparency International, corruption in the MENA region in general is "deeply rooted in the political infrastructure of the state, . . . the institutional infrastructure of the public sector, . . . and develops as a result of the relatively limited opportunities for public participation."[12] In such an environment, highly educated individuals who lack the requisite political 'connections' for attaining employment or a decent salary from the private or public sector are largely excluded. Over the last decade, the concentration of large amounts of wealth in the hands of a few further aggravated income inequalities and social exclusion. The system of cronyism-infused capitalism alienated citizens and increased resentment (UNDP 2009).

The explosion of socioeconomic and political demonstrations in the early 2000s—from which religious influence was almost entirely absent—was an important factor in the growth of new secular and youth movements. According to Ottaway and Hamzawy, Egypt experienced nearly one thousand demonstrations and sit-ins in 2009 and almost three hundred labor strikes in early 2010.[13] The early protests were mostly socioeconomic, lacking any political aspect for a long while. They were nevertheless vivid confirmation of the economic concerns of the poor and the working class, as well as the middle class and professionals.

While most of these actions were taken to protest income inequalities and poor standards of living, some were also politically motivated.

The Kefaya (Enough) movement emerged in 2004 to call for an overhaul of the Mubarak regime, but initially failed to develop a mass following.[14] Other movements followed suit, like the 9 March movement advocating for academic freedoms and autonomy from state security personnel. New social movements bypassed stagnant religious discourse by amalgamating the socioeconomic and political demands of a diverse range of people. The April 6 movement, for instance, did just that by framing its solidarity with the al-Mahalla textile workers with the ideals of social justice, equality of opportunity, and human dignity that lie at the root of both political and economic demands. The Reporters for Change movement called for independence of the press, the rule of law, and the separation of powers that are essential for the promotion of democracy in Egypt (Kheir 2011). The Anti-Globalization Egyptian Group focused on the socioeconomic problems of Egyptian workers and peasants that had resulted from privatization and globalization (al-Agati 2010). This was the popular discourse that emerged from these movements, which called for democracy and transparency in the hope that these would somehow alleviate social and economic problems. They were successful in framing human rights as the antithesis of injustice, inequality, and corruption—in other words, as a concept that did not clash with religious ideals. Thus, when the new social movements called for demonstrations against the police forces a few days before 25 January 2011, their notion of human rights was not pitted against religious identity, but presented citizens with an alternative view that could alleviate their social problems.

At the same time, religious institutions were busy trying to legitimize the political power of the Mubarak regime. The new preachers attempted to hypnotize the masses with precepts that defined what was and was not socially acceptable. The Muslim Brotherhood was devoting greater efforts to reconcile internal struggles between reformists and the old guard and trying to win seats in the 2010 parliamentary elections than to mobilizing the middle class or the poor against the regime.

New Secular Movements in the Post-Mubarak Period

Theorists describe new social movements as spaces in which new ideas are invented and developed: "Movements resemble safe, nourishing hothouses where non elites exchange ideas that elites deem silly, dangerous, or immoral" (Zirakzadeh 2006, 14). Their success lies in their ability to draw on cultural memory and moral systems, and to redefine situations to legitimate their actions against the regime (Oliver, Cadena-Roa, and Strawn 2003). An important feature of new social movements is their ability to negate a prevailing political order and construct alternative institutions and value systems. They are also able to develop alternative social and cultural subsystems or identities that coexist with the dominant order, even when tensions arise (Bayat 1998).

In the Egyptian case, new social movements have been successful in negating the authoritarian political system headed by Mubarak. The main question now is whether these movements can develop a new ideology that can overtake the prevailing radical religious discourse. Since the fall of Mubarak, this radicalism has increased sharply, especially with the politicization of the Salafi movements previously suppressed by the state security apparatus. The new social movements have made it very clear that they are not interested in gaining political office. It is still unclear, however, to what extent they will be able to influence society and Egypt's civil institutions gradually by exerting only moral and intellectual leadership, to inspire a process of democratization based on social inclusion and human rights ideals.

Conclusion

This study has shown that when an authoritarian regime encroaches on the public sphere, social movements find different avenues for expressing their ideas and gaining their freedoms. They develop new ideals, and are able to mobilize citizens by juxtaposing political culture with new principles. In Egypt, the regime monopolized the public sphere, including religious institutions, and retained social control for a long time. Eventually, both their dominance and their discourse became stagnant. Consequently, new social movements mobilized people in new ways, the Kefaya movement on the street and the April 6 movement in cyberspace and social networking as well as on the street. By moving into these spheres, they developed a new discourse that did not undermine Egyptians' religious consciousness.

The Egyptian Revolution will not, however, be truly successful unless the new social movements reach society at large. Their discourse needs to be extended to the political sphere—which comprises public authorities, the state police, and the ruling class—and the public sphere: the free realm between the family and the workplace, where citizens gather and organize to discuss public affairs and the common good, and thus develop a cohesive public opinion (Habermas 1989). The first goal can be attained by influencing the constitutional amendment process to enshrine political and religious freedoms, and by holding public office in order to influence institutions from within. The second goal requires an ability to influence the media, civil society, and educational systems, which are essential tools in any political socialization process and key to spreading intellectual and moral values.

The role new social movements have so far played in the post-Mubarak period reflects the embryonic development of a new political discourse that does not conflict with Egyptian religious identity. This can be seen, for instance, in the way these movements have cooperated with Muslim Brotherhood youth while criticizing and putting pressure on the Muslim Brotherhood old guard: they have been quick to accuse the latter of trying to co-opt the revolution for their own political advantage, especially following the referendum on constitutional amendments in March 2011. The Islamist movements, meanwhile, want to reaffirm their social base by gaining political power. This could be seen during the Friday 29 July 2011 demonstrations, where Islamists chanted 'Islamic nation' instead of 'unity,' reflecting their commitment to transforming secular Egypt into an Islamic state.[15] The political scene in Egypt today is polarized between the Islamists, mainly comprising the Brotherhood and the Salafis, against the so-called 'liberals,' made up of the right, the left, and Muslim and Christian centrists. The general picture is of Islamists against everyone else, whom the Islamists portray as atheists.[16]

Al-Azhar has been playing a pivotal role in national debates since Mubarak's fall. In March a group of Azhar sheikhs demanded that the institution be independent of the political establishment. Furthermore, in light of the growing distrust of new social movements and liberal intellectuals toward the Islamist movements, al-Azhar introduced a sort of 'vision statement,' the "al-Azhar Document," for post-revolution Egypt. Because it embraces Islamic teachings that are in harmony with liberal democratic principles, the document has won consensus from a variety of intellectuals, religious figures, and Islamists (Brown 2011). During the violence which flared in November 2011 between new social movements, revolutionaries, and the Supreme Council of the Armed forces, al-Azhar did not contest the power of the council directly, but did criticize the use of force against civilians. Fifty of its sheikhs have also mediated between the revolutionaries and the police to halt the bloodshed, and one of them,

Sheikh Imad Effat, was killed. This participation established al-Azhar as an important intermediary between the state and society. These developments are crucial, particularly since the Brotherhood abstained from demonstrating with the new social movements against the Supreme Council of the Armed Forces.

The Coptic Church, meanwhile, has been mobilizing Copts since the fall of Mubarak to participate in Egyptian politics. It has also shown its discontent with the use of violence against Coptic demonstrators. The Church, however, is fighting primarily for Coptic existence within a 'civil state,' that is, neither a religious nor a military state.

Having played a key role in ousting Egypt's autocratic leader, the challenge now for the new social movements is to build on that success to develop a new morality, new institutions, and new intellectual leadership based on democracy and human rights.

Notes

1 Interview with Muhammad Abdel Azim, undersecretary of the Ministry of Endowment, 4 April 2011.
2 Marina Ottaway and Amr Hamzawy, "Protest Movements and Political Change in the Arab World," *Carnegie Endowment for International Peace: Policy Outlook*, 2011, http://carnegieendowment.org/publications/?fa=view&id=42394
3 Sameh Fawzi and Samir Morcos, "Governance of Religious Diversity: The Copts of Egypt as Example," 2010, *Arab Reform Initiative*, http://www.arab-reform.net/spip.php?article5168
4 A. al-Habaal, "Maqass al-riqaba ya'tarid 32 'amalan ibda'iyyan fi 2010," *al-Shuruq*, 2010, http://www.shorouknews.com/ContentData.aspx?id=316130
5 Muhammad Badie, "Inauguration Speech," 2010, http://www.ikhwanonline.com/Article.asp?ArtID=59192&SecID=212
6 Ottaway and Hamzawy 2011, 16.
7 Badie, "Inauguration Speech."
8 Badie, "Inauguration Speech."
9 For more information regarding Islamic neoliberalism, see al-Hodaiby's analysis in chapter 7 of this book.
10 Ahmad Bayoumi, "Church Asks Immigrant Copts to Welcome Mubarak in Washington," *Al-Masry Al-Youm*, 2009, http://www.almasry-alyoum.com/article2.aspx?Article ID=209933
11 UNDP, *Human Development Report 2010*, http://hdr.undp.org
12 Transparency International, *Transparency International Middle East and North Africa*, 2011, http://www.transparency.org/regional_pages/africa_middle_east_and_north_africa_mena
13 Ottaway and Hamzawy 2011.
14 Ottaway and Hamzawy 2011, 8–9.

15 "'Jum'at tafriq al-shaml' . . . al-ikhwan wa-l-salafiyun yahtifun: 'islamiya islamiya' wa
    31 min al-quwa al-siyasiya tansahib," *Al-Masry Al-Youm*, 30 July 2011, http://www.
    almasry-alyoum.com/article2.aspx?ArticleID=305587
16 N. Mosaad, "Man khassar al-akhar? Al-Midan am al-Ikhwan?" *al-Shuruq*, 2 June
    2011, http://www.shorouknews.com/columns/view.aspx?cdate=02062011&id=
    60ba5abf-d2c6-46f3-8a99-4da3eef2d068

5

The Power of Workers in Egypt's 2011 Uprising

Dina Bishara

"Workers did not join the revolution; the revolution joined the workers," proclaimed a prominent labor activist when I asked him about the
role of Egyptian workers in the 25 January 2011 uprising, which forced
former President Hosni Mubarak—who had ruled Egypt for nearly three
decades—to step down.[1] This provocative claim, whether or not it is
true, reflects one side of a spirited domestic debate. To the labor activist
with whom I spoke, "the revolution joined the workers" in the sense that
workers had laid the foundation for the uprising through their continuous activism over the last five years. An equally pervasive view in Egyptian
domestic debates, however, demeans the 'late entry' of Egyptian workers
into the uprising and laments the fact that workers raised predominantly
economic rather than political demands.

This chapter suggests that these two views are not as mutually exclusive as their proponents might suggest. It argues that sustained and
widespread workers' mobilization, in the form of strikes and protests
during the last three days before Mubarak stepped down, was decisive
in bringing about this outcome, despite the fact that this type of mobilization did not uniformly embrace the slogan of 'toppling the regime.'
Notably, this mobilization occurred largely outside of the framework of
the official Egyptian Trade Union Federation (ETUF). In addition—and
in contrast to the widespread perception that workers joined the uprising

only at the end—individual workers as well as some workers' groups, especially those who had established independent organizations prior to 25
January, collectively mobilized at the start of the uprising and embraced
its political demands. Despite the fact that Egypt has not yet undergone
a 'democratic transformation,' these findings have important implications for theoretical debates concerning the role of the working class in
processes of democratization. First, these findings point to the limits of
the literature's narrow focus on the conditions under which labor adopts
a 'pro-democratic' stance (Therborn 1997; Rueschemyer, Stephens, and
Stephens 1992; Collier 1999; Bellin 2000). This narrow focus obscures the
fact that workers might play a consequential role in bringing down an
authoritarian regime without being at the forefront of a pro-democracy
movement. In addition, this literature assumes that 'organized labor,' in
the form of unions and labor-affiliated parties (Collier 1999, 15), is the
primary actor of concern. As this chapter demonstrates, however, this
assumption does not account for the possibility that consequential labor
mobilization might occur in the absence of strong, independent labor
unions or labor-affiliated parties.

On the eve of the 25 January uprising, the ETUF had become increasingly co-opted by the Mubarak regime, resulting in a growing disconnect
between EUTF leaders and rank-and-file workers. This disconnect had
led workers to defy ETUF leaders and organize numerous protests independently of their unions, and prompted some to establish 'independent'
unions to better organize themselves. Given this context, this chapter uses
primary sources and interviews with labor activists to investigate when,
how, and why Egyptian workers participated in the 25 January uprising. It
identifies three distinct modes of workers' mobilization in that uprising,
reflecting the fragmented nature of workers' organization in Egypt, and
explores the logic behind each mode of participation.

Early small-scale group participation was undertaken primarily by
'defectors' who had been involved in forming representative labor organizations or coordinating wildcat strikes and protests in various sites prior
to 25 January. These groups could capitalize on their existing networks
and act more collectively during the first two weeks of the uprising when
workplaces were shut down. Defectors articulated broad national and
economic demands. Militant rank-and-file workers participated individually as early as 28 January, but the lack of independent capacity to
organize and the fact that workplaces were shut down until the week of

6 February curtailed group mobilization of rank-and-file workers until 8 February. From then on, rank-and-file workers—both first-timers and those with a prior history of mobilization—organized a series of protests and strikes in almost all sectors. The fact that these actions were mostly about workplace-specific demands does not mean, however, that they had no impact on the outcome of the uprising. The mobilization of rank-and-file workers, in the form of strikes and protests at workplaces, starting 8 February, arguably constituted a tipping point in the Egyptian uprising. Their entry dealt a serious blow to a cornerstone of the regime's strategy in dealing with the Tahrir movement at the time—namely geographic and political isolation.

The chapter proceeds in five main sections. The first provides a brief overview of the history of workers' activism in Egypt prior to 25 January, thereby contextualizing the debate around workers' participation in the uprising. It also discusses the main features of current 'labor' organization in Egypt, and argues that Egyptian labor is particularly fragmented in light of certain structural and historical factors. The second places the Egyptian case in comparative perspective by discussing the theoretical literature on the role of the working class in processes of democratic transition. The third section provides an empirical analysis of the different modes of workers' participation in Egypt's January 2011 uprising, arguing that capacity to organize and history of prior mobilization largely determined the mode of workers' participation and the nature of the demands they articulated. The fourth section reflects on the impact of labor mobilization on the outcome of the uprising. The fifth section summarizes the findings of the chapter.

Context

Egypt has a long history of labor activism (Beinin and Lockman 1987; Posusney 1997). Since 2006, however, Egypt has experienced the "longest and strongest wave of worker protest since the end of World War II."[2] This wave was partly a response to the more aggressive adoption of neoliberal economic reforms since 2004, especially the accelerated rate of privatization of state-owned enterprises. Notably, these protests have taken place despite severe restrictions on striking. In addition, "the official ETUF institutions have rarely supported these protests although in some cases individual members of local trade union committees have done so" (Beinin

2010, 15). According to some estimates, more than two million workers[3] engaged in more than 2,100 strikes and other forms of protest from 2006 to 2009.[4] There were 530 labor-related incidents, including strikes, sit-ins, and demonstrations, in 2010 alone.

The timing of workers' activism since 2006 can be partly explained with reference to a broader political opening in Egypt, characterized by the holding of the first multi-candidate presidential elections in 2005 and the emergence of protest groups such as Kefaya (Enough). In addition, there was a marked shift in the way in which the Mubarak regime responded to labor protests. In contrast to the 1980s, the regime appeared to refrain from violently repressing workers' protests so long as they remained confined to workers' demands and did not join forces with political groups. This political environment contributed to a growing perception among workers that there was a greater opportunity for them to mobilize than there had been in the past.

The 2006–2010 wave of workers' protests was set in motion by a strike in December 2006 at the Misr Spinning and Weaving Company in al-Mahalla al-Kubra, "a public-sector firm and one of the largest enterprises in Egypt with about 25,000 employees." This and a subsequent strike in September 2007 were an inspiration to many other workers (Beinin 2010, 30). Notably, however, the 2006–2010 protests involved not only traditionally militant blue-collar workers, but also previously quiescent employees and workers from within the state's own administrative apparatus, such as ministries and government agencies. The most prominent case of this type of mobilization was that of real estate tax collectors, who went on strike in December 2007 and succeeded in securing a 300 percent pay raise. Although these protests mostly centered on workplace-specific economic demands, some advanced more politically ambitious goals, such as the recognition of independent unions.

In addition to the participation of previously quiescent constituencies, this wave of protests was characterized by two other important features. First, there was much more sustained activity than previous waves of labor protests in Egypt, notes an independent labor-affairs journalist.[5] This continuity, in addition to increased coverage by independent media outlets, allowed labor activists to learn from others' experiences, thereby contributing to an increase in the level of awareness and organization. Second, as noted above, the Egyptian government could no longer afford to violently repress labor protests, given the growing independent media coverage of these protests and increased scrutiny of the Egyptian government by international labor organizations.

Notably, workers' mobilization in the five years preceding Mubarak's ousting remained largely separate from mobilization by anti-Mubarak groups such as Kefaya and other similar initiatives. The only major exception to this trend was an attempt by a group of political activists (who later formed the April 6 movement) to call for a general strike on 6 April 2008, in solidarity with a strike organized by textile workers in Mahalla scheduled for the same day. The call for a general strike was spread through Facebook and was supported by the Kefaya movement and the Labor, Karama, and Wasat parties.[6] At the time, Mahalla workers were opposed to this call; some were concerned about the security repercussions, while others saw their demands as largely separate from those of the political activists.[7] Relations between labor and political activists were thus characterized by a degree of mutual distrust during the 2006–2010 period. While some political activists have accused labor activists of advancing narrow demands, some labor activists have accused political activists of adopting a condescending view of labor activism. Labor activists might also have believed that their demands were more likely to have been suppressed if they were tied to a more explicit political agenda. The seeming disconnect between the labor activism and political forces in Egypt was the topic of a lively discussion hosted by the Center for Trade Union and Workers' Services (CTUWS) in October 2010. Several labor activists attending the event were eager to denounce frequent attempts to construe their activism as 'apolitical.'

Indeed, workers' mobilization during the 2006–2010 period had significant political implications. Regardless of the specific demands raised, the collective mobilization of workers and government employees repeatedly contested the boundaries of political action set by the Mubarak regime and constituted an important form of political participation, understood as an "activity by private citizens designed to influence governmental decision-making" (Huntington and Nelson 1976, 4). In addition, the fact that workers started protesting outside of their workplaces and in front of the 'centers of decision-making,' namely government agencies in Cairo, such as parliament and the council of ministers, brought their activism to the public realm and signaled their willingness to resort to more confrontational approaches to resolve their grievances. Workers had also succeeded in introducing new repertoires for protest. Finally, workers' mobilization sometimes posed an institutional challenge to the

Mubarak regime's monopoly over workers' representation by calling for the establishment of independent unions.

The unprecedented frequency and scope characterizing the wave of labor protests prior to 25 January 2011 has led some observers of the Egyptian uprising to wonder about the role of workers. Internationally, media coverage of the uprising has focused almost exclusively on the role of the 'Facebook generation,' thereby obscuring the role of other actors. Domestically, the precise nature and impact of workers' participation in the uprising remains highly controversial.

First, however, it is important to provide a brief overview of the present state of labor organizing in Egypt. There are important structural conditions that have curtailed the emergence of truly representative labor organizations. First, Egypt's state–labor relations have long been governed by a state-corporatist system, according to which the state eradicates multiple or parallel associations in favor of "continuous interposition of state mediation, arbitration, and repression" (Schmitter 1974). Not only does this mean that the formation of labor unions is contingent upon state recognition, it also suggests that associations lack administrative independence from the state (Schmitter 1974). As a result, the state-controlled ETUF has long held a monopoly on the representation of workers in Egypt. The ETUF's ties with Mubarak's regime and the increasing disconnect between its leadership and the concerns of rank-and-file workers have led some observers to argue that the ETUF has lost its legitimacy.[8] In addition, labor activists have pointed out that whereas in the past, fraud was limited to elections at the level of general unions and beyond, electoral fraud has recently extended to union committees.[9] "In these elections almost all members of local union committees opposed to the enactment of the Unified Labor Law, which had been hotly debated, were removed from office either because they were administratively barred from running for office or because the elections were manipulated" (Beinin 2010, 42).

The legacy of state-corporatism in Egypt has thus resulted in growing rank-and-file distrust of ETUF union representatives, as well as some efforts on behalf of labor activists to exit official union structures. An analysis of the role of Egyptian workers in the uprising must thus take into account the variety of labor actors in Egypt. Notably, on 27 January, ETUF president Hussein Megawer instructed ETUF leaders to quell any labor protests.[10] Megawer is currently in jail on charges of conspiring to kill protesters during the famous 2 February 'Battle of the Camel.'[11]

In addition to ETUF union leaders, there are at least three distinct sets of labor actors in Egypt. The first consists of what could be referred to as 'defectors.' Defectors include a growing number of labor leaders who have been active in challenging state-controlled labor organizations through the establishment of independent trade unions. The last two years have witnessed heightened activism toward the establishment of independent unions. In April 2009, real estate tax collectors announced the establishment of the first independent trade union in Egypt since the 1940s. Other groups followed suit, including health technicians, pension holders, and teachers, establishing independent unions in 2010. The number of independent unions has increased exponentially since Mubarak stepped down on 11 February. Labor leaders within this set often have a history of political activism, ties to political parties, and extensive contacts with the broader activist community in Egypt. As a result, they possess the necessary tools to build bridges both among workers and between workers and other activists in Egypt. In addition, defectors include members of newly established independent unions, some of whom have withdrawn their formal membership from state-controlled unions, a politically risky move in the Egyptian context. Defecting rank-and-file workers in this set are unique in that they have started to become socialized in independent labor organizations. As a result, some have begun to develop a clear sense of group identity, even if they work in different locations. Defectors also include labor leaders who have been involved in organizing strikes in specific workplaces or who have been involved in informal strike committees.

The second set of labor actors consists of rank-and-file workers who maintain their formal membership in state-controlled unions, but who have been actively engaged in wildcat strikes and protest activities over the last several years. Although these workers have acquired important experience in collective mobilization, they may not exhibit the same level of group cohesion shared by defectors. Members of this group have various degrees of commitment to broader political change that goes beyond their sector or firm-specific demands.

The third set of labor actors in Egypt comprises rank-and-file workers who had not engaged in any protest activities prior to the 25 January uprising.

The diversity of actors described above makes it analytically difficult to speak of a unified 'working class' in Egypt, at least functionally. Any analysis of the role of the 'working class' in the Egyptian uprising must thus begin with an understanding of these various actors and their respective interests. The fragmented nature of 'labor' in Egypt is clearly reflected in the nature and scope of workers' participation in the uprising.

The Egyptian Case in Comparative Perspective

The impassioned debate in Egypt regarding the role of workers in the 2011 uprising is mirrored in rich theoretical debates surrounding the role of the 'working class' in processes of democratization. As Eva Bellin observes, "a long tradition in political science put social forces—and more specifically social classes—center stage when explaining democratic outcomes" (Bellin 2000, 176). Bellin identifies two schools of thought, one liberal and one Marxist, that examined the role of social classes in democratization, primarily drawing their insights from the early wave of industrialization in western states. While some scholars viewed the "capitalist class" as the "class agent of democracy," others attributed that status to the "working class" (Bellin 2000, 176). More recently, other scholars (Collier and Mahoney 1997; Collier 1999; Rueschemeyer, Stephens, and Stephens 1992; Bellin 2000) have reinvigorated this debate, in response to what they perceived as an excessive focus on elite-centric explanations of democratization, especially in the dominant paradigm on democratic transitions. Ruth Berins Collier makes a valuable contribution to this debate by pointing out that the role of labor might have been overestimated in early cases of democratization and underestimated in later ones (Collier 1999). Eva Bellin convincingly suggests that the conditions under which labor might support democratization differ in late-developing countries from those in early-industrializing countries (Bellin 2000).

Although it is premature to refer to the Egyptian case as one of 'democratic transformation,' it serves to highlight two serious limitations in the existing literature on the role of the working class in processes of democratization.

First, rooted in a specific theoretical debate regarding the role of elites versus social classes in democratization, this literature focuses primarily on analyzing labor's 'pro-democratic' actions (Collier 1999, 15). Bellin offers a very compelling explanation for why 'organized labor' might act as a "contingent democrat" (Bellin 2000) in late-developing countries, such as Egypt. The willingness of labor to play an active role in democratization, according to Bellin, is contingent upon two primary factors:

(1) its dependence on the state, and (2) its aristocratic position. The latter refers to the "degree to which organized labor is economically privileged vis-à-vis the general population" (Bellin 2000, 183). Specifically addressing the Egyptian case, Bellin documents a decline in labor's aristocratic position, which may drive it to support democratization. Bellin's analysis helps explain why Egyptian workers might have been inclined to support democratic demands, given the decline in what she calls the "authoritarian bargain" (204). At the same time, however, Bellin's assumption that a decline in labor's aristocratic position or its dependence on the state might push it to support democratization seems to obscure the range of other actions that such a decline might induce. These actions might include, but are not limited to, an explicit demand for democracy. For instance, labor groups might engage in disruptive protests, thereby exerting pressure on authoritarian incumbents without articulating a pro-democratic position. The literature's narrow focus on the conditions under which labor might adopt a pro-democratic stance is theatrically problematic because it obscures the potential for labor to play a consequential role in bringing down an authoritarian regime without being explicitly 'pro-democratic' at the forefront of a pro-democracy movement, as this chapter suggests has happened in Egypt. The Egyptian case thus extends the focus of the existing literature to situations where labor's engagement in contentious politics more broadly can have a consequential impact on the fall of authoritarian incumbents.

Second, conceptually, both Collier and Bellin treat 'labor' as an organized force, one that is capable of acting purposely. This conceptualization serves the authors' analytic aims, namely their attempt to document the important role that labor can play in democratization (Collier 1999) or to explain the conditions under which it might play such a role (Bellin 2000). Collier defines labor as a "collective concept," not an "aggregation of workers." As a result, labor's participation in democratization does not refer to

participation by atomized individual workers, but rather purposive action in which some sense of solidarity or identity or collective purpose must be involved. This notion of class solidarity or identity can take the form of a common construction of meaning in the participatory act, as in the understanding of democratization as a workers' issue, as a benefit to workers as a collectivity. Usually (but not always) it is expressed organizationally. Hence, in most cases we are talking about the organized class and pro-democratic actions led or undertaken by unions and labor-affiliated labor-based parties. (Collier 1999, 15)

If Collier's definition is taken seriously, it would be difficult to speak of the 'role of labor' in Egypt's uprising against Mubarak's authoritarian regime. For Collier, discussing the 'role of labor' presumes a degree of class solidarity and a level of labor organization that are not fully present in the Egyptian context. As the analysis in this chapter will demonstrate, some workers organized collectively during the 25 January uprising while others acted individually. This does not mean, however, that workers' mobilization over the course of the uprising did not have an impact on its outcome. The close control exerted by the state over labor organizations in Egypt (prior to Mubarak's stepping down) had curtailed the emergence of representative labor organizations and the development of cross-sectoral identities. This does not prevent Egyptian workers in various individual workplaces from sharing a common identity, nor does it undermine the fact that a sense of class solidarity may be increasing among members of the Egyptian working class.

The Egyptian case thus presents a challenge for conceptions of labor as a unified actor, whose actions are coordinated through strong organizations. The empirical evidence that will be presented in this chapter suggests that the term 'labor' must be broken down into more nuanced concepts to reflect the heterogeneous nature of the actors involved and their respective, and sometimes conflicting, interests. Doing so is the first step toward an explanation of the various forms of participation (as well as the timing of participation) undertaken by members of the Egyptian working class during the 25 January uprising.

Who Participated, How, When, and Why?

On the most general level, workers' participation in the Egyptian uprising can be classified along two primary axes—namely, individual versus group participation—and according to the degree of support or sympathy for the broader political message of the uprising. As well as drawing a distinction between participation by individual workers and collective action, Collier also differentiates between "labor protest centered around economic or workplace demands or non-democratic revolutionary goals" and cases in which the "working class (or the relevant part of it) took a pro-democratic position" (1999, 16).

More specifically, in Egypt, workers' participation can be classified into three categories: (1) individual participation in anti-regime protests across Egypt prior to 8 February 2011; (2) limited group participation in Tahrir Square and outside of Cairo prior to 8 February 2011 (as the evidence below suggests, this form of participation was primarily undertaken by defectors); and (3) large-scale participation in strikes, protests, and workplace sit-ins starting on 8 February 2011. Another layer of complexity can be added if one takes into account the degree to which each form of participation was sympathetic to the broader political goals of the uprising. As will be demonstrated below, there is variation in the degree to which workers adopted the uprising's political goals, even if they participated in the same way.

Various labor activists and observers assert that individual workers participated in anti-regime protests across Egypt as early as 25 January 2011, and more prominently starting 28 January. A long-time labor activist and active member of the Coordinating Committee for Trade Union and Workers' Rights and Liberties recounts that he saw, and could possibly name, sixty to seventy prominent labor leaders in Tahrir Square on 25 January.[12] He adds that these were either "politicized" labor leaders or ones who had been involved in spearheading labor mobilization between 2006 and 2011. He cites the example of the employees of Council of Ministers information centers, who mobilized repeatedly in 2010. In fact, some information center leaders had attended a training session on collective bargaining, led by the labor activist with whom I spoke; it was held at the Egyptian Center for Economic and Social Rights (ECESR) only a few days prior to 25 January 2011. "I met some of the colleagues who attended the training on 25 January and a large number of them on January 28," recalls the same labor activist (pers. comm.).

Workers from a variety of sectors and firms were present in Tahrir Square prior to the resumption of work on Sunday 6 February 2011, contends a prominent lawyer at the ECESR.[13] These workers came from the industrial cities of Suez, Mahalla, Alexandria, Shibin al-Kom, and Kafr al-Dawwar. Steel workers, public transportation workers, and pension holders were also present. These workers "refused to raise any demands other than the demands of the square," in order not to undermine the broader goal of the protest, he argues. Critiquing the widespread accusation in Egyptian domestic debates according to which workers usually advance "narrow" demands, the lawyer points out that "when they [the workers] stopped doing so and participated in the revolution without raising those demands, people started wondering about the role of the workers. . . . Workers like to be soldiers," he added. They, along with Egypt's poor, are the "unknown soldiers of this revolution."[14]

Another labor activist at the CTUWS notes that in Suez and Helwan, workers participated in the 28 January protests as "individuals."[15] According to some accounts, thousands of workers in the Suez industrial zone took to the streets and joined other protesters.[16] This mode of participation, he argues, was "natural" given the absence of organized labor forces that are independent of the ETUF. Commenting on why individual workers responded to the call for anti-Mubarak protests, this activist noted that drivers of the uprising were "clever" to have used the inclusive slogan, "Bread, freedom, and social justice," at the beginning of the uprising. This slogan resonated quite powerfully with Egyptian workers, he said.

In addition to the participation of workers as individuals during the early days of the uprising, there is some evidence that groups with a history of mobilization capitalized on their networks and acted more collectively—albeit on a small scale—as the uprising continued. This is particularly evident in the case of the four nascent independent unions that had formed prior to 25 January, namely the Independent Union of the Real Estate Tax Authority (RETA), the Independent Teachers' Union, the Independent Union of Health Technicians, and the Independent Union of Pension Holders. Small blocs of active members in these unions participated in anti-Mubarak protests in Tahrir Square, notes an independent labor affairs journalist.[17] Notably, this mode of participation did not include a large-scale mobilization of rank-and-file union members, largely because the teachers' and health technicians' unions were still in the process of developing their capacity to organize. Nonetheless, active union members did coordinate and mobilize collectively to some degree. This was particularly true of RETA members, who had been mobilizing since 2007, even before their union was formally established a year later.

Various RETA members have asserted that they took part as a collective in anti-regime protests prior to 8 February. A leading RETA member from Daqahliya asserts that union members participated as a group in these protests across various governorates.[18] One member from Cairo argues that although union members initially mobilized individually, there was more coordination and communication among union members as the uprising continued. She recounts that in Cairo, union members aggregated around two banners on two different sides of Tahrir Square. RETA members also had a tent on Tahrir Square, asserts an independent labor-affairs journalist.[19] Another union member from the governorate of Daqahliya recounts that she and her colleagues participated in protests and were involved in community initiatives, such as local defense committees, which formed over the course of the uprising to protect public and private property after the withdrawal of police forces from the street.[20]

In addition, there was some degree of coordination among the four independent unions over the course of the uprising. On 30 January, representatives of the four unions and independent groups representing workers in a variety of industrial sites met in Cairo and announced the establishment of the founding committee of the Egyptian Federation of Independent Trade Unions (EFITU). Union representatives and labor activists distributed a leaflet announcing the formation of EFITU's founding committee in Tahrir Square on 1 and 2 February.

This mode of participation seems to have been primarily motivated by national grievances rather than workplace-specific ones. RETA members, for instance, had no group-specific economic demands when they joined the Tahrir protest on 25 January, argues a high-ranking member of the union.[21] In addition, the leaflet announcing the formation of the EFITU asserts that the federation "adopts all of the demands of the revolution of the Egyptian people and its youth, announced on 25 January." The statement pays special attention to workers' specific national demands, including Egyptians' right to work, the adoption of a minimum wage of LE1,200, and Egyptians' right to just social security.

Given this set of grievances, I hypothesize that the early mobilization of groups such as RETA can best be explained with reference to the organizational capacity that RETA had started to develop, as well the group's highly politicized leadership. Organizational capacity is especially important for quick mobilization, especially when group members are geographically distant from each other (either because they work in different locations or because they cannot gather in their common workplaces; the latter was the case for all Egyptian workers during the uprising, until the resumption of work on 6 February 2011). For instance, the fact that RETA members live and work in different governorates would have made the task of ensuring their presence in Cairo on 25 January particularly difficult. Since its formation in 2009, RETA has been engaged in organi-zation-building efforts, capitalizing on the successful strike of 2007. The group has built its organizational capacity by electing union committees in all of Egypt's governorates and has built independent financial resources by collecting membership dues. I further hypothesize that the collective nature of this form of mobilization is facilitated by prior socialization in a group or organization. Such socialization makes it more likely that group members act purposely and articulate the same set of demands. RETA members have started to develop a sense of group identity through their socialization in a representative organization over the last two years and through their previous experience in organizing various strikes and sit-ins. Some aspects of the group's professionalization, such as the facts that members have identification cards and meet periodically irrespective of whether a strike or sit-in is planned, have also contributed to developing this identity. At one RETA weekly meeting in December 2010, I met with members from the governorates of Cairo and Daqahliya, among others. The members were eager to share that they had made friends from various governorates through their participation in union activities. The union has also created a network of contacts among individuals who previously did not know each other.

The hypothesis advanced here requires further empirical testing. Its primary implication is that early group mobilization is more likely to have involved already-formed groups (formal or informal) with a history of collective mobilization. The existence of an independent union or an informal collective forum, such as a strike committee, can help facilitate group mobilization.

Notably, only a few independent labor organizations (formal or infor-mal) existed prior to 25 January 2011, making an organized large-scale mobilization of rank-and-file workers almost impossible. This was further impeded by the limited organizational and mobilizing capacity of the independent unions that had only recently been established.

Perhaps the most widely referenced labor actions during the upris-ing are the strikes and protests by rank-and-file workers in workplaces across Egypt beginning on 8 February 2011, three days before Mubarak stepped down. This is the form of participation that some observers have in mind when commenting on the 'late entry' of Egyptian workers into the uprising. As will be discussed below, the mobilization of rank-and-file workers during this period does not necessarily mean that they endorsed the uprising's political message. Their actions would be better understood as large-scale disruptive activities that coincided with the last three days of the uprising.

In what some accounts described as acts of "civil disobedience,"[22] thousands of Egyptian workers and employees across almost all sectors staged major work disruptions—strikes, sit-ins, and demonstrations—in more than twenty of Egypt's twenty-nine governorates. According to one estimate, between 250,000 and 300,000 workers engaged in these types of protests on 9 February 2011 alone.[23] Notably, whereas the largest protests took place in governorates with a large concentration of workers and a clear history of labor activism, including Alexandria, Suez, Gharbiya, and Helwan, they also spread to governorates that had been far less involved in any protest activities since the start of the uprising: Aswan, Sohag, Qena, Beni Suef, and Minufiya, among others.

Strikes took place in several vital sectors, including public transportation. Railway workers in Cairo and Alexandria went on strike, bringing all train activity to Upper Egypt to a halt.[24] In addition, two military production companies (nos. 63 and 36) went on strike on 9 February and two others (nos. 45 and 54) announced that they would go on strike on 10 February 2011. Soon after the announcement, the minister of military production designated 10 February an official holiday. Giza cleaning workers also went on strike. Protests and demonstrations were also held in numerous important sectors, including Suez Canal companies.

It was not only industrial workers who participated in these actions. Protesters included employees and workers from within the government's own administrative apparatus.[25] This is especially significant because the government had issued a decision on 7 February 2011 to increase wages for state employees. In Cairo, hundreds of employees of the Central Agency for Public Mobilization and Statistics held a sit-in to demand permanent contracts.[26] In Suez, all employees in government agencies stopped working, paralyzing the governorate's administrative agencies.[27] Employees in the ministries of Social Solidarity, Agriculture, Electricity, Religious Endowments, Education, and Health also staged protests.

It would be "incorrect" to assume that all of these protests took place to support the uprising directly, argues labor analyst Mostafa Basyouni.[28] For the most part, they were motivated by workplace-specific economic grievances against corruption. The uprising provided workers with an opportunity to voice these grievances more forcefully.

Despite the diversity of workplaces involved, however, the demands mostly converged around improving working conditions, removing corrupt leaders, and providing permanent contracts to temporary workers. The clearest indication that these were the dominant demands is that these types of protests have continued even after Mubarak stepped down. Between 11 and 14 February 2011, there were forty to sixty such workers' protests a day, and they are still ongoing.[29] Indeed Egypt's ruling Supreme Council of the Armed Forces has issued a communiqué urging workers to go back to work and approved a decree issued on 23 March 2011 by the Egyptian cabinet, criminalizing protests that "disrupt work."

At the same time, some of the groups that joined strikes and protests from 8 February onward explicitly voiced political demands. Egypt Telecom employees called for the "removal of the regime" and threatened to join protesters in Tahrir Square.[30] Public transport workers, who went on strike on 9 February, issued a statement expressing their complete solidarity with the demands raised by revolutionaries in Tahrir Square.[31] The statement expresses support for the demand that Mubarak step down and calls for an end to the state of emergency, the removal of National Democratic Party leaders from all government agencies, and the disbanding of the people's assembly.

In this sense, then, only one segment of the workers who participated in strikes and protests in the last three days took what Collier would describe as a "pro-democratic position" (Collier 1999, 16). A prominent labor activist argues that only a "minority" of workers added the removal of Mubarak to their list of demands. In analyzing the "role of labor in democratization," Collier emphasizes that "it is insufficient if labor protest centered around economic or workplace demands or nondemocratic revolutionary goals, which may have been a threat to capitalism or destabilized authoritarianism by threatening the government's capacity to maintain order but did not constitute a demand for democracy" (16). Despite the fact that only a minority of Egyptian workers adopted a 'pro-democratic' stance while most raised workplace-specific demands, their actions had an important impact on Mubarak's decision to step down, an impact that will be explored in more detail in the next section.

The timing of these protests, during the third and final week of the uprising and only three days before Mubarak stepped down, can best be explained with reference to two factors: the shutting down of workplaces during the first two weeks of the uprising, which impeded workers from staging localized protests and strikes, and the fact that most rank-and-file workers lacked the capacity to independently organize collective action during this period.

A newsletter issued on 22 February 2011 by the CTUWS points out that shutting down workplaces before the week of 6 February meant that workers "lost a weapon that could have settled matters early on. This weapon is their presence in their workplaces as organized human blocs. But this did not prevent them from leading the popular protests on the streets of Suez, Mahalla, Alexandria, Naga Hamadi and almost all of Egypt's governorates."[32] Whether workers' presence at their workplaces could really have "settled matters early," there is reason to believe that the resumption of work in the week of 6 February is closely tied to the timing of workers' mobilization.

By contrast, defectors—given their involvement in independent workers' organizations and their politicized leaders—were better equipped to mobilize collectively during the first two weeks of the uprising, despite the fact that they were also deprived of the ability to meet in their workplaces.

Beyond the issue of timing, however, the sheer volume and geographic reach of workers' protests and strikes between 8 and 11 February raises an intriguing question. It is not clear exactly *how* this mobilization took place, especially since in several of the workplaces where these actions took place, there was neither a history of collective action nor any organization that could easily mobilize the workers. Preliminary evidence suggests that the large-scale mobilization during this period was not the product of central coordination, although there were efforts by some non-governmental organizations (NGOs) and independent labor unions and activists to encourage workers to demonstrate. On 7 February, the CTUWS, a labor NGO, and two of Egypt's independent unions disseminated a statement that linked workers' demands to the need to topple Mubarak's regime and called on workers to take action to support the uprising.[33]

Did Workers' Mobilization Affect the Outcome of the Uprising?

Perhaps the most controversial question regarding workers' participation during the uprising relates to the impact of their mobilization, in its various forms, on Mubarak's decision to step down. Two competing narratives have emerged domestically. The first sees workers' participation, especially during the last three days before Mubarak stepped down, as decisive in hastening that outcome. The second contends that the fact that workers were 'slow' to mobilize and did not explicitly support the political goals of the uprising meant that their mobilization had no impact on Mubarak's stepping down. This narrative suggests that workers' actions are better seen as opportunistic attempts to secure narrow, workplace-specific demands at a time when the regime was vulnerable.

These two narratives might not, however, be mutually exclusive. On the one hand, the uprising did provide an opportunity for workers to voice their workplace-specific demands more forcefully. On the other, workers created a new dynamic through their strikes and protests, activities that were largely detached from Tahrir Square. The mere fact that these actions focused largely on workplace-specific demands does not prevent them from having a broader impact.

It is arguable instead that the mobilization of workers from 8 February onward served as a tipping point in the Egyptian uprising. The entry of rank-and-file workers dealt a serious blow to the Mubarak regime's strategy in dealing with the Tahrir movement at the time, which, as mentioned earlier, relied heavily on geographic and political isolation. The Mubarak regime had tried to 'isolate' the movement by spreading rumors that protesters had foreign agendas.[34] The geographic range of labor action (in twenty-nine governorates as noted above) signaled the possibility of large-scale civil disobedience. That workers' protests and strikes took place simultaneously across a wide variety of sectors, including vital ones, in the days before Mubarak stepped down greatly heightened the pressure on the regime, even without a coordinated national strike.

The regime had also tried to take measures to appease employees in the state's administrative apparatus, and distance them from the movement in Tahrir Square. Aware of these challenges, the Tahrir movement was looking for alternative strategies, including expanding beyond the square by marching on key state buildings, such as parliament. Notably, Tahrir youth groups issued a statement on 8 February, titled "From the Revolutionaries of Tahrir to Our Brothers, the Dignified Workers of Egypt."[35] The statement called on workers to announce a general strike starting the week of 13 February. This indicates that there was recognition on the part of the Tahrir youth that workers' mobilization was important in sustaining the momentum and supplementing their efforts in the square.

Conclusion

Not only has workers' activism in Egypt predated the 25 January uprising, it has continued even after Mubarak stepped down. The role of Egyptian workers in the uprising has fueled great domestic debate, a debate that is mirrored in the theoretical literature regarding the role of social classes in processes of democratization. This chapter has argued that sustained and widespread labor mobilization, which occurred primarily during the last three days before Mubarak stepped down, played a critical role in bringing about this outcome, despite the fact that this form of mobilization did not uniformly adopt the goal of toppling the regime. This analysis contributes two important insights to the broader theoretical literature on the role of labor in democratization.

First, the Egyptian case highlights the potential for labor to play a decisive role in bringing down an authoritarian incumbent without being at the forefront of a pro-democracy movement and without uniformly and purposively articulating a pro-democracy stance. The existing literature accords little attention to this possibility, because it focuses solely on the conditions under which labor explicitly advocates for democratic change.

Second, the Egyptian case highlights that, contrary to the position of much theoretical literature, labor mobilization need not be orchestrated or coordinated by organized groups, such as unions or parties, in order to have a consequential impact on democratization. Successive authoritarian regimes in Egypt had maintained a tight grip on workers through state-controlled labor organizations, which had led to a growing discontent between rank-and-file workers and union leaders and curtailed the emergence of representative labor organizations. Egypt nonetheless witnessed a great deal of sustained workers' mobilization, organized independently of the official union structure. Indeed, one of the striking features of the labor action that swept Egypt in the last days of Mubarak's rule is that it took place in the absence of strong, representative labor organizations. The real question is therefore how this mobilization took place, rather than what explains its delay.

Notes

1   Interview with author, February 2011. All sources in personal interviews remain unnamed in accordance with the research guidelines of George Washington University.
2   Joel Beinin and Hossam El-Hamalawy, "Strikes in Egypt Spread from Center of Gravity," *Middle East Report Online*, 9 May 2007, http://www.merip.org/mero/mero050907

3   Mostafa Basyouni, "al-Tabaqa al-'amila fi qalb al-thawra," *al-Akhbar*, 27 February 2011, http://www.al-akhbar.com/node/5181

4   Data compiled by author from the following reports published by the Land Center for Human Rights: 54 (2006); 56 (2007); 58 (2007); 65 (2008); 78 (2009); 84 (2010); 88 (2011). http://www.lchr-eg.org

5   Interview with author, September 2011.

6   Nadine Abdallah, "Quwa al-ihtijaj al-ijtima'i: muqarana bayn Misr wa Polanda," *al-Dimuqratiya*, Al-Ahram Center for Strategic and Political Studies, October 2010, http://digital.ahram.org.eg/articles.aspx?Serial=341316&eid=5603

7   Interview with a member of the Coordinating Committee for Trade Union and Workers' Rights and Liberties, June 2011.

8   'Alaa Al-Din Salem, "Muzaharat al-'ummal . . . azmat ittihad faqada mashru'iyyatahu li-irtibatihi bi-l-sulta al-siyasiya," *al-Ahram*, 15 February 2011, http://gate.ahram.org.eg/News/40330.aspx

9   Interview with members of the Independent Union for Real Estate Tax Collectors, December 2010.

10 Mohammed Azouz, "Trade Union Federation Calls on Union Presidents to Prepare to Stop Any Labor Protests," *Al-Masry Al-Youm*, 27 January 2011.

11 "Egypt's State-Controlled Union Dissolved," *Ahram Online*, 4 August 2011, http://english.ahram.org.eg/NewsContent/1/64/18129/Egypt/Politics-/Egypts-State-controlled-trade-union-dissolved-.aspx

12 Interview with author, June 2011.

13 Interview with author, March 2011.

14 Interview with author, March 2011.

15 Interview with author, February 2011.

16 "al-'Ummal fi qalb al-thawra al-misriya, kalam sanay'iya," Dar al-Khadamat al-Niqabiya wa-l-'Ummaliya, 22 February 2011, 7, http://www.ctuws.com/uploads/Magazine/112/112-P1-16.pdf

17 Interview with author, September 2011.

18 Interview with author, September 2011.

19 Interview with author, September 2011.

20 Interview with author, September 2011.

21 Interview with author, February 2011.

22 "Misr al-lati qalat la," *al-Shuruq*, 11 February 2011.

23 "Thawrat al-'ummal: ihtijajat 'ummaliya li akthar min 300,000 'amil fi 60 mawqi' 'ummaliyan bi 9 muhafazat," *al-Badil*, 9 February 2010.

24 "Mawja jadida min al-ihtijajat al-'ummaliya tajtah al-Qahira wa-l-muhafazat," *Al-Masry Al-Youm*, 11 February 2011, http://www.almasry-alyoum.com/article2.aspx?ArticleID=287569

25 "Majlis al-wuzara' yuwafiq 'ala ziyadat al-ma'ashat wa rawatib al-jihaz al-idari li-l-dawla 15% . . . wa wazir al-maliya yaltaqi shabab 25 yanayir," *Al-Masry Al-Youm*, 8 February 2011, http://www.almasry-alyoum.com/article2.aspx?ArticleID=287248&IssueID=2039

26 "al-Muwazzafun yarfa'un rayat al-'isyan," *al-Shuruq*, 11 February 2011.

27 "al-Suez tu'lin al-'isyan al-madani . . . alaf al-'ummal fi 27 shirka wa masna' yu'linun al-idrab . . . wa shalal tam fi al-masalih al-hukumiya," *al-Badil*, 10 February 2011.

28 Basyouni, "Limadha."

29 "al-'Ummal wa-l-thawra al-misriya, mu'asasat awlad al-ard li-huquq al-insan wa-l-markaz al-masri li-l-huquq al-iqtisadiya wa-l-ijtima'iya," *al-Badil*, 16 February 2011.

30 "Muwazafu al-masriya li-l-ittisalat yatazaharun amam al-sintralat li-l-mutalaba bi huquqihim al-maliya wa yahtifun did al-nizam," *Al-Masry Al-Youm*, 9 February 2011, http://www.almasry-alyoum.com/article2.aspx?ArticleID=287311&IssueID=2041

31 Bayan li-'ummal al-naql al-'am bi midan al-Tahrir yu'ayyid al-thawra wa yu'akkid dukhulahum fi idrab shamil 'an al-'amal," *al-Dustur*, 9 February 2011, http://www.dostor.org/society-and-people/variety/11/february/9/36078

32 "al-'Ummal fi qalb al-thawra al-misriya, kalam sanay'iya," 7.

33 "Yawm al-'ummal al-misriyin," Dar al-Khadamat al-Niqabiya wa-l-'Ummaliya, 7 February 2011, http://www.ctuws.com/default.aspx?item=713

34 "al-'Ummal wa-l-thawra al-misriya," 6–7.

35 "al-Ghadab yasil ila al-'ummal," *al-Shuruq*, 9 February 2011.

6

Youth Movements and the 25 January Revolution

Dina Shehata

The 25 January revolution was described by many observers as a youth revolution due to the prominent role played by youth activists and youth movements in organizing the protests that led up to it and their role in framing the demands and strategies used by the protesters. In the decade preceding the revolution, youth-led movements such as Youth for Change, Tadamon, the April 6 movement, the ElBaradei campaign, and We Are All Khaled Said played an important role in mobilizing a new generation of Egyptians into politics. They helped to introduce innovative tools of mobilization and organization that allowed activists to bypass many of the constraints imposed by the authoritarian regime. Youth movements were also able to overcome many of the traditional weaknesses and divisions of the Egyptian opposition by adopting a cross-ideological discourse that allowed activists from different political backgrounds to work effectively together to achieve common objectives. Finally, they helped to create important linkages between political and social activism in Egypt.

This chapter seeks to explore the current wave of youth activism, which began with the outbreak of the Palestinian Intifada in the autumn of 2000 and reached its peak when Mubarak stepped down on 11 February 2011. The chapter will highlight how youth movements were able, through the introduction of new methods of mobilization and organization and through the framing of a new political discourse, to mobilize

Egyptian youth and create conditions conducive to the outbreak of broad-based popular protests on 25 January 2011.

Youth as a Unit of Analysis

The use of youth as a unit of analysis has been a source of controversy in the debate that has emerged around the Egyptian Revolution. Some analysts have argued that labeling the revolution as a 'youth revolution' and giving youth a privileged place in staging it masks the broad-based nature of this revolution and blurs the class basis of the different groups that have participated.[1] Some of the youth activists who have played an important role during the revolution have also rejected the label of 'youth revolution,' arguing that although youth activists and movements may have called for the protests that sparked the revolution, in reality this was a genuine popular uprising in which Egyptians of all age groups and different class backgrounds took part.[2] One activist has argued that the use of the label 'youth revolution' is of little analytical use: all revolutions can to a large extent be similarly characterized, since young people always constitute the bulk of the revolutionaries; what matters is not the age of the insurgents but rather their class background and the nature of their grievances.[3]

However, in spite of these compelling arguments, there are good reasons to use youth as a unit of analysis, as long as it is not used to the exclusion of other class-based or ideological categories that are also relevant to the study of the Egyptian Revolution. Youth activists and movements were only some of the many groups and individuals who carried out the revolt; but as such, their role deserves to be studied independently.

The study of the roles of different age groups and political generations in driving social phenomena is not unusual, either in the social sciences or in the study of Egyptian politics. Analysis of student movements, for instance, has long been a fixture in the subfield of social movement studies. In fact, the student movements of the late 1960s are credited with the emergence of this academic field in Europe and the United States. Similarly the study of political generations, generational change, and youth values has been used to explain the shift from modernization to post-modernization in the post-industrial world (Inglehart 1997).

In the field of Egyptian politics, multiple works have examined the role of the Egyptian student movement in the shaping of national politics at various historical junctures, especially in the decades leading up to the 1952 revolution, and during the late 1960s and early 1970s (see, for example, Abdalla 2009). In recent years, the study of youth in Egypt and the Arab world has grown in importance in light of the 'youth bulge' that the region is undergoing, and which has created a number of challenges pertaining to the social, economic, and political inclusion of young people throughout in the region. The life and death of Muhammad Bouazizi, the young Tunisian man who is credited with setting off the Tunisian uprising in December 2010, makes clear that youth exclusion has become one of the driving forces for change in the Arab world.

Youth Exclusion in Egypt

Egypt is experiencing a dramatic rise in the proportion of fifteen- to twenty-four-year-olds in the total population. Today, more than half of the Egyptian population is under the age of thirty, and a third is between the ages of fifteen and twenty-four (Assaad and Roudi-Fahimi 2007). This youth bulge has created numerous pressures and needs in the economic, social, and political domains. The failure of the Mubarak regime to address these created a widespread feeling of alienation and exclusion among youth.

The predicament of youth in Egypt has been accentuated by increased educational and communications capabilities, on the one hand, countered by a lack of economic opportunity on the other. Egypt and the Middle East boast the fastest-rising levels of schooling in the world (Salehi-Isfahani and Dhillon 2008), but also suffer from the highest levels of youth unemployment in the world.

Primary education is almost universal in the region. The gender gap in education has all but disappeared, and in some countries the number of female university graduates exceeds the number of males. In Egypt, school enrollment at the primary level is at 94 percent, at the secondary level 88 percent, and at the tertiary level 35 percent (Salehi-Isfahani and Dhillon 2008). Yet despite these impressive figures, the average youth unemployment rate in the region is one of the highest in the world: 25 percent, compared to the world average of 14.4 percent (Salehi-Isfahani and Dhillon 2008). Unemployment in the Arab world tends to be highly concentrated among young people, and especially those entering the labor market for the first time. In Egypt, the number of new entrants into the labor market has more than doubled since the 1970s. Currently there are 850,000 new entrants in the labor market per year; 75 percent of these will have to wait an average of five years before they find their first job. Moreover, youth unemployment tends to be highest among educated youth, especially those with university education. According to Assaad and Barsoum (2007), "unemployment in Egypt is primarily a problem of educated youth." Educated youth, that is, those with a secondary education or above, constituted 95 percent of the jobless young in 2006, up from 87 percent in 1998.

In Egypt, even young people with jobs suffer from low pay and poor working conditions, primarily because most are employed in the informal sector. In 2005, 72 percent of labor market entrants had only informal or low-wage employment (Assaad and Roudi-Fahimi 2007).

High unemployment rates and low pay have had detrimental effects on the ability of young people in Egypt to marry and to form families. Young men are often unable to meet the high costs of marriage, which include providing for housing and a dowry. Thus, many have to wait until well into their thirties and sometimes into their forties before they can afford to marry. According to Salehi-Isfahani and Dhillon, the Middle East has the highest rate of delayed marriages in the developing world: the percentage of Middle Eastern men aged twenty-five to twenty-nine who are married has declined from 63 percent in the 1980s to 53 percent in the 1990s, compared to an average decrease from 76 percent to 73 percent for the developing world overall. They also cite a recent study which found that in urban areas in Egypt, 57 percent of men were not married by age twenty-nine and 22 percent were still unmarried by thirty-four (Salehi-Isfahani and Dhillon 2008).

Egyptian youth also suffer political exclusion. According to a recent survey conducted by the Population Council (2010), only 2 percent of young people participate in volunteer work and only 16 percent of all eligible young people voted in a previous election. Another survey of youth (ages fifteen to twenty-four) conducted by Al-Ahram Center for Political and Strategic Studies (2004), found that 56 percent of the sample had never participated in student union elections, 67 percent had never participated in any student activities, and 84 percent had never participated in a public protest or demonstration. Another study found that 67 percent of youth do not have a voting card, and that 80 percent had not participated in parliamentary elections (Abdel Hay 2001).

Youth Mobilization since the 2000 Intifada

Student and youth movements have played an important role at a number of critical intervals in Egyptian politics. The most recent wave of youth activism, which reached its peak with the events of 25 January to 11 February 2011, can be dated back to the outbreak of the Palestinian Intifada in the autumn of 2000. Youth activism since 2000 may be divided into four distinct stages. During the first phase (2000–2003), youth mobilization focused primarily on external issues—namely the Palestinian Intifada and the war on Iraq. In the second phase (2004–2006), it shifted toward issues of domestic political and constitutional change, and youth began to organize themselves independently from older activists by creating youth-led movements such as Youth for Change, which was created under the umbrella of Kefaya. The third phase (2006–2009) saw a rupture between older activists and their young counterparts, as well as the emergence of youth-led movements such as Tadamon and April 6, which sought to bridge the gap between political and social issues and build linkages with the rising labor movement. The fourth and final phase of youth activism (2010), which directly preceded the 25 January revolution, saw a return to issues of political democratization in anticipation of the upcoming parliamentary and presidential elections and the mobilization of an ever-increasing number of independent youth in movements such as ElBaradei Campaign and We Are All Khaled Said. In the following sections we discuss these four phases in more detail.

Phase one: 2000–2003

With the beginning of the new millennium, and after nearly a decade of political demobilization, youth activism gained renewed momentum. The outbreak of the second Palestinian Intifada in 2000 and the invasion and occupation of Iraq in 2003 played a crucial role in propelling a new generation of activists into politics. In 2000 and 2001, Egyptian students staged a large number of demonstrations in support of the intifada. Thousands of younger Egyptians also joined the newly established Egyptian Popular Committee for the Support of the Palestinian Intifada (EPCSPI). EPCSPI was notable for having spearheaded a new model of political mobilization that subsequent movements adopted and developed. EPCSPI eschewed formal channels of participation and relied instead on direct political action. Moreover, EPCSPI tried to overcome longstanding divisions within the opposition by embracing a cross-ideological framework for mobilization. Membership in the movement was open to activists from all political orientations in their individual, as opposed to their institutional, capacity.[4] The movement also succeeded in attracting a large number of youth activists, many of whom were students and graduates who were participating in a political activity for the first time (Abdel Rahman 2007). Finally, EPCSPI adopted a horizontal and decentralized model for organizing that allowed the various committees created under the movement's umbrella to operate with a great deal of autonomy from the Cairo-based steering committee. The activities of EPCSPI in 2000 and 2001 included a campaign to boycott American and Israeli products, the collection of donations, a number of aid caravans to the Occupied Territories, and a large number of protest activities against the Israeli and U.S. governments.[5]

With the invasion and occupation of Iraq in 2003, political mobilization continued to gain momentum. On 20–21 March, tens of thousands of Egyptians staged large demonstrations in Tahrir Square in downtown Cairo—the largest since the bread riots of 1977.[6] In 2003, new movements such as the 20 March movement and the Cairo Campaign (also known as the Popular Campaign for the Support of the Resistance in Palestine and Iraq and against Globalization) were established to mobilize opposition to the war on Iraq. These movements were notable for the linkages they created with the global anti-war movement and for organizing a number of successful conferences that attracted the various factions of the Egyptian opposition, as well as a large number of international activists.[7]

Phase two: 2004–2006
In 2004, as western powers and domestic opposition movements began to press Arab regimes to adopt democratic political reforms, youth activism shifted away from external issues toward domestic issues of political and constitutional reform. In 2004 and 2005, hundreds of youth activists joined new movements, such as Kefaya and Freedom Now, which called for comprehensive political change. Youth for Change, a subgroup of the Kefaya movement, became a vocal actor during the pro-reform protests of 2005–2006 (Hassabo 2009).

Youth for Change included hundreds of youth activists from the various factions of the opposition, many of whom had previously been active in EPCSPI and in the anti-war movement. It also included a large number of independent activists who were not affiliated with any political party or movement. Youth for Change adopted the horizontal organizing framework initiated by EPCSPI and developed by Kefaya. This framework consisted of a steering committee that was elected every six weeks and a number of specialized committees, including the popular mobilization committee, the socialization committee, the artistic committee, the communications committee, and the committees for the governorates.[8]

Youth for Change endorsed the comprehensive political change that Kefaya advocated, but the movement also adopted a number of youth-specific demands. According to its founding declaration, Youth for Change

> considers itself part of the Kefaya movement. It adopts its demands and shares in its activities and is tied to it democratically without hierarchy or authoritarianism. . . . The movement is open to all political forces and to independents without exclusion or hegemony. . . . The movement believes that rights cannot be given but must be wrested and that popular peaceful struggles such as protests, strikes, sit-ins, and civil disobedience are the path to Freedom.[9]

The declaration also stipulated that the youth movement was advocating for the achievement of "political democracy both within society and within the university and against corruption and for the realization of equality of opportunity." It also listed a number of demands important to young people, such as restoring democracy inside the university and guaranteeing equality of opportunity and access to education, health care, housing, and employment.[10]

In 2005, Youth for Change helped Kefaya to organize a large number of peaceful protests which, though relatively small, attracted a great deal of national and international attention and broke with many of the practices and taboos that had characterized public life in Egypt for several decades. Most importantly, Kefaya protesters called for change rather than reform, thereby abandoning the opposition's longstanding strategy of trying to encourage the regime to enact reforms from above. They believed that protests and popular mobilization were the means to achieve change, rather than trying to work through the system by creating parties or nongovernmental organizations (NGOs) or by participating in elections. By staging popular demonstrations in public spaces without official permission, Kefaya succeeded in breaking the regime's clampdown on popular protest and forced the regime to tacitly accept them as a legitimate form of expression. Finally, Kefaya protesters chanted slogans that denounced the president, his family, and the security establishment, thereby challenging the taboo against directly criticizing these 'sovereign' institutions (Shaaban 2006; Siyyam 2006).

In 2006, as a result of a general crackdown on political parties and movements in the wake of the 2005 elections, political mobilization began to lose momentum. This, alongside repression by the regime, drove many youth activists to turn to blogging as a way of expressing their disenchantment with social and political realities. In 2008 there were approximately 160,000 blogs produced by Egyptians, 20 percent of which were political in nature (Al Masry 2008). Youth blogs were distinct from the mainstream media because of their bold criticism of public officials and official practices. Bloggers used colorful language to criticize public figures, including the president and his son. They also relied on audiovisual media such as photographs, videos, and cartoons to make their message heard. Some blogs became sites for posting footage of torture and various human rights violations by state security officers. Such footage helped put the question of torture on the national agenda. Blogs were also used to publicize protests and other events organized by opposition movements and parties.

Phase three: 2006–2009
As mobilization around political democratization receded in the wake of the 2005 elections, mobilization around social and economic issues began to gain momentum. The Mahalla workers' strike in September 2006 ushered in a new wave of labor mobilization unseen in Egypt since the 1950s. Worsening economic conditions triggered unprecedented protest activities among blue-collar workers, civil servants, and the urban poor. The number of protest activities by workers increased from 222 in 2006 to nearly six hundred in 2007 and 2008, and more than seven hundred in 2009 and 2010 (El-Mahdi 2010a).

The spike in labor protests in 2007 led to a fundamental change in the outlook of many youth activists. Those who had previously been associated with opposition parties and movements such as Kefaya began to question the model for change adopted by these movements, which they deemed elitist, abstract, and out of touch with the grievances and needs of the masses. Youth activists concluded that real change could only happen when real linkages were made between political mobilization, on the one hand, and labor mobilization and people's movements, on the other.[11] Youth activists thus endeavored to create a number of youth-led movements that sought to bridge the gap between political and social issues and between the democratic movement and labor movements. In 2007, a number of activists previously associated with Youth for Change established the Tadamon movement. Tadamon, which means 'solidarity' in Arabic, was conceived as a group whose primary task was to support labor activism and other forms of grassroots mobilization by providing legal and media support and by helping to build linkages and exchange experiences with one another. In its founding declaration, the movement maintained:

> The task of [the] Tadamon movement is to support the rising labor and social movement, to learn from it and to try to transfer experiences to it and from it, and to help it look ahead and make gains. This is our task and this is what we dream of: a single popular movement that seeks freedom, bread, and dignity for us and for our children. To achieve our dreams we must exert all our effort in this small initiative, which we are financing with our limited resources. But we believe that this small initiative is the right path to change . . . the path of relying on people's struggles from below.[12]

Tadamon's declaration states that it is unifying the various grassroots movements into a single popular movement that will bring about real change. It also declares that economic demands must be linked to political demands and grassroots movements must become aware that their interests can only be realized through political change:

> All the struggles that are budding in all of the factories and companies and farms in Egypt are the beginning of the long road to change. These struggles are the basis of our strength and the foundation for any real change. What is needed is for these struggles to become unified and networked as one hand: . . . property tax collectors linking with Mahalla workers, . . . Mahalla workers building bridges with administrators in the ministry of education, . . . both of these groups showing solidarity with Qursaya fishermen, . . . because our problems are the same and those who steal from us are the same. We must unite and we must also think about the future of

Egypt: . . . all of Egypt, not just our factory, company, or neighborhood. . . . We are the owners of this country and we must determine its future. . . . Politics is not something for other people. If politics means the future of Egypt then we are all politicians and we will not allow them to poison our lives and the future of our children.[13]

Tadamon adopted a very loose organizational model, which consisted of individual working groups for mass action, communications, and dialogue. From its founding, Tadamon included activists from the leftist Revolutionary Socialist movement, liberals from the al-Ghad Party, and Islamists from the Labor Party. In 2007 and 2008, Tadamon was active in supporting a number of grassroots movements, including the Suez fishermen's movement, the Tanta textile workers' movement, and the Qursaya and Gazirat al-Dahab movements. Tadamon lent legal and media support to these movements and helped them publicize their cause through its monthly forum, newsletter, and website.[14]

Shortly after Tadamon was established, however, al-Ghad and Labor party activists quit the movement, opting for a more radical approach to change. Unlike Tadamon activists, who believed that change must be fostered gradually from the bottom up through the emergence of a broad-based popular movement, al-Ghad and Labor party activists believed that the country was ripe for radical political and social change.[15] In March 2008, youth activists from al-Ghad and the Labor Party called for a general strike in solidarity with a strike organized by textile workers in Mahalla scheduled for 6 April 2008.[16]

The call for a general strike was broadcast via a Facebook group created especially for that purpose by al-Ghad Party activist Esraa Abdel Fattah, in coordination with Ahmed Maher, the former head of al-Ghad's youth committee.[17] Within a few days, the Facebook group had as many as seventy thousand members. The call for protests was endorsed by a number of political groups, including Kefaya and al-Ghad, and was picked up by the mainstream media. Some of the main opposition groups, however, including the Muslim Brotherhood, al-Wafd Party, and the leftist Populist Unionist Party (PUP), refused to endorse the call for protests, and some even dismissed the members of the group as "a bunch of crazy kids."[18] The regime for its part responded forcefully to the call for protests. On 5 April 2008, the Ministry of Interior issued a declaration in which it warned that it would take "immediate and strict necessary measures regarding any attempts to protest or to disrupt traffic or interrupt work in public facilities or to incite any such actions."[19]

On 6 April 2008, Cairo and other major cities were quieter than usual. Many people stayed at home, either in response to the call for protests or out of fear of clashes between protesters and the police, or simply because of the sandstorm that blew that day. In Mahalla, state security forces forcefully prevented workers from striking in their factory. As a consequence, violent protests broke out on the streets of Mahalla, and confrontations with the police ensued. Hundreds were arrested that day and at least fifty injured in confrontations with the police. Those arrested included activists from what came to be known as the 'April 6 movement,' including Esraa Abdel Fattah, the cofounder of the Facebook group that had called for the strike, who was arrested for three weeks.

In the wake of the 6 April protests, activists from the movement decided to formalize the group and transform it into a fully fledged political movement.[20] The group drafted a founding declaration in which it stated that it sought to change Egypt through youth activism, since youth have a real interest in such a change. In its declaration the group maintained that there is no substitute for systemic change, which will be brought about not by the intellectuals and politicians, who are disconnected from the masses, but rather through the struggles of the simple people who have a real interest in change.[21]

The April 6 movement adopted an organizational structure similar to that of Kefaya. It elected a general coordinator, four sub-coordinators, a steering committee, and a number of specialized committees and governorate committees. According to Ahmed Maher, the general coordinator of the group, in 2009 the movement had approximately two thousand active members across twelve governorates.[22]

Since its inception in 2008, the April 6 movement has been able to expand its following among youth and to initiate a number of successful political campaigns, including annual 6 April protests and the annual 'Subversive Minority' conference that took place parallel to, and as a challenge to, the annual conference of the ruling National Democratic Party (NDP). The group also initiated the "Your Voice Is Your Demand" campaign, which aimed to mobilize youth to vote in elections. Finally, April 6 joined a number of events and protest activities focusing on social and economic demands like raising the minimum wage and tackling rising prices and unemployment.[23]

Phase four: 2010–2011

In 2010, and in anticipation of the upcoming 2010 parliamentary elections and the 2011 presidential elections, which many expected would lead to the transfer of power from Hosni Mubarak to his son Gamal, the April 6 movement joined other political movements to launch the ElBaradei for President campaign. Dr. Mohamed ElBaradei, the Nobel Peace laureate and former director of the International Atomic Energy Agency (IAEA) had expressed in late 2009 an initial interest in running in the 2011 elections. Youth from April 6 and other political groups welcomed this declaration and saw in ElBaradei a figure who could rally and unify the opposition. In February 2010, activists from April 6 and Kefaya, alongside independent activists, oversaw the organization of a large rally at Cairo airport on the occasion of the return of Dr. ElBaradei to Egypt after his retirement from the IAEA. In subsequent months, youth activists in the ElBaradei campaign helped to organize a number of rallies and initiated a door-to-door campaign aimed at acquainting voters with ElBaradei, hoping to get them to sign the declaration for change that he introduced. The ElBaradei campaign gained support among a large number of secular and liberal youth and also among many leftists and Islamists who felt that he represented a viable alternative to both Hosni and Gamal Mubarak. Its Facebook page had more than 250,000 members, and 800,000 people signed the declaration for change issued by ElBaradei and the National Society for Change, which called for legal and constitutional amendments to guarantee free and fair elections.

In parallel, in the summer of 2010, tens of thousands of people joined the 'We Are All Khaled Said' Facebook page. The campaign was launched on Facebook in June 2010 to protest the death of Khaled Said, a young man who was beaten to death by plainclothes policemen in Alexandria. The picture of Khaled Said's deformed face was widely circulated on the Internet alongside a picture of his face before the beating. The brutality used against Said, who was not a militant nor an activist nor a criminal, caused a stir among youth, first in Alexandria and then, as the story spread, elsewhere across the country. A group of anonymous activists, who were later identified as members of the ElBaradei Campaign, created a Facebook group to protest the incident and called it 'We Are All Khaled Said.' Within a short time the group had become the largest Egyptian political grouping on Facebook, with more than three hundred thousand members.

In the summer of 2010, We Are All Khaled Said organized a series of protest activities across the country, which attracted a large number of young people. The administrators of the group called on the members to wear black clothes and stand for an hour in silence, facing the Nile or the sea. For several Fridays in a row, thousands of young people stood apart from one another dressed in black and facing the Nile or the sea to protest the murder of Khaled Said. In July 2010, We Are All Khalid Said and April 6 organized a large protest to commemorate the death of Khaled Said in Alexandria. The protest was attended by many of the leading figures in the opposition, including Mohamed ElBaradei and Ayman Nour.

Thus by the end of 2010, there had emerged in Egypt a fairly broad-based youth movement that consisted of a wide array of youth-led groups such as April 6, the ElBaradei campaign, and We Are All Khaled Said, and which boasted a fairly distinctive approach to mobilization that set it apart from the older generation of activists. Youth activism in the new millennium also differed in significant ways from previous waves of youth mobilization in Egypt. Most importantly, it occurred largely outside existing parties and movements, including the Muslim Brotherhood. The stringent restrictions imposed by the regime on political parties and movements during the 1990s, coupled with those restricting student activism on university campuses, significantly weakened the links between university students, on the one hand, and political parties and movements, on the other. Moreover, during the 1990s, most political parties and movements experienced internal divisions and fragmentation, partly as a result of the continued domination of an aging leadership and the marginalization of younger activists with bolder ideas. This dissuaded young people from joining these parties and led them to explore other avenues of participation.

Youth were important actors in some of the new informal movements, like EPCSPI and Kefaya, which chose to operate outside the existing institutional structures. These movements were led by 1970s-generation activists, many of whom had split from older parties and movements in the 1990s. The movements they created tended to be more action-oriented in their discourse and to adopt a more consensual approach that focused more on what united Egyptians rather than on what divided them. Moreover, these movements were less conciliatory in their approach to the regime and favored comprehensive political change emanating from below rather than gradual reform introduced from above.

A second distinguishing characteristic of youth activism over the last decade is that it occurred largely off university campuses. For most of the twentieth century, university campuses had been the primary sites of youth activism in Egypt. Since the early 1990s, however, and largely as a result of the strict constraints imposed by the regime on political activism on campus, youth activism within the university was severely limited. And although students continued to stage some demonstrations on university grounds, the most significant youth actions since 2000 have occurred elsewhere. Furthermore, whereas in previous decades, student unions had played a central role in leading student activism in Egypt, they have been largely absent from the current wave of youth activism. Dominated by pro-regime activists for most of the 1990s, student unions appear to have become largely ineffective and delinked from student activism in the new millenium.

The third major characteristic of the new youth activism is its largely non-ideological or cross-ideological nature. Many of the youth who joined movements such as EPCSPI, Kefaya, Youth for Change, and April 6 did not clearly subscribe to well-defined ideologies. Most seemed to share a general commitment to the values of human rights, pluralism, democracy, and social justice, and some expressed watered-down leftist and Islamist views. Unlike previous generations of activists who were steeped in the writings of Marxist or Islamist writers, this new generation—at least, prior to the 2011 revolution—has focused more on consensus building and direct action rather than on ideological squabbles.

Most of the youth movements that emerged since 2000 tended to be internally diverse and inclusive of all ideological orientations. Youth movements such as Youth for Change and April 6 tended to bring together activists with different beliefs who shared a commitment to common objectives, such as support for the intifada or political reform. Moreover, unlike the older cross-ideological coalitions that were formed in the 1980s and 1990s through alliances among existing parties and movements, membership in youth movements was based on individual rather than institutional membership. Youth activists hoped that by structuring their movements thus, they would be able to overcome many of the long-standing divisions that have weakened the Egyptian opposition.

The final distinguishing characteristic of the most recent wave of youth activism is its extensive use of information and communication technology as a tool to both organize and mobilize, and also as a means of expression. Given the strict constraints on formal political participation, youth were able to use the Internet and social networking sites such as Twitter and Facebook to create an alternative political space. This was most apparent during the 6 April youth protests, which were organized wholly online, and during the events leading up to the 25 January revolution, in which Facebook was used to communicate and to mobilize action.

Youth Activism and the 25 January Revolution

During the eighteen days from 25 January to 11 February 2011, three groups of actors came together in opposition to the Mubarak regime: youth movements, labor movements, and the political parties and movements that had been excluded from the 2010 parliament, including the Muslim Brotherhood.

Youth activists, inspired by events in Tunisia, were the first to call for popular protests on 25 January 2011. According to Khaled Abdel Hamid (pers. comm., 17 Feb 2011) and Shady Ghazaly Harb (pers. comm., 23 Feb 2011), activists from five youth movements—April 6, the Popular Campaign for the Support of ElBaradei, leftist youth from the Freedom and Justice movement, and a number of youth activists from the Muslim Brotherhood and the liberal Democratic Front Party—met after the events in Tunisia and agreed to call for popular protests on the occasion of Police Day on 25 January.[24] Youth activists agreed that the day would be devoted to protesting police brutality and agreed to raise the slogan, "Bread, freedom, human dignity." The protests were then advertised on the widely read 'We Are All Khaled Said' Facebook page. The organizers expected a large turnout given recent events in Tunisia, but none expected a revolution to ensue.[25]

During the next three weeks, and in spite of a total communications shutdown and excessive use of force by the regime, a series of large demonstrations took place across the country. Protesters were successful in occupying Tahrir Square in the center of Cairo for the duration of the uprising, and in resisting a violent attempt by thugs and plainclothes police to evacuate them from the square on 2 February 2011.

In the course of the protests, youth activists formed the 25 January Youth Coalition, which included all the major youth movements that had called for the protests. The coalition presented the regime with a series of demands that included Mubarak's resignation, lifting of the state of emergency, release of all political prisoners, dissolution of parliament, appointment of a government of independent technocrats, drafting of a new constitution, and punishment of those responsible for violence against protesters. The coalition rejected all pressures to enter into negotiations with the newly appointed vice president and insisted that there would be no negotiations until the president stepped down.[26]

While youth activists were the principal driving force behind the revolution, political parties and movements also played an important role. In the early days of the protests, parties and movements were divided about whether or not to participate. Some groups, including Kefaya, the National Society for Change, the Democratic Front Party, and the al-Ghad Party, endorsed and joined the 25 January protests; others, such as the Muslim Brotherhood and the leftist Tagammu' Party, did not join the protests until 28 January, although many of their younger members participated on the 25th.[27]

There were also divisions among movements and parties about the demands of the revolution and about how best to achieve them: Kefaya, Mohamed ElBaradei, Ayman Nour, the Democratic Front Party, and the National Society for Change were among those who endorsed the demands of the 25 January Youth Coalition and refused to negotiate with the regime until Mubarak stepped down; the Muslim Brotherhood, al-Wafd Party, the Tagammu' Party, and a number of independent public figures who formed the Committee of Wise Men agreed to enter into negotiations with the newly appointed vice president, Omar Suleiman. However, the refusal of the regime to make any real concessions to the opposition, coupled with the escalation of the street protests, ultimately drove the various opposition groups to withdraw from the dialogue and to endorse the demands of the protesters for the immediate resignation of the president.

The third main category of protesters comprised labor groups and professional associations. As mentioned above, labor activism had been on the rise for the past five years. In 2010 there were approximately seven hundred strikes and protest actions organized by blue- and white-collar workers across the country. Labor protests had, however, tended to focus exclusively on labor-specific demands and to shy away from political ones. During the first two weeks of the revolution, labor groups and professional associations did not play a visible role in the demonstrations. This was partly due to the fact that the regime had shut down all economic activity during that time. As the protests entered their third week, however, and as economic activity resumed, workers and professionals began to organize strike actions in their workplaces. In the two days preceding Mubarak's resignation, the country was approaching a state of total civil disobedience, with workers' protests taking place in the transportation, communications, and industrial sectors and among judges, doctors, university professors, lawyers, journalists, and artists. According to Shady Ghazaly Harb, one of the youth activists, it was this development that finally convinced the military to oust Mubarak and to assume control over the political system.[28]

Youth Activism in the Post-Mubarak Era

The 25 January Youth Coalition, which was formed by youth activists during the second week of the revolution, continued to play a visible role during the weeks following Mubarak's ouster. The coalition issued a number of declarations and organized a series of protests with the aim of exerting continued pressure on the Supreme Council of Armed Forces (SCAF) to implement the revolutionaries' demands and to proceed with the dismantling of the old regime. However, as divisions between political activists regarding the course of the transition and the desired social and political order in the post-Mubarak era began to deepen, the youth coalition began to disintegrate. Many of the groups who were active in the coalition, such as the April 6 movement and the Muslim Brotherhood youth, dropped out, and their members began to focus instead on the creation of new political parties that reflected their different political views and orientations.

Liberal youth were engaged in creating a number of new political parties, including the Egyptian Social Democratic Party, al-'Adl (Justice) Party, and the Egypt Freedom Party; leftist youth helped to found the Popular Alliance Party, the Workers' Party, and the National Front for Justice and Democracy; while Islamist youth helped establish the Freedom and Justice Party and the Egyptian Current Party. Some youth movements, including April 6, officially announced that they would neither form nor participate in creating any political party, but would instead remain an informal protest movement seeking to influence the political process and the various new parties indirectly.[29] Not all members of the group agreed with this decision, however, and some took an active part in the creation of new parties.

The fragmentation of youth activists in the wake of the revolution and the subsequent emergence of a large number of liberal, leftist, and

Islamist parties has substantially weakened the leverage of youth and opposition groups in the face of the SCAF and the interest groups allied with it. Polarization among Islamists and secularists over the sequence of the transition, and between liberals and leftists over social and economic policy, has enabled the SCAF to successfully play off the different groups against one another and thus to monopolize the decision-making process in the post-Mubarak period.

Another important challenge confronted by youth after 11 February was the inadequacy of their mobilizing tools post-Mubarak. Whereas the use of social media and direct political action were necessary to bypass the constraints imposed by the Mubarak regime on political parties and movements, in the post-Mubarak era they have proved insufficient. Their limitations were underscored during the 19 March referendum on constitutional amendment, which set the course for the transitional period. The main questions that were put to Egyptian voters was whether parliamentary elections should be held *before* the drafting of the new constitution, and whether the elected parliament should therefore select the members of the constituent assembly that would be charged with drafting the new constitution.

Youth activists and many of the secular and liberal groups that had participated in the revolution rejected these amendments and called for an inclusive committee to be selected to draft the new constitution before holding elections, to ensure that no one group would be able to monopolize the process of drafting a new constitution. In contrast, Islamist groups, the SCAF, and members of the defunct NDP supported having elections prior to the drafting of the new constitution. Youth activists relied on social media and protests to rally popular opposition to the amendments, whereas the Islamist movement, in tacit collaboration with the SCAF, used the country's vast network of mosques and religious institutions to mobilize support for the amendments. The state-owned media were also used extensively to rally public opinion in favor of the amendments, as were the traditional networks associated with the old ruling party. The outcome was a scathing defeat for the youth and secular groups that opposed the amendments, with 77 percent of the electorate voting yes and only 22.8 percent voting no.

The limited ability of the tools and strategies favored by youth activists to access and mobilize broad segments of the population outside major cities and beyond the reach of the Internet has raised fears that youth activists will perform badly in the coming electoral contests.

Thus while youth movements played an important role in fomenting the revolution and creating a space for democratic change, the fragmentation of youth activists and the inadequacy of their mobilizing strategies in the post-Mubarak era have significantly limited their power to shape Egypt's future course. Confronted with a divided opposition, with its limited capacity to rally the population on key votes, the SCAF has been able to determine the course of the transition and has pitted different groups against one another quite effectively in order to consolidate its own power and inhibit a fully fledged restructuring of the political system.

Notes

1 Rabab El-Mahdi, "Orientalizing the Egyptian Uprising," *Jadaliyya*, 11 April 2011, http://www.jadaliyya.com/pages/index/1214/orientalising-the-egyptian-uprising
2 Personal interview with Khaled Abdel Hamid, 17 February 2011.
3 Presentation by Hossam El-Hamalawy at the conference "From Tahrir: Revolution or Democratic Transition," held at the American University in Cairo, 4–6 June 2011, http://www.youtube.com/watch?v=9hTv25REXe4&feature=relmfu
4 Interview with Gamal Abdel Fattah, 2 November 2003.
5 Personal interview with Khaled Abdel Hamid, 8 July 2009.
6 Abdel Hamid interview, 8 July 2009.
7 Interview with Mohamed Waked, 4 July 2006.
8 Abdel Hamid interview, 8 July 2009.
9 Founding Declaration of Youth for Change, http://www.ournormandy.com. p4.hostingprod.com/forum/showthread.php?t=733
10 Founding Declaration of Youth for Change.
11 Personal interviews with Ahmed Maher, 6 July 2009, and Khaled Abdel Hamid, 8 July 2009.
12 Founding Declaration of Tadamon Movement, 2007, http://tadamonmasr. wordpress.com
13 Founding Declaration of Tadamon Movement, 2007.
14 Personal interviews with Khaled Abdel Hamid, 9 July 2009, and Mohamed El Saeed, 19 July 2009.
15 Personal interviews with Khaled Abdel Hamid, 9 July 2009, and Mohamed El Saeed, 19 July 2009.
16 Personal interviews with Esraa Abdel Fattah, 21 July 2009, and Ahmed Maher, 6 July 2009.
17 Personal interviews with Esraa Abdel Fattah, 21 July 2009, and Ahmed Maher, 6 July 2009.
18 Ramadan Khairy, "Shwayet 'eyal lasa'a," *Al-Masry Al-Youm*, 4 May 2008, http://today.almasryalyoum.com/article2.aspx?ArticleID=103870& IssueID=1030
19 "Text of Declaration of Ministry of Interior Regarding April 6 Protests," *al-Ahram*, 5 April 2008.
20 Interview with Ahmed Maher, 6 July 2009.

21 Founding Declaration of April 6 Movement, 2008, http://shabab6april.wordpress. com
22 Interview with Maher, 6 July 2009.
23 Interview with Maher, 6 July 2009.
24 Interviews with Abdel Hamid, 17 February 2011, and Shady Ghazaly Harb, 23 February 2011.
25 Interviews with Abdel Hamid, 17 February 2011, and Mostafa El Naggar, 9 March 2011.
26 Interviews with Abdel Hamid, 17 February 2011; Ghazaly Harb, 23 February 2011; and Ahmed Maher, 9 March 2011.
27 Interview with Abdel Hamid, 17 February 2011.
28 Interview with Ghazaly Harb, 23 February 2011.
29 Interview with Maher, 9 March 2011.

7

Islamism in and after Egypt's Revolution

Ibrahim El Houdaiby

Introduction

Egypt's revolution is transforming the country's Islamist landscape. The first wave of protests, which lasted for eighteen days and successfully ousted Mubarak after three decades in office, triggered revolutionary changes within the country's Islamist movement. The Muslim Brotherhood (MB), Egypt's largest organized political group, serves as a good example. The group—which stood united despite (or because of) long decades of oppression—witnessed major transformations in just a few months. After years of insisting on the all-encompassing nature of the organization, it was only a few days after Mubarak's ousting that the group announced its intention to establish an independent political party and to retreat from politics and focus on social activities.

The Freedom and Justice Party (FJP) was soon established, and its leaders had to resign from the MB's executive council. The party's platform avoided controversial stances adopted earlier by the draft manifesto released by the Brotherhood in 2007, including banning women and Copts from running for president. Within a few months, and parallel to the establishment of the FJP, some major splits took place within the MB; most important was the dismissal of Abdel Moneim Aboul Fotouh, the group's iconic reformist leader, after he announced his candidacy for president. This was followed by the dismissal of many young cadres who had

125

played a role during the eighteen days in Tahrir Square and who later came to form their own party: the Egyptian Current.

Revolutionary impact was not limited to the MB. Traditionally apolitical Salafi groups began to seek a political role in revolutionary Egypt. With no significant participation in the early days of protests, some Salafi groups joined the uprising a few days before Mubarak stepped down. Their politicization became more obvious later, when they started institutionalizing their political activities and formed different political parties, the potential of which is yet to be seen.

Attempting to understand these changes requires proper scrutiny of the internal dynamics and ideology of both movements, as well as the governing external context. This chapter argues that two sets of variables affect the political outlook of Islamist movements: perceived identity threat and political opportunity. The definition of the former varies due to differences in ideological orientation and political maturity, and its presence leads to the increased detachment of Islamists from society and, consequently, their stagnation and organizational unity. The latter, on the contrary, leads to inclusion and attachment that breeds diversity stemming from the emergence of more sophisticated forms of affiliation to Islamic identity. Post-revolutionary Islamism is therefore likely to witness further sliding transformation that will eventually lead to the transcendence of identity-based Islamism and the emergence of a new wave of diverse, policy-based Islamist activism.

Pre-revolutionary Islamist Movements
The landscape of Islamist organizations prior to the Egyptian Revolution was composed of five main groups. First among them was the official religious establishment, at the heart of which lies al-Azhar. Despite its legacy of centuries of scholarship, the institution had become increasingly disempowered and discredited since the 1950s. The MB, established in the late 1920s, represents, along with its offshoots, the second key player in the pre-revolution Islamist domain, being the country's largest opposition group and the world's oldest Islamist group. Third was the Salafi trend, which has been on the ascent in Egypt since the 1970s. Despite having a handful of institutional incubators, Salafism remains a largely social movement, with the vast majority of Salafis not being attached to any organization. Fourth were the Sufi orders. While dominating the socioreligious scene until the

turn of the nineteenth century, Sufi orders have been on the decline ever since, as they have come increasingly under the control of the state and have lost social legitimacy. Neoliberal Islam—manifested in the discourse and audience of new preachers—represents the last group of pre-revolutionary Islamist actors. The trend emerged in Egypt in the 1990s and developed a strong presence among the urban upper middle classes. Other groups, including al-Jama'a al-Islamiya and al-Jihad, were significant during the 1980s and 1990s, but have been on the decline ever since, and have established close ties with either Salafi or MB groups.

While outlining major transformations in different groups, this chapter will focus primarily on the MB and Salafis. Being more dynamic due to their breadth, large membership, and heavy involvement in political affairs, these groups serve better as case studies for transformations within Islamist movements in post-revolutionary Egypt. This section will survey the history of different groups and scrutinize their political stances before the revolution.

The Sufi orders

When Sufism was first institutionalized in Egypt during the rule of Saladin, Sufi orders had only limited sociopolitical significance, as their primary focus was the restoration of Egypt's Sunni identity. It was not long before Sufi sheikhs became social leaders, and enormous endowments were established to sponsor the orders' activities, thereby leading to a steady growth of Sufism (Amin 1980, 204–205). The role of Sufi orders was magnified with the rapprochement between those orders and al-Azhar scholars (Youssef 1994, 93), who were widely viewed as the scholarly and social elites from whom the "Mamluk and Ottoman military elite sought political legitimation" (Hatina 2003, 51). This rapprochement had colossal effects on the roles and popularity of Sufi orders, allowing them to play a huge role in mobilizing against the French in 1798–1801 and later against the Ottomans.

While the influence and power of Sufi orders continued to rise in the first half of the nineteenth century, this trend was later reversed. Only one Sufi order had significant presence with Ahmed 'Urabi's forces against the British in 1882, and Sufis participating in the 1919 revolt had no significant presence in leading or extending it. This decay in their roles is largely attributed to the erosion of their independence. Sufi orders originally relied on three forms of independence: financial independence via endowments; intellectual independence via rapprochement with al-Azhar; and the autonomy of their administrative hierarchy through independence from the state.[1] Over the course of two centuries, these pillars of independence were compromised.[2]

For decades, Sufi orders lost all their social and political significance. Subordination to the state left them with no margins of influence and kept them out of political formulae. A few months before the revolution, however, turbulence erupted in Sufi circles, leading to a mild degree of politicization. Following the death of the Grand Sheikh in November 2008, a dispute erupted between two potential successors. Sheikh Abu-l-Azayim was elected as Grand Sheikh, but the decision was then contested by Sheikh al-Qasabi, a member of the policies committee of the ruling National Democratic Party (NDP); President Mubarak recognized al-Qasabi as Grand Sheikh. In protest, Sheikh Abu-l-Azayim nominated himself for parliament against a key NDP figure, declared his support for a handful of Sufi candidates,[3] and established the Sufi Reform Front (SRF).

The official religious establishment
Al-Azhar is Islam's oldest existing scholarly institution, with a legacy of over a thousand years of scholarship. Throughout history, al-Azhar scholars have played instrumental roles in politics, particularly in the anti-colonial struggle (Bayat 2007, 37). With its immense power, an independent al-Azhar was increasingly viewed as a threat to the Egyptian rulers. From Muhammad Ali to the British governor Lord Cromer, consecutive rulers therefore attempted to weaken the organization, or to co-opt its leaders (see, for example, Farah 2009; Rabie 1992; al-Awwa 2006; Bayat 2007).

By the time Nasser came to power in 1952, al-Azhar was already too weak to resist the changes he would impose. The institution became more dependent on the state when Nasser "abolished religious courts, [and] put all endowments under state control" (Bayat 2007, 37). Within a very few years, the regime had "undermined the traditional influence of the Ulama by reforming the historic Al-Azhar University," transforming it into a state university in 1961 after expropriating religious authority from the ulama (Jefferis 2009, 49). Nasser believed that "religion should be part of a political ideology which he directs to support his policies and achieve required political mobilization" (Rabie 1992), and consequently fought hard to subordinate al-Azhar to his power.[4]

After losing its independence, al-Azhar's political role was redefined. Instead of focusing on people's empowerment and resisting colonialism, the institution became increasingly engaged in legitimizing rulers (al-Awwa 2006). With the country's largest opposition—even at that time—being the Islamist MB, Nasser's regime relied heavily on al-Azhar to construct a religious discourse that legitimized state policies and delegitimized the Brotherhood. This eventually put al-Azhar into direct confrontation with political Islamists and, coupled with the deteriorating academic standards of the university (as well as other public schools), pushed Islamists toward other schools of thought in their pursuit of scholarship. Among other factors, this led to the rise of Salafism and Qutbism in the 1970s, as well as the continuing erosion of al-Azhar's legitimacy under presidents Sadat and Mubarak. Mubarak also tended to appoint al-Azhar scholars who were known for their hostility to the Brotherhood, as well as Salafis, to key positions.

The Salafi movement

Scholars argue that Salafism is "par excellence a modern phenomenon and the result of the objectification of religion" (Meijer 2009a, 16–17). Egypt's first wave of Salafism came in the early twentieth century at the hands of Sheikh Hamid al-Fiqi, who established Gam'iyyat Ansar al-Sunna in 1926 with the intention of reviving 'orthodox' Islam. While that planted the movement's first seeds, it was only in the 1970s that Salafism became a popular movement. A few reasons contributed to the Salafi rise. Besides the disempowerment of al-Azhar highlighted earlier, Egypt's 1967 defeat in the war against Israel created an identity crisis that caused many Egyptians to turn to Islamism (al-Tayyib 1968). During his presidency, Sadat encouraged Salafism as an apolitical discourse that would nonetheless delegitimize both Nasserists and Muslim Brothers, especially after the latter reorganized. The return of Egyptian workers and professionals who had exiled themselves to the Gulf during Nasser's presidency further contributed to the rise of Salafism, alongside the 'petrodollar effect.' (The term 'petrodollar effect' refers to the sponsorship of religious textbooks and the like by rich Gulf states, and the resulting export of Salafi ideology.)

Salafism grew in Egypt as a 'new social movement.' Instead of relying on an organization—as the MB did—Salafis relied on a multi-polar network of preachers, largely connected to Saudi Wahhabi scholars.[5] While the number of organizations proliferated, only a few had real significance. Most important are the Ansar al-Sunna organization—with branches all over Egypt—and al-Da'wa al-Salafiya in Alexandria (DSA). Due to the way it was revived under Sadat, Salafism had no significant political presence; its role was limited to the socioreligious domains. Most Salafi scholars preached political quietism and kept themselves away from the contentious issues, focusing instead on ritual and individual salvation in their proselytizing. The attacks of 11 September 2001 swiftly transformed their relationship with the Egyptian regime, as their intellectual ties with Salafi jihadists were more closely scrutinized, leading to aggressive interrogation and recurrent imprisonment of Salafi leaders and members.

With the evident failure of Mubarak's regime in the months preceding the 2011 revolution, socioreligious tensions emerged, which triggered the politicization of Salafis. Lack of transparency and rule of law transformed the tensions that surrounded the case of Kamilia Shehata in September and October 2010 into serious religious strife, where Salafi antagonism was targeted at the Church instead of the failed state.[6] It was only a few weeks later that terrorist attacks targeted a Coptic church in Alexandria, a Salafi stronghold, on New Year's Eve. State Security soon assumed a link between earlier Salafi protests and these attacks, and hundreds of Salafi activists were rounded up and held in custody. Some were seriously tortured during interrogation, and one follower of DSA—Sayed Belal—died in prison.

Fearing a confrontation with the regime, key DSA figures decided not to join the protests denouncing the murder of Belal. Only a few days later—and following the ousting of President Ben Ali in Tunisia—Abdel Moneim al-Shahhat, DSA spokesman, made a statement rejecting calls for protests on 25 January, raising questions about the organizers' aims and insisting that they would cause more damage to the Salafis and to the country.[7] DSA and other Salafi groups maintained their hostility toward the revolutionaries until the second week of protests.

Neoliberal Islam
The trend of neoliberal Islam emerged with the emergence of 'new preachers' in the 1990s. With fewer scholarly qualifications and less training, a more modern facade, moderate discourse, and strong interpersonal skills, new preachers were "thick on ritual and remarkably thin on dissent," focusing primarily on "personal salvation, ethical enhancement and self-actualization" (Bayat 2007, 149). Televangelist preachers soon became popular among the conservative upper middle classes. Operating on the same modern, materialist paradigm of Salafism, advocates of neoliberal Islam stressed integration more than identity, leading to a complete shift in

discourse that matched their audience, which was "inclined toward a piety that could accommodate their privilege and power" (151). Their discourse provided a "safe alternative" for conservative upper-middle-class families and the Islamist business community (Haenni and Tammam 2003). On the one hand, a focus on morality and individual salvation meant detachment from the 'un-Islamic' aspects of their 'globalized' lifestyle. On the other hand, the Protestant-like neoliberal discourse provided them with enough legitimacy to sustain their lifestyle and retain their social networks despite their new religiosity (see, for example, Hennai 2005 and Lotfy 2005). In other words, new preachers advocated a form of Islam that provided its followers with "safe religiosity which entails no confrontation with the state or society" (El Houdaiby 2009, 48).

Guided by audience interests, new preachers adopted an apolitical discourse that focused on charity and development efforts. Over the past decade, a few attempts have been made by some new preachers to step into the political domain. These attempts were met with fierce opposition from the regime, which attempted to use new preachers as a stabilizing force, both because they operated within the dominant neoliberal paradigm and hence provided the regime with Islamic legitimacy, and because their charitable and development activities compensated for the regime's failures at a very low political price, especially when compared to the MB. New preachers and their neoliberal Islamic audience were therefore operating on the margins of politics, focused more on covering the regime's shortcomings than on challenging the regime or questioning its very legitimacy. This stance has consistently put neoliberal Islamists at odds with other Islamists, who have deemed them to be government elements that corrupt Islam.[8] While the neoliberal preachers, who were focused on integration, had programs on liberal satellite channels, other Islamists, who focused on identity, were increasingly retreating from this public sphere, choosing to present their shows on 'Islamist' satellite channels. Eventually, new preachers were not welcome to appear on Islamist channels, and were left with no option but to increasingly side with the regime's business cronies and other elements maintaining the status quo. Their neoliberal discourse, lack of scholarly qualifications, focus on integration (which seemed to jeopardize or dilute their Islamist identity), and mild stance toward the regime have provoked Sufis, Azharis, Salafis, and Muslim Brothers respectively. Criticism by these groups delegitimized the new preachers, who with their audience were then pushed further away from the other Islamists. Conflict between the new preachers and other Islamist groups escalated in the months preceding the revolution. Being more attached to the regime, some new preachers supported ruling NDP candidates against the MB in the 2010 parliamentary elections, further widening this schism.[9]

The Muslim Brotherhood

The MB is Egypt's largest opposition group, and the world's oldest existing Islamist movement. Over time, at least four different schools of thought, or what could be seen as ideological leanings, have come to coexist within the MB.[10] First is the founder's school: a relatively modernist school that existed on the margins of al-Azhar in the early twentieth century. It rejects *turath* (the accumulated heritage of Islamic knowledge) as the defining authority, and calls for a return to the Quran and Sunna as original sources, and to practicing *ijtihad* (independent judgment) with guidance from, rather than slavish adherence to the ideas in, *turath*. Second is the traditionalist school, championed by al-Azhar's long history of scholarship. It is characterized by heavy reliance on *turath* and acceptance of the full authenticity of the four main Sunni schools of jurisprudence. The school also promotes the notion of 'balanced identity,' arguing that each individual belongs to different circles of affiliation, including schools of jurisprudence and theology, Sufi order, hometown, profession, guild, family, and so on. Qutbism, the third school, is characterized by its highly politicized and revolutionary interpretation of the Qur'an, which divides people into those who belong to/support Islam/Islamism and those who oppose it, with no gray areas in between. This school emphasizes the necessity of developing a detached vanguard that focuses on recruitment and ways to empower the organization while postponing all intellectual questions. While hardcore Qutbism opens doors for political violence, Qutbis within the MB follow a demilitarized version of the ideology, clearly distancing themselves from notions of *takfir* (denunciation as apostates) and violence.[11] The Salafi/Wahhabi school made its way to the MB (and to broader Egyptian society) in the 1970s, forming the fourth leaning within the organization. It is a modernist Islamist ideology that has minimal respect for *turath*, relying instead on "a direct interface with the texts of revelation," which leads to "a relatively shallow and limited hierarchy of scholarly authorities" (Haykel 2009, 36). Salafism is characterized by a conservative reading of shari'a because it relies on "a textual approach, which uses text more than wisdom and reason in understanding it, and adage more than opinion" (Emara 2008, 130), leaving little room for diversity. Salafi and Qutbi acceptance of notions like democracy and diversity are minimal, and they generally believe in a strong, broad central state that plays a major role in defining and upholding public morality.

The MB responded to years of threats and actual persecution by state authorities by developing a "pyramid-shaped hierarchy [which] ensures that members dutifully execute the aims of its national leadership at the local level" (Trager 2011, 119). Through its strategy of centralizing decision-making and decentralizing the implementation of those decisions, the MB has sought to sustain unity within the organization. Centralized decision-making was intended to keep disputes contained in limited domains, while the decentralization of action was an attempt to avoid the possible consequences of security crackdowns, to create a sense of belonging and empowerment among members, and to develop members' executive capabilities. This was reflected in the group's recruitment and promotion criteria, which are based on standards of religious practice and organizational discipline. Observers note that "becoming a full-fledged Muslim Brother is a five-to-eight year process during which aspiring members are closely watched for their loyalty" (Trager 2011, 119).

Arguably, only a few principles kept the MB united as an organization despite the varied ideological leanings of its members: a belief that Islam is an all-encompassing system; rejecting violence as a means of political change in domestic politics; accepting democracy as a political system; consequently accepting political pluralism; and supporting resistance movements operating against foreign occupation.

This search for common ground among the different MB factions had a structural impact on the Brotherhood. It led to the emergence of a heavyweight organization, with exponentially growing membership and enormous room to maneuver due to the diversity of activities in which the group is engaged. Yet with the high centralization of its decision-making, the MB was easily pressured by successive regimes who wanted to control its decisions. Over the course of decades, this led to the emergence of unspoken rules of engagement that enabled the MB to oppose the regime while not seriously challenging it.[12]

Over the past decade, the MB has had to undergo serious transformations. It was part of the opposition that united around a "common foreign policy agenda" following the Palestinian Intifada in 2000 and the invasion of Iraq in 2003 (Shehata 2009, 315). Its domestic agenda has also increasingly prioritized democracy since 2005 (Shehata 2009, 325). After the Brotherhood secured 20 percent of parliamentary seats in the 2005 elections, it faced a vicious crackdown from the regime. This swift change between inclusion and exclusion sparked dissent among members as they became more focused on questions of policy and reform (al-Anani 2009). While some chose to resign, others remained in the group and added their critical discourse to its internal dynamics.

Another wave of Brotherhood changes came from within. In mid-2009, former chairman Mahdi Akef announced his decision to step down. This was significant not just because of the precedent it set, but also because Akef was the last MB leader with the historical legitimacy gained by joining the group at an early stage and working directly with its founder. Muhammad Badie, Akef's successor, who follows the Qutbi tendency and has strong ties with the Salafis in the group, also belongs to another generation that lacks the gravitas of Akef and his predecessors,[13] a quality that had helped them to resolve internal disputes within the MB. Without this authority among its leaders, it became more difficult for the MB to postpone intellectual and political debates while maintaining unity, particularly in light of the narrow decision-making structures (described above) and the absence of proper internal governance structures.[14]

The subsequent executive council elections took the competition between different MB factions to another level. Elections took place in a context of exclusion, where the regime was fiercely cracking down on the organization and the path for integration seemed occluded. The Salafi–Qutbi faction—being the most powerful, as it was operating in its ideal historical moment—adopted an exclusionary position, fearing that diversity in decision-making would lead to organizational rifts. The newly elected executive council did not include key reformist figures like Aboul Fotouh and Muhammad Habib, the former deputy chairman. The chairman's selection of deputies also reflected this trend: all three belonged to the Salafi–Qutbi school.

The new leadership was soon faced with a wide range of challenges. The start of 2010 saw the return of Mohammad ElBaradei, former president of the International Atomic Energy Agency, and the establishment of the National Society for Change (NSC). The MB's political calculation—highlighted above—inspired it to keep one foot in line with ElBaradei and the NSC, who were focused on challenging the regime, and the other in line with the group's social activities.[15] The year ended with parliamentary elections in which the MB won no seats, which had a serious impact on its membership. Having no parliamentary representatives for five years meant that street presence was the only way for the organization—officially outlawed—to remain heard. This, in turn, meant that the MB needed to move one step closer to the NSC and other opposition groups. Occlusion of political opportunity was met with despair and helplessness by senior MB members, but the reaction of juniors was fury—and this anger was soon transformed into hope with the ousting of Ben Ali.

Conclusions on the pre-revolutionary scene

Islamists were generally excluded from the Egyptian polity prior to the 2011 revolution. Not a single Islamist political group was legally recognized, and tolerance for their extralegal integration was dictated by the regime's need for legitimacy. During the 1980s, Mubarak's regime "needed a measure of legitimacy to help it maintain stability," and sought it partially by tolerating nonviolent groups (al-Awadi 2004, 194). Islamists—primarily the MB—exploited the opportunity by strengthening their organization and securing de facto legitimacy by participating in parliamentary, student union, and syndicate elections (al-Awadi 2004, 194). Other symptoms of Islamic ascent included the rise of a 'parallel Islamic sector,' which "had begun to coalesce in the interstices of Egypt's authoritarian state" (Wickham 2002, 95), and an unprecedented boom in the number of private mosques and Islamic associations, as well as growth of a parallel Islamic banking sector. Bayat notes that Islamic revival had "reached its peak by the early 1990s" (2007, 33). Islamists started "politicizing their achievements of social legitimacy in society" (al-Awadi 2004, 140), which contributed to the gradual erosion of the regime's legitimacy.

The Islamists' threat to the regime's legitimacy inspired a strategic transformation during the 1990s: while crushing radical Islamists, the regime resorted to less violent measures to sideline moderates. Components of the exclusion strategy included "divide-and-rule tactics to break the ranks of the opposition and prevent sustainable alliance building between Islamists and non-Islamists," and adopting policies that "significantly raised the costs of cooperation with Islamists" (Shehata 2009, 321). This was coupled with crackdowns on Islamist strongholds, including student unions, syndicates, private mosques, the banking sector, and private enterprise. The alignment of some secularists with the regime legitimized these efforts (Shehata

2009, 320), leading to both the exclusion of Islamists and the emergence of a dual public sphere phenomenon that defined both the political and socio-religious domains. The exclusion of moderate Islamists created space for more extreme elements to flourish. Apolitical Salafism capitalized on its historical moment and grew steadily—alongside neoliberal Islam—during the second half of the 1990s. This, in turn, led to further divisions between Islamist and non-Islamist opposition factions.

The new millennium witnessed the ascent of a new generation to the front lines of Egyptian politics. Disenchanted with established political divisions, this generation (usually referred to as the '1970s generation') was more focused on issues of national consensus, as highlighted in the previous section. Its ascent increased "the prospects for effective alliance building . . . [as activists] demonstrated a greater propensity for pragmatism and compromise, despite their varying ideological commitments" (Shehata 2009, 324–25). Islamists belonging to this generation were challenging the tactics of their respective organizations and their focus on divisive identity politics instead of joining forces to achieve nationwide goals. Operating against the backdrop of their own historical moment, these activists were increasingly marginalized within Islamist circles, only to regain their influence in post-revolutionary Egypt.

Islamists in the Revolution

Inspired by Muhammad Bouazizi, the Tunisian street vendor whose self-immolation sparked that country's revolution, a few Egyptians set themselves on fire in front of the parliament, to protest their living conditions and the country's socioeconomic problems. Politicians and activists soon followed by calling for a massive demonstration on Police Day, 25 January—a call that elicited different responses from different Islamist groups.

While some Salafi groups were fast in their denunciation of the call for protest (including the influential DSA), the relatively insignificant Salafi group Hafs issued a statement encouraging Egyptians to participate.[16] Consistent with the regime's strategy to downplay the significance of calls to protest, Sufi orders and the official religious establishment remained silent.

The Brotherhood's reaction was more sophisticated. The group's leadership was cornered between two choices: extreme provocation of the regime, or detachment from the broader nationalist movement. It therefore issued three statements between 15 and 23 January in escalating tones.

The first statement congratulated the Tunisian people for the successful ousting of Ben Ali and called upon Arab regimes to "listen to the voice of wisdom" from their people calling for reform; the second statement, issued 19 January, included a ten-point roadmap for reform to be enacted immediately; the third condemned the interrogation and threats faced by MB leaders being pressured to boycott the protests, and called for dialogue (Rabie 2011, 174–78). While these official statements remained ambiguous about the degree of the group's own participation, a group of MB youth members were quick to endorse the protest calls and begin rallying for the cause.

The turnout on 25 January exceeded expectations and thereby altered the political calculation of the various parties. Between 25 and 28 January, the co-opted official religious institution and politically inexperienced Salafis were slow to react, while the MB was modifying its position around the clock. In a statement on 26 January, the Brotherhood asserted that its members were participating in their personal capacity and that the regime should "comply to people's will" (Rabie 2011, 178). On the eve of 28 January, the group announced its endorsement of the calls for nationwide demonstrations. The regime responded by preemptively arresting a large number of key MB leaders and activists, including a handful of executive council members.

Islamists responded differently to the unprecedented clashes that took place on 28 January and the shocking death toll of that day. Despite its conservative nature, the MB's political experience facilitated a swift change of rhetoric. Four increasingly strident statements were made between 29 January and 1 February, the last outspokenly calling for Mubarak to step down (Rabie 2011, 179–82). Meanwhile, a statement issued by the DSA on 30 January condemned the "destruction of public property," while not declaring a stance vis-à-vis the protests, a position that the group maintained in its statement following Mubarak's second television appearance. Again, the official religious establishment and Sufi orders remained largely silent.

When Mubarak addressed the nation in his second televised speech, following the "million-man march" on 1 February, he made some minor concessions.[17] He offered a roadmap for change that was more aligned with Islamists' conservative thinking, as the apparent 'unconstitutionality' of his stepping down made calls for him to do so seem irrational, especially given the absence of a clear alternative. The official establishment used the pro-Mubarak demonstrations that followed this speech to confirm its loyalty to the regime. Both the Grand Sheikh of al-Azhar and the Grand Mufti issued statements hailing the president's speech and the changes it promised. The Sufi establishment remained silent, although some Sufi sheikhs and al-Azhar scholars joined the protests, giving rise to dissent within the institutions upon which the regime depended.

The positions taken by the MB during this period reflected an internal divide. On-the-ground activists played an instrumental role in defending revolutionaries when thugs attacked Tahrir Square the following day; they chanted alongside other protesters and rejected talks with regime officials, thereby moving closer to the core of the revolutionary movement. The MB leadership, however, was shaken by Vice President Omar Suleiman's carrot-and-stick interview in which he offered the Brotherhood a seat in negotiations while accusing them of political opportunism and jeopardizing the country's national interests. Their statement of 3 February reflected a return to their earlier conservative position: while it clearly rejected the regime's threats and endorsed the revolutionary demands, it opened the door to a "constructive, productive and sincere dialogue," with the regime (Rabie 2011, 183). The persistence of the revolutionaries was shaking the balance of power, however, and caused the retreat of MB leaders from talks with Suleiman after only one round.

Salafis emerged in support of the protests only a few days before Mubarak stepped down. Clearly departing from its earlier anti-revolutionary stance, the DSA issued two statements on 2 February. While the first condemned violence by protesters, the second outlined a rather conservative roadmap for reform that including abolishing the emergency law, combating corruption, and hiring the competent and the pious for various state positions in order to end corruption (Rabie 2011, 214). A few iconic Salafi figures began to appear at protests.[18] The official religious establishment remained silent all the while, while facing serious pressure from those among its scholars who joined the demonstrators.

Immediate Revolutionary Impact on Islamists

The eighteen days preceding Mubarak's fall had a deep impact on the Islamists who took part in protests. Most significantly, it pushed them beyond the borders of identity politics. Through their interactions with other groups and activists, Islamists realized that their social and political counterparts were not hostile toward Islam, and that their agendas were not anti-Islamic. Although legal barriers to inclusion were removed, allowing the MB to form a legal political party, this inclusive dynamic lasted no longer than a few weeks. A few days after Mubarak's resignation, the Supreme Council of Armed Forces (SCAF) established a committee to draft constitutional amendments that would facilitate the transition process. The committee was headed by retired judge Tariq al-Bishri and included a handful of judges and law professors, as well as Subhi Salih, lawyer and former MB parliamentarian.[19] While the MB accepted the proposed roadmap, other political groups remained opposed. Soon the procedural debate was transformed into an ideological one: supporters of the amendments were considered Islamists; those who opposed it were branded anti-Islamists. This re-polarization revived the split in the public sphere, which in turn had an impact on Islamists.[20]

The short era of inclusion had a significant impact on all of the different Islamist groups, but most importantly on the MB, which had relied on identity politics to maintain its organizational unity. One week after Mubarak's fall, the Brotherhood declared its intention to establish a political party, and the Freedom and Justice Party (FJP) was born. While the nomination of leaders (all of whom were members of the MB executive council) raised serious questions about the party's autonomy, the establishment of a political party reflected a major shift in the group's political thinking.

The structure and leadership of the FJP was met with dismay by different reformist figures within the group. Ibrahim al-Za'farani, Khaled Dawood, and Hamid al-Dafrawi—three prominent reformist figures from Alexandria, all considered disciples of Aboul Fotouh—decided to split with the MB and form their own political party. Soon enough, and as they moved beyond identity politics, they realized that the question of religious moderation was not the only one governing the political domain: political orientation was also crucial. They consequently split into three different political groups: two consider themselves center-right (the Nahda and Riyada parties); the third (the Society of Peace and Development Party) considers itself center-left.

Younger members who had operated for a far shorter time in the context of oppression found it much easier to move beyond identity politics and to rediscover Egypt's political landscape in light of revolutionary inclusiveness. A first wave of protest came from a group of Cairene youth, who called for a nationwide conference for MB youth with workshops that would focus on two main themes: transforming the MB from an organization to an institution, and discussing different scenarios for the relationship between socioreligious and political activities.[21] This conference, held on 26 March, was followed by the dismissal of key figures, young and old, who refused to join the FJP and formed their own parties, or who joined Aboul Fotouh's presidential campaign.[22]

If the moment of inclusion was the main trigger for change within the MB, it was a combination of perceived identity threat and political opportunity that altered Salafi dynamics. Dozens of secular activists gathered in a demonstration in late February and called for the second article of the constitution, establishing the principles of shari'a as the primary source of legislation, to be amended. Salafis, who perceived this as a threat, responded with a massive demonstration after prayers in Abbasiya the following Friday—the first Salafi demonstration since 25 January. The widening split in the public sphere that emerged during the referendum on constitutional amendments further politicized Salafis. With the MB supporting the amendments and most 'secular' political forces rejecting them, Salafis—operating on identity politics—decided to side with the MB. This decision was further encouraged by some marginal voices on the 'No' campaign calling for the wholesale removal of Article 2, and other, more significant, voices basing their opposition to the amendments on the assumption that a 'Yes' vote would empower Islamists. Over 77 percent of Egyptians voted for the constitutional amendments. Instead of reading these figures as representing the broader public's choice of a less risky path to change, mainstream media insisted that the outcome reflected the overwhelming electoral power of Islamists. This, in turn, fed into the Salafis' perception of themselves and highlighted the opportunities that appeared to be associated with political integration. Initially, however, and aware of their political inexperience, Salafis were still hesitant to establish their own political parties and instead announced their support of the MB.[23]

Subsequent events, however, illustrated the divergence of MB and Salafi positions. The resurfacing of the case of Kamilia Shehata and the state's failure to resolve it provoked Salafis to demonstrate again, calling for Shehata's release from 'church arrest.' Demonstrations in front of the Coptic church in Abbasiya led to clashes between Salafi and Coptic youth. The silence of the MB provoked Salafis to pursue an independent political track. They started establishing their own political parties, most significantly al-Noor Party (NP), which was affiliated with leaders of the DSA. Despite these moves, Salafis remained marginal on Egypt's political scene as the MB retained its hegemony over the political Islamist discourse. But with the increasingly loud call by some secular intellectuals and public figures for a set of supra-constitutional articles, Islamists who viewed this as threat decided to respond. Salafis, resorting again to identity politics, magnified the practically nonexistent fear of the marginalization of shari'a—the adoption of supra-constitutional articles that would restrict the application of shari'a. And on 29 July, hundreds of thousands of pro-Islamist activists responded to a call by the DSA for a demonstration in Tahrir Square opposing these supra-constitutional principles, joined by other Islamist factions including the MB.[24] The predominantly Salafi parade sent alarming signals to some political and social groups, who feared that a Salafi ascent would jeopardize their civil liberties and alter the political system in undesirable ways.

The ousting of Mubarak took Egypt's religious establishment by surprise. Its primary challenge in the revolution's aftermath was to regain both its political and its scholarly legitimacy. Al-Azhar's Grand Sheikh adopted a multidimensional strategy for personal and institutional relegitimization. On the one hand, he reversed his position, insisting that he had always been a strong supporter of the revolution, citing incidents such as sending an imam to lead the Friday prayers in Tahrir Square as proof. To avoid scrutiny of these claims, a key component of his strategy was to divert attention to other issues. He formed a committee to revise the laws governing al-Azhar, and pledged to revitalize the organization in order to enable it to regain its position as a leading scholarly institution. This was welcomed by observers who feared Salafi assimilation into the institution after long years of institutional disempowerment. He also relied on independent credible experts to revisit laws regulating al-Azhar and propose new legislation that would offer a wider margin of financial and administrative independence. A shift was also effected in the broader discourse, with al-Azhar and the Grand Sheikh's bureau issuing statements supporting Arab revolutions and condemning the dictatorship of Arab regimes.

Meanwhile, al-Azhar's efforts to increase its legitimacy as an academic institution were based on positioning itself as the guardian of religious authenticity and moderation, and the patriarch of Islamists. Hence it launched initiatives that brought together iconic figures from all Islamist groups, including Salafis and the MB. It also embarked on a discussion about the 'nature of the state,' which provoked significant debate in the public sphere. Al-Azhar contributed to this debate by issuing a declaration representing its perception of the role and nature of the state.[25] Egypt's Grand Mufti, who had initially waged intellectual battles against Salafis, later followed in the footsteps of the Grand Sheikh and hosted Salafi preachers in his office, emphasizing the need for unity and cooperation.

The Sufis, like the Salafis, were politicized as a result of the perceived threat to their identity. The split in the public sphere between Islamists and secularists catalyzed their politicization. Realizing there was an opportunity to oppose the Salafis on a more moderate and inclusive platform while still enjoying Islamist authenticity, Sufi orders began to increase their political presence.[26] Following a strategy similar to al-Azhar, their politically active elements chose to align themselves more closely with secularists than with Islamists, since their identity was constantly threatened by their religious rivals, the Salafis. This rivalry was further fueled by the Salafis' show of force in the 29 July demonstration, which the Sufis avoided. To no one's surprise, the first Sufi political party was formed by the sheikh of the Azmiya order, who had been growing increasingly politicized in recent years. With little political experience and limited capacity to organize and mobilize, the party has not yet left the margins of Egypt's political landscape.

Islamists' Post-revolutionary Challenges

The split in the public sphere has led to an identity-based polarization, with political actors characterized on one side as Islamist, and as secular on the other. This has had the effect of polarizing and/or marginalizing serious questions of reform and policy that Islamists will have to face in post-revolutionary Egypt. These include the relationship between state and religion, and between authenticity and modernity, as well as the challenge of developing a coherent political program and the unprecedented empowerment of individuals within organizations.

Various scholarly attempts have been made to define the term 'secular' and assess how it relates to religious values. Of these attempts, perhaps the most important in the Egyptian context is that of Abdel-Wahab Elmessiri, who distinguishes between two layers of secularism: the procedural and the absolute (2002). While procedural secularism amends procedures without challenging the governing value system, absolute secularism aims at constructing its own frame of reference, challenging the transcendental religious values that governed societies in pre-secular times. For Elmessiri, these forms exist on a continuum, with theocracies at one end, procedural secularism somewhere in the middle, and absolute secularism at the other end. This clustering has a much greater illustrative capacity than traditional Islamist–secular polarization. Arguably, the notion of 'absolute secularism' has only marginal (if any) presence in Egypt's public debate. The question is therefore not *whether* religion should have a role in the political system, but rather *how* this role should be managed, and which domains it should cover.

Islamists have responded differently to these questions. While Salafis refuse terms designed to bridge the gap (such as the 'civil state,' a vaguely defined term coined to end the secular–Islamist dichotomy, and intended to mean a state that is neither theocratic nor hostile toward religion), Sufis tend to bypass the entire question in their political discourse by avoiding any discussion on the matter. The MB and al-Azhar, meanwhile, demonstrate higher levels of sophistication. With the experience of years of debate and discussion on the matter, the MB presented its vision for a 'civil state with an Islamic frame of reference.' While this articulation is still considerably vague, the group has successfully distanced itself from the traditional Salafi stance and is working hard to present itself as a mainstream movement capable of acting as a bridge between both sides of the political spectrum.[27] Al-Azhar—with solid academic credentials, insufficient political experience, and a dire need to re-legitimize the institution—took part in the debate through its declaration on the political system. The declaration successfully grabbed the attention of both secular and Islamist activists, yet was harshly criticized by Islamists on both political and scholarly grounds.[28] An earlier attempt by al-Azhar to approach this rather contentious question had been made by Ali Gomaa before the revolution. Focusing on the 'uniqueness' of Egyptians' understanding of religion, Gomaa examined modern history, arguing that "Egypt had not detached itself from Islam, but was only trying to respond to contemporary challenges" (Gomaa 2008, 27) through its legislation. He argued that the contemporary Egyptian legal system presents a successful model for a civil state that upholds shari'a.

This question of the relationship between religion and politics will play an instrumental role in shaping the future for Islamist groups. The scholarly question of what constitutes shari'a and the political question of how much the state—rather than the individual and society—should be involved in the application of shari'a are likely to spark real debates among Islamists. Upcoming events will encourage Islamists to scrutinize this relationship between religion and politics, and will eventually lead to the redefinition of the Islamist landscape.

Another major factor that will affect the future of Islamism is the authenticity–modernity dialectic. Long decades of exclusion from the polity have hindered Islamist scholarship in sociopolitical domains (al-Bishri 2005). However, since authenticity is such an integral component of Islamism, Islamists cannot simply discard authenticity and unconditionally accept modern notions such as democracy. If more politically experienced groups do so, they are criticized by less experienced, more stagnant ones as 'inauthentic,' and their 'Islamist legitimacy' is consequently jeopardized.

This authenticity–modernity dialectic is most clearly manifested in the relationship between neoliberal Islamists and all the others. While the neoliberals' unconditional pursuit of relevance to modern societies has boosted their popularity among globalized, modern segments of the society, their lack of focus on authenticity has almost completely discredited them among other Islamists.

Striking a balance between authenticity and sociopolitical relevance is a major challenge for different Islamist groups. Attitudes toward notions like 'democracy' and 'the state' reflect different groups' positions on the matter. Al-Azhar—the symbol of authenticity—issued a statement outlining the principles of an 'Islamically acceptable' political system. While the definition was widely accepted by different social groups and by intellectuals, signaling success on the moderation parameter, it was criticized by Islamists, and particularly by Salafis. More significantly, none of the Islamist activists or intellectuals were invited to the first round of talks and workshops that al-Azhar held in the run-up to the publication of this key declaration. Arguably, al-Azhar made a political calculation—influenced by long years of disempowerment and state control and the difficulty of fighting Islamists in the struggle for legitimacy—to side with other social actors, and to win the battle for religious authenticity and representation on non-Islamist grounds.

The MB, being the most experienced political Islamist group, approached the challenge differently. The group resorted to the writings of Yusuf al-Qaradawi[29] and other credible scholars to justify its acceptance of a 'civil' state and emphasize the authenticity of that position. On other matters, including questions of public morality, the group's position remains vague, as they attempt to appease audiences on both sides. The separation of the FJP from the MB has given the group more room for political maneuver, wherein the party could adopt a politically correct stance while the Brotherhood as a whole stresses religious authenticity.

The question of identity governs the Salafi approach to this dilemma. Salafi leaders seize every possible opportunity to highlight differences between their position and those of other sociopolitical forces—including other Islamists—always attempting to emphasize their own authenticity. On the question of the nature of the state, for instance, they continue to reject the 'civil' state, promote the 'Islamic' state, and stress their rejection of democracy.[30] It is al-Azhar's lack of credibility that allows Salafis—arguably presenting less scholarly sound and religiously authentic stances—to play the identity card in post-revolutionary Egypt.

Sufis, meanwhile, have adopted a stance contradictory to that of Salafis. Attempting to emphasize their moderation—their key political strength—Sufis seem to endorse democracy while emphasizing their authenticity in other domains, including their reliance on al-Azhar as a reference in religious practice. Consequently, their rhetoric is hardly competitive on Islamist grounds, as they make no serious attempts to authenticate their political stances. On the question of the nature of the state, they too emphasize their acceptance of the 'civil state' with equal citizenship rights for all citizens regardless of religion and gender. They do not, however, provide any religious authority for this stance.

Neoliberal Islamists, operating through al-Hadara Party, have adopted more progressive political stances (in contrast to their conservative economic ones): one party spokesman announced his rejection of state intervention in cultural and moral affairs, and insisted that movies and art should not be censored.[31] Credibility of this discourse among Islamists is minimal, as it is hardly viewed as religiously authentic.

Developing coherent political programs is a key challenge for Islamists in the aftermath of the revolution. While the current polarization of the Egyptian public sphere is causing the retreat of most into identity politics, some remain persistent in their focus on policy and reform. As events progress, however, more Islamists are likely to be forced out of identity politics. With the abolition of legal barriers to participation and legal recognition already being granted to a handful of Islamist parties, public debate will eventually reshape alliances in a way that shifts the focus to policy rather than identity. Questions of economy and foreign policy, among others, will prove to be more important to Egypt's public debate than Islamist identity politics. Nonetheless, Islamist movements venturing beyond identity domains will have to be cautious as they move into these new fields. A too-sudden shift will cause them to lose their constituencies, which would then resort to more rigid forms of Islamism.

The current scene suggests that al-Azhar, together with the more sophisticated elements of the MB, would be better able to navigate this path than other Islamist groups. Al-Azhar's authenticity and historical legacy, alongside its pursuit of moderation and social reconciliation, in combination with the MB's political experience and credibility among Islamists, could serve toward that end. Nonetheless, the political thinking of the current MB leadership seems to be more concerned with identity and organization, and consequently allies itself with more conservative elements. This kind of alliance therefore seems unlikely.

Egypt's revolution has caused a major shift in the thinking of Islamist organizations. The pre-revolutionary context—with its identity politics, split public sphere, and state oppression—led to the emergence of autocratic organizations, in which leaders wielded tremendous power. This power was challenged by the decision of individual members to join the mass protests, usually against the will of their leaders, as highlighted in earlier sections. This decision by MB youth altered the group's chain-of-command legitimacy, with events proving the youth to have been right. Small, marginal Salafi groups, and junior members of the more prominent ones, who joined the protest in its earlier days came to be viewed by Salafis as political lifesavers: preachers who had begun by denouncing the demonstrations later pointed to a few martyrs broadly identified as Salafis as evidence of Salafi participation. The same applies to junior al-Azhar scholars who participated in the demonstrations from the beginning, as well as the former spokesman for the Grand Sheikh, who resigned and joined the protests. These and other incidents have challenged the governing perceptions of leadership and led to a redistribution of power within Islamist groups, whereby individual choice will have a major role in their decision-making and limit top-down authority.

Post-revolutionary Egypt has already witnessed a few manifestations of this shift: When a few Salafis established al-Noor Party, they were met with criticism from the leadership, which soon afterward endorsed the idea and supported the party. And MB youth conferences were initially boycotted by the group's leadership, which later decided to organize similar conferences in different provinces. The power of initiative-taking has been inspired and magnified by the revolution, and poses a clear challenge to the leadership of Islamist factions.

Impact of Key Future Milestones

While several details have yet to be defined, the context of freedom and inclusion will inevitably lead to further political evolution of Islamist trends. The removal of legal barriers to participation, alongside the marginalization of the threat of physical oppression, will catalyze this evolution. While an inclusive discourse from other societal and social elements would further facilitate the process, its absence will not necessarily be fatal. Milestones highlighted in this section—most significantly parliamentary elections and their aftermath—will encourage Islamists to focus on politics and not identity. The future of Islamism in Egypt will be shaped by the ways in which Islamist groups react to their parliamentary experiences and electoral exposure, whether in parliamentary or presidential elections, as well as by the nature of the alliances they will have to build in their pursuit of ending military rule—the most serious challenge currently facing Islamists.

Polarization within the public sphere in the run-up to parliamentary elections had a huge impact on the performance of Islamist groups and candidates. As highlighted earlier, polarization has tended to encourage Islamists to resort to identity politics. This led to an easy electoral victory for Islamists since, according to a 2008 Gallup world poll, 98 percent of Egyptians say that "religion is an important part" of their "daily lives," while 87 percent say that traditions and customs associated with Islam play a central role therein (Esposito and Mogahed 2007, 7). Religion in Egypt is therefore not merely a set of rituals, but rather a *Weltanschauung*, with its value system and legislative guidelines. According to the same statistics, the vast majority of Egyptians want to have shari'a as a source of legislation, and a majority want it to be "the only source of legislation." Post-revolution polls show similar results: only a small minority of Egyptians (9 percent) want to see an absolute separation between religious and political institutions that gives religious scholars no authority whatsoever over political affairs. A slightly larger minority (14 percent) seems to support theocratic rule (where religious scholars have full authority over political affairs), while Egypt's mainstream (70 percent) stands somewhere in between, demanding that religious scholars play a role in advising those in power.[32] With the election hinging on identity rather than on policies, the vast majority of Egyptians voted for Islamists, and the FJP and al-Noor Party collectively won around 70 percent of parliamentary seats. Moving from the opposition into the decision-making role will, however, have a significant impact on Islamists, obliging them to engage in serious political debate on questions including military budgets, education, health care, subsidies, scientific research, infrastructure, national security, and foreign relations. This very participation will force them out of identity politics, and while the impact might not be immediately visible, it is likely to affect their political alliances in the following election.

Election campaigns also contribute to this development. During the parliamentary campaign, the MB had to walk a thin line, with 'secular' forces on one side and Salafis on the other, where their traditional election slogan, "Islam is the solution," became a double-edged sword, helping them to capitalize on the large degree of pro-Islamic support but impeding their efforts to present themselves as a mainstream movement. A less Islamist slogan, however, would increase the risk of losing much needed 'Islamist' voters to the more identity-focused Salafis. During the parliamentary elections, the FJP resorted to the latter option, reflecting their keenness to pose as the mainstream national movement.

Egypt's presidential elections had a greater impact on Islamists than parliamentary elections. Initially, there were three competing 'Islamist' candidates, none of whom was backed by any political party. The MB had announced it would not field any candidate of its own, yet all three Islamists were mildly affiliated to the group. Muhammad Salim Al-Awa, secretary general of the International Union of Muslim Scholars (IUMS), resigned from the MB in the 1960s and has been viewed ever since as an independent moderate Muslim thinker. Abdel Moneim Aboul Fotouh was an iconic reformist in the Brotherhood, but was dismissed from the group after announcing his candidacy. Hazem Abou Ismail is an inactive member of the group who ran on the Brotherhood's behalf in the 2005 parliamentary elections.

The positioning of Islamist presidential candidates reflected diversity within Islamism. Looking at these three candidates only through the traditional lens of religious moderation—ranging from moderate to extremist—does not get us very far, since Al-Awa and Aboul Fotouh are both widely viewed as moderate. To differentiate between them requires a different analytical framework. If we assess them on a political scale,

Al-Awa appears to be the right-wing candidate due to his condemnation of political protests, discouragement of labor protests, calls for stability, and lack of serious challenge to the status quo.[33] Aboul Fotouh, in contrast, is widely viewed as a leftist-Islamist candidate because he endorses sit-ins, repeatedly emphasizes social justice as a priority, and calls for radical change in state institutions—most significantly security institutions.

Shortly before the elections, however, the MB decided to file its own candidate. Failure to find a 'consensus candidate,' coupled with the ascent of Aboul Fotouh, posed a serious organizational threat to the MB, which was threatened by the possibility of a dismissed member making it to the presidential palace and hence proving the group's leadership wrong. The MB therefore nominated its strongman and vice chairman Khayrat El-Shater for the post. He was then disqualified, alongside Abou Ismail, only to be replaced by the FJP's chairman Muhammad Morsi. The al-Noor Party, also based on organizational calculation, decided to support Aboul Fotouh, the candidate closer to the mainstream national movement and revolutionary groups. In response, the MB attempted to detach al-Noor's leadership from its grassroots, by emphasizing that Mursi was the 'only Islamist candidate' in the election. However, when Morsi made it to the second round (with Ahmed Shafik, Mubarak's last prime minister), the MB rebranded its candidate as the 'revolution' candidate, and emphasized—once again—the necessity of broad consensus, downplaying the previously emphasized Islamization.

Parliamentary and presidential races have both contributed to the redefinition of Islamism, a process that will continue in the coming months. Legislative empowerment meant that Islamists were faced with people's daily problems, which made them realize that Islam is *not* the solution, that is, it does not automatically provide solutions for the country's problems. The presidential race witnessed the challenging of the predominantly right-wing nature of Islamist movement, with Aboul Fotouh (who won some 18 percent of the total vote, only 7 percentage points behind the leading candidate) defending leftist economic principles, emphasizing redistributive measures, and opting for a more 'independent' foreign policy. These policies clearly contrasted with Mursi's emphasis on privatization, reliance on international financial institutions, and vowing not to threaten regional stability. The coming months are expected to witness a power struggle between the MB and the SCAF, as well as intra-Islamist conflicts over policy. The alliances governing the first battle—that is, the nature and orientation of the groups who decide to side with the Islamists in this battle—will have a huge impact on the dominant political discourse within Islamism, while the existence of the internal conflicts will ensure the continuation of diversity within Islamism. Eventually, the forced focus on policy and issues will discourage identity politics. Islamism as a phenomenon will eventually be transcended, to be replaced by more sophisticated forms of religiously-influenced political participation.

Notes

1 Ammar Ali Hassan, "Changes in Sufi Orders' Orientations," interview by Ibrahim El Houdaibi, 27 November 2010.

2 For more on state control over endowments and its impact on al-Azhar see Ghanem (1998) and El Bayoumy (1998).

3 Alaa Abu-l-Azayim, "La ulzim atba' al-tariqa al-azmiya bi-l-taswit li-murashah mu'ayyan, wa-lakinni uzaki murashahin," interview, 11 November 2010, Islamyoon.net

4 A new law regulating al-Azhar was issued in 1961, fully subordinating it to the state. For more on this subject, see al-Awwa (2006).

5 Wahhabism is a school of Islamism that follows Muhammad ibn 'Abd al-Wahhab. It calls for the rejection of accumulated *turath* (accumulated heritage of Islamic sciences) and the return to the original sources of Islam to understand them. It is widely viewed as rigid, and while it claims to represent orthodox Islam, its authenticity is contested by various competing schools, including al-Azhar.

6 Kamilia Shehata was the wife of a Coptic priest who allegedly converted to Islam, but was held in custody by the regime before being sent back to the Church. Salafist groups started mobilizing their supporters and staged demonstrations calling for her 'release' from church.

7 Abdel Moneim al-Shahhat, "Lan nataraja', lan nustadraj, lan nuwazzaf," 19 January 2011, http://www.salafvoice.com/article.php?a=5105

8 Husam Tammam, "Tayyar al-du'ah al-judud lan yantahi, wa-huwa namuzaj jadid li-l-'almaniya al-muslima." Interview with El-Sayyed Zayed, 10 February 2010, http://www.islamismscope.net/from-media/447.html

9 Amr Khaled, icon of the new preachers, supported NDP member and former minister Abdel Salam al-Mahgoub against the MB's Subhi Salih in Alexandria, provoking a variety of Islamist groups (see, for example, Ahmad Fathi and Muhammad Khayal, "Inqilab bayn muridi Amr Khaled bi-sabab muhadaratuh fi jam'iyyat al-mahjub," *al-Shuruq*, November 2010, http://www.shorouknews.com/ContentData.aspx?ID=337802)

10 For more on different ideologies within the MB, see Ibrahim El Houdaiby, "The Muslim Brotherhood's Trial on Pluralism," *Ahram Online*, 23 April 2011, http://english.ahram.org.eg/NewsContentP/4/10662/Opinion/The-Muslim-Brotherhoods-trial-of-pluralism.aspx

11 For more on the MB's version of Qutbism, see Bayat 2007, 36–42, and Ibrahim El Houdaiby, "Four Decades after Sayyid Qutb's Execution," *Daily Star Egypt*, 28 August 2008, http://dailystaregypt.com/article.aspx?ArticleID=16062

12 For more on the 'rules of the game,' see, for example, Khalil al-Anani, "al-Nizam wa-l-Ikhwan fi Misr: hal tataghayyar qawa'id al-lu'ba?," *Al Jazeera*, 3 August 2009, http://www.aljazeera.net/NR/exeres/D25AB80C-7A5B-41B9-893E-23A8FFCE1727.htm; and Ibrahim El Houdaiby, "al-Mawqef al-estrateigy li-l-ikhwan," *al-Shuruq*, 23 July 2010.

13 Tammam, "Tayyar al-du'ah al-judud lan yantahi."

14 For more on the impact of leadership change in the MB, see Ibrahim El Houdaiby, "Egypt's Brotherhood Faces Leadership Challenges," *Arab Reform Bulletin*, Carnegie Endowment, 10 November 2010, http://www.carnegieendowment.org/2009/11/10/egypt-s-brotherhood-faces-leadership-challenge/9k8

15 Abigail Hauslohner, "Egypt's Opposition: Will the Islamists Join ElBaradei?," *Time World*, 14 April 2010, http://www.time.com/time/world/article/0,8599,1981368,00.html

16 Eman Abdelmonem, "Harakat Hafs al-salafiya tad'u li-l-musharaka yawm 25 Yanayir wa-tu'akkid: al-nizam wasal li-mada ba'id fi-l-zulm," *al-Dustur*, 20 January 2011, http://www.dostor.org/politics/egypt/11/january/20/35443

17 In his televised statement, Mubarak made it clear that he would not be running for a sixth presidential term, nor would his son Gamal run for the presidency. He also announced that he intended to make some constitutional changes.

18 Mohammed Hassan, an iconic Salafi television preacher, appeared in the square, and was interviewed by Al Arabiya on 31 January 2011: http://www.youtube.com/watch?v=DZInCkm5vm8

19 The committee suggested that nine articles of the constitution be amended, and that the transition begin with the election of a new parliament. That parliament would name a committee to draft a new constitution. A new president would be elected as a final step.

20 On the controversy preceding the referendum, see, for example, Salma Shukrallah, "Will Egypt Vote 'Yes' or 'No' to Constitutional Amendments?," *Ahram Online*, 15 March 2011, http://english.ahram.org.eg/NewsContent/1/0/7707/Egypt/0/Will-Egypt-vote-Yes-or-No-to-constitutional-%20%20amendm.aspx

21 Hanaa Souliman, "The Muslim Brotherhood's New Guard Rocks the Boat," *Daily News Egypt*, 3 April 2011, http://www.thedailynewsegypt.com/egypt/the-muslim-brotherhoods-new-guard-rocks-the-boat.html

22 Jeffrey Fleishman, "In Egypt, Muslim Brotherhood Showing Cracks in Its Solidarity," *Los Angeles Times*, 6 July 2011, http://articles.latimes.com/2011/jul/06/world/la-fg-egypt-brotherhood-expelled-20110706

23 Key figures, including al-Shahhat and Hassan, openly declared their intent to support the MB (see, for example, "Abdel Moneim al-Shahhat, al-mutahaddith bi-ism al-Jama'a al-Salafiya bi-l-Iskindiriya: Sa nad'am al-Ikhwan fi-l-intikhabat," Umma wahda, 20 April 2011, http://ummahwahda.blogspot.com/2011/04/blog-post.html).

24 Anthony Shadid, "Islamists Flood Square in Cairo in Show of Strength," *New York Times*, 30 July 2011, http://www.nytimes.com/2011/07/30/world/middleeast/30egypt.html

25 Comprising eleven points, the declaration supported the establishment of a national, constitutional, democratic modern state with respect for civil liberties; emphasized al-Azhar's role as the key scholarly Islamic institution; and announced its support for the Palestinian struggle. A copy of the declaration can be found at http://www.jusur.net/index-Dateien/image/azhar.pdf

26 Ammar Ali Hassan, "al-Dars al-siyasi li-l-turuq al-sufiya ba'd thawrat 25 yanayir," Aljazeera.net, 30 July 2011, http://www.aljazeera.net/NR/exeres/21FA3618-C1B2-4D1B-82E6-00699D58A650.htm

27 The MB's attempts to outline the role of state can be traced in their political documents. The most significant attempts include the 2004 reform initiative, the draft manifesto of 2007, and platforms presented in different parliamentary elections. Main ideas of these arguments are summarized in Essam el-Erian, "al-Ikhwan al-Muslimun wa-mafhum al-dawla," *Sina'at al-fikr*, 30 November 2010, http://www.fikercenter.com/fiker/index.php?option=com_k2&view=item&id=141:%D8%A7%D9%84%D8%A5%D8%AE%D9%88%D8%A7%D9%86-%D8%A7%D9%84%D9%85%D8%B3%D9%84%D9%85%D9%88%D9%86-%D9%88%D9%85%D9%81%D9%87%D9%88%D9%85-%D8%A7%D9%84%D8%AF%D9%88%D9%84%D8%A9-/-%D8%AF-%D8%B9%D8%B5%D8%A7%D9%85%D8%A7%D9%84%D8%B9%D8%B1%D9%8A%D8%A7%D9%86&Itemid=72

28 Mohammed Anz, "al-Jadal hawl wathiqat al-Azhar yastammir bi-raghm al-tawafuq," *al-Ahram*, 19 August 2011, http://www.ahram.org.eg/Al-Mashhad-Al-Syiassy/News/96106.aspx

29 A reputable al-Azhar scholar and former member of the MB who fled the country to Qatar in the late 1960s and later resigned from the group to become the Mufti of Qatar, and the chairman and founder of the International Union of Muslim Scholars.

30 Prominent Salafi figures, including al-Shahhat, Yasir Burhani, and Abu Ishaq al-Huwayni, have made recurring appearances denouncing democracy, and insisting that it violates the sovereignty of God. The most frequently cited examples include the legalization of gay marriage and extramarital sexual relations in democratic countries.

31 For more insights on different views of Islamists on this matter, see Reem Magued's interview with representatives of four Islamist parties at http://www.youtube.com/watch?v=5F6e1LwlQoY

32 Statistics from Gallup Report, "Egypt from Tahrir to Transition," 2011, http://www.abudhabigallupcenter.com/147896/egypt-tahrir-transition.aspx

33 For more on al-Awa's political stances, see his statements on his campaign's Facebook page: http://ar-ar.facebook.com/pages/%D8%A7%D9%84%D8%B5%D9%81%D8%AD%D8%A9-%D8%A7%D9%84%D8%B1%D8%B3%D9%85%D9%8A%D8%A9-%D9%84%D8%AF%D8%B9%D9%85-%D9%85%D8%AD%D9%85%D8%AF-%D8%B3%D9%84%D9%8A%D9%85-%D8%A7%D9%84%D8%B9%D9%88%D8%A7-%D8%B1%D8%A6%D9%8A%D8%B3%D8%A7%D9%8B-%D9%84%D9%85%D8%B5%D8%B1/232811033412520

8

Women Are Also Part of This Revolution

Hania Sholkamy[1]

Introduction

The revolution was planned, executed, and supported by both men and women. Gender was not a factor that influenced the decisions to revolt or to protest. That is at least the impression that prevails when contemplating the Egyptian Revolution that erupted on the streets of various Egyptian cities on 25 January 2011 and is still ongoing. With hindsight it is now clear that the protest movements that had been taking place for a decade, and that were initiated by rights activists belonging to workers' and civil liberty groups and other social movements, became the revolutionary agglomeration that toppled the elite echelons of the regime. The eruption of people onto the streets and into the squares demanding the end of the Mubarak era was an unexpected expression of social, gender, and generational inequality. Men and women, old and young, rural and urban, rich and poor were on the streets voicing their demands for change. This chapter ponders the relevance of gender to post-revolutionary political and social transformations by presenting a brief history of women's rights in Egypt and the structures and agents representing the politics of these rights, as they are re-evaluated through the revolutionary prism.

Publicly and privately, women young and old gave different reasons for their participation in the public protests that became the revolution. "I am here to support these youth"; "I want to help because of the brutality of the regime's attack on the protesters"; "My friend died and I will not have his death go in vain"; "I hate this regime because it is corrupt"; "I want a dignified future for my kids"; "I am here because this is the best place to be"; and "I have never before been in a crowd and not been harassed" are some of the responses that women gave when asked why they continued to stand in Tahrir Square.[2] These and other women were protesting in their capacity as citizens, not in their sex roles. They were not protesting in the name of gender equality, women's empowerment, or right to political participation. These are the buzzwords of gender work that probably make no sense outside the narrow confines of gender politics. In fact, these protests have discredited formal politics and therefore have implications for a revised understanding of women's political empowerment.

The images from Tahrir Square defined international and local perceptions of the revolution. They were images of jovial, tenacious, carefree solidarity against autocracy. There were always enough people in this and other squares all over Egypt to keep the spirits of Egyptians alive and optimistic. There were always women beside men, chanting, listening, making speeches, distributing food, making banners, tending the wounded, and maintaining this popular stand of defiance. There were hundreds if not thousands of women involved in organizing supplies, medications, banners, marches, international contacts, and general mobilization for this movement. There were no distinctions between women who were veiled, face-veiled, not veiled, women alone and with children, very young and elderly.

Such moments of solidarity, equality, hope, and popular mobilization are also 'liminal' moments in which hierarchies and structures of distinction are temporarily suspended (Turner 1969; 1974); they are also moments that are impossible to sustain as they are temporally and spatially bounded. Turner developed further the interpretation of ritual provided by Van Gennep in which the process of moving from one cultural stage to another (in other words, a rite of passage) is a three-stage process of separation, transition, and reintegration (Van Gennep 1960). The liminal phase is the middle one in which, as Turner puts it, "anything is possible!" (Turner 1969, 97). Although both Van Gennep and Turner were describing rituals, in particular those developed to mark and celebrate rites of passage such as coming-of-age ceremonies or religious rituals such as pilgrimage, the Egyptian Revolution lends itself to this analytical framework.

Liminal moments are wedged between two states of normalcy as they mark the disruption of one order and clear away the debris of what used to be the norms of this order to permit the creation of a new set of norms. The social actors/participants in this symbolic space/time are suspended between structures as they separate from one social order but are yet to become part of another. While thus suspended they are equal in all ways and are free from strictures and structures that had defined their personhood, a condition that Turner refers to as one of "communitas." This is the necessary condition from which a transformed order emerges and into which the initiates are reintegrated.

During the eighteen days of protest, a condition of near-communitas prevailed on the streets and squares where people had congregated. Sharing sleeping space and food, men and women bracketed their old gender norms, as evinced, for example, by the total absence of sexual harassment and the acceptance of women as equals in the face of the autocracy that was about to be ruptured and decimated. A better illustration of this communal spirit is the merging of a vast array of political ideologies—left, right, and center—who organized the rank and file to stand together with few, if any, marks of difference or distinction. The best proof of the prevailing communitas is the continued rejection of figureheads and leadership in the squares. It was only toward the end of the protests, when a new order seemed to be emerging, that a nascent structure developed in which some names and faces became prominent. But during the surge of protests, there were no leaders, just some organizers, champions, and communicators.

Soon after the presidential exit and the entrance of an interim leadership, the square was transformed into a space of contention and one in which distinctions and politics appeared. The liminal moment ended and a semblance of structure and hierarchy returned. This chapter looks at one particular hierarchy and the significance of its suspension and interruption: the structure that dictates gender differences and imbalances. The chapter discusses the condition of gender politics before the revolution, ponders the revolutionary moment itself, and wonders whether a new norm of gender justice has emerged since the presidential exit. In so doing the chapter attempts to gauge the extent to which transformations in the narrative of gender politics have occurred or are yet to take place in a new Egypt. It may be premature to define this new narrative, if indeed it emerges as new. This chapter will, however, identify the direction of change and the forces that will (or that could) most influence a new gender regime.

In its first chapter, this collection posed an argument about contentious politics as an alternative (or additional) paradigm to explain the Middle East. The social movements that have been influential, although external, to the way formal politics are framed are the prime example of how contestations voiced through social and or economic idioms can influence political structures. The examples of gay/lesbian struggles, environmental radicalism, and racial liberation movements illustrate the process whereby contestation upends the normative to create a political force with which formal politics must contend.

Feminism is one of the early precursors of social forces challenging the official structures of power. Women (and some men) challenged patriarchy not only as a social dogma but also as a political hegemony that excluded women from public domains where power, wealth, and privilege are transacted. Excluding the role of feminists in the framing of politics from below would not only be a historical oversight, but also an epistemological shortcoming in our understanding of contestation and protest.

The persistence of gender injustices before and after, if not during, the Egyptian Revolution is the focus of this analysis. The framing of women's rights to equality and freedom as a dimension of liberation was a challenge before the revolution and continues to be one in the subsequent transition period. The exegesis of this omission (of women) is quite different for each of these phases. Before 25 January the quest for gender equality was identified as a pet project of the regime, and was alien to the population at large precisely because of this association. The landscape of gender politics was defined by the tug of war between state and civil society on one hand and, on the other, by the confrontation between conservatism and liberal values. These debates rotated around axes of power and religiosity. The multiple frontlines along which gender justice was contested and asserted created uncomfortable alliances between unusual partners. So state-sponsored feminism at times became the defender of liberal values and thus won the backing and support of civil society activists who would otherwise not be amenable to cooperation with the state and its self-imposed elites. This situation meant that demands for gender justice were transacted in a contest-free environment. For example, in 2009–10 a decision was taken by the Ministry of Justice to break a long-held taboo and allow women to accede to the bench of administrative courts. On the one hand, this decision was greeted by women's rights advocates as one that rectified a longstanding wrong. On the other hand, however, the fact that this decision complied with the wishes of the state elites, particularly Suzanne Mubarak, soured the victory for activists: this right was won through the state-sponsored gender lobby, and not by the activism of civil society feminists. Although these state-sanctioned initiatives and institutions included some well-regarded feminists, the latter were overwhelmed by the pomp and circumstance that was an important aspect of their affiliation with the president. The minister and his minions were just trying to please powerful elites and were not transforming the judiciary. This has become most evident in the very quick and relentless backlash against these legal reforms. This backlash was spearheaded by members of the judiciary, specifically some who presided over family courts.

Despite the perceived strength of the former first lady and her entourage, hard-line conservatives among judges and commentators viewed this innovation as the scandalous slaughter of a sacred cow. Judges can only be men, they argued, as women lack the ability to judge. One judge was quoted as saying that a woman cannot be pregnant and sit on the bench! Another said that women lack rationality at "certain times of the month." A third noted that women have chores and social responsibilities that distract them from their professional lives and that can detract from their ability to reflect on complicated cases and make hard decisions (Sholkamy 2010).

Such anecdotal and sadly eccentric points of view were considered merely to be the iterations of hard-headed 'outliers' until the three hundred or so highest and most senior judges and members of the state council general assembly vetoed the appointment of women in their revered institution.

Feminists took to the streets in modest protest and forced the National Council of Women (NCW) to make public statements denouncing this U-turn. But these feminists found themselves siding with the powerful against the conservatives. The contestation was muted by the nature of the contest.

These elisions between gender inequality as a feature of the pre-revolutionary order and gender equality as a social justice demand that should fit comfortably in the post-revolution world continues to confound any analysis of women and the revolution.

The first part of this chapter presents a brief account of the landscape of gender and politics before the revolution. The focus of this account is on formal political representation and influence, whether it was connected to the state, to a para-state, or to civil society. The issues espoused by these forces and the international processes that legitimated their agency and activities will be discussed. The second part presents the immediate post-revolution stage in which questions about women and gender justice are asked and answered. These tumultuous times are not easy to interpret or summarize. The chapter will focus on media and documented initiatives and positions. Needless to say, there are hundreds of meetings, plans, projects, and policies that are not included in this account since they have yet to make a public appearance. The conclusion will address the articulation of gender and national politics by tracing this troubled relationship and suggesting a framework in which the struggle to protect women's rights to freedom, equality, and citizenship can inspire the transformation toward a liberated Egypt.

Separation!

There are no avenues to women's political empowerment that do not traverse the landscape of politics as a whole. Quotas in a rigged election, access to high office in the absence of transparency and accountability, local council representation without good governance, or voice without freedom—all of which have been practiced in Egypt—do not deliver gender justice. There has been a disconnect between the components of the gender narrative on politics, voice, and representation and the macro-social and political landscape in Egypt. The agendas of gender politics fade when faced with genuine will and radical transformation. "An autocratic regime cannot deliver justice to any of its citizens," activists and analysts argued after the revolution. Women in Egypt are now coming to terms with this nugget of wisdom. But what are the lessons of the recent protests for the study of women's empowerment? To answer this question we need to describe the institutional and formal arrangements in which decisions on women's empowerment and gender were transacted.

The Eurocentricity of the narrative of gender may be put down to this association between women's rights and the liberal political philosophy of the nineteenth century. The early liberal thinkers extended the debate on individual rights to encompass women and argued for their right to education and public participation. Later on, their work would inform the movement to grant women full political rights, including the right to vote and to run in elections. A quick succession of ideas favoring equality and questioning the basis for discrimination and subjugation laid the foundations for both a feminist movement and an analytical project in the social sciences that sought to understand how and why women were less active in public life, had fewer political rights, less access to jobs, more burdens and responsibilities, specific health burdens, restricted mobility, fewer assets, little control over decisions, and a litany of other observable markers of difference (see Wollestonecraft 1792; Mill 1869; Amin 1899).

The ladies of the suffragette movement in Britain took to the streets to contest patriarchy from below. They eventually forged a broad enough alliance with formal political actors and won the right to vote early in the twentieth century. Similarly, activists like Margaret Sanger and Mary Stopes fought for women's rights to control their bodies and their fertility. The legalization of abortion in non-Catholic western countries was slow in coming, but that right was also won at the cost of personal sacrifice and persecution. These rights were then framed as constitutive of what we now think of as human rights and liberal values (de Beauvoir 1949; Freidan 1963; Greer 1970).

Since the work of radical early feminists appeared and proliferated in the minds and hearts of women and men, several waves of feminism and strands of critical philosophy have contested the subjugation of women. Marxists have posited patriarchy as a mode of production that reproduces inequalities (Kabeer 2004; Pateman 1988). Black American and third-world feminists have contested the supremacy of the white woman and the Eurocentricity of the gender discourse (Mohanty 2003; De Veaux 2004, 174).

Postmodernist feminists like Butler and Kristeva have questioned the substantive meaning of sex and sexuality and posited language as the vehicle of gendering (Butler 1997; Kristeva 1995). The diversification and complexity of feminist reflection and analysis established the feminist point of view as an analytical lens that can explain and change oppressions based on gendered experiences and assumptions.

This potted history of feminist thinking serves to remind us that there are genuine intellectual and political issues that point to the existence of a social injustice that pervades many societies and that has to do with women. We cannot dismiss this reasoning or trivialize it. There are good grounds for engaging with the narrative of gender injustice, but not for falling under the sway of its western hegemonic influence. In this sense, we can read the efforts to internationalize the policies of gender justice as a means to counter the use of cultural relativism as grounds to enable injustice. Feminists and women's groups have been active in shaping this international agenda and have fought against the culturalist orientations of groups and authorities who wish to avoid the whole issue of women and their rights.

Gita Sen, a renowned Indian activist, feminist, and advocate of the poor, noted in her speech at the 2009 Organization of Arab Women conference in Abu Dhabi that the covenants on human and women's rights cannot possibly be western, as it is not the white man who was enslaved or the white woman who was the victim of genocide and impoverishment.[3] The contestations of feminism have filtered into the formal international politics of development and aid. The principle of gender equality was enshrined in the Convention on the Elimination of All Forms of Discrimination against Women (CEDAW), which is the benchmark used to gauge the situation of women and was used at the OAW conference to report on the progress of women at Beijing. Egypt signed CEDAW on 16 July 1980 and ratified it on 18 September 1981, reserving the right not to implement certain points if they counter Islamic shari'a law.

The Beijing Platform for Action also adopted the notion of human security to promote the rights of women and called for concrete developments that would improve women's health and their social, economic, and political security, thus boosting the calls for gender equity that were heard in Cairo in 1994 at the International Conference on Population and Development.

Soon after the 1994 conference, the United Nations led the international community in approving the Millennium Development Goals (MDGs) as a tool for holding the world accountable for its efforts to realize development for all. The third MDG is to promote gender equality and empower women. Its target is to end the disparity between boys and girls in primary and secondary education by 2005, and at all levels of education by 2015. Thus women's progress, rights, and empowerment were established by the end of the 1990s as a global priority for development.

The agency of women and their representation in public forums and in private decisions is a broad subject. Women's representation in national, regional, and local politics is one part of it. Another is the representation of women in culture and the media. A third is women's citizenship and legal equality. A fourth is women's mobility, freedom, and right to express public opinions, engage in public protest, and make public choices. The first area is one on which there has been by far the most action, mainly because it is the most measurable rendition of voice. Global actors such as the United Nations and its Development Fund for Women (UNIFEM, now part of UN Women), the United States through its aid and foreign policy, and the European Union, most significantly through its Gender and Development (GAD) program, have identified benchmarks that measure progress on expanding women's voice. Access and presence in public offices, quotas in legislative bodies, and universal suffrage are some of these benchmarks. This focus is problematic because it ignores context and its own exposure to subversion.

This journey from radicalism to dogma has had a profound influence on how gender is perceived in a country such as Egypt. Somehow a denial developed that shrouded the fact of gender inequality in a veil of exceptionalism. The cause of gender justice was not a field of protest but rather a boon given by royal or presidential fiat. The 1952 revolution in Egypt set the tone, when universal suffrage was granted to women by President Nasser in 1956 and when the constitution adopted the demands of the women who had been fighting for equality since the turn of the century. The state remains to this day the champion of women's equality. First the 1952 revolution, then the socialist state, followed by the seemingly liberal (and female) face of the increasingly autocratic Egypt of the 1980s onward became the guarantors of women's rights.

The past decades have seen the development of a critique of this manipulation by autocrats of the principles of gender equality espoused by the international narrative of gender and development.

Recently attention has been drawn to Iraq and Afghanistan, where women's quotas in parliament, set by invasion-appointed legislators, have become a tool for tribal and family forces to maintain their own hold on power. This and other experiences have raised questions about the virtue of involving women in 'less than virtuous' political processes. What is the point of being appointed to a parliament that is not representative of society? Moreover, the focus on the outcome of the political process is less important than the process itself. Goetz and Cornwall have argued that women's participation in politics and political parties and the inclusion and prioritization of women's issues and demands is a more significant indicator of gender justice and voice than are the numbers of women in elected or, even worse, appointed bodies (Goetz 2008).

Islamist feminists have expressed their own critique of a feminist interpretation of voice and agency that accuses this religion in particular of oppressing women through the imposition of the veil, the segregation of women, the emphasis on women's reproductive and family roles, and the constraints it places on women's ability to arbitrate and lead. Islamist scholars questioned the universality of feminist definitions of power and agency, taking the position that agency and voice are about the ability to realize goals and roles and not subscription of roles chosen by western women. It follows therefore that the rights of Muslim women to acquire the kind of agency and voice that they want and that is religiously sanctioned should not be ignored or subverted. Most Muslim women prize their religiously sanctioned gender roles and will agitate to realize that which Islam provides and which they have been denied by secularist and despotic regimes (Hafez 2011; Mahmoud 2004; Mir-Hosseini 2006).

This critique of the limited paradigm of gender and development has echoed in other circles. This approach to gender justice has become the focus of a critical narrative that espouses women's empowerment (Kabeer 2004; Sholkamy 2009). Gender and development ignores the possibility of transforming gender relations in favor of a recipe that seeks to mitigate injustices rather than negating the institutions that enable it.

Institutional arrangements in Egypt

The suspended Egyptian constitution of 1971 states in Article 11 that the state will enable women to fulfill their public and private roles and ensure equality in all walks of life. The constitution thus permits and indeed guarantees gender justice. The state has been the fairest employer and the most gender-blind arbitrator and champion of women's economic and legal rights since the revolution of 1952. This large state presence, however, somehow stalled the creation of a strong feminist movement or consciousness. Moreover, the impact of a strong religious movement partly created and fully promoted by the state has thwarted the modernist discourse of gender rights. The labor migrations into Egyptian cities from the south and north and out of Egypt to the Arab Gulf also had an impact on how gender roles and rights came to be constructed and enacted. Meanwhile, the international movement toward gender equality infiltrated the UN bureaucracy, and successive international conferences were held in Mexico in the 1970s, Kenya in the 1980s, and then in China in the mid-1990s—so as to forge an international agenda or roadmap to guide all member states toward gender equality. The agenda agreed in the 1990s is known as the Beijing Platform for Action (BPFA). One important item on this roadmap is the creation of national women's machineries as part of the state apparatus to ensure that women's rights are recognized and realized at the highest possible levels of executive and legislative power.

In response to the BPFA, a National Council for Women (NCW) was established in Egypt by Presidential Decree no. 90/2000. The NCW is comprised of thirty persons, or rather public figures, selected for their expertise in women's issues and appointed for a three-year term. It reports directly to the president. The thirty founding members included the president's wife, who was immediately elected by the other members to chair the council. She retained this 'elected office' until the regime fell in 2011. This national machinery is dedicated to promoting women's issues and ensuring that state bodies and policies realize the goals of gender justice.

The NCW was given a broad mandate to promote women's rights. At the national level, this mandate included proposing a national action plan to improve the status of women, feeding into national legislation to ensure it was sensitive to women's needs and concerns, and proposing public policies whereby the government could integrate women into Egypt's development in a way that was empowering and allowed women to fulfill their economic and social potential. The council also had a monitoring function that would allow it to measure the implementation of women-friendly policies and programs. It was tasked with both collecting information and statistics about women and educating policymakers and the public about women's needs, women's rights, and the situation of women in Egypt.

The NCW was backed by strong political will and directly supported by Suzanne Mubarak, which gave it teeth enough to have an impact. This was probably the most significant institutional rearrangement in the two decades that preceded the revolution as far as women in Egypt are concerned.

The council succeeded in mobilizing both the executive and the legislative to effect significant legal reforms that favor women. Through its concerted work, rights and legal mechanisms that had previously been denied to women became available to them. Article 20 of Personal Status Law no. 1 of 2000 gave women the right to obtain divorce through *khul'* in exchange for forfeiting their rights to the dowry and the three-month post-divorce spousal maintenance *(idda)*. Article 17 gave women who have entered into an unregistered marriage the right to file for divorce, thereby recognizing—for the first time in Egypt—the rights of women in these illicit unions. In 2004, Personal Status Law no. 10 introduced new family courts. Law 11 of the same year established a family fund administered by the government, which collects alimony payments from ex-husbands and transfers these to divorced women. In 2005, a law extended women's rights to keep custody of both male and female children up to the age of fifteen.

And in 2004, a presidential decree enabled Egyptian women married to men of foreign nationality to pass their citizenship to their children.

More recently, Egyptian women finally gained the right to be judges and prosecutors. This was a truly stubborn frontier for professional women, and one that met significant resistance due to the prevalent misinterpretation of religious texts, both Qur'anic and Prophetic (see research papers issued by the NCW of Egypt). Despite that resistance, thirty women judges were appointed to the administrative courts in 2007, opening the door for others to follow. But, as noted earlier, the best efforts of the NCW to open the judiciary to women were met with vocal opposition and successful resistance from judges.

The NCW was also instrumental in ensuring that women had the right to freedom of movement by successfully advocating for the repeal of the administrative decree that required a husband's approval for his wife to be issued a passport. In effect, the NCW set about implementing the recommendations of CEDAW and the BPFA by undoing some of the persistent and anachronistic legal and administrative arrangements that had legalized the subjugation of women and institutionalized gender injustice.

Even with the passing of the parliamentary quota in 2010, the NCW has had less success in enabling women's political participation. Most women in legislative bodies and in both houses of parliament are appointed, not elected. A very limited number of women have contested and won local elections. These women are mostly supported by non-governmental organizations (NGOs), many of which are donor-funded and are part of a program to open village and local councils to women in line with good governance initiatives. There is even one female village head (*'umda*) in Asyut in Upper Egypt.

Despite this impressive record, one assessment notes that the NCW suffered from three main limitations (see Konsouah 2006, 28): a top-down approach to policy and engagement with the affairs and rights of women that resembles that of a centralized bureaucracy; an uneven relationship with civil society, which sees the NCW sometimes squandering its political capital and building only limited alliances as a result of micromanagement; and a lack of popular legitimacy.

Thus, under the authoritarian regime there were advances in women's rights to freedom of movement, political representation as a fixed quota, and unilateral divorce. These gains were perhaps the most that could be accomplished within the strictures of a restrictive and elitist system. But genuine equality and solidarity of men and women could only exist if the system was challenged as a whole because of socioeconomic and political inequities in the determination of voice. Gender is one factor in these inequities, but class, family, and power are even more important. In other words, elite women may surface as parliamentarians or judges, but poor women still lack the power to express their collective predicaments universally. Poor women suffer from unequal relationships within the family, from the tyranny of state security forces, from the indignities of poverty, and from marginalization in local politics and public spaces.

In other parts of the so-called global South, women's voices and their impact on national and local politics were amplified by the strong popular base enjoyed by activists seeking to change politics and balance the distribution of power in society. For example, in India the Panachiyat movement worked to include women in all local village and regional councils. Over a million women were thus inducted into local politics with varying degrees of efficacy, but with a certain success in engendering local-level issues and decisions. Placing women in positions of power at the village level placed women at the forefront of real politics (Goetz 2008). They were given the power to make decisions that affected daily life and countered local despots. Not all women appointed have been effective or just, but the process has changed the reality on the ground, broken political constraints, and become an illustrative model of the level at which women need to engage in order to avoid simply becoming a part of patriarchal political elites. The contrast with Egypt is stark: the power enjoyed by Egyptian women derived from the power of the elites who comprised the national women's machinery, and not from civil society or from the grassroots (or grassroots organizations such as unions, syndicates, or associations).

Another important means by which voice can be acquired and heard is through collective action and representation. For example the Self-Employed Women's Association (SEWA) in India has strengthened the leverage of poor women and enabled them to realize the power that unions have enjoyed for a century. This is another example of how poor women can make their voices heard and gain the influence that accrues to those who can act collectively (Bhatt 2006). In Egypt, poor women benefited from the legal changes or social services implemented by the national women's machinery, but they were never members of or activists within this machinery; rather, they were its passive clients (Sholkamy 2008).

The problem in Egypt was the disarticulation between classes and generations of women. The NCW 'imposed' a progressive agenda on an unwilling population. In other words, the message (a progressive one) and the messenger (a propped-up elite with no popular base of rank-and-file supporters) were in conflict, because the NCW could not communicate with the constituency whose circumstances they were trying to transform, and therefore could not encourage collective action.

Civil society has always been present in gender politics in Egypt. Donors and analysts have noted the hard and distinctive work of civil society activists in fields such as reproductive, economic, personal, and political rights (al-Ali 2000; Abdel Rahman 2004). The history of state–society partnerships and enmities in the context of gender politics is not covered in this chapter; suffice it to say that while this relationship has at times been complementary, it has more often been a competitive one in which the might of the state often supersedes the self-perceived rights of civil society. There is, however, a credible bevy of organizations that have acquired international recognition and whose work has had an impact on the status of women. The Alliance of Arab Women, the Women and Memory Forum, the New Woman Association and Research Centre, the Legal Research and Resource Center for Human Rights, and the Egyptian Women Association are some of the acknowledged players in this field.

Like the NCW, many of these organizations were donor-dependent and therefore committed to working on projects rather than enacting programs. Jad has described the impact of this model as the "NGO-ization" of women's activism (Jad 2007). She describes a shift whereby women's NGOs ceased to be coalitions of women who built political alliances and will through solidarity and became implementers of development policies and intervention. The result is that these groups no longer strive toward the creation of a critical, radical, or political agency but rather are enmeshed in a bureaucratized development industry (Mostafa 2011).

The decade that preceded the revolution witnessed high levels of female participation in industrial action and workers' strikes. Women unionists and workers were at the forefront of what are now acknowledged to have been the first flutters of a popular rebellion. The workers of Mahalla (textiles and yarns) and of the tobacco industry took to the streets and spent a month in picket lines, protesting management practices, privatizations, and low wages. Unionists struggling for freedom of association and the right to collective action included women such as Fatma Ramadan, who has spent more than a decade in courts fighting for the right to membership in unions and workers' committees—a right that is still denied to women.

The landscape of political action on gender was rich, but fragmented and fractured. The co-optation of gender justice by government and para-governmental elites was contested by other elites located in civil society. Meanwhile, women workers were independently voicing their protest at economic injustices and locating their struggle within that of the workers' movement.

The elections of 2010 — now acknowledged as 'the last straw' and the tipping point at which the anger of both young and old at policies and at the police came to a head—was also unfortunately the election that shepherded sixty-four women into parliament. For the first time in history women were 'fairly' represented in a legislative body, but this came about only as a result of rigged elections and thus did not reflect an authentic expansion of women's political rights or representation. This discouraging association between autocracy and women's right to political participation as enacted in the worst elections ever seen in Egypt (by some accounts) has remained to haunt women's rights advocates and has cast a long shadow over the immediate post-revolutionary future.

It is important to note, however, that the clear fragmentations in the women's movements between state-sponsored pseudo-feminists, civil society researchers, feminist activists, and women active in protest and politics but not self-identified as feminists have greatly damaged the cause of gender justice in Egypt. There is also a schism that results from the conflicts between women who cite religion as the foundation of their feminism and those who do not (Sholkamy 2010). This fault line lingers in the current climate of dissent in which religion has become a pivot of future social and political arrangements.

The Liminal Phase

Esraa Abdel Fattah, Nawara Negm, Noha Atef, and many others who use real or fictitious names are some of the women bloggers who have been publishing their political reflections and rejection of hegemonic norms for many years. Women bloggers have contested the conventions that have governed sexuality, privileged chastity, and permitted sexual harassment since the beginning of this century.[4] Previously, there existed a level of segregation that facilitated women's participation in critical forums because they were viewed as a safe space, which may have empowered and cultivated the female voice. However on 25 January the call made online was to take to the streets and leave the comforts of home and seclusion. Abdel Fattah reiterated calls previously made by bloggers and Internet activists and asked men to join her on the streets in an almost flirtatious request for male protection.[5] If a woman was going to risk her safety to protest police brutality and government, then the least men could do was to come to the streets and protect her. Indeed, Asmaa Mahfouz, another woman blogger, in her own accounts claims the credit for inviting people to take to the streets.

The eighteen days of protest were days of class, religious, and gender parity and solidarity. But after the ecstasy of victory came some sobering events. A few weeks after Mubarak left power, protesters who remained in Tahrir Square were attacked and some of the women among them were subjected to 'virginity tests' by the army. One of these women, Samira Ibrahim, took her case to court, but tragically lost her case against the doctor who allegedly performed the test; the judge pronounced the physician innocent on 12 March 2012. The explanation offered by the army was that the army officer in charge wanted to prove that they were 'good girls,' not prostitutes! Even if this explanation made any sense, the humiliation that these women endured is undeniable. But that was not the first crack to appear in the gender solidarity of Tahrir Square.

The demonstrations by women commemorating International Women's Day on 8 March 2011 were attacked, and the two hundred or so women and men participating were harassed, ridiculed, shouted down, and ultimately chased out of the square. No other demonstrators in the square since the revolution had been heckled, told that their demands were unjustified, unnecessary, a threat to the gains of the revolution, out of time, out of place, and/or the product of a 'foreign agenda.' No other demonstrators were told to 'go back home and to the kitchen.' No others were heckled for how they looked or what they were wearing. In unison, hecklers were saying "*batil*" (illegitimate) to the demands for gender equity and "*awra*" (ignominy) to women demonstrating with their frankly innocent and almost idealistic demands. "Back to the kitchen" and "Off the square" were also among the chants. One elderly gentleman stood in the midst of the protesters on the pavement and said that the posters they held were an offense to the good women who are "mothers of the martyrs" and who deserve respect and rights, not like these women who deserve nothing. Then young men, fired up by the imagery he was invoking, started snatching the placards and bits of paper from women in the square, tearing them up, and throwing them at the silenced, baffled, dejected, astounded men and women.[6]

This reaction shows the paradox of people supporting women as revolutionaries but not as activists asking for women's rights. It challenges us to answer some important questions. How do we reconcile the wide acceptance of women as activists and instigators of the revolution with the denial that women are entitled to demand their rights within the context of wider revolutionary change? How do we sustain gender justice and women's rights? How do we support the broad values of the revolution in the face of the neglect or animosity of some revolutionaries? There is a fear that by demanding their rights during this delicate transitional moment, women will become a fifth column or fracture an edifice that is still under construction. Why were they ridiculed and attacked on 8 March? Why was their demonstration singled out, from among the five others taking place at the same time and in the same vicinity, to be attacked and dispersed? These are questions that need an honest answer.

Under the influence of optimism and immersed in Internet-fueled naiveté, hundreds of women and men sought to go to the square and actually say what they had not dared speak in the past. The demonstrators dropped the veil of caution and voiced demands for equality and for civil rights and equal rights of citizenship. Perhaps their protest was badly presented or wrongly timed, but what remains is the fact of differences among Egyptians who are now building a new Egypt. Evidently the space of protest is not a neutral one when it comes to questions of gender. But there are more important lessons with which we need to contend.

Reintegration:
Popular sentiments and stereotypes prevailing in the new order
What is thirst but fear of thirst itself! (Omar Khayyam)

There is either a backlash against women's rights or a fear of a backlash. But as the poet Khayyam says, the difference between the actual event and fear of that event is slight. There are rumblings of a rebellion against women. The laws that expanded and protected women's rights and that were enacted under the aegis of the NCW with Suzanne Mubarak at the helm are now discredited as her laws. The council itself has been swept under a mat of silence. It has not, however, been dissolved, although a new council was appointed in February 2012 and a new secretary general was elected from among its members. According to the UN Women representative in Egypt, calls by gender activists to dissolve the NCW because of its ties to the old regime were silenced by fears that if it were dissolved, future governments and parliaments would not reconstitute it. This dilemma succinctly illustrates the fear that women have of rejecting the old only to find that the new is worse. Could women actually lose out in a democratic order?

The press is replete with calls to repeal progressive personal status laws, cancel women's quotas, disband family courts, and reinstitute patriarchal laws and practices. According to Mulki Sharmani, the personal status laws were imposed by presidential fiat and are therefore inherently unjust or anti-democratic. This argument ignores the substantive impacts of these laws on gender justice. Moreover, it ignores the tremendous influence and sustained actions of women's rights groups and of civil society, which were somewhat stifled by the NCW but continued to work. Another argument is that these laws do not conform to Islamic codes and principles. These protestations not only ignore the difference between *fiqh* (the interpretation by scholars of the laws of God), shari'a (the will of God and what it signifies in terms of moral action), and *maqasid* (objectives, intentions), but also the fact that scholarly interpretations are by definition historical and variable. Rejection of the new personal status laws based on historical precedent is unjustifiable (Sharmani 2011).

There are also demands to change Law 10 of 2004, which created family courts, and Law 4 of 2005, which extended the legal age of guardianship and thereby permitted women to be legal guardians of their children up to the age of fifteen, for sons, or until marriage, for daughters. A new NGO called the Family Protection Association, created by retired judges from the family courts, is spearheading this challenge. The argument is that these laws, along with the *khul'* law, which granted women the right to unilateral divorce, have disempowered men to the extent that they empower women. There have been problems with visitation rights, which many Egyptians find too restrictive from the father's point of view, but could that be a reason to permit fathers automatic guardianship for children as young as seven?

The call to reintroduce patriarchal institutions such as spousal obedience *(bayt al-ta'a)* and repeal *khul'* is made under the pretext that freedom and rights have enabled women to undermine the institution of marriage. There are claims that divorce rates have gone up, child destitution has increased, and morality has crashed because women have the option to divorce. As Sharmani (2011) points out, this is a typical condition of denial. The increase in divorce rates, if real, may reflect a problem in the institution of marriage itself. Can there really be an argument against rights based on the protection of common wrongs? Can keeping women in relationships despite their desire to leave be better for the relationship or its offspring?

There are other signs of a confused post-revolutionary discourse of gender. The question of women's quotas, for example, is an interesting one. Women appeared on all party lists for the parliamentary elections, even those of the ultra-conservative Salafis. This was mandated in the new election law. The women may be veiled, face-veiled, or so 'covered' that their images are absent from party posters altogether.[7] But they are almost all in the bottom half of the lists, if not at the very end. Only the Muslim Brotherhood's Justice and Freedom Party can claim that they have seriously fielded women candidates, since they may expect to win larger percentages of the vote, and thus allow candidates lower on the list to gain a seat in parliament. There is only one woman heading a party list, who is running on behalf of the Egyptian Social Democratic party.[8] The fact that parties have failed to use the party-list quota as it was intended—to give women a real opportunity to be elected to political office—suggests that there was real comfort with the original quota system. The change did not challenge politics as usual, but only confirmed each party's ability to pay lip service to women's political participation.

There are, however, a number of women contesting parliamentary seats as independents, and even one running for president. Those in urban areas stand a good chance of winning a seat (but not the presidency).[9]

There are concerns among elites, observers, and activists about the implications of a new constitution for gender justice and alarm at the exclusion of women from the process. But the most serious issue is the denial of the very notion of gender as a facet of a democratic order. There is a clear nostalgia for an older political discourse—now discredited by world experience and by global standards—that sought to subsume gender rights in a larger discourse of citizenship. There are many historical lessons that illustrate the importance of a conscious pursuit of gender justice rather than a naive assumption that we will all go to the ballot box and happily accept the outcome, whatever it may be.

Besides these new concerns, some old problems persist that reflect gender gaps and imbalances. Gender gaps are the distinctions and inequalities between females and males that disempower women and girls and restrict their options and choices. Education, work, health, and security are four aspects of life that affect an individual's freedom and agency, much of which is also determined by class as well as gender. Some activists and revolutionaries may deny the existence of such a thing as a 'gender gap,' but meanwhile the gaps and differential burdens persist. Although girls have overtaken boys in the formal education stream, it should be noted that only 24.9 percent of students are enrolled in this stream; the other three-quarters of the student body are enrolled in the al-Azhar secondary education stream or in technical secondary education (Sholkamy 2010). In these other two streams a gender gap persists. The ratio of girls to boys in technical and vocational training overall is 8:10. However, disaggregating this figure shows that the enrollment ratio of girls to boys in the more industrial and agricultural concentrations in technical education falls to 1:2. In other words, the sections that give a more competitive advantage in the job market are the ones where there is a large gender gap. Girls are enrolled in the Azhar stream, but in far lower numbers than boys, and those numbers are falling: there were 59.8 girls for every hundred boys in 2000–2001, but only 54.4 in 2005–2006 (UNDP 2010, 21–22).

Gender bias is still a pervasive practice even if it is clouded by vast differences between the urban and well-to-do, who seem to have achieved some form of gender parity, and the rural and poor, who have not.

Conclusion

Audiences and activists can draw two lessons relating to gender from the unfolding events in Egypt. The first is that democracy may not deliver equal rights for women. Democracy can become a tyranny of the masses if not tempered by a commitment to basic principles and freedoms. Despite the regeneration of politics and participation, there is no guarantee that the political process will be a fair one to women. It was easy to get millions to agree to jettison Mubarak. It will be hard to get them to agree on what comes next. Whatever the politics of our future governments and legislatures may be, some basic principles of rights and freedoms must be clearly stated and not left to the vagaries of elections. All free nations have imposed limits on the ability of people to harm or undermine their compatriots. This is a position Egyptians need to realize and cement into our national psyche.

The second lesson is that women should focus on demanding democratic processes that enable us to have voice and realize achievements. We should perhaps have demonstrated to dissolve the national machinery known as the National Council for Women and create a new body formed of civil society organizations with an elected board that is accountable to its constituents. We should insist on quotas for women within every new and old political party so as to insure that all politics are gendered, as the existing quotas are insufficient. We should lobby for participatory policy councils that oversee the services we require from the state. These local councils would consult their citizens when planning health, social protection, education, policing, and housing policy through a legally binding process. Perhaps women can realize citizenship-focused democracy by demanding the mechanisms that deliver justice to all.

How can commitment to greater fairness to women be built among voters, policymakers, and public- and private-sector institutions? What does it take to successfully build constituencies for a commitment to equality and justice, and to hold those who make these commitments to account?

Of course it will take time, and there are five factors that will make it a difficult process. The first might be called the 'generation factor.' There are differences in the ways that the young and the old identify and perceive the gender roles and disparities. The second is the 'globalization factor,' which prioritized international standards and demands over national ones. There is the 'domain factor,' whereby women are torn between the recognition that they enjoy in the public domain and the private burdens that they experience as women. The fourth is the 'consciousness factor,' the absence in Egypt of feminism as a widespread political ideology. Finally, there is the challenge of structures of representation for women and lingering questions concerning the reinstatement of formal female representation in legislative and political bodies.

It will take time to rebuild a platform for gender equality in Egypt. But if this platform emerges from the participatory politics of the revolution, it will be a solid foundation built on a basis of integrity, dignity, debate, and action. It is therefore worth building, as it will not be a frail edifice as vulnerable to disintegration as the pre-revolutionary formal structure.

In conclusion, and with reference to the new paradigm of politics structured by the Arab transformations, there are two points that pertain to women. The first is that the women's movement in Egypt was orphaned at the moment when the state assumed the mantle of champion for women.

This was when the call for gender justice ceased to be a grassroots, street-evident movement that crafted a feminist conscience through collective action and became a formal politic that was a feature of government and a set of individual rights transacted through a discourse on citizenship. The second is that this genesis may explain why the protesters of Egypt have chosen to deny the gendered domains in which injustices occur and therefore continue to frame women's rights in apolitical terms.

Notes

1   Tahrir bystander.
2   Informal interviews conducted by the author, mainly in Tahrir Square, during the first ten days of protests.
3   Speech given at the OAW conference, Abu Dhabi, 2009.
4   For women's anti-harassment blogs and radio, see "Nermeena" (nerro.wordpress. com), "Nazra" (Nazra.org), "Banat we bas" (banatwebas.mam9.com), and "Teet" (www.facebook.com/...203915789659795/تيت).
5   "Gabhet el-tahyis el-shaabeya" (blog), tahyyes.blogspot.com
6   All of these comments come from the author's own observations.
7   In the case of the al-Noor party the women's pictures are replaced by a red rose!
8   Party lists were yet to be finalized at the time of writing.
9   The outcome of the elections was announced on 21 January 2012. Only eight women won seats on party lists. Two independents won seats, and two women were subsequently appointed. The new Egyptian parliament has one of the lowest rates of representation for women in legislative bodies, at only 1.5 percent. The world average is 19 percent, and the Arab-world average is 13 percent.

9

Back on Horse? The Military between Two Revolutions

Hazem Kandil

The military's abandonment of Hosni Mubarak's regime was essential to his downfall. At the very least, it provided an opportunity for the 25 January uprising to continue long enough for the ruling elite to step down. The position of the Supreme Council of the Armed Forces (SCAF) was welcomed at first, but the frustrations associated with the transitional period invited comparisons with the July 1952 coup. Once again, a vibrant (yet ineffective) opposition was reduced to making demands and waiting for a council of officers to respond; once again the country was ruled via military communiqués. Are we back to square one, some justly wonder?

I contest this analogy here on two grounds. The first is too obvious to merit elaboration: despite the violence of the social unrest in Egypt during the 1940s, the enormity and persistence of the recent uprising remain unmatched in the country's modern history. One can confidently state that such popular empowerment makes it difficult for officers to reestablish the same type of authoritarian regime they erected six decades ago. It is hard to imagine that the millions who have thrust themselves so decisively onto the center stage of their own history could be dismissed so easily.

But what makes the claim that officers are back in the political saddle truly doubtful is the change that has occurred within the military itself. It is true that in both 1952 and 2011, officers had enough professional grievances against the regime to contribute willfully to its overthrow. Also, in both cases the military as an institution signaled its intention to return to the barracks as soon as the necessary reforms were carried out. The main difference between the two 'revolutions,' however, lies in the fact that in 1952 a secret society of politicized officers (calling themselves the Free Officers) rode the crest of military support to consolidate its power, and succeeded in doing so by immediately installing its trusted lieutenants in the security apparatus. So the crucial factors at that time were: (1) that the security regime under the monarchy had neither the determination nor the capacity to prohibit activism within the ranks, thus allowing the development of politicized cliques among officers; and (2) that the Free Officers promptly seized the rudimentary security structure they had inherited and developed it into an expansive and ferocious establishment to safeguard their power. In 2011, by contrast, this same security apparatus had effectively sealed the army from politics and had become too entrenched to be seized from above. Soldiers had no recourse to an in-house political movement with the ambition and organization of the Free Officers, nor could they rein in Egypt's unruly security agencies and turn them to their own purposes.

So while the January uprising presented a golden opportunity to dismantle the regime, no political group within the corps had the agility to see it through. Instead, the military, shepherded by SCAF, behaved as a self-centered institution narrowly concerned with its corporate interests, which had long been undermined by the political and security components of Mubarak's regime. This leads us to conclude that while the military might certainly enhance its autonomy and leverage in future Egyptian politics,[1] it simply has neither the vision nor the tools to restructure the established order.

To illustrate the differences between yesterday's Free Officers and today's SCAF, I apply a historical institutional approach, which underlines the interests of the corps as a whole rather than the reputed desires of a handful of generals. I begin by discussing the merits of this approach, then use it to analyze military grievances on the eve of the two seizures of power, and the changes enacted thereafter. So far the evidence suggests that the crucial variable in both cases was the security institution: its suppleness in 1952 enabled the military junta to establish a domineering new regime, and its intransigence in 2011 prevented the army from acting likewise. Hence, the question that should occupy us now is not whether officers will 'steal' the 25 January uprising as they did in 1952, but rather whether the two victims of the old regime, the army and the people, are likely to fare any better at this point if the main oppressor—the security apparatus—is still at large.

The Military: An Institutional Approach

What motivates military intervention in politics? Class theorists, beginning with Karl Marx's classic study of Louis Bonaparte's 1851 coup and continuing through Antonio Gramsci's later elaborations on Bonapartism, have held that officers act in the interests of the economic elite, whether that elite comprises those eager to preserve their power or those still hoping to impose it. Marxist commentators on postcolonial coups have emphasized in particular the army's role in paving the way for the rise of the bourgeoisie in societies traditionally dominated by the landed class (see Hobsbawm 2001). So in Egypt, for instance, a nascent capitalist class blocked from power by the tenacity of a handful of large landlords supposedly invited the 1952 coup, which was carried out by middle-class officers on behalf of the entire bourgeoisie (Abdel-Malek 1968; Botman 1988). Liberal scholars, on their part, have claimed that militaries act as political proxies in institutionally undeveloped nations (Finer 1962). Whenever the army is more organized and disciplined than political institutions proper, it shoulders the burden of modernizing society before passing on the mantle to civilians—or so did liberal optimists believe at first (Pye 1962; Huntington 1968; Trimberger 1978). Not-so-optimistic liberals warned that once officers get a taste of power, they tend to hold on, thus corrupting political life irrevocably and arresting economic development (Janowitz 1967; Rapoport 1982). Perlmutter (1974) was the first to apply this 'praetorian army' thesis to Egypt, and was followed by a horde of liberal analysts (most recently, Cook 2007; Droz-Vincent 2007).

Marxist and liberal interpretations therefore portray military men as "obediently enacting . . . roles assigned to them by vague and impersonal systematic forces" (Thompson 1975, 459). They are either prompted to action by their class loyalties, or drawn into the political fray by an institutional vacuum. What is missing from both perspectives is the view of the military acting on its own behalf, a premise supported by the fact that the intense socialization and indoctrination of soldiers cause them to identify with the military as an institution. So while class interests or political ambitions might animate a few officers, we have little reason to doubt that the critical mass within the armed forces intervenes in politics largely to defend and promote its corporate agendas. What we need therefore is an institutional perspective that takes seriously officers' belief that their duty "consists in the first instance of the defense of national security, [which] entails the maintenance of a strong military force" (Needler 1975, 67–71).

An institutional approach, in general, stresses how the structures within which individuals operate shape their outlook, interests, and strategies (Brooks 2008, 15). The more concrete the institution, and the more clearly defined its interests, the greater its sway over its followers. This applies especially to the military, which constitutes a supremely organized "'estate' with positive professional interests" within society (Vagts 1959, 295). The military as an institution commands greater loyalty from its members, and exerts greater influence over them, than social class, civil associations, political parties, or any other social group, and it does so for three reasons. First, its control over and proficient use of the most devastating means of violence allows it to perceive itself as the "single most powerful group in society" (Nordlinger 1977, 46). Second, compared to other social groups, it is remarkably cohesive. The military chain of command allows a "small group of men who hold the chain's uppermost links" to treat the largest and most diversified army as a single entity whose resources can be deployed in a unitary fashion, and thus "maneuver the whole enterprise" with relative ease to meet their ends (Poggi 2001, 188). This sense of unity is of course enhanced by the military's physical separateness from society in heavily guarded barracks. Third, contrary to other social organizations, the typical domain of the armed forces, which is war preparedness and conduct, is shrouded in secrecy. Even in advanced democracies, no government could afford to divulge completely what the military does, nor could legislators and opinion makers claim to have the expertise or information to contest military estimates (Zegart 1999, 129). This leads officers to imagine that only they can appreciate the challenges that must be overcome to protect the country against foreign aggression, and that civilians must defer to them regarding these matters. For all these reasons, officers are more inclined to identify with their institution and to jealously guard its interests than the members of any other social organization.

Much ink has been spilled to underline this special status. A few scholars have noted the peculiarity of the 'military mind' with its conservative professionalism (Huntington 1957; Janowitz 1960). Some have detailed how socialization in the corps was infinitely more thorough and extensive than in other social groups (Ricks 1998; Poggi 2001). Others have provided nuanced analysis of how the army pursues its interests in the face of political resistance (Kolkowicz and Korbonski 1982; Allison and Zelikow 1999; Zegart 1999). More relevant to our purposes here are the sociological studies illuminating the intricate links between a society's war-making capacity and its socioeconomic, ideological, and political order (Anderson 1979; Mann 1986; Tilly 1990; Downing 1992). In this latter batch of studies lies the answer to our original question regarding why the military intervenes in politics: it is because the way a society is organized determines its ability to conduct war. If war represents the military's raison d'être, it is only natural for officers to occupy themselves with the type of social order that will optimize their combat readiness and battle performance.

This is not to suggest that officers are naturally disposed toward governing. Even if there were no prohibition on military participation in politics, it is unlikely that "officers as a type have the ability, the suppleness, the temperament, or the time for a continuous application to politics" (Vagts 1959, 294). Soldiers are made for war, not politics, but they are driven toward politics because they can only flourish in a state that devotes considerable resources toward war. While on occasion a small faction of officers might seek power for its own sake (as aptly demonstrated by Latin American juntas), whenever the military as a whole intervenes in politics, it does so because it views the world through the eyes of German historian Otto Hintze, who stated: "In the foreseeable future, matters will remain as they have been throughout history: the form and spirit of the state's organization will not be determined solely by economic and social relations and clashes of interests, but primarily by the necessities of defense and offense, that is, by the organization of the army and of warfare" (1975, 215). The custodians of violence thus insist that "all of politics ought to reflect the absolute priority of the question whether the political entity, confronted with the challenge of war, is capable of prevailing militarily" (Poggi 2001, 196).

If we apply this institutional framework to Egypt, we can clearly discern why the army felt in 1952 and 2011 that the political elite threatened its interests, and therefore Egypt's national security. Let us consider each case separately.

The King's Sword? A Snapshot of the Military in 1952

Conventional accounts of the July 1952 coup run as follows: although the army was the bastion of social privilege and the ultimate guarantor of the monarchy, a group of patriotic officers chose country over crown and seized power to transform Egypt into a modern independent state. This version is not entirely unfounded. Under the last monarch (r. 1936–52), and with his blessing, the military became increasingly politicized. Officers were exposed to all sorts of ideological currents and debated vigorously the type of sociopolitical system their country deserved. Politicized officers, from various ideological strands, gravitated toward the Free Officers, a secret society conspiring to overthrow the regime. The movement's core leadership envisioned a new Egypt with a centralized bureaucracy, state-led industrialization, giant national ventures, and the rest of the modernization package.

But instead of the traditional focus on the Free Officers and their ambitious state-building project, we ought to ask: Why did the rest of the military go along with their junior colleagues? After all, it takes more than a few dozen middle-ranking officers to carry out a coup. Three issues seemed particularly pressing for the corps on the eve of July 1952: the regime's responsibility for their humiliation at home (the February 1942 debacle, when British tanks surrounded the royal palace to install their preferred cabinet) and abroad (the 1948 defeat in Palestine); employing the army for domestic repression (especially after the 1951 abrogation of the Anglo-Egyptian Treaty); and, most importantly, the unconstitutional expansion of the king's jurisdiction over military affairs (in 1950) and the deeply unpopular hiring and promotion decisions he took afterward—decisions that led Mohamed Naguib, the nominal leader of the coup, to accuse the monarch of "openly ridiculing the military" (Naguib 1984, 67; for details see Al-Bishri 2002, 390–95).

It is not surprising, then, that military sociologist Eric Nordlinger proclaimed that the coup was "largely motivated by the king's interference in military affairs" (1977, 71–72). Or more generally, as Amos Perlmutter put it, that the coup was "planned, organized, and executed entirely by the army, strictly for its own benefit" (1974, 127). Indeed, a close observer of the post-coup days, Miles Copeland, stated that the coup "had not been a matter of upsetting discipline, but a matter of establishing it . . . [its] main contribution . . . in the eyes of [its] followers, was to make a respectable institution out of the army . . . to make it into the kind of organization they thought they were joining when they first enlisted" (1970, 66–69). So regardless of the specific motivations of the ringleaders, acting as a political movement within the ranks, the hundreds of officers who supported the coup were acting in defense of the military as an institution. Now, was the military under Mubarak any better?

Exposing the Myth of Military Privileges under Mubarak

The military's desertion of the regime during the 2011 revolt confounded observers. Sentimentalists found comfort in the belief that the Egyptian army, being overwhelmingly a conscript army, was exceptionally patriotic and loath to use violence against civilians. This is of course historically inaccurate because, on the one hand, the Military Police was brutally repressive under Nasser, and, on the other hand, the police-managed Central Security Forces, the state's striking arm against civilians, is also composed of conscripts. This idealistic image of the armed forces was further undermined after the revolt, when the Military Police applied (measured) violence against demonstrators, beginning with the forced evacuation of Tahrir Square on 9 March.

Skeptics therefore found many adherents to their claim that the military was and remains complacent; that while it might have shed a few liabilities (Mubarak and his cronies), it was ultimately determined to salvage a regime that had furnished it with wealth and privilege. Advocates of this view ask: What did the military have to complain about under Mubarak? Did it not run an economic empire? Did it not receive countless social benefits? Did it not enjoy a special relationship with the world's mightiest power? Did its arsenal not include M1A1 Abrams tanks, F-16 fighting Falcons, and other state-of-the-art weapons? These legitimate questions overlapped nicely with the scholarly consensus that the regime had bought off the military with financial and symbolic rewards (see Springborg 1989; Sadowski 1993; Cassandra 1995; Richards and Waterbury 1996; Weiss and Wurzel 1998; Frisch 2001; Cook 2007; Droz-Vincent 2007; Richter 2007).

In this section, I draw on empirical evidence to refute this claim and demonstrate that the army's corporate interests had been undermined enough to justify intervention against the political elite. Here it is necessary to keep in mind our original stipulation that even if a few members of an institution are corrupt, the critical mass within it lean toward fulfilling its raison d'être, and that the corrupt few cannot hold their institutions at bay forever—unless of course this corruption goes hand-in-hand with realizing the institution's mission and interests. So in the Egyptian case, for example, as corrupt as the political and security components of the regime were, they still fulfilled their basic institutional goals: the former ruled, and the latter applied violence to preserve public order. Only the military had been deprived of that right. If we assume for a moment that those who join the army are indoctrinated to care about war preparedness, rather than building bridges, tending farms, or raising poultry, then we will immediately realize that they have been suffering professionally from the mid-seventies onward. Let us consider some of these misgivings.

An economic empire?

In 1978, the National Service Projects Organization (NSPO) was created to redirect the military from war to economics, after Sadat declared that the 1973 October War would be Egypt's last. The portfolio of this budding military-economic complex included activities as diverse as construction, land reclamation, agro-industries, and, most importantly, over thirty factories producing civilian durables and weapons (small weapons and ammunition, mortars, armored vehicles, assembled helicopters, and short-range missiles). Halfway into Mubarak's reign, the arms industry covered perhaps 60 percent of Egypt's needs, and the surplus was exported (a purported $1 billion-a-year business). In addition, officers received discounted apartments and vacation homes and subsidized services, and some were offered short stints in the civil service after retirement (Springborg 1989, 104–18; Droz-Vincent 2007, 200–205). So what was there to rail about if a military career promised so much prosperity?

The public debate that raged in the summer of 1984 regarding the army's economic role sheds light on officers' views. To start with, military spokesmen underlined the official rationale (stated in a 1979 Presidential Decree) that the military was now responsible for attaining self-sufficiency (looking after its own members), as well as aiding economic development through the provision of cheap products and services. This was followed by an article by Major General Ibrahim Shakib arguing that it was the absence of war that forced the army to seek civilian work for its conscripts;[2] and another by Major General Ahmed Fakhr explaining that the army cannot abandon its modestly paid officers to the mercy of market forces.[3] In a subsequent interview, Defense Minister Abd al-Halim Abu Ghazala emphasized that the conspicuously humble privileges his men received were scarcely enough to afford them a decent life against sky-rocketing inflation. The field marshal also complained at the ruling party's 1986 conference that diminishing defense budgets barely covered army wages (quoted in Baz 2007, 64–70).

The credibility of these statements was supported by Central Auditing Authority reports, which revealed that military-run projects did not generate a noteworthy surplus (Farouk 2008, 288). Also, a *Financial Times* analyst admitted after Mubarak was deposed that the military's

> reputed economic 'empire' . . . is considerably more modest in volume than is commonly believed, and has probably shrunk in proportion to a national economy that has grown by more than 3 percent annually since 2003 . . . [and] although a few generals are *rumored* to have become rich, the main purpose [behind the army's economic activity] . . . is to ameliorate the impact of a rapidly privatizing economy on the living standards of officers.[4] (my emphasis)

Further evidence could be drawn from casual observations of the disparity between the army's shabby discount stores, automobiles, apartments, and vacation cabins, and those enjoyed by upper-middle class citizens, and the fact that the military has consistently failed to attract members of this class (Frisch 2001, 6). Critics who point indignantly to military 'privileges' forget that Mubarak's inflationary policies, which eroded the value of all public incomes, were partially overcome by government employees by moonlighting or taking bribes, while officers—who could do neither—were the only ones stuck with their meager wages.

But regardless of what officers said, the army's economic complex was reduced in size after 1989 to pave the way for the privatization program that began in earnest after 1991. Little wonder that the top brass remained "largely hostile to economic liberalization and private-sector growth," and were therefore wholeheartedly opposed to being ruled by the political representative of neoliberalism in Egypt, Gamal Mubarak (Anderson 2011, 4). The regime's economic policies not only hurt military interests, but also its public image: "the military revolutionaries of July 1952 had taken power in the name of the Egyptian people and pursued social and economic policies which benefited the middle and lower-middle classes from which they had originated. Now the military was being called upon to sustain a regime, which was identified in the popular mind with upper- and upper-middle-class interests" (Dekmejian 1982, 39).

What about the supposedly giant arms industry? We know that arms manufacturing began in the 1950s and expanded significantly when Egypt convinced three Gulf countries in 1975 to contribute $260 million each to the Arab Military Industries Organization (AMIO). The organization received a heavy blow, however, when the Arab partners withdrew in protest of Egypt's unilateral peace treaty. Naturally, the capital of the new exclusively Egyptian Arab Organization for Industrialization (AOI) depreciated significantly (McDermott 1988, 170–72). Not only that, but the arms export business did not provide the military with an independent economic powerhouse because the president kept it under his control via Article 108 of the constitution, which gave him ultimate say over weapons contracts, and Law 146 of 1981, which established his power over arms exports (Sirrs 2010, 130–31). To add insult to injury, officers soon realized that the end goal of the arms industry was no longer to guarantee Egyptian independence, as originally intended, but rather to become a regional arms dealer for the benefit of those on top.

Another unsubstantiated claim is that military spending remained high under Mubarak. But even if we accept some of the highest estimates, this allegation appears to be wide off the mark, as table 9.1 demonstrates:[5]

Table 9.1: Egypt's defense expenditures, 1980–2010

Year	GDP ($ bn)	Defense Expenditure ($ bn)	Defense Expenditure/ GDP (percent)
1980	17.82	3.47	19.47
1985	31.75	3.71	11.68
1990	34.00	4.30	12.64
2000	92.40	2.39	2.58
2005	93.20	2.76	2.96
2010	188.40	4.10	2.20

In the mid-1970s, the defense budget was as high as 33 percent of GDP. By the time Mubarak was sworn in, this figure had been cut in half. During his three-decade reign, military expenditures oscillated between $2.4 and $4.3 billion, regardless of inflation, the increased cost of technology, or the tenfold increase in Egypt's GDP. In fact, defense expenditures as a percentage of GDP fell considerably, from 19.5 percent in 1980 to 2.2 percent in 2010, reaching its "lowest level in the country's modern history" (Wahid 2009, 137–41). Furthermore, if we consider that the celebrated $1.3 billion provided annually by the United States has depreciated in real terms by over 50 percent since 1979 we can begin to grasp how bleak the picture seemed. Rather than basking in wealth, the army lived with the fear that merely to "balance accounts," it might be forced one day to "slash military salaries severely" (Frisch 2001, 2). In fact, frantic efforts to reduce costs led Israeli military analysts to note that "a striking factor about the Egyptian Armed Forces' combat arsenal is that a portion of it, including aircraft, is kept in storage . . . [because of] budgetary constraints" (Eytan, Heller, and Levran 1985, 91), and that because of these constraints, "cost-effective simulation training took priority over live training" (Eytan and Levran 1986, 131).

Sociopolitical limitations

Intimately related to the problem of economic resources is the problem of recruitment. Although the Egyptian military is largely conscript-based, this particular pool of human resources has been suffering from "serious manpower quality, readiness, and sustainability problems" (Cordesman 2006, 159). This issue was temporarily sidestepped during the 1973 war preparations by allowing the military to enlist university graduates. Following the war, however, most of the country's 1.2 million war-seasoned conscripts were demobilized, shrinking Egypt's active forces to 450,000 by 1980. Ignoring their role in improving the army's combat performance, the conscription formula was revised so that university graduates would serve less than a year. Once again, the military was stuck with illiterate peasant conscripts (Barnet 1992, 125–44).

Numerous complications followed. To begin with, this group of conscripts was perceived to be able to handle only menial duties and so received almost no training (Cordesman 2006, 159). This in turn affected the army's ability to absorb advanced training and weaponry. To make things worse, even the innovative skills and technical know-how of educated Egyptians had deteriorated because of the regime's backward education methods (De Atkine 1999, 15). Then there was the problem of specialization. An effective military requires qualified technicians, but the regime's provision of free access to universities—offered mostly as a social bribe—dissuaded Egyptians from pursuing vocational training

(De Atkine 1999, 15). Also, the regime's suspicions regarding political and security studies—manifested by the fact that Egypt's twenty-three universities have only two full-fledged political science programs and no security studies—deprived the army of the services of 'defense intellectuals,' who in open societies defend military interests and help formulate strategic doctrines. In short, the corruption and incompetence of the regime produced a dysfunctional education system that could hardly provide the military with the required manpower, and its authoritarian bias against allowing educated citizens to receive adequate military training (lest they turn against the government) or specialize in subjects related to military strategy forestalled the upgrading of the army.

This is not mere speculation. The army's general command struggled bitterly for the right to offer special rewards to persuade qualified conscripts to reenlist, but it was turned down by the political leadership under the pretext that no national emergency justified increased spending (Barnet 1992, 143–44). Army recruiters expressed frustration at their inability to draw in members of country's urban elite due to lack of resources. In fact, the military began in 1996 to send delegates abroad to recruit members of Egypt's expatriate communities, since the "local educational system was not yielding the quality of soldiers the armed forces thought necessary"—but to no avail (Frisch 2001, 5–6). The social situation created by the regime thus led to the unsettling fact that a considerable part of the military's order of battle was now composed of "relatively low-grade and poorly-equipped units, many of which would require substantial fill-in with reservists—almost all of which would require several months of training to be effective." The structure of the Egyptian forces thus became static, assuming the status of "a garrison army" (Cordesman 2006, 162).

Moreover, authoritarianism even affected the military's strategic doctrine. Insecure regimes cannot tolerate 'born in battle' war mavericks with inflated egos and popularity within and outside the corps. They preempt the rise of this type of ingenious officer by centralizing warmaking in the hands of a few trusted generals. This rigid war doctrine disallows the implementation of the superior 'war of movement' strategy, which relies on dynamic and spontaneous maneuvers and therefore requires autonomous middle-ranking officers who can improvise in battle without prior orders. The effectiveness of this type of warfare has not only been proven historically (by Roman legions, American Union troops, and the German Wehrmacht), but it has also been Israel's preferred fighting strategy since

1948. In contrast, the set-piece offensives and trench-style defense strategies that have characterized Egyptian warmaking have repeatedly proven substandard. No student of Arab–Israeli wars has failed to notice that Egypt's strength lies in its "tenacious defensive ability," while its chief weakness can be attributed to its "equally persistent inability to conduct a war of movement" (Insight Team 1974, 145, 164). An over-centralized command-and-control structure that prohibited unauthorized initiatives by field officers led to the "total stultification of the initiative of junior officers—precisely the cadre on whose wits mobile warfare depends" (Insight Team 1974, 341; Boyne 2002, 185). U.S. Colonel Norvell De Atkine, who accumulated years of experience training Egyptian officers, observed mockingly that "a sergeant first class in the U.S. Army has as much authority as a colonel in an Arab army" (De Atkine 1999, 17). Curiously, when asked about the most important position in Israel, David Ben-Gurion responded without hesitation: "Battalion leaders . . . . Those are the men who protect the future of Israel" (Imam 1996, 33).

The Egyptian military was certainly aware of this pervasive weakness. Its chief military historians (led by major generals Hasan al-Badri and Gamal Hammad) reviewed the army's battle performance and concluded that the military "was poor at executing operations that relied on offensive maneuver, despite its inherent advantages on the battlefield" (Brooks 2008, 130–31; see Hammad 2002 for details). Officers were also aware that under Mubarak, distinctive performance and popularity among troops jeopardized their career. The president relied heavily on security organs to monitor those who 'stood out' and sent them packing.[6] It is no wonder that one analyst commented, tongue-in-cheek, that during the last two decades of Mubarak's reign, "the most popular military officer . . . in Egypt [was] Colonel Sanders of Kentucky Fried Chicken" (Shatz 2010, 6).

In short, officers understood that "until Arab *politics* begin to change at fundamental levels, Arab armies, whatever the courage or proficiency of individual officers and men, are unlikely to acquire the range of qualities which modern fighting forces require for success on the battlefield" (De Atkine 1999, 20, my emphasis). Improving the status of the soldier and his warmaking ability is intimately linked with improving the status of the citizen, and indeed the sociopolitical system as a whole. It is not by accident that the armies of democratic states have repeatedly proved their worth on the battlefield in the face of those of autocracy. Armies thrive in democracy and wither under the shadow of authoritarianism.

Geopolitical constraints

Although any type of foreign assistance comes with strings attached, U.S. aid remains particularly problematic for the Egyptian army. In the summer of 1997, Defense Minister Abu Ghazala confessed in an interview that the officer corps was naturally disturbed by the fact that their primary military supplier was committed to keeping the power of all Arab countries inferior to that of Israel (Baz 2007, 207). This pledge was not only mentioned in the memoirs of leading American figures like Henry Kissinger (1994, 737) and Robert Komer (quoted in Scott 2009, 30),[7] but also recorded officially in a 1986 letter from President Ronald Regan to Israeli Premier Menachem Begin "guaranteeing Israeli superiority in armaments over all the Arab states combined" (photocopy of text in Heikal 1983, 71).

This commitment haunted Egyptian–American military relations. For example, the number of U.S.-supplied F-16 fighters was carefully kept at less than two-thirds of the number supplied to Israel. In many cases, the Egyptian military was also denied specific weapons due to Israeli objections: Egypt's request for Advanced Medium-range Air-to-Air Missiles (AMRAAM), which the Bill Clinton administration provided readily to the UAE but not to Egypt, is one recent example. More importantly, the United States assisted Israel in producing advanced missiles by, for instance, furnishing 70 percent of the costs of its Arrow missile program, while obstructing Egypt's ambitions to develop its own. So while the arsenal in both countries has many weapons in common, Israel's lot is not only superior in quantity and quality, but it is also supplemented by an advanced homegrown arms program, as well as America's determination to maintain "a technology gap" in its favor (Frisch 2001, 3–5). One needs to remember that Abu Ghazala lost his job when he attempted to smuggle U.S. missile technology (a Scud-B variant with extended range) into Egypt under the radar of a reluctant Pentagon, and that his dismissal for that specific reason infuriated scores of Egyptian officers (Colonel Selim, pers. comm. 2009).

Even when the Egyptian military turned to other sources, driven by its "expressed dissatisfaction with the pace of weapons supplies from the United States and its desire to avoid excessive dependence on a single supplier," the U.S. government was quick to sabotage its pursuits (Eytan, Heller, and Levran 1985, 87). For instance, the Pentagon blocked the Egyptian–Russian deal to upgrade Egypt's air defense system in 1997 with S-300 anti-tactical ballistics missiles, which were particularly effective in countering Israel's cruise missiles. Despite several pleas, it was not until 2003 that the Egyptian military was permitted to use U.S. funds to refurnish some of its obsolete, low-quality SA-3 Russian missiles. U.S. missile-transfer policy to Egypt, in the view of American military analysts themselves, has set "serious limitations" on its ability to face an Israeli strike (Cordesman 2006, 175–77). A more general version of this conclusion was recorded in an Israeli report, which stated that Egypt's reliance on the United States had caused it to "fall behind Israel and other Arab states in the Middle East arms race" (Eytan, Heller, and Tamari 1984, 89).

An even subtler analysis by the Jaffe Center for Strategic Studies noted that American assistance assigned priority to the air force and the navy (which received perhaps 80 percent of the annual grant), and to a lesser extent the armored corps, to the detriment of air defense and artillery. Air defense, which had proved so crucial to Egypt's security during its war with Israel between 1967 and 1973 that it was organized into an independent service, continued to rely on outdated Eastern-bloc surface-to-air missiles, especially the SAM-6, with only a handful of state-of-the-art U.S. Improved Hawks. Similarly, in the 1990s, of Egypt's 2,200 artillery pieces, only two hundred were American (Eytan, Gazit, and Gilbo 1993, 136–42). It is interesting to note the correlation between the inattention of the United States to Egypt's air defense and artillery—the two services that have repeatedly proven essential to Egypt's defense and deterrence power—and its support for the air force and navy, those technology-intensive services with which Egypt has no hope of outperforming Israel. Moreover, American military aid to Egypt proved overly expensive. While it cost Egypt only $1.7 billion worth of Russian weapons to fight the Suez War (1956), the Yemen War (1962–67), the Six-Day War (1967), the War of Attrition (1967–70), and the October War (1973) during its two-decade relationship with the Soviet Union, the first five years of its alliance with the United States left it $6.6 billion in debt, even though it neither went to war nor planned to do so (Handoussa 1990, 114).

What made things worse is that officers felt that their patron was not only committed to keeping them inferior to Israel, but was also informing Israel about Egypt's weapons portfolio and training (Springborg 1989, 95). This discomfort is perfectly understandable when one considers that the military still classifies Israel as an important threat. Abu Ghazala said so himself in parliament in February 1987.[8] In addition, annual military exercises, such as Badr in 1996 and Gebel Farun' in 1998, explicitly named Israel as the training target and took place on a terrain similar to that of

Sinai. It is also no secret that the greatest concentration of Egyptian forces lies in the area between Cairo and the Suez Canal. In short, "almost all of Egypt's capabilities, equipment, and deployment of forces are concentrated on one front to engage one force only: the Israeli Defense Forces" (Frisch 2001, 6). Heavy reliance on the United States therefore makes the army feel exposed and somehow defenseless. As summarized by renowned military expert Anthony Cordesman: "In spite of Egypt's firm commitment to peace, it cannot ignore the risk of some unexpected political crisis or strategic shift that could again make Israel a threat. It must maintain a suitable deterrent and defense capability to deal with the risk of some unlikely breakdown in the peace with Israel" (2006, 200).

It certainly does not help that the political basis for U.S. military aid to Egypt (the peace agreement with Israel) almost demilitarized Sinai: military airfields were prohibited, and only one mechanized infantry division could be deployed along the eastern bank of the Suez Canal, while the rest of the peninsula could hold no more than three lightly armed border patrol units and policemen (Gamasy 1993, 374–81). These constraints made it impossible for Egypt to amass troops in Sinai, even for training purposes. Not surprisingly, one of the first military recommendations following the 2011 revolt was to revise Israeli restrictions on the deployment of troops in Sinai.[9]

Israel aside, the army nonetheless recognizes that its alliance with the United States prohibits it from projecting regional power in any direction. As a superpower, the United States vigorously defends its interests throughout the region, from Sudan to the Gulf, and does not welcome other interventions. Even when Egypt was summoned, along with twenty other countries, to facilitate America's liberation of Kuwait, it was not subsequently allowed to play a more active role in Gulf security via the ill-fated Damascus Declaration (Frisch 2001, 6). To add insult to injury, the performance of the two divisions Egypt had sent to war against Iraq was assessed by American sources as "middling" (Eytan, Gazit, and Gilbo 1993, 141). U.S. Colonel De Atkine, who had personally supervised the training of Egyptian troops, actually described their performance as "mediocre" (De Atkine 1999, 13). It was clear that after years of U.S. upgrading, the Egyptian armed forces had not advanced very far.

To conclude this section, it is clear that the military suffered from what one analyst described as "rank disequilibrium": a psychological dissonance that spreads among members of an institution whose position becomes at odds with their original duties (al-Mashat 1986, 64). Egyptian officers were training for war, while knowing full well that they were never meant to fight one; they were asked to defend the nation, while being deprived of the conscripts, arms, and funds necessary for combat; they were made dependent on a country sworn to preserve their key rival's superiority; and they were serving a regime that kept them under constant scrutiny by obtrusive security organs that influenced their careers through intelligence reports. Although Mubarak tried to guarantee army loyalty by appointing his trusted head of the Republican Guard, Hussein Tantawi, as defense minister in 1991, the military grievances catalogued above provide strong reason to suspect that Tantawi (like everyone else who assumed the top military post in Egypt) ultimately chose the military over political loyalty. Instead of protecting the president's back, he sided with officers whose corporate interests had been undermined by the political rulers.

Now that we have uncovered why soldiers had an institutional interest in turning against their civilian masters in 1952 and 2011, let us turn to how they behaved in each case.

The Free Officers in Power

On the night of 23 July 1952, junior officers spearheading the Free Officers' movement overtook army leadership, detained all generals (except for two), and cashiered all brigadier generals and lieutenant colonels outside their group. Before February 1954, another 1,100 officers were retired, 2,300 were removed from combat formations, and 1,200 were appointed to civil service (Hammad 1990, 32–34). As if this were not enough to guarantee the loyalty of the army, in June 1953, Major Abd al-Hakim Amer was promoted to major general and appointed commander-in-chief in order to place the officers under tight surveillance and purge suspect elements periodically. In the same month, the Republican Guard, in the words of its first chief, Abd al-Muhsin Abu al-Nur, was created to protect the regime against the rest of the army (Abu al-Nur 2001, 34).

The success of the coup occasioned an immediate split within the ranks. The majority, led by the strongest services (artillery and cavalry), was determined to return to the barracks after implementing needed reforms, whereas the ringleaders, supported by disparate elements (mostly from the infantry and air force), aspired to create an authoritarian regime in order to transform Egypt from above. The primary reason the latter group ultimately prevailed is because it seized the security apparatus and used it to crush military opposition.

Gamal Abd al-Nasser, the movement's effective leader, installed himself as interior minister right after the coup to revamp the security infrastructure the British had built over the past seven decades. Nasser then passed on the mantle to his close lieutenant, Zakariya Muhyi al-Din in October 1953, whereupon the methodical Zakariya purged four hundred of the three thousand security officers and restructured the entire apparatus, notably by refashioning the notorious Political Police into a ruthless domestic intelligence organ (it eventually became the State Security Investigations Sector), and placing this crucial agency under the supervision of trusted military colleagues. Zakariya also redirected the Military Intelligence Department toward domestic control, aided by the country's first civilian intelligence agency, the General Intelligence Service, which he founded in December 1953. Zakariya then charged a group of junior military confidants to run Nasser's home-based intelligence unit, the so-called President's Bureau of Information, and another group to help Amer make the military invulnerable to coups through the security-oriented Office of the Commander-in-Chief for Political Guidance (Sirrs 2010, 25–44). Dozens of security-oriented military officers were later implanted throughout the bureaucracy to preempt peasant or working-class disturbances. Even the loosely organized mass-based Liberation Rally, which Nasser established in January 1953 and managed through two military aides, was primarily responsible for submitting security reports against subversive elements and manhandling opponents (Hammad 2010, 652 and 886–88).

It is this "veritable pyramid of intelligence and security services" that formed the cornerstone of the post-coup political order (Vatikiotis 1978, 164–65). Without the scheming and daring of this newly empowered security establishment, especially against the artillery and cavalry mutinies (in January 1953 and March 1954, respectively), the new regime did not stand a chance against a military that was determined to withdraw from politics.

The Military and the January Revolt

After four days of street fighting, it became clear that the interior ministry was unable to stem the popular uprising that began on 25 January 2011. The president was forced to summon his gravediggers—the military—in a final attempt to restore order. The fact that members of the general staff were doubtlessly loyal to Mubarak (or at least indifferent to his policies) did not prevent them, under the weight of general opinion within the armed forces, to abandon their old political master to his fate. Acting otherwise risked fracturing the corps. From day one, combat units were visibly supportive of the revolt, without waiting for instructions from above, and those higher up in the chain of command prudently issued a number of communiqués describing the people's demands (the overthrow of the regime) as legitimate, and pledging not to use violence against demonstrators, contrary to what their colleagues did in Syria, Libya, Yemen, and Bahrain. On 10 February, the Supreme Council of the Armed Forces (SCAF) convened without its supreme commander (the president) in what was deemed a soft coup, and the next day Mubarak was forced to resign. As one member of the SCAF later explained, "The armed forces took charge before the president stepped down in accordance with the communiqué that stated that the military acknowledges the legitimacy of the [demands of the] Egyptian people."[10] The military then proceeded to isolate many of the powerful players in the old regime by dissolving the ruling party and putting many of its leaders on trial (mostly for financial corruption). The SCAF declared its intention to withdraw from politics after a six-month transition period, which would supposedly end with the passing on of power to an elected authority. In the meantime, military rule received legal sanction via a referendum that paved the way to replacing the old constitution with a SCAF-issued Constitutional Declaration.

Over the next few weeks, the military took several bold foreign policy steps in a clear indicator of its frustration with Egypt's diminished geopolitical role, and its determination to project regional power. These steps included allowing two Iranian vessels (rumored to be carrying missiles to Syria and Lebanon) to sail through the Suez Canal for the first time since the Islamic Revolution, despite vehement opposition from the United States and Israel; sending popular delegations to Tehran to mend Egyptian–Iranian relations; dispatching the new intelligence director to Syria and Qatar (two countries Mubarak almost considered enemy states) to explore means of resuming cooperation; opening up the borders with Hamas-controlled Gaza against Israeli protests; brokering national accord between Hamas and Fatah after the old regime's unconditional support for the latter had stalled its prospects for years; brokering a prisoner swap that freed over a thousand Palestinian activists for one Israeli solider; encouraging public discussion of the necessity of reversing the demilitarization of Sinai decreed by the Egyptian–Israeli peace agreements; arresting an alleged Mossad officer (who was also an American citizen) in Cairo for the first time in decades, and trading him for Egyptian detainees in Israeli prisons; raiding foreign NGOs and banning nineteen Americans from travel for receiving illegal funding (though it had to release them under U.S. pressure two months later); and other similarly controversial steps.

One remarkable incident is the military response to the killing of six Egyptian soldiers in Sinai by Israelis on 17 August 2011. The military insisted on an official Israeli apology, and received one. Although this does not display particular bravado, one should note that between September 2004 and August 2011, twenty-two Egyptians were killed in similar border incidents with little complaint from Mubarak's diplomatic corps. Moreover, in an angry rejoinder published the following month in the military's mouthpiece *al-Nasr*, Major General Abdel Moneim Kato warned that Israel could no longer act with impunity, and attacked the United States for "offering all its support to Israel . . . as usual," adding that the Egyptian–Israeli peace agreements grant the military the right to revise the articles governing the size of forces in Sinai, "even though,"—he concluded resentfully— "the old regime never utilized that right" (Kato 2011, 14–15).

Even though these erratic endeavors did not add up to much, they at least reflected the high command's desire to rock the boat a little after the political leadership had taken the wind out of Egypt's sails for over three decades.

On the domestic front, the assistant defense minister for legal affairs made it clear in an interview with *Al-Masry Al-Youm* on 17 March 2011 that his colleagues refused to involve themselves in party politics, and that— unlike the Free Officers—the SCAF rules in the name of the military as a whole, not as a revolutionary actor:

> Some believe that the armed forces took charge by virtue of revo-
> lutionary legitimacy, but what happened was that . . . when the
> armed forces found the country collapsing, they intervened by
> virtue of being the only power on the ground capable of protect-
> ing the country. They managed the country's affairs in accordance
> with a declaration based on Article 88 of the constitution, which
> holds the military responsible for the security and protection of

the country. . . . What happened in 1952 was in fact revolutionary legitimacy, because the Free Officers . . . carried out the revolution and seized power. . . . Now we have a different situation, where those who revolted on 25 January 2011 were not the ones who seized power.[11]

What the general did not explain is *why* the army could not pursue a course similar to that of July 1952. Three reasons held the military back, and all had to do with the security apparatus (rather than camaraderie with the deposed president). To start with, the armed forces had been sealed off from all political currents through the relentless surveillance of officers and the weeding out of politicized elements; this had effectively ruled out the creation of a movement with the daring and political imagination of the Free Officers. Hence, those who came to the helm in 2011 had neither an alternative vision for Egypt's future, nor an adequate understanding of its political terrain and socioeconomic complications. Also, contrary to the malleable security infrastructure that fell into the coup-makers' laps in 1952, the military now faced an overbearing and hydra-headed establishment, capable of resisting a takeover from above with great ferocity. The menace represented by today's Interior Ministry was further enhanced by the fact that police officers have become too closely wedded to public officials, thugs, and petty (and not-so-petty) criminals to go down without stirring up intolerable havoc. Most important of all, perhaps, is that the extent of economic distortion, inequality, and deprivation produced by the Mubarak era compelled the military to think twice about the social forces it might unleash by opening up avenues for participation, and the turmoil that might result if security organs were weakened to the point where they could no longer suppress this popular stampede. The SCAF dared not open Pandora's box.

This military apprehension is manifest in the increasingly paternalistic tone of SCAF generals, summarized in the defense minister's comment that "the revolutionaries are our sons and brothers, but probably lack a clear and comprehensive understanding of the situation."[12] The army's rigid response to popular demands, its violent response to any form of resistance, and its endorsement of the continued brutality and impunity of the Interior Ministry provide another piece of evidence. Despite continued police violence against citizens, the SCAF only authorized limited purges, which stuck to the letter of law, and cashiered mostly officers close to retirement age.

We might therefore conclude that although the interests of the armed forces dictate the dismantling of a security apparatus that has been employed by politicians to curb military influence, and although those interests per se are not incompatible with democracy (as long as military prerogatives are constitutionally guaranteed), the un-politicized and inexperienced SCAF fears that the weakening of the police coupled with full transition to democracy (in a deeply impaired society) could lead to domestic instability, which would in turn drag army officers into protracted policing activities—a nightmarish scenario the SCAF is determined to avert. This means that despite the cosmetic changes applied to the Interior Ministry so far, and despite the army's encouragement of demonstrators to raid State Security headquarters, the military is still hesitant to conquer, dismantle, and restructure the security forces. And, one has to add, the leaderless character of the uprising, which caused popular demands to become fragmented immediately after Mubarak stepped down, makes it easier for the SCAF to skirt this thankless task and hope that an elected civilian authority could carry it out whenever circumstances allow.

Regrettably, this sets serious limitations on how far the military can alter the balance of forces maintained by Mubarak, whereby the security force rules, its political auxiliaries enjoy status and wealth, and the military watches powerless from a faraway corner. After all, the security apparatus was not just a supporter of the regime; it was the throbbing heart of the regime itself. Without the rigging of elections, the suppression of civil society, the intimidation of political contenders, the containment of mass unrest, and the close monitoring of the armed forces, the political apparatus was likely to crumble—which it did after the Interior Ministry was temporarily defeated by the revolt. Indeed, one might be justified to treat the presidency and ruling party as no more than parasitic bodies living off this formidable security establishment. We can therefore expect that as long as this institution persists, there remains a high probability that future elected officials will be corrupted or blackmailed into submitting to its omnipotence.

Although the military was driven by its institutional interests to support the uprising, the overwhelming challenges it confronted after coming to power—most crucially the entrenched security apparatus— have deterred it from following through on demands for reform. The price that both soldiers and citizens will pay for this timidity is likely to be dear and painful—a truly sad outcome for such a heroic episode in Egypt's history.

Notes

1 This was signaled by Article 9 of the military-inspired Governing Constitutional Principles (whose first draft surfaced in October 2011), which gives exclusive power to SCAF over all military-related issues, including its budget and governing laws.

2 Ibrahim Shakib, "Shukran ayyuha al-sada," *al-Ahali*, 7 November 1984.

3 Ahmed Fakhr, "al-Fikr al-'askari al-masri wa idarat al-sira': al-ahdaf al-istratijiya li-l-'askariya al-masriya," *al-Jumhuriya*, 20 January 1985.

4 Yazid Sayigh, "Egypt's Army Looks Beyond Mubarak," *Financial Times* 37 (532), 3 February 2011. Needless to say, there has not been one documented case of officers amassing wealth under Mubarak.

5 The figures are based on Eytan and Heller (1983, 74–90); Eytan, Heller, and Levran (1985, 74–93); Eytan and Gazit (1991, 218–31); Kam and Shapir (2003, 191–93); Shtauber and Shapir (2005, 113–16); Cordesman (2006, 157–63): Wahid (2009, 137–41); and Roula Khalaf and Daniel Dombey, "Army Torn Between Loyalty to Egyptians, President and US," *Financial Times* 37 (532), 3 February 2011.

6 Personal interview with Muhammad Selim, Los Angeles, 7 March 2009.

7 CIA operative Robert Komer, who served on the Kennedy and Johnson National Security Councils, noted in an internal memorandum in May 1967: "No one who has an insider's view could contest the proposition that the US is 100% behind the security and well-being of Israel. We are Israel's chief supporters, bankers, direct and indirect arms purveyors, and ultimate guarantors" (quoted in Scott 2009: 30). Kissinger noted in *Diplomacy* that Arabs must understand that "Israel was too strong (or could be made too strong) to be defeated even by all of its neighbors combined" (1994, 737).

8 Musa Gendy, "Dajja fi Isra'il hawl tasrihat al-mushir," *al-Ahram* 45392 (3), 18 February 1987.

9 Mohamed Abd al-Qader and Hossam Sadaqa, "Lajnat al-quwwat al-musalaha bi mu'tamar al-wifaq al-watani tusi," *Al-Masry Al-Youm*, 6 January 2011.

10 Dalia Osman and Pasant Zein al-Din, "Masdar 'askari: nabhath ta'dil mu'ahadat al-salam," *Al-Masry Al-Youm* 2633 (1), 29 August 2011.

11 Dalia Osman, "Musa'id wazir al-difa' li-l-shu'un al-qanuniya wa-l-dusturiya fi hiwarih," *Al-Masry Al-Youm*, 17 March 2011.

12 Abd al-Gawad Tawfik, "al-Mushir: al-quwwat al-musallaha musammima 'ala taslim al-sulta," *al-Ahram* 45524 (1), 28 July 2011. The paternalistic attitude of the army reached comic proportions when Mamdouh Shahin, a member of SCAF, tried to justify the council's harsh response to the 8 July uprising: "[We deal with the revolutionaries] as a father whose son goes to school. He encourages him to study every once in a while, pleading: 'Study, my dear, for my sake.' Then exams draw near, and he has to yell at him in a sharp tone: 'Attend to your studies!'" (Quoted in Ahmed Bahnasawy, "Maham a'da al-a'la li-l-quwwat al-musallaha," *al-Shuruq* 895 (7), 15 July 2011.)

10

Egypt's Civic Revolution Turns 'Democracy Promotion' on Its Head

Sheila Carapico

Did western political aid agencies encourage the 25 January uprising with their civil society promotion projects? Did they encourage mass mobilization against the regime, or perhaps tutor dissidents in how to organize grassroots opposition? At the same time as the United States and other NATO powers were providing economic and military assistance to the Egyptian regime, did they also foment popular defiance? Some people seem to think so; different narratives about foreign provocation of Egypt's uprising circulated in Arabic and in English.

First, as Egyptians filled the public squares with cries for the demise of the Mubarak administration, his government's officials flailed about, seeking to blame the disturbances on outside troublemakers and foreign infiltrators. Disorder was blamed variously on foreign journalists, global rights-monitoring organizations, U.S.-based democracy brokers, and, most disparagingly, the latter's Egyptian partners and grantees.

From another angle, soon after Mubarak's resignation, American journalists hunted for shreds of evidence that U.S.-funded civil society promotion projects had "nurtured young democrats" prior to the uprising by offering training on organization, social networking, and new social media; by some U.S. news accounts, American government-funded non-governmental organizations (NGOs) like the National Endowment for Democracy, the National Democratic Institute (NDI), the International Republican

Institute (IRI), and Freedom House played a role in fomenting Egypt's revolt.[1] A related story line credited a private citizen, Gene Sharp, the Boston-based author of an impressive and widely translated compilation of 198 tactics for nonviolent resistance, with devising the 'playbook' that toppled the Egyptian government.[2] The connection to a successful, populist, western-backed anti-authoritarian drive in Serbia, where Sharp's techniques had evidently been put to effective use, seemed especially intriguing.[3]

Even more ominously, during the long, hot summer of 2011, the transitional military government seized on international news reports that some leading protesters had attended training sessions sponsored by the European Union, U.S.-based quasi-NGOs, the U.S. Agency for International Development (USAID), Sharp's International Center on Nonviolent Conflict, or Serbian youth associated with the Center for Applied Non-Violent Action and Strategies (CANVAS) as grounds for investigating their 'seditious' activities and accounts. Sketchy secondhand evidence of 'working with foreign agendas' and 'secret bank accounts' was propagandized to slander some Egyptian protest organizers and human rights defenders. Egyptian organizations that received American and/or European training or funding, whether before or since the revolution, were brought to a military court.

The notion that western efforts to promote civil society had offered resources for insurrectionary mobilization seemed logical to some western liberal internationalists, even though they were taken aback by the 'Arab Spring,' because it was consistent with their hope that the United States and Europe support popular aspirations for liberty and justice abroad. At the same time, the suggestion was plausible to some Egyptians who, according to conventional wisdom, had been taught never to rebel against their rulers. Yet many scholars familiar with foreign donor activities would doubt that the United States or the European Union had actually helped to incite unruly, contentious, bottom-up mobilization. To the contrary, observers in Latin America, Africa, Palestine, and elsewhere had associated civil society promotion with the anti-revolutionary interests of great powers.

Some critical scholars argued that donors' NGO funding practices sidelined welfare and services, instead enlisting professional non-profit think tanks to rationalize neoliberal economic agendas that often disadvantage the poor. According to this analysis, civil society promotion was designed to cloister intellectual counter-elites into non-confrontational, white-collar activities outside the body politic (Guilhot 2005; Kamat 2003; Petras 1999; Robinson 1996; Encarnación 2000, 2003). Concurrently, the separation of welfare and labor issues from advocacy for procedural democratization seemed to delegitimize pleas for social programs and economic justice. The 'professionalization' of cosmopolitan Arab NGOs working in spaces where English is the lingua franca, humanitarian norms are shared, and metropolitan office practices prevail was a form of "depoliticization" of Palestinian activism, according to Rema Hammami (1995). Islah Jad, another Palestinian activist intellectual critical of donor practices, called this the "NGO-ization" of politics (2004). Another analyst pointed to the consequent political and economic competition among Palestinian civil society groups (Jamal 2007). Echoing these concerns about the effects of foreign funding on civic activism, Maha Abdelrahman worried about the effects of foreign funding on Egyptian civil society: "The idealized space where the weak are supposed to be fighting their battles for freedom and justice has been hijacked by segments of the (petite) bourgeoisie who have found their niche in the growing sector of NGOs." By these and similar reckonings, civil society promotion was designed to forestall disruptive mass uprisings, not to encourage them.

Other scholars and activists have argued persuasively that American military aid and European cultivation of formal partnerships with Arab autocrats belied their rhetorical commitments to democratization, favoring authoritarian stability over the vicissitudes of the popular will (Hamid 2011; Khalidi 2004). The Egyptian government received $1.3 billion annually in American assistance alone, much of that budgeted for the armed forces. America and also Europe seemed to be betting on the status quo. Western powers clung to the Mubaraks even after the writing was so starkly written on the wall, and then seemed to back the military government that took over after 11 February. Many participants and commentators noticed that tear-gas canisters lobbed at protesters from January through November 2011 were 'made in the USA.'

The analysis presented here takes these points into account, but offers another perspective centered on two radically different conceptions of civil society. The first is the donor-driven reification of civil society as 'CSOs' (civil society organizations) and 'NGOs' with office suites, websites, letterhead, boards of directors, mission statements, and official licensure by the United Nations, the World Bank, the European Union, or American agencies, as well as the relevant Egyptian government ministries. International democracy brokers and professional transitologists frame civil society as an assembly of organizations. This frame is almost a grid. Civil society seems to consist entirely of institutions, not people. Actions are planned in advance by leaders, and audited by international agencies. They are emphatically not improvised from the bottom up. Even before the upheavals, this managerial model was almost inevitably detached from popular aspirations in Palestine and in Egypt (Challand 2010; Tadros 2010; Abdo 2010). This way of framing civil society as comprised of formal, professional advocacy organizations pays no attention to the contentious politics analyzed in other chapters in this book.

An alternative, people-centered conceptualization of civil society includes workshops for professionals, but also incorporates other, more fluid, horizontal forms of activism in the public civic sphere, including civil disobedience and grassroots mobilization. Using such a model we can see how popular appropriation of the national commons challenged not only longstanding Egyptian laws and regulations inhibiting rights of association, assembly, and expression, but also the ways in which outsiders thought about civic participation and, indeed, donor-driven ideas of orderly transition to democracy.

The 25 January revolt invites us to consider a more contentious, concentric, dynamic view of civil society. In this chapter, therefore, I explain why it is ludicrous to assert that 'civil society promotion' projects prompted revolutionary upheavals. Instead, the civic revolution in Egypt ought to prompt western democracy experts to reconsider their operational definitions of 'civil society' and to move beyond the paradigm of managed, incremental 'transitions.' The public civic sphere needs to be understood as a site of contentious politics and transformative potential rather than a sphere of management. My overall thesis is that the revolution in Egyptian public civic life fits with this dynamic notion of mobilized civic activism, not the managerial model of civil society.

In particular, this chapter contrasts the kinds of programs, organizations, and procedures supported by international democracy brokers in the name of 'civil society promotion' with the actual praxis of civic self-organization during a tumultuous period. The first part of this chapter describes American and European projects that encouraged the 'professionalization' of formal NGOs and CSOs—encouraging them to produce audited accounts, three-year strategic plans, technocratic credentials, bureaucratic procedures, and counter-terror pledges—and explores their repertoires, rhetoric, and institutional practices. While some political aid indubitably supported worthy partners harassed by the Egyptian regime, the bureaucratic, managerial procedures for funding CSOs and NGOs were not meant to encourage sweeping or sudden political change. If anything, like Latin Americans and Africans, some Egyptians might argue that they were designed to forestall rather than foment revolutionary turmoil. While Sharp's more progressive populist ideas for mobilization were somewhat more relevant to Egypt's revolution, they seem to have reached Egyptians indirectly via contacts with youth leaders of the Serbian crusade that ousted a tyrant. The evidence is that their model was only one among many diverse influences on Egypt's *shabab* (youth).

In the second section I show how the boisterous, adaptive strategies of agitation—even if they began among tech-savvy dissidents—relied on vernacular energies to devise ways of breaching security barricades, organizing marches, self-managing camp-outs and sit-ins, protecting protesters and neighborhoods, directing traffic, disposing of trash, caring for the injured, deploying music and art, reaching the international media, defending themselves against police brutality, and so forth. I rely mainly on my own notes, observations, and conversations to tell the Tahrir story as I saw it. The narrow objective is simply to show that these activities went far beyond the projects and organizational formats recommended by international trainers: civil society and pro-democracy activism burst out of the boxed-in model of planning and management created and exemplified by formal, professionalized institutions to encompass mass acts of defiance. In a particular place and time, 'Midan al-Tahrir,' literally 'Liberation Square,' signified the liberation of the public civic sphere. This approach reaffirms a nuanced definition of 'civil society' and presents the Egyptian experience as a civic revolution. In other words, although there has not yet been a full-scale political regime change, nor a social revolution redistributing wealth among socioeconomic classes, Egyptians have reconfigured the public civic sphere and widened the scope of civic activism. If international democracy brokers want to prove themselves relevant to the anticipated political transition, they ought to think outside the box.

Understanding Civil Society

Civil society is a classic social science construct, broadly defined as an associational space situated between governments and households, and also between the public state sector and the commercial economy. Thus when we think of civil society we think of professional associations, charities, universities, interest groups, media outlets, and community betterment groups; of public gatherings or displays in civic-minded parades, concerts, or museums; and of suffrage, labor, civil rights, anti-war, and environmental movements. Often called the non-profit, non-governmental, or 'third' sector, civil society is driven by neither the profit motive of businesses nor the political ambitions of political parties or revolutionary movements. It is a place for voluntarism, philanthropy, and public-spirited activism, a sphere of civil discourse, a metaphorical public square (Seligman 1992). Some imagine it as a distinctively modern phenomenon that has gradually replaced primordial associations grounded in ascriptive bonds of caste and clan with individualist membership in the organizations of mass, bourgeois society. In many conceptualizations, a vibrant civic associational network and a lively public intellectual sphere of civility are the sine qua non for democratic development; in other words, the test of civil society is its ability to enable democratic transitions. By this criterion, Egyptian civil society seemed, in 2010, rather moribund.

We also know, however, that when the circumstances demand it, civil society can enable communities to cope with physical or political adversity, to navigate bureaucratic obstacles, and even to challenge authoritarianism. Indeed, comparative and historical research in Europe, the Americas, and elsewhere shows that civil society is not a constant, unchanging cultural attribute, but rather a variable that changes shape and size according to political and economic conditions (Carapico 1998). At different moments German civil society, for instance, marched for Nazism, cowered from a police state, and breached the Berlin Wall. In the United States, civil society operated differently in colonial days, the Jim Crow era, the Great Depression, the Second World War, the Vietnam protests, and the age of electronic networks, and it still assumes different forms in contemporary rural Wyoming, Manhattan, and New Orleans. Civic networks in the old Soviet Union and postcolonial Africa have at times been fully penetrated by central governments, but then found outlets in religious or cultural expression or enclaves inside totalitarian state systems. Likewise, in Egypt and the greater Arab region, by 2010 we had already recognized that even though governments worked very hard and vigilantly to contain, co-opt, or suppress independent energies, people still found outlets for civic impulses in everyday ways of working for common purposes either within the system or in enclaves outside it; moreover, when legal avenues for complaint and lobbying were exhausted and conditions become intolerable, Egyptians and their neighbors did take to the streets in exceptional civic moments of mass engagement (Carapico 2010; El-Mahdi 2009a, 2009b).

Civil Society Promotion

Regarding foreign support for civil society, in Mubarak's Egypt there was a complex dynamic among a regime determined to co-opt both civic activism and foreign aid, international democracy brokers caught between their reformist mission and American realpolitik, and the bilingual strata of activists enmeshed in both national and transnational regimes of governmentality (Carapico, forthcoming). Time and again, the Mubarak administration regulated and re-regulated which civil society groups could operate legally, fought to monopolize distribution of all forms of foreign aid, and prosecuted intellectuals for 'taking foreign money' or violating the strict regulations on non-profit associations (Abdelrahman 2004b; Pratt 2006). The United States and the other major NATO powers tended to favor the stability of the regime over activities that would rock the boat. Labor activism was certainly not part of their agenda.

Political aid donors borrowed the logic of civil society funding from the economic stimulus paradigm that underlies much conventional development assistance: financial and institutional resources would stimulate 'demand' from extra-governmental lobbies, public action committees, watchdog groups, businesswomen's associations, investigative journalists, and advocates for the poor. This template called for grants, training, and conference interactions to motivate think tanks to generate empirical evidence and ideological arguments for liberal democracy. Accordingly, projects encouraged publications and training by professional research centers, media institutes, offices of gender analysis, human rights monitors, opinion survey companies, educational foundations, law academies, legal counseling centers, and other such bodies. Particularly in the Middle East, think tanks were considered "useful organizational vehicles" for influencing public opinion "through the sponsorship of specific research agendas and policy dialogues" (Schlumberger 2000, 253, 255). Yet in Egypt, Palestine, and elsewhere, research showed that the main impact of civil society programs was neither on the 'macro' level of national reform nor the 'micro' level of grassroots sentiments, but rather on the 'meso' level of elite advocacy (Brouwer 2000; Carapico 2002). Further research in Palestine suggested a political paradox of 'heteronomy' whereby the success of NGOs in the donor circuit was inversely related to grassroots concerns, and disproportionate resources were funneled through pyramidal 'multiplicator' NGOs relaying messages from donors and filtering bottom-up communications (Challand 2010).

Let us look into this more closely. Although the discourses of civil society among international democracy brokers reflect a fluid understanding of the concept, institutional practices promote very particular organizational rubric. The Foundation for the Future, for instance, a U.S.-led multilateral civil society funding mechanism for the Middle East, explained in its 2010 annual report that:

> The civil society is the arena of voluntary collective actions, whose institutional forms differ from the state, the family and the market. Civil society organizations (CSOs) include nongovernmental organizations (NGOs), community-based organizations (CBOs), faith-based organizations, charitable organizations, foundations, labor unions and professional associations, advocacy groups, research institutions, as well as more informal political, social and religious movements.[4]

Although on the one hand this definition includes informal 'off the grid' movements, on the other the term 'civil society' becomes equated throughout the donor literature (and much academic writing as well) with organizations. All three acronyms used in the definition above imply a degree of formality and permanence inconsistent with many voluntary collective actions. The common substitution of the neologisms 'CSO' or 'NGO' for the written terms 'civil society' or 'activism in the civic arena' encourages a highly institutional conceptualization of civil society.

Moreover, while acronyms made from initial letters are commonly used in English or French, they do not work in Arabic. They tend therefore to be creolized, with the effect that the Latin-alphabet expressions 'NGO' and 'CSO' become disembodied abstractions with no literal meaning at all. Using these terms interchangeably with 'civil society' reduces the latter to particular kinds of organizations and excludes acts of resistance from the picture.

In Egypt, all associations and civil companies were required to undergo cumbersome, intrusive procedures for registering with the Ministry of Social Solidarity and/or the Ministry of Interior. In addition, the Egyptian government had long insisted that only organizations that were 'legally licensed' should qualify for external funding, and that all foreign aid must be distributed through central government ministries. There had been many disputes between the Mubarak regime and American, European, and other foreign donor agencies over this issue (Abdelrahman 2004b; Pratt 2006). A long campaign financed by the World Bank and the European Union and joined by groups like the International Center for Not-for-Profit Law, the Fredrich Naumann Stiftung, and the Club de Madrid, among others, failed to convince the Mubarak administration to liberalize its byzantine laws governing civic associations (Carapico, forthcoming). In the end, the Obama administration agreed to Cairo's demand to maintain government control of all official aid earmarked for extra-governmental associations. Taken together, Egyptian and international policies seriously restricted access to foreign assets by oppositional groups or quasi-underground movements.

Furthermore, under their own operating procedures, donor agencies developed very precise bureaucratic criteria for CSOs to be eligible for small grants and/or inclusion in NGO conferences and networks. Indeed the term 'NGO' was originally coined by the United Nations to distinguish member-state institutions from other entities working with the international body. To register as an observer at a UN convention or to obtain funds from European or American agencies, NGOs needed to submit paperwork to document goals expressly consonant with the those of the sponsors, three years' worth of financial records, certification of elections for their board of directors, and a suitable program or plan of activities. Those that made the grade—formal organizations with professional translators and accountants, a 'track record,' and organizational mandates consistent with donor objectives —could compete for dollars and euros.

Not surprisingly, by the twenty-first century the procedures for registration with international agencies had become routinized and also politicized. After the turn of the millennium, America's Middle East Partnership Initiative (MEPI) outlined its grant application process in a forty-page instruction manual. It explained why and how NGOs should engage in "strategic planning" based on a clear "mission statement" and well-kept "financial accounts"; called for proposals for "reform programs" addressing MEPI's four pillars of democracy, economic growth, education, and women's empowerment; and specified admissibility criteria of accounting, bylaws, and anti-terrorism pledges.[5] Like other U.S. government-funded agencies MEPI issued a 'transparency directive' requiring grant recipients to make the relationship visible by displaying the donor's logo on bumper stickers, posters, websites, pamphlets, or other materials.[6] To applicants, these rules ever more closely approximated Egyptian requirements for associations and companies to be certified. To Foucauldian scholars, they looked like rubrics of regimentation and surveillance. In retrospect, we can see how far they were from revolutionary praxis.

Such conditions were widely if variably replicated. The thematic categories of the Anna Lindh Foundation's (ALF) Euro-Mediterranean Foundation for the Dialogue between Cultures were somewhat different from MEPI's; one year its objectives of improving mutual perceptions, youth and artist exchanges, and coexistence between European and Mediterranean partners seemed more creative and perhaps more progressive.[7] But the call for proposals consonant with "strategic fields" and the lengthy application form with its rubrics of "target groups" and "long-term multiplier effects" as well as financial, managerial, and technical "proficiency requirements" (ALF 2009) paralleled the parameters of MEPI, the Foundation for the Future, and other transnational CSO grant-making agencies. NGO organizers needed to mimic certain kinds of knowledge and bureaucratic institutional structures and practices. Formal organization was the sine qua non to qualify for funding; no mass movements of students, workers, peasants, or faith congregations need apply.

Similarly, the NGOConnect guidebook—USAID's civil society promotion program—defined NGO "networks" as "civil society groups, organizations and sometimes, individuals that come together voluntarily to pursue shared purposes of social development or democratic governance."[8] Although this notion might seem to apply to revolutionary mobilization, the manual also underscores planning and organization. "Successful networks are not created overnight," it cautions, advising that "[n]ew networks should consider the level of social capital existing among members and the extent to which the environment can be considered 'enabling' for the network's aims and prospective activities" (11). Finally, "Even the most collaborative network will fail if it does not have a sound technical program strategy and the expertise to achieve its desired social impacts."[9] Especially when coupled with rigid procedural rules, this advice proved utterly irrelevant to the progressive commotion stirred up by the very absence of an 'enabling environment' and carried out without a 'sound technical program.'

It is not my contention that *no* American or European organizations funded activities relevant to Egyptians' mass protests in 2011, much less that there was no contact between some protest leaders and foreign agencies. Perhaps training in how to upload video captured on cell phones to the Internet and use Google Earth as a mapping device were of some use to Egyptian activists, for instance.[10] Clearly, grantees or partners of USAID, the European Community, MEPI, the Anna Lindh Foundation for the Dialogue between Cultures, the Soros Foundation's Open Society Institute, and so forth, acting either as individuals or as institutions, took part in the vigils in Tahrir Square, helped organize the logistics, defended those arrested, and documented human rights abuses. Of course there were contacts, and some funding arrangements. But the projects of international democracy brokers were hardly revolutionary.

The Nonviolent Playbook

Some of the tactics of nonviolent resistance against dictatorships that Sharp first collected and put into a handbook for Burmese dissidents in Thailand in 1993—later widely publicized, translated, and updated—did feature in the repertoires of Egyptian protesters (Sharp 2010, 79–86). I identified from his numbered list of 198 tactics at least fourteen activities that I observed in Cairo in January and February 2011:

7. Slogans, caricatures, and symbols;
8. Banners, posters, and displayed communications;
20. Prayer and worship;
35. Humorous skits and pranks;
36. Performances of plays and music;
37. Singing;
38. Marches;
43. Political mourning;
47. Assemblies of protest or support;
122. Literature and speeches advocating resistance;
158. Self-exposure to the elements;
167. Pray-in;
180. Alternative communication system; and
184. Defiance of blockades (or, notably, in the Egyptian case, though not explicitly in Sharp's pacifist list, of police barricades).

These practices and the spirit of Sharp's recommendations on how to exploit the weaknesses of authoritarian dictatorships were certainly more relevant to the revolution than the tame and managed institutional practices and white-collar round tables of the democracy-promotion industry. But Sharp did not invent these strategies or patent them; they are activities Egyptians, Yemenis, Tunisians, Palestinians, and many other people imagined and enacted on their own.

A version of Sharp's message of nonviolent resistance reached Egyptians via associates of the Serbian youth movement associated with CANVAS, in Belgrade, some of whose leaders had been active in the briefly successful but now defunct *Otpor!* movement for change. Evidently with at least some support from American agencies like NDI and IRI, representatives of the Egyptian 'Youth for Change' movement attended a CANVAS meeting in New York and a week-long course for international activists in Belgrade.[11] These workshops featured interesting ideas about breaking obedience patterns, tips on assembling flash demonstrations to confuse security police, and stories from the revolt sometimes called the 'bulldozer revolution' in remembrance of the day a lone, brave heavy-equipment driver blocked the way of Serbian army tanks.

However, CANVAS's "basic curriculum" does not seem like a blueprint for the Egyptian intifada. Apparently reflecting the logic of its own funders, the description of the lesson plans read in part:

> There is rarely victory for nonviolent movements without a strategic plan. Therefore, an understanding of basic strategic principles (Lesson 7) as well as tools and techniques to analyze their past and current situation (Lesson 8 and Lesson A1) is important as movements develop their strategic plans. An essential part of those plans will be communications. How do movements effectively communicate what they stand for? Developing effective messages and analyzing audience segments (Lesson 9) and understanding the tools and types of targeted communications (Lesson 10) are essential. Targeted communication is one of the most important parts of any movement's strategic plan.[12]

This is a manual for a long-term, well-organized campaign. Its motto is "unity, discipline, and planning." It assumes centralized leadership and a relatively hierarchical organizational structure. As I will demonstrate shortly, this does not correspond to what happened in Tahrir Square and other public spaces across Egypt.

Furthermore, there were significant differences between the Serbian and Egyptian democratic movements (Hamid 2011). Serbs had stronger labor unions and political parties. Serbian 'youth' were energetically encouraged and subsidized by American and European governments to overthrow a regime hostile to the European Union and the United States. NATO had already bombed Serbia to halt its aggression in Kosovo, and western leaders had belligerently denounced the fraudulent election of the dictator Slobodan Milošević. Not so in Egypt, whose government and military were beneficiaries of so much western largesse and support.

At most, according to activists, CANVAS and Sharp's manuals were two among many diverse inspirations for the 25 January uprising, and in any case not thanks to any direct foreign funding. In a forum on the Egyptian Revolution at the Massachusetts Institute of Technology Center for International Studies Starr Center on April 29, 2011, Tahrir activists Ahmed Maher and Waleed Rashed mentioned that an April 6 Movement colleague attended an *Otpor!* training and talked about having studied the Serbian tactics of peaceful protest. They spoke as much or more about American civil rights leaders Rosa Parks and Martin Luther King, Jr., contacts with Palestinian, Tunisian, Sudanese, and Cuban dissidents, Mahatma Gandhi's passive anti-colonial struggle, the anti-authoritarian movement in Chile, movies and documentaries about social protests and police crackdowns, the importance of mass and social media, and, especially, the hard lessons learned during several years of organizing protests against the Mubarak regime. Specifically questioned about help from American funding agencies and Gene Sharp, they replied that they avoided contradicting U.S. foreign policy by encouraging the Egyptian opposition to engage in civil disobedience; on the question of non-violence, they emphasized the difference between armed resistance in Libya and unarmed resistance in Egypt. Digital activist and blogger Hossam El-Hamalawy told the conference "From Tahrir: Revolution or Democratic Transition?" at the American University in Cairo (AUC) on June 4, 2011 that he had never heard of Gene Sharp until western journalists began crediting him with inspiring the revolution, pointing out that the 25 January movement was not purely *silmiya*, 'peaceful': citizens fought back against police and set fire to police stations and ruling party offices. Other speakers and participants at the conference cited the protests in neighboring Tunisia sparked by a desperate suicide. They also referred to earlier models familiar to Egyptian intellectuals, including the worldwide protests in 1968, Marx's writings on the Paris Commune of 1848, two decades of anti-apartheid struggles in South Africa, the works of Franz Fanon and the famous Gilo Pontecorvo film *Battle of Algiers*, revolutionary heroes as different as Gandhi and Che Guevara, and Iranian demonstrations in 2009. Most centrally, in their presentations Saber Barakat, May AbdelRazik, and Dina Shehata joined El-Hamalawy in reviewing the ways in which Egyptian labor, popular defense, and youth movements had learned from their own successes and setbacks how to mount effective protest and civil disobedience campaigns.

The Civic Revolution, in Stages

While professional transitologists insisted on the necessity of planning and organization, in Egypt in 2011 necessity was the mother of invention. A demonstration planned for 25 January—a nationwide movement demanding the downfall of the regime—gained its own dynamic forward thrust. Of course, before, during, and after the mass outpouring launched on 25 January, different groups and individuals had been poring over a range of historical, social, and even entertainment sources and also analyzed the tactics and weapons wielded by police and security forces against demonstrators in Egypt in recent years. All of this was vital. Nonetheless, after 25 January, the horizon for naming and handling the logistics of the next demonstration was defined by evolving exigencies and opportunities. At least initially, the 'strategic objective' was simply to register mass discontent.

The medium or the mother's message

Several astute commentators have questioned the image of an online virtual revolution (Herrara 2011; El-Ghobashy 2011).[13] Certainly, purposeful bloggers and members of Facebook, including the "We Are All Khaled Said" page, relied on computers to reach online audiences in Egypt and abroad. Nonetheless, the metaphor of a digital revolt tends to confuse the medium with the message. I personally became aware that something dramatic would happen on 25 January from a YouTube video distributed via Facebook. In the clip, the mother of Khaled Said, a handsome woman perhaps fifty years of age dressed simply in a grey hijab, spoke clearly, earnestly, eloquently to the camera from a sofa in her Alexandria living room. She implored patriots to mark Police Day by showing popular solidarity against police brutality. She appealed to the galvanizing moral outrage at the senseless murder of her son, who could be anybody's son. While the Internet brought Umm Khalid's message to me and to countless Egyptians, her plea was more warmly human than the cold, electronic medium of its delivery.

Mass rallies: 25, 26, 27 January

Others besides Umm Khalid, her family, and the April 6 and Youth for Change coalitions spread the word to demonstrate on Police Day—an official holiday—via cell phones and face-to-face conversations. Taxi drivers passed the news. The stratagem for Police Day was to maximize turnout by assembling in scores of accessible public squares around central Cairo and then marching along major thoroughfares toward the heart of the city, gathering numbers along the way. This kind of acephalous, decentralized preparation to mobilize crowds for a day relied more on neighborhood-level interpersonal networks than hierarchical organization. Moreover, as many have observed, members of labor unions, political parties, and other established institutions participated in great numbers, but in their capacity as citizens, not as members of official groups. Once things got underway, small collectivities in different locations needed to think on their feet.

The momentum of 25 January exceeded organizers' dreams. After tens of thousands marched toward Tahrir Square that Tuesday, defying the Interior Ministry's riot police, thousands returned on Wednesday and Thursday; hundreds never left Tahrir. Between the famed Mugamma' building and the even more renowned Egyptian Museum, and in central plazas in Suez, Alexandria, and other cities, they coalesced into a multitude, a *sha'ab* ('people') with a newfound sense of collective solidarity and togetherness. The spectacle of hope was a major global news story.

With a couple of days' notice, people used Facebook, Twitter, and old-fashioned interpersonal or landline communication to spread calls for mass rallies on Friday 28 January, named a "day of rage." The message, complete with tips for self-defense against the weapons fired on the 25th, went viral. It was picked up by Al Jazeera and western news outlets. The wide posting also tipped off the regime, which blocked Facebook, then pulled the plug on the Internet, and finally suspended cell-phone service. By dawn on Friday, tens of thousands of riot police were positioned around major intersections, key government buildings, bridges, and Tahrir Square. The challenge for the demonstrators was to break through these concentric barriers of intimidation and constraint. In the heat of a veritable battle, new tactics specific to the social geography of Cairo and Egypt were devised on the spot.

Storming the barricades: Friday 28 January

I witnessed the security police force firsthand. While Egyptian colleagues planned to congregate at Opera Square to march across the bridge to Tahrir, I formulated my own half-baked plan to go directly to the AUC campus in Tahrir Square. I packed some very healthy peanut butter breakfast cereal (Panda Puffs), water, eye drops, and scarves, and at about 10:30 a.m. hailed a taxi in Maadi and asked the driver to take me to the metro station. He asked where I was headed and I said Tahrir Square. He said the metro would not be stopping there "due to Friday prayers," and the usual route along the Corniche was impassable, but he could take me via the Autostrad and the Qasr al-'Aini Bridge.

Along all but deserted roads, we drove by paddy wagons and police lined up in riot gear on overpasses and at major crossings. The lines of men armed with gas masks, shields, helmets, jackboots, and batons thickened as we approached Tahrir. The worried taxi driver very reluctantly let me off near AUC's Falaki campus. I bought a kilo of bananas and another bottle of water and walked, an invisible, naive expat out buying groceries, back to Tahrir, past uniformed formations, armored vehicles, and obvious security thugs in expensive suits talking on their own cell phones or walkie-talkies. This was a formidable defense of the central public space in Egypt from the Egyptian citizenry. I personally was stranded, safely, inside the police cordon. The guards at AUC's Tahrir campus would not open the gates for me, but I found refuge in the Falaki facility a couple of blocks off the square. From the Falaki roof, I could see police, shoulder to shoulder, outside the gates, and every fifty meters on surrounding streets. But a guard told me I had been spotted from the roof of AUC's Oriental Hall building (on Tahrir Square itself) and sternly advised me to stay inside.

Tumultuously, the tide turned at the end of that tense day. Two things occurred nearby, but beyond my direct line of vision—although I could hear, smell, and feel parts of both—and far from either Sharp's nonviolent playbook or expert recipes for civil society engagement. My colleagues and thousands of others who assembled at Opera Square attempted to cross the formidable barricades on the bridge leading to Tahrir Square. As Rabab El-Mahdi said at AUC's "From Tahrir" conference on 4 June, by

5:00 p.m. they had almost lost hope of entering the square until sports fans accustomed to scuffles with the police took the lead with aggressive tactics like setting cars on fire and erecting barricades. At last, despite being pummeled with tear gas and live ammunition, the demonstrators stormed through the rows of riot squads on the Qasr al-Nil Bridge. Subaltern forces had breached police lines there, in front of the Arab League building, and perhaps at other spots. Within a few minutes, the ruling National Democratic Party headquarters situated between the Nile and Tahrir Square was set ablaze. As dusk settled in, blocks away and several stories up, I saw flames, sneezed from tear gas, and heard a human roar. As police who had been given orders to stand down fled their positions pell-mell, citizens occupied the central plaza.

What happened next was not planned. AUC's dedicated guards, who all afternoon had kept me inside the safety of the Falaki campus, announced that since a "state of emergency" and a 6:00 p.m. curfew had been declared I needed to "go home." Out on the streets it was pandemonium. The riot police had broken ranks, thrown down their helmets and shields, taken off the sweaters bearing their insignia, and were running in the opposite direction from civilians swarming toward Tahrir. Burning tires spewed flames and smoke. There were hardly any cars on the usually crammed streets of central Cairo. Failing to "find me a taxi," an AUC guard instead prevailed upon a kind Egyptian family, with their infant and three young children, who had been visiting family downtown, to give me a ride. Yasir, the father, behind the wheel, drove far out of their way (their home was in Giza, where he owns a small fish shop) along a backstreet route full of twists and turns because so many roads were blocked, to deliver me safely to Maadi. All the while he was complaining to a foreign stranger about the Mubarak policies that led the people to revolt. I was glad to share my bananas and Panda Puffs with the kids, Yara, Yasmine, and Yassin.

On the way to Maadi, we witnessed the other significant development of that evening, which was emerging extemporaneously in neighborhoods across greater metropolitan Cairo. On the spur of the moment, amid fires, confusion, blocked streets, families driving or walking to safety, and general disorder, citizens took matters into their own hands to direct traffic. This was utterly organic and localized: bottom-up activism. Men at intersections waved us toward the safer routes. Sometimes they peeked at who was in the vehicle. By the time we reached Maadi an hour later, civilian sentries manned almost every intersection. Twenty neighbors on guard outside my building at a railroad crossing called Mazlaqan Digla nodded me safely indoors. Overnight, they erected makeshift roadblocks from found objects: fencing, buckets filled with concrete and rebar, disembodied car parts, oversized potted plants, tables and chairs. Reacting to events on the spur of the moment, micro-level auto-organization was quite distinct from the demonstrations downtown. It was not necessarily part of the revolutionary movement as such, but certainly an important element in the popular seizure of the commons.

Occupying the commons: 29 January–2 February

From Maadi we could take the metro to Nasser Station, just north of Sadat Station at Tahrir, and walk the few blocks down along the Egyptian Museum entrance to the square with thousands of others. More and more people assembled in Tahrir Square: thirty thousand, forty thousand, fifty thousand, more. Banners and slogans declared: *Irhal!* (leave), *Batel!* (illegitimate), "Prosecute Mubarak" and "Honor international treaties" (both in two languages), and "Game over" (in English). People chanted in unison: "The people and the army are one" was a popular slogan. Others included "The people want to stomp on the president" and "God is great." Posters displayed photographs of slain martyrs. Egyptian flags, red-white-and-black headbands, and face paint signified nationalism. Little boys were going around collecting "garbage for Mubarak"; the refuse was dumped into a few burned-out vehicle carcasses near the museum, which were then set alight again. Other more serious clean-up brigades appeared, with people wielding brooms and trash bags against the accumulating refuse. Megaphones and drums amplified sound. It was electrifying, but more folksy than choreographed.

February 2 was later dubbed the 'Battle of the Camel' for the mounted thugs who thundered into the square in an absurdly dramatic and excessively brutal but pathetically futile effort to break up the sit-in. I was not there that day. When I returned two days later the level of organization and self-defense was markedly higher. The public geography and architecture of the square evolved quickly. By this time, cell phones and Internet had been restored. Cutting them had not quelled the mass mobilization.

Self-protection: 3–6 February

As May AbdelRaziq told the "From Tahrir" audience in June, this violent effort to disperse demonstrators spurred civil society to organize more formally both in Tahrir and in the neighborhoods. In the protest zone, popular committees variously took responsibility for sanitation, emergency medical care, security, food, and other necessities to keep the space viable for the multitudes. Men and women established checkpoints at the several entrances to Tahrir, checking identity cards, searching bags, and patting down entrants. It had been raining, so in addition to blankets and sleeping bags, more people were setting up tents or plastic tarps. Soon, campsites filled the green in the center of the square. Trash collection points were designated at the closed entrances to the metro and a spot just outside the AUC science building. A makeshift emergency medical clinic at the mosque on the southern side of the square was resupplied and staffed by field hospital professionals who volunteered their services. Kitchens and bathrooms were commandeered at several fast-food restaurants on or very near Tahrir whose glass fronts had already been smashed. Arrangements were made for procuring groceries, water, and other supplies. Although no weapons whatsoever were brought into the square, the popular defense committee established one area where volunteer brigades broke up sidewalk bricks and honed them into sharp-edged projectiles intended for self-protection. Sentries were on guard around the clock.

Civil society was very much in motion, then, but not in the ways encouraged or even conceived of by international experts.

The size and density of the Tahrir demonstrations swelled to astounding proportions. A quarter or a half million people were in Tahrir every day; some said numbers peaked at over a million in the afternoons. More and more tents were pitched, in concentric circles spilling beyond the green. The somewhat haphazard security measures were reinforced: rubble, vehicles, and other physical barriers and lines of men created multiple, well-marked concentric circles of resistance against unruly intrusion. Thus the physical layout of the public civic sphere evolved along with its sociology. Different groups set up stages for speeches and performances. By now there were loudspeakers. Large printed banners festooned buildings and bridges. Photographs of the martyrs were everywhere, and one grassy median was dedicated to a vigil for the martyrs. Graffiti decorated paved surfaces. There were songs, with some musical accompaniment: "Baladi," a familiar Egyptian national folk tune, was a favorite. Spaces for public prayers were designated and protected. The iconic popular slogan became "The people want the downfall of the regime." American and European governments were not in support of this demand.

By now, however, the cameras of Al Jazeera, CNN, and the BBC were trained from balconies in the Semiramis Hotel and other high-rise buildings overlooking Tahrir Square for a panoramic God's-eye view of the scene. Down below, key activists took calls from international journalists. Foreign camera crews and interviewers followed an undergraduate political science student at AUC, Gigi Ibrahim. The eyes of the world were now on Egypt's extraordinary popular assembly in the vast clearing at the heart of its megalopolis. Global audiences were mesmerized by the force of the popular outpouring they could see on television (Carapico 2011).

In neighborhoods, off camera, where groups of men had been rotating guard duty armed with sticks, shovels, or kitchen knives, neighborhood committees formed, too. Prompted partly by rumors of marauding escaped convicts, they reinforced community defense. Simultaneously, other specialized popular committees routinized street cleaning, traffic direction, and emergency services during the curfews imposed from 5:00 p.m. to 5:00 a.m. They kept tabs on the positioning and movement of Defense Ministry tanks through the neighborhoods and monitored deserted police stations. Groups of high-school students in particular collected garbage and swept streets clean, and would soon begin repainting the curbs.

During this time, the ruling party apparatus spread rumors of foreign instigation of the protests. Foreign news reporters and human rights monitors were harassed, and there were instances of intimidation, detention, and mistreatment. Mindful of the risks, I personally chose not to burden my Egyptian friends by tagging along with them, lest my presence entangle them in a distracting altercation. So during the eighteen days and on subsequent Fridays through June, I usually went to Liberation Square with resident-expat AUC colleagues. We moved freely and inconspicuously. I was never harassed at all. To the contrary, my personal experience of the revolution was quite charmed. I felt protected by the neighborhood watch teams, both in Maadi and in Zamalek where I sometimes spent the night. In Tahrir Square, people smiled or welcomed me by the hundreds if not thousands. (When I had friends visiting as actual tourists on a long-planned visit from London in March, they were greeted warmly, asked their opinions, and invited to pose for countless cell-phone photographs.) The spirit of solidarity was contagious.

Persistence and determination: 7–11 February

Egypt's military played a role in the uprising that toppled Mubarak with few parallels in other revolutionary situations. Tahrir's demonstrators embraced the soldiers positioned around the perimeter of the square. People kissed them and gave them flowers. The Egyptian colloquial slogan "The people and the army are one hand" was utterly vernacular, and for a time it seemed that saying it could make it come true. Tanks and soldiers stationed just beyond Tahrir Square and at other locations also shaped the new revolutionary urban landscape. Soldiers manned some of the checkpoints at the entrances to Tahrir, particularly from the north toward the Egyptian Museum and the 6 October Bridge. People spray-painted the tanks or climbed on top to pose for pictures. By this time there was a relatively festive atmosphere in the square, especially in the daytime. The nights, especially the evening of Thursday 10 February, when Mubarak gave a speech to the nation in which he disappointed the demonstrators by not resigning, could be tense and uncertain. Perhaps ironically, while tens of thousands defied the curfew by camping out in protest zones, neighborhoods and malls were dark and empty but for roaming army tanks and the citizen police who kept the night watch. By now, clearly, those in Tahrir Square were determined to stay until the president did resign. But even on 10 February, or the afternoon of the 11th, it was impossible to predict when that would happen or what would follow.

I had been staying in Zamalek for several days to be closer to the action and friends while avoiding an after-curfew commute. The evening of the 10th I had dinner with two American friends working for international monitoring organizations, whose personal experiences that week had not been as trouble-free as mine, at one of the few restaurants in this usually bustling part of town that were still serving food; we were the only customers, and the lights were dimmed. Our cell phones kept ringing, especially after the president's speech. Despite the good meal I went to sleep dejected and awoke Friday morning full of anxiety. Later in the day I walked with a colleague along the Nile to Qasr al-Nil Bridge, crossed, waited with the throngs to pass through a series of civilian and military checkpoints, and joined the demonstration. Once again it was uplifting, because people were still optimistic, holding their banners high and shouting their slogans loudly. "Raise your head high," one mantra ran, "you are Egyptian." After a few hours we wove our way out of the crowd again to be back in Zamalek by sundown.

As it happened, I was getting into a taxi to go to Maadi when the news broke that the president had resigned. I was driven through Opera Square toward Giza as waves of jubilant youth and whole families streamed into the streets waving flags, blowing horns, cheering, and throwing flames from cans of hairspray using cigarette lighters. When we got to the usually sleepy but central Victoria Square in the Digla area of Maadi, a spontaneous street party of a few thousand neighbors lit up the traffic circle. Evidently there were similar celebrations throughout Cairo and Egypt.

Conclusions: Homegrown and Organic
In this essay I have offered a theoretical argument, a critique of civil society promotion, and a political point. The theoretical argument is that civil society needs to be understood as an arena of engagement, not a set of organizations. By this line of reasoning, in Egypt the popular seizure of the commons has constituted a kind of civic revolution, a genuine reconfiguration of public engagement, an extraordinary, earth-shattering, take-to-the-streets moment. It will be significant regardless of the outcome of the next phase of Egyptian politics, whether or not democracy is achieved, and even if stratospheric levels of popular engagement are unsustainable. The 2011 Egyptian Revolution, along with the movements in other Arab countries, ought to liberate our understanding of civil society from the narrow confines of formal membership in organizations with offices and bank accounts. We will, in the future, give much more attention to the potential for public-spirited individual and networked activities to have transformative effects, and scholars will spend a long time now discovering the ways in which civic culture and spaces of public expression in Egypt have been revolutionized by the heady experience of being part of a *sha'ab* as never before.

As for the critique of the bureaucratic framing of civil society as organizations that file quarterly reports, I have suggested that international democracy promotion efforts have been largely irrelevant to the antiauthoritarian rebellions in Tunisia, Egypt, Yemen, Bahrain, Syria, and Libya. Expert transitologists from the United States and elsewhere are now designing projects to facilitate an orderly transition to democracy in Egypt, and meeting quite a lot of resistance from the military government, which has vowed to enforce Mubarak-era rules banning international elections monitors, foreign funding of domestic associations, and other 'violations of national sovereignty.' It is not my intention to give policy advice, but since some readers become frustrated with critical analysis of programs not accompanied by any better ideas, here's a radical concept: instead of inviting activists to come indoors to attend round-table workshops, perhaps American or other foreign experts could explain some of the basic principles and practices of democracy to career military officers who are making political decisions about constitutions and elections for which they have no professional training or experience.

Egypt may not have had a political revolution that unseats the ruling class. There is little evidence that the country is headed toward a full-fledged socioeconomic revolution that will redistribute wealth and power from the privileged elite to the teeming lower classes. Whether or not the country is experiencing a transition to democracy remains an open question. Nonetheless, there has been what might well be termed a civic revolution. Diverse, raucous popular forces have appropriated public civic realms and proclaimed ownership of the commons. Citizens have taken charge of street corners, public squares, expression in cyberspace, and channels of communication with global audiences. This has been and will continue to be a contentious, even messy process. Regardless of the outcome, it has wreaked havoc with the regulatory and disciplinary regimens of both the Cairo bureaucracy and international 'civil society promotion' programs. Many Americans empathized from afar with the revolutionary aspirations of the pro-democracy demonstrators and also the mostly non-revolutionary solidarities of neighborhood defense or betterment committees. I hope my first-person account deepens that empathy, but also that how I have told the story makes clear that this was a civic uprising of, by, and for Egyptians.

Notes

1   See, for instance, Charles J. Hanley, "US Training Quietly Nurtured Young Arab Democrats," *Washington Post*, 12 March 2011, http://www.washingtonpost.com/wp-dyn/content/article/2011/03/12/AR2011031202234.html; Ron Nixon, "U.S. Groups Helped Nurture Arab Uprisings," *New York Times*, 14 April 2011, http://www.nytimes.com/2011/04/15/world/15aid.html?pagewanted=1&_r=1&hp

2   Ruaridh Arrow, "Gene Sharp: Author of the Nonviolent Revolution Rulebook," BBC News, 21 February 2011, http://www.bbc.co.uk/news/world-middle-east-12522848; Sheryl Gay Stolberg, "Shy U.S. Intellectual Created Playbook Used in a Revolution," *New York Times*, 16 February 2011.

3   Tina Rosenberg, "Revolution U: What Egypt Learned from the Students Who

Overthrew Milosevic," *Foreign Policy* 19, February 2011, http://www.foreignpolicy. com/articles/2011/02/16/revolution_u?page=full

4. Foundation for the Future Visibility Guidelines, 2007, p. 5, http://www.foundation forfuture.org/?q=en/node/289/menu_id=214

5   Middle East Partnership Initiative (MEPI), "Guidebook for Applicants," 2007, http://www.medregion.mepi.state.gov/uploads/images/vxi1jzmXnk6nQQ4O4D-V3hQ/Microsoft_Word_-_Guidebook-Applicants-Eng_Dec1707.pdf

6   Foundation for the Future.

7   Anna Lindh Foundation Euromed, "Guidelines for Grant Applicants Responding to ALF Call for Short Term Project Proposals, ref. no ALF/CFP/2009/ST1, Deadline for Submission of Proposals 30 April 2009."

8   Darcy Ashman et al., "Supporting Civil Society Networks," in *International Development Programs*, Academy for Educational Development Center for Civil Society and Governance, December 2005, http://www.ngoconnect.net/c/document_library/get_file?p_l_id=42617&folderId=36287&name=DLFE-3337.pdf

9   Ashman 2005, 12.

10 Maryam Ishani, "The Hopeful Network: Meet the Young Cyberactivists Who've Been Planning Egypt's Uprising for Years," *Foreign Policy*, 7 February 2011, http://www.foreignpolicy.com/articles/2011/02/07/the_hopeful_network?page=0,3

11 Rosenberg 2011.

12 CANVAS Core Curriculum http://www.canvasopedia.org/legacy/content/special/core.htm

13 See also Rabab El-Mahdi, "Orientalising the Egyptian Uprising," *Jadaliyya*, 11 April 2011, http://www.jadaliyya.com/pages/index/1214/orientalising-the-egyptian-uprising; and Mohamed Elshahed, "Tahrir Square: Social Media, Public Space," The Design Observer Group, 2011, http://places.designobserver.com/feature/tahrir-square-social-media-public-space/25108/

11

Democratization and Constitutional Reform in Egypt and Indonesia: Evaluating the Role of the Military

Javed Maswood and Usha Natarajan

Introduction

The Middle East was in the throes of pro-democracy protests in 2011, from Tunisia in the west to Syria and Bahrain in the east. Two long-standing authoritarian leaders were deposed: Tunisian president Zin El Abidine Ben Ali and Egyptian president Hosni Mubarak were forced out of office on 14 January and 11 February respectively. The popular anger that toppled these leaders and inspired violent protests across the region was fueled by high levels of corruption, nepotism, poverty, and unemployment, and a pattern of governance and development that benefited the elite but failed the majority.

In Egypt, Mubarak's departure created an opening for democratic transition. A seminal obstacle to successful transition is the military's entrenched engagement in political processes. While Egypt was not technically governed by a military dictatorship, Mubarak was a decorated and respected military officer and military support was indispensable to his rule. A litmus test for transition from this military-backed system to democracy is "civilian control of the military."[1]

The end of the Mubarak regime came when the military withdrew its support. Mubarak was forced to resign and appoint a transitional authority, the Supreme Council of the Armed Forces (SCAF), led by field Marshal Muhammad Hussein Tantawi. In effect, the military has been asked to bring in democratic reforms but may be unprepared to give up its political and economic privileges easily and become a professional institution. For the past thirty years, Egypt's powerful military has enjoyed domestic popularity as well as support from the United States. Any potential transformation is likely to be premised on both internal and external demands for change. In the months immediately after the so-called January revolution, there was little domestic or international pressure on the military formally to abnegate its political role. In November 2011, however, popular anger resurfaced, creating greater uncertainty about future political developments.

The Egyptian transition benefits from comparison with Indonesia's democratization. In May 1998, President Suharto resigned from his thirty-two-year autocratic rule and Indonesia commenced a series of democratic reforms. The country's transition to democracy, although accompanied by large-scale violence and instability, is largely acclaimed as a success today. Indonesia's successful democratization was assisted by combined domestic and foreign pressure on the military to vacate the political space. We argue that without similar pressure, Egypt's reform efforts risk disappointment. The future is uncertain, but it is interesting to note that while the United States, with its close links to the Egyptian military, equivocated and appeared to hedge its bets, in November U.S. president Barack Obama was quick to call upon the Egyptian military to vacate the political space. Whether this will be sufficient remains to be seen.

By comparing the development and evolution of the political role of the Indonesian and Egyptian militaries, it is possible to appreciate the central role the military has played in both maintaining and dismantling authoritarianism. First, we consider the politicization of the military in the postcolonial Indonesian and Egyptian states and the military's relationship with authoritarianism. Second, we examine the decisive role of the military in unseating the Suharto and Mubarak regimes. Lastly, we conclude that, in light of its history, depoliticization and professionalization of the Egyptian military will be decisive in determining democratic transition in Egypt.

Our analysis is undertaken through the lens of constitutionalism, as constitutions provide a vision for governance and a framework within which state institutions such as the military operate. Egyptians are turning to constitutional reform as an important tool for democratic transition. While such reform could play a significant role in instituting civilian control over the Egyptian military, the link between constitutionalism and military power is far from straightforward. Comparative analysis of the Indonesian and Egyptian experiences indicates that while constitutional guarantees of civilian government are important, they are ineffective if unaccompanied by other substantive and procedural guarantees regarding constitutional drafting, amendment, derogation, and interpretation. Before commencing this analysis, we briefly introduce the concepts of democratization and constitutionalism that form the background to our argument.

Background: Democratization and Constitutionalism

While there is no universally accepted definition of democracy, most scholars agree with Diamond (2008, 22–23) that it is a combination of electoral contestation and civil and political rights. In democratic governance, accountability and transparency are aided through the guarantee of basic human rights, including the freedom of thought and speech, the right to assemble, to participate in public affairs and vote, to be free from unjust detention and torture, and to have access to fair legal process. In order to guarantee these rights, one of the hallmarks of democratization has been an elected and accountable civilian government, which exercises supreme control over a professionalized military.

Military professionalization is the process whereby the role and mission of the military are constitutionally constrained to ensure that it remains accountable to the state, and ultimately, in a democracy, to the people. The constitution expresses the fundamental values and rules of the political life of a nation. As such, it is an exercise of, and metaphor for, collective national self-definition. The constitutions of the United States and France typify constitutionalism as a lofty ideal. The constitutions of Belgium and Germany typify a functional and perhaps more prosaic view that constitutionalism makes governance more predictable and efficient. Constitutions, including those aforementioned, combine elements of both these goals in differing degrees.

The principle of civilian control is to minimize the interference of an inherently powerful institution in domestic politics, through coups, repression, rights abuses, resource appropriation, fomenting internal conflicts, and so on. A professional military's role is confined to protecting state sovereignty from external threats. It is separated from other domestic security forces such as the police and state intelligence agencies. The state maintains control over both the actions and resources of a professionalized military, thereby increasing military transparency and accountability.

Transitions to democracy are frequently accomplished through, among other things, reformed or new constitutions. Thus, constitutionalism has become an important concept in the modern democratization process. Existing scholarship predominantly treats constitutionalism as a phenomenon of western origin. Histories of constitutionalism typically describe its development in Western Europe and the United States, followed by a gradual process of universalization through colonization and decolonization. While non-western civilizations evidenced similar traits in their histories, it is the western tradition that has shaped contemporary understanding and gives meaning to the term 'constitutionalism' today. Thus, in the Middle East, for example, the only states without constitutions are those that escaped direct colonial rule: Oman and Saudi Arabia. Even there, 'Basic Laws' were issued in the 1990s that bear some approximation to constitutions.

Given that democratic transitions are often accompanied by constitutional reform, it is useful to examine the role of the military in Egyptian and Indonesian political life against the backdrop of constitutionalism. The national ideals expressed in the constitution have been used in different ways by the Egyptian and Indonesian military during the three phases examined below. Such an examination is useful in reevaluating what type of constitutional reforms would be effective in shaping the military's role in a democratic Egypt.

Evolution of the Military's Political Role

Protecting the postcolonial state
In the thirty-two-year Suharto regime in Indonesia and the thirty-year Mubarak regime in Egypt, the constitutions of both nations technically guaranteed civilian supremacy over the military by declaring the president's supreme control over the armed forces. Nevertheless, the military has played a dominant role in both nations' politics, not only because most presidents came from the armed forces, but for longstanding historical reasons. Rather than being simply irrelevant, constitutional provisions were often used as a tool for oppression by autocrats and the military; less frequently, the constitution also provided an avenue for resistance against the state.

Egypt: Military presidents and 'constitutions without constitutionalism'

Egypt's first constitution in 1882 was the outcome of a long and arduous struggle at a time when Egypt was administered by the Ottoman Empire as an autonomous monarchy. Egypt had recently emerged from a state of bankruptcy. The resulting foreign intervention and domestic strife led parliament to push for a constitution to guarantee more rational, predictable, legal, and fiscally responsible state behavior (Brown 2003, 36–37). Thus, while the constitution did set constraints on the monarch's power, this was not its primary aim.

The second constitution, in 1923, was an 'independence constitution,' as Britain had taken direct control of Egypt in the intervening period. This constitution was written with British influence and aimed at balancing the powers of the Egyptian monarch and parliament upon decolonization. It instituted a liberal democratic government, but provisions were too vague to allow effective governance by elected governments. Some of the primary reasons were the lack of broad participation during drafting; strong executive powers allowing the monarch and some ministers to override elected parliamentarians; executive control over constitutional interpretation; and easily claimable emergency powers (Brown 2003, 38–39). These issues were harbingers of the still unresolved constitutional problem for Egypt today. For a brief period from 1930 to 1935, parliament attempted to assert itself by instituting a new constitution, but the monarch soon reinstated the 1923 constitution, which remained in effect for nearly three decades.

In 1952, a revolutionary group led by young military officers declared Egypt's independence from the monarchy and suspended the constitution. This group of Free Officers provided Egypt's first three presidents, Muhammad Naguib, Gamal Abdel Nasser, and Anwar Sadat. As revolutionary leaders, they claimed direct representational authority and denied the need for a constitutional 'buffer' between the people and their state (Brown 2003, 40). Eventually, Nasser used constitutions to formalize and institutionalize his rule, rather than to place reasonable constraints on state power. Egypt's first republican constitution was enacted in 1956. In 1958, the United Arab Republic constitution was promulgated to declare the merger of Egypt and Syria. The 1963 constitution allowed the government to proclaim its commitment to Arab socialist ideals and the breaking down of class barriers. This type of constitution was common across the

Arab world in the 1950s and 1960s and was, to a large extent, ideological posturing rather than a genuine exercise in constitutionalism.

In 1971, the socialist state was overthrown and President Sadat, another senior member of the Free Officers group, promulgated an ostensibly liberal democratic constitution. With some amendments, the 1971 constitution remained in effect in Egypt for the following four decades. It was maintained by Sadat and, after his assassination, by President Mubarak, who was Sadat's vice president and a high-ranking air force officer. While supposedly liberal and democratic, in reality, constitutional mechanisms such as elections merely allowed the executive to allege a democratic facade behind which the basic contours of governance remained unchallenged and unchanged. Subsequent decades saw experiments in constrained and reversible liberalization, where the text of the 1971 constitution was gradually tinkered with to allow for greater participation and freedoms on paper. The reality, however, saw the powers of the president steadily increase.

Since 1952, the Egyptian military has been intimately involved in domestic political processes. It never limited its role to dealing with external threats. As defense minister, Tantawi stated that the military had a rightful role in dealing with internal tensions as well (Kechichian and Nazimek 1997, 128). This principle of insulating the military from civilian control resurfaced again in late 2011 when Tantawi headed the transitional SCAF-led government. The release of the so-called Selmi document, which had been prepared by the deputy prime minister and which presumed to serve as a guide for constitutional revision, included the principle of military autonomy from parliamentary oversight. Understandably, this became the trigger for renewed protests.

In recent decades, the military in Egypt has presented itself as the only domestic institution capable of keeping in check both internal and external threats, whether emanating from monarchists, fundamentalist Islam, or neighboring countries such as Israel. In this way, the military has projected itself as a symbol of Egyptian nationalism, unity, and stability. The success of this strategy is evidenced by the fact that all of Egypt's presidents so far have come from the military.

To some extent, the nature of postcolonial states contributed to the development of strong militaries and authoritarian rulers, in the Middle East and in other parts of the Third World. The experience of colonization—the exploitation and subordination, the 'divide and rule' policies

used by empires to maintain domination, and the creation of artificial pol-
ities and destruction of older alliances—meant that upon decolonization,
many postcolonial states found themselves to be artificial, weakened, or
divided societies. Joel Migdal (1988, 24) states that, in order to overcome
structural weakness and prevent state failure, some postcolonial leaders
"adopted the ambitious goal of making their organizations overpowering
in their societies," which frequently involved cultivating a strong, well-
resourced, and politically active military. Oftentimes, the exigencies of the
independence struggle—or the republican struggle in the case of Egypt—
created strong nationalist militaries in postcolonial states.

The military in Egypt arrogated to itself powers that had previously
been exercised by the monarchy, an appropriation that was subsequently
consolidated by means of financial independence. The military used its
political clout to secure significant economic interests; its involvement
in the civilian economy escalated rapidly after Nasser nationalized major
industries, and continued during the Sadat and Mubarak regimes. The
economic interests of the military range across a number of agricultural and industrial sectors, including petroleum, cement, electronics,
construction, automobiles, olive oil, bottled water, and hotels. The military budget is not disclosed to the parliament, but experts estimate the
military to have interests in at least one-third of the Egyptian economy
(Brownlee and Stacher 2011).[2]

The military participated in the development process and acquired a
stake in an economic system that failed to benefit a large section of Egyptian society. Trickle-down benefits were few, and the living condition of the
poor was further exacerbated by inflationary pressures which subsidies on
some basic food items were insufficient to curb. Economic policies failed
to deliver inclusiveness. A small civilian minority did prosper by hanging on
to the coattails of government and this group enriched itself particularly
over the last decade, taking advantage of Mubarak's economic reforms
and liberalization that ushered in a period of high economic growth. For
the majority of Egyptians, however, high youth unemployment and poverty on one hand and monopolistic political control on the other fueled
perceptions of 'elite blocking,' a situation in which it was impossible to
share in either political power or the benefits of economic growth.

As with many other autocratic regimes in the Middle East, Mubarak
had little broad-based political or economic legitimacy. His longevity
was grounded in a combination of military power and police repression,

rentierism, popular apathy, and American support. Of these causes, rentierism is most frequently identified as the defining feature of Middle Eastern and Egyptian politics that allowed authoritarianism to flourish. Premised on that, Diamond (2010) suggested that democratization might have to await a dismantling of the rentier compact between state and society. However, military involvement in politics is an equally important part, and democratization will require reform of the civil–military relationship.

Apart from political and economic interests, the powers of the Egyptian military and its budgetary independence owe a great deal to support from the United States, which includes the provision of military weapons, training, and logistical support as well as a yearly injection of about $1.3 billion in financial aid. U.S. support to the Egyptian military—and the dictators it produced—evidences longstanding American ambivalence toward democratization in the Middle East because of the uncertainty that transition entails. The United States became wary of such uncertainties after Iran, a country with which it had had a special relationship, went through a revolutionary upheaval in 1979 that ousted a friendly authoritarian regime and replaced it with a hostile Islamic republic. After the Iranian revolution and in the backdrop of the Camp David peace accord between Egypt and Israel, the United States established a close relationship with Egypt with the objective of preserving regional stability.

The Americans viewed Mubarak's strong military ties and authoritarian rule as a guarantor of secular politics, whereas democracy risked unleashing hostile religious forces, as in Iran in 1979 and Algeria in the early 1990s. Mubarak positioned Egypt as a moderate Islamic country and a bulwark against fundamentalist and firebrand versions of Islam. He cultivated domestic and international fear of Islamic fundamentalism to justify suppressing his main political threat, the Muslim Brotherhood. The party was banned despite its renunciation of extremism and violence. As Shehata states, the Brotherhood is a large organization, made up of people from all walks of life and political beliefs. It was suppressed less for its religious extremism than for its capacity to organize against the ruling regime.[3]

Alongside strong military and external support, Sadat and Mubarak maintained power through regular and clever political reform initiatives, including constitutional amendments, in an attempt to waylay opposition movements. Whenever possible, the regime stepped back from 'unmitigated coercion.' Citizens either consented to these ostensible reforms or embraced apathy in a state–citizen compact that produced a system of 'liberal autocracy' or 'illiberal democracy,' defusing the possibility of democratic transition (Diamond 2010, 99). At the same time, the heavy hand of repression was never too distant and was applied ruthlessly against those who defied the implicit compact. The ability to deploy indefinite state-of-emergency powers allowed the regime and the military to escape constitutional constraints, including the protection of the freedom of movement and assembly, habeas corpus rights, and the right to a fair trial by a civilian court. Thus, the number of political prisoners in the final stages of the Mubarak regime mounted to the tens of thousands. Indeed, Egypt has been in an almost continuous state of emergency since the late 1960s, effectively rendering the state of so-called emergency as the constitutional norm.

Experiments in constitutionally controlled liberalization under Sadat and Mubarak were tightly monitored. Reforms never targeted the military, ensuring that one of the primary domestic pillars supporting Egyptian autocracy remained untouched. Yet these reforms sometimes allowed openings for progress beyond those that had been anticipated and pushed political life in a more constitutionalist direction. One such endeavor was the creation by the 1971 constitution of a new court at the top of the Egyptian judicial hierarchy: the Supreme Constitutional Court (SCC). It was meant to be an instrument of executive oversight over the judiciary, but it became a more autonomous body than had been intended. In the 1980s, the SCC twice struck down electoral laws, causing the dissolution of parliament and new elections. The rules of electoral competition had been designed to secure the president the parliament that he wanted, through party-list systems, gerrymandering, proportional representation with high requirements to enter parliament, restrictive rules on founding parties, rejection of international monitoring, and assignment of oversight of balloting to interior ministries. The regime designed rules that would guarantee a small, loyal opposition. Those efforts were dealt a series of blows by SCC rulings striking down provisions of the electoral law for unconstitutionality. In the early 1990s, an activist court president led the court to declare over half of the contested laws to be unconstitutional. It was not the SCC's interpretation of the constitution that troubled the regime so much as the court's translation of the constitution's broad but vague civil and political rights provisions into more effective protections. By the late 1990s, the regime had to take counter-measures to constrain the court.

During the Bush administration's 'war on terror,' the United States made tepid demands for further democratic reform in Egypt, accompanied by large aid packages to some non-governmental organizations (NGOs). However, the NGOs that received U.S. assistance had to avoid anything that could be construed as either supporting regime change or curtailing the power of the military (Hamid 2011). The latest in Mubarak's attempts at reform culminated in the 2005 constitutional amendment allowing for multi-candidate presidential elections. This brief move toward democracy, which resulted in opposition gains in parliament, was firmly quashed by 2007 amendments of thirty-four articles reversing earlier moves toward democratization. The regime was therfore able to consolidate its overwhelming power in the 2010 parliamentary elections.

The regime created only the appearance of reform, rather than its substance. Democratization, including constitutional reform, was defensive and managed. It was not meant to lead to democracy, but rather to prevent its emergence. What resulted was continual piecemeal reform that did little to change the underlying power structure. Regime opponents found themselves ensnared in a process of endless transition. By directing public attention toward manageable reform issues, the regime could control dissent and obfuscate the real sources of state power, including the military. In light of this checkered history, as Brown accurately observes, while Egypt may have grown rich in constitutions over the past century, it has grown poorer in constitutionalism (2003, 41).

Indonesia: Pancasila and the military's dual function

Unlike Egypt, Indonesia functioned under the same constitution that established it as an independent unitary republic in 1945. In stark contrast with Mubarak, during the thirty-two-year period when President Suharto was in power, the constitution was never amended. The constitutional preamble declares the Pancasila, meaning 'five principles' in Sanskrit, as the official philosophical foundation of the Indonesian state. These five inseparable and interrelated principles proclaim belief in the one and only God; a just and civilized humanity; the unity of Indonesia; democracy guided by unanimity and deliberations among representatives; and social justice for all Indonesians. These five concepts proved immensely resilient, surviving both military dictatorship and democratic transition. Their breadth and flexibility meant that, with creative interpretation and emphasis, both autocrats and democrats were able to use Pancasila to further their interests.

Pancasila has been an object of philosophical discourse since 1945, and its content is continually being reinterpreted. It was created by Indonesia's independence leader and first president Sukarno during preparations for independence. Sukarno led Indonesia's independence struggle against the Dutch, and then the Japanese, who had taken the islands from the Dutch during the Second World War. Initially, Sukarno intended to apply Pancasila to the independent island of Java (Smith 1974, 174–83). Upon independence, however, the newly created Indonesian state encompassed a much bigger, culturally diverse archipelago, the size of the United States, and with a much larger population. While sometimes critiqued for privileging Javanese philosophy, Sukarno argued that Pancasila reflected all of Indonesia's cultures, including indigenous, Indian–Hindu, western–Christian, and Arab–Islamic traditions, in an attempt to unify the nascent state.

The Indonesian military played a central role in securing independence and sovereignty for Indonesia. It also kept the massive archipelago together by putting down insurgencies in the early years. Thus, the military had a large governance function from the earliest days of the state. It did not consider itself apolitical (Crouch 2007, 344). Indeed, it did not court political neutrality as a desirable trait, as it has always been accepted as a legitimate player in domestic politics. This role was promulgated and formalized through the concept of *dwifungsi*, or dual function, which recognized that the military had a role in defending Indonesian sovereignty not only from external threats but also from internal threats. On this basis, the military exercised control over the domestic security apparatus, including the police force and state intelligence agencies. It saw itself as the guardian of the unitary state as manifest in the Pancasila.

Articulating the dual role of the military, General Nasution in the late 1950s stated that the military was not an instrument of the government, but an instrument of the state—a view that undermined supreme civilian control over the military. Nasution argued that the military was one of many social groups with a legitimate claim to political involvement (Singh 2000, 615). The armed forces secured guaranteed representation in parliament and, over time, also became financially independent through participation in the national economy. When industries were nationalized by Sukarno in 1958, military officers were dispatched to manage them, and the military has since increased its economic stake in the country. In the mid-1990s, 70 percent of annual military spending was internally funded (Webber 2010, 400; Carnegie 2010, 58).

Sukarno had pronounced socialist tendencies and, while he did not curtail military power, he allowed a powerful rival to grow in the shape of the Indonesian Communist Party (PKI). Tensions between the PKI and the military came to a head in 1965 when, allegedly to prevent a communist coup, the military engineered a counter-coup. The actual circumstances of the 1965 coups remain shrouded in mystery. They resulted, however, in General Suharto seizing power, ending the domestic political presence of the PKI, and securing a prominent role for the military in Indonesia's future. Sukarno was progressively marginalized until his death in 1970, and for the next three decades, Suharto exercised absolute control. These were the golden years for the military as it consolidated its political and economic role.

Suharto's 'New Order' government was established on the foundations of extreme violence, dispensed through the all-powerful military and the police that it controlled. It is estimated that half a million alleged PKI members were eliminated in the mid-1960s as Suharto asserted his control over Indonesia. Suharto tasked the Department of Education and Culture with finding purely indigenous or *adat* origins for Pancasila from across the country. He harnessed these findings to assert the inherent unity of Indonesia and to create an ideological underpinning for his strongly centralized form of Jakarta-based governance. Suharto was a strong supporter of Pancasila, making it mandatory in the constitutions of all social and religious organizations, thus undermining opposition efforts to institutionalize or organize against his regime.

Unlike the socialist Sukarno, Suharto followed the path of economic liberalization. With economic liberalization there was some relaxation of political controls. Like Egypt, Indonesia had regular elections that were largely stage-managed. Public-sector employees were obligated to vote for the ruling party, ensuring that its dominant position was never threatened. Any sign of dissent, including claims for regional autonomy or self-determination, was ruthlessly suppressed by the army and police.

Just as Sadat and Mubarak were able to hold up the threat of radical Islam to garner international support, Suharto's anti-communist stance won initial favor with the United States, which was grateful to see the PKI cut off at the pinnacle of its strength. Like Mubarak, Suharto preserved a secular polity, steering his country away from strict shari'a law, through either legal reform or open suppression. Both Mubarak and Suharto promoted secular forces, but where Egypt managed to maintain a special relationship with the United States, Suharto's relationship was much more troubled. Indonesia under Suharto was certainly an ally of the west but, as observed by Robert Elson (2006), it simultaneously always "trouble[d] the West." Suharto was suspicious of western-style liberal democracy, which he claimed was alien to Indonesian political culture. While Indonesia was not at the forefront of the 'Asian values' debate, Suharto sent a clear message that unwelcome foreign interference in Indonesian's governance and economy would not be tolerated.

Economically, there were points of similarity between Egyptian and Indonesian autocracies, as both instituted an extensive and elaborate network of patrimonial politics, where the military and immediate family and friends were the main beneficiaries. Cronyism and corruption were rampant in both countries and, once removed from office, Mubarak and Suharto were alleged to have amassed huge personal fortunes by stealing from the treasury. Despite corruption, however, Suharto's regime oversaw a period of development and prosperity in Indonesia, achieving vast improvements in infrastructure, industrialization, agriculture, income, education and literacy, gender equality, and access to health. Economic growth lifted average Indonesians out of poverty and gave them a share of the country's wealth. Eventually, the Asian financial crisis that was to be Suharto's downfall reversed some of these gains, but few would deny his contribution to Indonesia's overall development. In comparison, the Mubarak regime squandered Egypt's economic wealth and potential, bringing little benefit to the average Egyptian.

Egyptian and Indonesian militaries have played a seminal role in shaping their states. They have profoundly influenced modes of governance and economic development paths and have helped to shape domestic society, culture, and understandings of constitutionalism. They maintained power and influence by creatively interpreting their constitutionally mandated role, arguing that they were indispensable to maintaining the unity, integrity, and stability of the sovereign state. Undoubtedly, the military played a positive and constructive role in the formation and maintenance of the Egyptian republic and the independent Indonesian state. Their immense and unaccountable power, however, has also been deeply destructive to popular sovereignty, enabling the institution and maintenance of autocratic and corrupt regimes for decades. The subsequent two sections examine the military's role in autocratic collapse and the democratic transition that follows.

Withdrawing support from the dictator

Crises are important triggers for democratic transition. Economic crises in particular undermine authoritarian regimes, as the latter typically have shallow roots of internal legitimacy and support. Democracies, in contrast, have a domestic legitimacy that is grounded in process, rather than performance. An economic crisis in a democracy may weaken support for an incumbent government, but a similar crisis in an authoritarian regime can be fatal to the structure of government itself (Haggard and Kaufman 1995, 7, 107).

In Indonesia more than in Egypt, legitimacy of authoritarianism was predicated on good economic performance, but crises in 1997 and 2011, respectively, shook those foundations in both countries. Authoritarian dominance had also been weakened by the way Suharto and Mubarak distanced themselves from their predecessors. Thus, when faced with a crisis, neither was able to appeal to any sense of domestic loyalty. Sukarno and Nasser, by contrast, inspired popular respect and a feeling of affinity. Both were well-respected global figures as leaders of the Non-Aligned Movement, and they symbolized the struggle of Third World countries to gain freedom from western economic exploitation. They were visionaries who inspired a sense of national pride in the people. While Indonesia prospered economically under Suharto, without Sukarno's global vision, Indonesia's role in the international arena was greatly diminished. Similarly, Mubarak did not endow Egyptians with any sense of domestic or international vision or purpose; neither did his economic achievements, meager compared to Suharto's, translate into political support. Both regimes were, therefore, vulnerable to crises.

Worried about the contagion of Arab uprising, regimes across the Middle East tried to garner political support through economic incentives. Kuwait, Bahrain, and Saudi Arabia promised cash bonuses to citizens, and Saudi Arabia also announced new employment schemes. States lacking abundant oil revenues, such as Egypt, had less capacity to purchase internal legitimacy with economic largesse. Regardless, the uprising that toppled Mubarak was not preceded by economic crisis or sudden loss of performance legitimacy. The economy was performing reasonably well in terms of GDP growth when protests started in January 2011. Although the preceding years saw growth accompanied by increasing inequality, industrial disputes, and strikes, most experts did not predict revolution and regime change, except in very general terms. When Mubarak responded to protests by promising public-sector employees a 15 percent salary increase, this failed to mollify them because they simply wanted an end to authoritarian rule.

In Indonesia it was a threefold crisis in 1997 and 1998 that undid the New Order regime. It started as a financial crisis and swiftly developed into an economic crisis, which ultimately led to a political crisis. The domestic legitimacy of the Suharto government was based on impressive economic performance (Crouch 2007, 353). However, the financial crisis reversed many of the state's development gains and led to large-scale factory closures and unemployment. The disproportionate effect of the crisis on the poor fueled resentment toward the wealthy Chinese minority and the Suharto government, and eventually fomented a political crisis. In order to stabilize a free-falling economy, the government was forced to secure a bailout package from the International Monetary Fund (IMF), with accompanying conditionality.

While the IMF could not call for regime change, it offered a structural adjustment package that was unprecedented in both the size of the bailout and the number of conditionalities imposed. Indonesia was forced to implement not just economic, but also political reforms. These aimed to ensure government transparency and accountability and reduce corruption and nepotism, and asked for removal of regime members from lucrative government posts. The IMF argued that it could not use funds provided by taxpayers in democratic countries to maintain authoritarian regimes. While the United States did not press for Suharto's resignation directly during the financial crisis, it signaled through the IMF that business as usual was no longer acceptable.

Both Suharto and Mubarak faced mass domestic protests calling for their resignation, and both attempted to placate such calls by announcing that they would not seek another presidential term in the next election. Each tried to leave office on his own terms, but the public would not brook delay and continued to agitate for regime change. The standoff was resolved only when the military withdrew its support and coerced the longstanding dictators into resigning. Suharto was determined to ride out the economic crisis but, as violent protests escalated, military leaders signaled to Suharto in May 1998 that they could no longer ensure order unless he resigned (Freedman 2007, 208). Mubarak's decision to resign came eighteen days after protests began on 25 January. It was the military that ended his regime, only one day after he defiantly reiterated his intention to continue in office until the presidential election later in the year.

When Suharto stepped down, he handed power to his recently appointed civilian vice-president, B.J. Habibie. Mubarak, however, ceded powers to the military in the form of the SCAF, headed by General Tantawi. While General Tantawi and other senior military officers were loyal to their commander-in-chief for years, relations between the president and the military had gradually soured. The generals resented Mubarak's reliance on the police, which enjoyed great privileges as an important part of his domestic security apparatus. More importantly, they feared the ascent of powerful civilian elite businessmen, personified in Mubarak's son Gamal. Not only did increasingly powerful private business interests impinge on the military's economic turf but, more importantly, Gamal's own aspirations to leadership endangered the military's long-held claims on the presidency. The revolution was in some ways welcome to the military establishment, as it allowed them to outmaneuver the Mubarak family's succession plans.

In chapter nine, Hazem Kandil describes the military's diminishing institutional and economic power under Mubarak and the rise of a strong domestic security apparatus. We agree with Kandil's observations that Mubarak undermined the military's institutional and economic power so as to prevent further coups and protect the Mubarak family's succession interests. Kandil concludes, however, that in its current diminished capacity the military is incapable of restructuring the existing order in post-Mubarak Egypt, either to safeguard its own interests or to respond to popular demands for reform. We argue that the military is capable of restructuring the existing order and is attempting to do so. It is merely unwilling to prioritize reforms that come at the expense of strengthening and safeguarding the military's own interests. While military capacity may indeed have diminished today when compared with its abilities in 1952, it remains a powerful institution.

The military took over the reins of power in 2011 with popular support, goodwill, and trust that it would safeguard the revolution. It welcomed the opportunity to shepherd the transition process. In the immediate aftermath of Mubarak's ouster, much of the general public also welcomed the transfer of power to the military. Senior ministers, including the vice president, were deeply mistrusted by most Egyptians. The military, while in reality equally implicated in Mubarak's rule, managed to distance itself from the embattled president and keep a comparatively clean reputation during the eighteen-day uprising. It took up a seemingly neutral stance in the ensuing standoff, setting up tanks and barricades between the protesters and regime supporters. By refusing to openly put down the protests or openly support the regime, it preserved an image of political neutrality and professionalism, thereby maintaining much of its popularity. Protesters looked upon the military as a valued strategic partner in the process of revolution. Indeed, this was a wise calculation, as Mubarak was only unseated when the military was forced to abandon its ostensible neutrality and take sides. In addition to the absence of domestic critique, there were also no international calls for civilian government, or for the military to abstain from taking up an overtly political role when Mubarak finally resigned.

The Egyptian uprising caught the United States unprepared, and it responded with a series of ambiguous and contradictory statements. Over a few weeks in January and February, it called alternatively for peace and stability, major democratic reform, and regime change. In March 2011, President Obama commented that, while there was no certainty as to the ultimate direction of change sweeping across the Middle East, "I do know that change is not something that we should fear."[4] Again, in May 2011, he stated that unfolding events in the Middle East required a shift in U.S. foreign policy. What its new policy is or will be remains unclear, as the United States was only unequivocal in its support for regime change in the case of Libya, with a more muddled approach in Bahrain, Egypt, Jordan, Syria, Yemen, and particularly Saudi Arabia. To the extent that external support has been one of the determining factors in the longevity of authoritarianism in some Middle Eastern countries, transition will be aided by the withdrawal of such support.

In Indonesia, the United States played a very different role during the crisis. Given that there was no special relationship to preserve, with either Suharto or the powerful military, the United States took the crisis as an opportunity to intervene in Indonesia's economic and political future. Once Suharto stepped down, the United States openly demanded that post-Suharto Indonesia embrace democratic reform and guarantee civilian government. It supported domestic demands for human rights and military accountability, imposing congressional sanctions on the export of weapons and aid to Indonesia to press for reforms and civilian control of the military. When Suharto stepped down, domestic and international scrutiny ensured that power was transferred to a civilian authority, as mandated in the 1945 constitution.

As was the case in Indonesia, the Egyptian constitution also stipulated in Article 84 that the president must hand over power to a civilian authority. Mubarak's transfer of power to the SCAF violated the constitution and has placed Egypt in a temporary state of military dictatorship. On 13 February, two days after taking power, the SCAF suspended the constitution and parliament. The SCAF proposed nine constitutional amendments to prepare the way for parliamentary and presidential elections, which were passed in a referendum on 19 March with 77 percent support. None of the amendments dealt with the issue of genuine civilian control. On 30 March, the SCAF adopted the Provisional Constitution of the Arab Republic of Egypt to govern the transitional period. This declaration comprises sixty-three articles, including articles from the 1971 constitution and those amended by referendum. It stipulates that after elections, the new parliament is to form a constituent assembly to write a new constitution. In the meantime, the provisional constitution preserved all the executive powers of the past regime, and created a vaguely defined Defense Council, whose powers were equated with that of the president. The state-of-emergency provisions also continued to operate.

Both Egyptian and Indonesian history evidence that constitutions can espouse lofty ideological principles, but fail to translate to real benefit for their polity. Rights may be declared, but they may be either too vague to be enforced, or later constrained by legislation or states of emergency. Elections may be guaranteed, but stacked parliaments and no real electoral choice make them meaningless. The various Egyptian constitutions have all been state-enabling instruments, helping autocrats negotiate internal and international pressures. The constituent assemblies that drafted past constitutions were elite factions eager to support and legitimate authoritarianism.

Despite this history, Egyptians are devoting significant public attention to constitutional matters during the transition. They remain committed to the idea of constitutionalism, both its sociocultural and symbolic role in defining Egyptian identity, and its function to regulate politics and the powers of the state. In the immediate aftermath of Mubarak's ouster, public attention focused on the looming constitutional referendum; the composition of the constituent assembly; the role of religion in the state; human rights, including religious freedom and minority protection; and curtailing excessive use of state-of-emergency provisions. While these are all important constitutional issues, the seminal issue of the role of the military in a democratic Egypt was largely sidelined. The following section considers the planned reforms for Egypt's transition and lessons that Egypt could learn from Indonesia's democratization process.

Reform toward civilian government

Egyptian protesters won global admiration by dethroning a seemingly immovable pharaoh. They not only achieved what many experts deemed impossible, but did so with courage and principled nonviolent behavior in the face of aggression. Such momentous change is frequently followed by public desire for collective self-definition. Thus, the resurgent Egyptian interest in constitutionalism in recent months is unsurprising. Additionally, Mubarak did not cultivate a strong sense of political identity in Egypt. While the desire to topple Mubarak created some unity, his departure revealed a vacuum in the national psyche.

The revolutionary movement represented a broad cross section of Egyptian society. It was not unified, but rather a diverse multitude of small groups, and even solitary protesters with handwritten signs. Other than the vague demand for democracy and equity, clear alternatives to Mubarak are yet to emerge. His sudden departure has given Egyptians the opportunity to choose a different path, including that of constituting a democratic Egypt. Alternatively, the military may continue its longstanding tradition of reconstituting its own power with a new titular head.

The SCAF is in a schizophrenic position. In the aftermath of Mubarak's departure, Egypt is still simmering with protest and discontent as the nation attempts to formulate a new self-identity. Thus, to quell further unrest and remain in control, the SCAF must successfully present itself as the guardian of the revolutionary ideal and the facilitator of democratic transition. At the same time, it has to collude with remnants of the regime to some extent in order to protect itself, because it was a participant in Mubarak's oppression and economic opportunism. While facilitating an ostensible return to formal civilian control, the SCAF will attempt to ensure that military interests are safeguarded under any future government.

When Suharto was succeeded by his vice president, Habibie, many domestic and foreign observers were skeptical of Habibie's reform credentials and his presidency was carefully scrutinized. Habibie was a recent appointee, well known for his loyalty to Suharto, whom he saw as a father figure and referred to as "SGS," or "Super Genius Suharto." The fallen mentor may therefore have harbored some hope that Habibie might preserve the basic structure of the old regime. As president, however, Habibie rapidly undertook pivotal reforms toward democratization, as did his successor, President Abdurrahman Wahid, addressing human rights, legal and judicial reform, electoral reform, decentralizing state power, and, crucially, professionalizing the military. These reforms are examined below in terms of their relevance for the Egyptian context.

Since Suharto's fall from power, the Indonesian constitution has been amended four times, in October 1999, August 2000, November 2001, and August 2002. Habibie began by adding a bill of rights. In Egypt, the constitution already guarantees many basic civil and political rights, as well as economic, social, and cultural rights. Many of these rights have, however, been suspended by the longstanding state of emergency. Some were also limited in their application through subsequent legislation. Additionally, there was a lack of adequate remedy for violations. A formal bill of rights may help to codify clearly a full range of rights and raise awareness of them among the Egyptian citizenry. More importantly, however, the constitution would need to restrict when, how, and for how long states of emergency can be declared. As was the case in Indonesia, Egypt has suffered decades of corruption and injustice, where the constitution and the law were tools of the wealthy and powerful: a system of 'rule by law' rather than rule of law. Constitutional reform therefore becomes meaningless unless accompanied with broader justice system reform and restoration of the rule of law.

To restore faith in the legal system, Indonesia undertook massive legal and judicial reform programs. The bill of rights was accompanied by rights-implementing legislation and the creation of the National Human Rights Commission. A 2001 amendment created the Constitutional Court. Constitutional courts are particularly helpful during transitions, as they usually determine the constitutionality of legislation, results of a general election, and actions to dismiss a president from office. That is to say, Egyptians have to address the issue of who interprets their constitution, and whether the SCC has the institutional capability, strength, and independence to fulfill this function.

Indonesia has a plural legal system, with a complex confluence of three distinct structures: indigenous customary law (*adat*), the legacy of Dutch colonial law, and the post-independence law of the modern state. Post-Suharto amendments gave greater constitutional recognition to *adat* to help minorities gain recognition and protection, which they otherwise risked losing in a transition to democracy. While Egypt is smaller than Indonesia, in both geographic size and population, and lacks Indonesia's cultural diversity and ethnic tensions, it has religious and cultural minorities. Egyptian society faces the particular risk of polarization over religious issues. Minority protection provisions can calm growing fears of the 'tyranny of the majority.' The fear of Islamization, especially among religious minorities, can be addressed through human rights and legal pluralism. Such systems could also help tribes in areas such as the Sinai Peninsula, Upper Egypt, or the Libyan frontier, who may otherwise feel less integrated or underrepresented.

Alongside protection of human rights, Habibie prioritized electoral reform. Constitutional amendments instituted direct popular election of the president and vice president, who serve a maximum of two consecutive terms of five years each. Habibie removed all restrictions on political parties. More than sixty parties were set up in the first six months. The first free, fair, and independently monitored parliamentary elections were held in 1999, thirteen months after the fall of Suharto. They led to the formation of a coalition government led by moderate Islamic cleric and philosopher Abdurrahman Wahid, who continued the reform process. Indonesia has had three orderly and peaceful transitions of government: from Habibie to Wahid; from Wahid to Megawati Sukarnoputri, the daughter of Sukarno and a democracy campaigner; followed by the first directly elected president in 2004, the former army general Susilo Bambang Yudhoyono, who is currently serving his second term.

In Egypt, parliamentary elections were planned to commence in November 2011 and the elected parliament was to form a constituent assembly to revise the constitution and pave the way for presidential elections. Until presidential elections and transfer of powers, SCAF intended to govern alongside the elected parliament. There were concerns that November was too soon for new competitive political forces to emerge. The military, Mubarak's party, and the Muslim Brotherhood had the advantage of funds, structure, and organizational capacity compared with newly formed political parties. Interestingly, in the early transitional phase there were moments of agreement between sections of the Brotherhood and the SCAF on points of mutual advantage. Increasingly however, this was replaced with competition and conflict after parliamentary elections resulted in a parliament dominated largely by the Brotherhood. First,

SCAF blocked the constituent assembly on grounds that since it was dominated by Brotherhood it was not representative of Egyptian society. Then, shortly before the presidential election in mid-June 2012, the judiciary dissolved the newly elected parliament and the military blocked members of parliament from entering the building. Finally, after presidential elections but before results were announced, SCAF and the military arrogated to themselves sweeping powers that rendered them completely independent of elected representatives. None of these maneuvers inspire any confidence that Egypt is likely to make a quick or easy transition to democratic politics. In Indonesia, by contrast, there was a longer transitional period before parliamentary elections and the results were a split among six parties, including Suharto's former party, moderate and conservative Islamic parties, and democratic reform parties. With no individual party in a dominant position, a coalition government was inevitable, and this was ultimately beneficial to the consolidation of democratic politics.

While the Egyptian Revolution manifested widespread societal support, the transition process runs the risk of being hijacked by elites. This happened in Indonesia when student movements, demanding a new constitution and radical reforms, became gradually sidelined by elite networks and 'court politics' (Bunte and Ufen 2009a, 13). Moderates and regime soft-liners formed an alliance to manage processes that met minimal reform without completely overhauling the system. In Egypt, SCAF's control of the transition has meant that reforms were introduced in an incremental top-down manner. SCAF has also shown itself to be determined to protect its own interests from democratic accountability. The very real risk is that the military will not only retain control over the constitutional drafting process, but will remain directly involved in domestic politics, making a mockery of the Egyptian revolution and the democratic aspirations of the people.

The combination of domestic and international scrutiny meant that in Indonesia's case, attempts to depoliticize and professionalize the military were prioritized. This has met with some success. In 1998, the leader of Indonesia's armed forces, General Wiranto, proclaimed a 'New Paradigm,' which formally ended *dwifungsi* and the military's political role. The military no longer has representation in parliament and formally accepts the principle of civilian control. In 2000, the police was separated from the military, and both organizations were renamed and reconstituted to reflect their new and separate professionalized functions.

Despite significant reforms and diminishment of power, after thirteen years the political power of the Indonesian military remains formidable. Indeed, the main criticism leveled at Indonesia's fledgling democracy is the continuing power of the military (Honna 2009, 240), which has adapted to and manipulated the changing political landscape with great effectiveness. The current president, reelected by a strong majority, is a former army general.

The military's ability to remain politically engaged has affected the success of other democratic reforms. President Wahid delegated some authority from the central government to provincial and regional governments through constitutional amendment. A House of Regional Representatives was created, as well as special autonomous regimes in troubled regions such as Aceh and Papua. These amendments encouraged philosophical reinterpretations of Pancasila requirements of unity. However, the military has continued to interpret Pancasila strictly as requiring a unitary state, and therefore brutally putting down ethnic conflict in various regions. This has undermined constitutional provisions on regional autonomy, rendering them the least effective of Indonesia's constitutional reforms.

Significantly, Indonesia has not had great success in holding past regime members to account for human rights violations. The state has also failed to punish egregious military violations of human rights in East Timor, Papua, and other conflict-ridden regions. This is directly attributable to the continuing influence of the military. In Egypt there is an even greater risk of such injustice, as the SCAF is controlling the transition process. While the trials of Mubarak, his sons, and certain members of the former regime are underway, the SCAF has been careful to confine charges only to issues in which the military has not itself been implicated.

Despite formal submission to civilian control, the reason for the Indonesian military's continuing political influence lies in its budgetary independence. Only a third of the army's annual budget is reliant on parliamentary approval, while the rest is internally sourced (Webber 2010, 400; Carnegie 2010, 58). The military continues to be heavily involved in business ventures, including in the lucrative extractive and forestry sectors. Without parliament controlling the military budget, the military lacks transparency and accountability, undermining Indonesia's fledgling democracy and the principle of civilian governance.

Nonetheless, Indonesia is regarded as a democratic success story. Over the last thirteen years, it has emerged as a more liberal and democratic polity, with increasing respect for the rule of law, freedom of press and assembly, free and fair elections, and peaceful transfers of power. It will inevitably have to address some of the criticisms mentioned above to continue down the path to successful democratization.

Outside forces were deeply engaged in the Indonesian transition, assisting in extensive law reform, election, and development programs. Actors included the IMF, the World Bank, various UN agencies, and direct foreign government aid. Like Egypt, Indonesian institutions of governance had been undermined by decades of autocracy and corruption. The parliamentary, legal, and judicial reforms required to make the transition to a society governed by rule of law seem impossible without outside financial and technical aid. Alongside constitutional reform, a host of other issues were addressed, including training of courts, police, and prosecutors; institutional reform; technological efficiencies; and other similar topics. Egypt shares many of these needs. While foreign involvement brings funding and pressure for reform, it also comes with the danger of debt and self-interest. Egyptians are closely acquainted with both of these dangers and are understandably wary of outside involvement in the transition process.

The United States has not indicated that it will depart from past practices with regard to the Egyptian military. It may continue to shield the military from budgetary constraints by tying large amounts of aid to military spending. Despite its leverage over the Egyptian military, the United States has never used this influence to produce a professional armed force. Indeed, it is the army's political influence that has made it a valuable regional ally. Additionally, the close personal bond between the American and Egyptian armed forces, formed over decades of training together, cannot be underestimated or easily overcome.

Indonesia's experience thus far reveals the importance of prioritizing military reform and civilian government. Despite Indonesia's significant strides in addressing this problem, the power of the military remains the central challenge to Indonesian democracy. As Egypt's transition is being managed by the military, the challenge is even greater. While the SCAF may indeed shepherd Egypt toward democracy, there are reasons for skepticism. Military governments have never produced democracies before. While Egypt will undoubtedly undergo some democratization, the risk remains that, as in the past, the language of reform will be used to mask its absence.

In late November 2011, public disquiet over the future of reform unleashed a new wave of protests. In November, the biggest protests since February occurred. The trigger for these protests, which, unlike the initial uprising, quickly took a very violent turn, was the release of the so-called Selmi document. It was drafted by the deputy prime minister as a set of constitutional guidelines, and what infuriated the protesters was that it appeared to quarantine the military from parliamentary and civilian oversight. The resurgence of protests and violence just days before the start of parliamentary elections created fresh uncertainties about political developments, but also highlighted a popular determination not to accept anything short of full democratic transition. The United States has also, more plainly than before, aligned itself with democratic forces and called for the military to return to the barracks. How and whether this is achieved remains to be seen.

Conclusion

The constitutions of both Egypt and Indonesia guarantee a civilian government that exercises supreme control over the armed forces. An examination of the military's role in the evolution of Egyptian and Indonesian political life, however, reveals the pivotal role the military has played in the governance of both modern states. Thus, attempts to transition to a more just and equitable system of governance would do well to address what role the military should play in such a state. The military's role will necessarily be informed by the nation's broader vision of how its society should be reconstituted after the departure of longstanding dictators. Effective military reform is only possible if it is undertaken while addressing broader constitutional challenges at the same time.

Egypt's long history of constitutional reform and Indonesia's comparatively recent experience both reveal certain issues that Egypt should address to overcome past shortcomings and make a successful transition to democracy. First, the constituent assembly should ensure broad public representation in the drafting process. In the past, drafting privileged the input of political, military, economic, and legal elites, with the public participating only through referendum. Second, the constitution must have clear provisions for amendment, as previous regimes changed the constitution to suit themselves, making it an enabler of rather than a constraint on state and military power. Third, derogation provisions need to be stricter, since vague emergency provisions allow for indefinite departure from the constitution. Last, without proper restrictions on interpretation, the constitution is rendered meaningless. While judicial mechanisms exist in Egypt, their effectiveness is limited through both lack of judicial independence and deliberately vague constitutional provisions that baffle attempts at interpretation.

It is against this constitutional background that depolitization and professionalization of the military can take place. The Indonesian example shows that in nations such as Egypt and Indonesia, where the military plays a central role in governance, its power and influence are the primary hurdles to successful democratic transition. As Egypt is undergoing its transition under a military government, it is even more important that this issue be prioritized. The transition process has already evidenced abuse of power and a slow pace of reform. Among other things, the military has subjected civilians to military trials, exercised extreme violence against civilian protesters, and restricted freedoms of assembly and speech. As civic frustration grows, public attention is increasingly focused on removing the military from the political arena in the long term, in order to ensure that government can be fully accountable to its people.

The Indonesian experience also illustrates that professionalization of the military is necessarily a long and incremental process. Historical context explains the military's deeply entrenched role in these two states. Assumptions about the appropriate relationship between civilian government and the military in a democratic state stem from western political history. As the respective histories of Indonesia and Egypt show, these assumptions cannot easily be translated to non-western states. The legacy of colonization and decolonization shaped militaries in postcolonial states in ways that were fundamentally different from their western equivalents. With this perspective, it is possible to appreciate the unique role the Egyptian and Indonesian militaries have played. In both states, while military depoliticization is indispensable for accountable and transparent government, professionalization is only feasible if accompanied by effective civilian government. For the military to accept a subservient position, constitutional and legal reform must not only unseat entrenched military interests, but also create a civilian government that is able to protect the strength of the state and provide for people's needs.

Notes

1 Clement Henry and Robert Springborg, "The Tunisian Army: Defending the Beachhead of Democracy in the Arab World," *The Huffington Post*, 7 March 2011, http://www.huffingtonpost.com/clement-m-henry/the-tunisian-army-defendi_b_814254.html

2 See also C. Simpson and M. Fam, "Egypt's Army Marches, Fights, Sells Chickens," *Bloomberg Businessweek*, 17 February 2011.

3 Dina Shehata, "Islam and Politics in Egypt," interview with Toni Johnson, *Council on Foreign Relations*, 24 February 2011, http://www.cfr.org/egypt/islam-politics-egypt/p24229

4 "Remarks by the President to the People of Brazil in Rio de Janeiro, Brazil," 20 March 2011, http://www.whitehouse.gov/the-press-office/2011/03/20/remarks-president-people-brazil-rio-de-janeiro-brazil

12

Authoritarian Transformation or Transition from Authoritarianism? Insights on Regime Change in Egypt

Holger Albrecht

The litérature on authoritarian regimes in the Middle East and North Africa (MENA) has emerged, in the past two decades, as if in a Hegelian dance between democracy and authoritarianism.¹ In the 1990s, scholars accepted the broad assumptions of the 'democratic-transition paradigm'— developed in studies on Southern and Eastern Europe, and particularly on Latin America—to search for the prospects, and later the setbacks, of democratic change in the region. In the past decade, scholars responded by criticizing assumptions borrowed from the 'transition paradigm' and demanded analytical inquiries into what was empirically present, rather than into the absence of a phenomenon, that is, democracy. The author-itarian-regime literature therefore searched for the sources of regime stability, rather than the prospects of systemic change. Based on the upris-ings that brushed aside the authoritarian rulers in Tunisia, Egypt, Libya, and Yemen, and other revolts challenging autocrats in Bahrain and Syria, it is tempting to revive the debate on the prospects of democratic change and proclaim the 'fourth wave' of democratic transition.

This chapter demands a more cautious perspective at a time when dynamic developments are still unfolding. Broader conceptual frame-works appear to be inapt to fully grasp the political earthquake that shook the authoritarian regimes in the MENA region. The 'authoritarian-per-sistence' literature has apparently confused the longevity of some of the region's authoritarian regimes with an assumed stability of their political orders, thereby overestimating both coercive and adaptive capacities of authoritarian incumbents and, at the same time, underestimating the people's power and determination. In turn, the 'transition paradigm'—at least in its mainstream perspective, which assumes a particular sequencing of events and in which systemic regime change seems to be the product of elite negotiations (O'Donnell and Schmitter 1986)—proves ill-equipped to explain the conditions of regime change in the region. Egypt is a telling case in point. At the outset of the 25 January uprising, the country had not experienced a distinct phase of political opening. Rather, since 2006 Egyptian society had lived through a period of political de-liberalization culminating in increasing restrictions toward opposition activism and in the rigged parliamentary elections of 2010 (see chapter 2). Moreover, preliminary insights into the transformation process in the immediate post–25 January period do not offer enough empirical support for a 'pacted transition' hypothesis (Przeworski 1986), that is, a democratic transition along the path of particular elite constellations that would find reformers in the authoritarian regime to side with parts of civil society.

This chapter discusses some preliminary insights on the ongoing process of regime change in Egypt. While the conceptual value of an account investigating the unfolding process is naturally limited, I identify some core elements of the Egyptian transformation process in the immediate aftermath of the 25 January uprising. My argument is that the repercussions of the uprising itself, the dominant nature of the political discourse during the transition period, the internal stakes of the interim regime, and challenges in the formation of political organizations render democracy as the outcome of the transformative period unlikely. Thus, we witness an authoritarian transformation of sorts, rather than a transition toward democracy.

Before inquiring into the post–25 January period, I will address the reasons for regime breakdown in Egypt and discuss two distinct but related questions: Why was mass participation sustained in the 25 January uprising? And why did the uprising result in the fall of Hosni Mubarak? A comparative perspective that employs a limited set of cases in the MENA region is helpful in order to reach beyond over-simplifying explanations that would invoke the state of economic development and the lack of civil rights and liberties as major reasons to explain the mass uprising in the region. Rather, I argue that the particular regime type (monarchies vs.

republics), the age of incumbent leaders, and choices made by the respective military establishments are decisive for the process and outcome of the recent uprisings.

It's Not the Economy, Stupid

In order to explain the mass uprising of Egyptians that led to the ousting of Hosni Mubarak, two interrelated puzzles need to be solved. First, one must understand why the protests—which started on 25 January, and came to a tentative conclusion on the day of Mubarak's resignation, 11 February—turned into a mass movement that quickly grew into a systemic threat for the Egyptian authoritarian regime. Then one must determine why the uprising in Egypt, at a relatively low level of violence (compared to other Arab revolts), was ultimately successful in bringing down Hosni Mubarak. The first question is intriguing for two reasons: first, the Egyptian regime has experienced, in its more recent history, but also during the late Nasser years and the late Sadat years, a significant degree of popular protest that never turned into a revolutionary force of the kind and extent witnessed in early 2011. Second, in a more comparative perspective, one wonders about variance among countries in the Middle East, which range from the Egyptian case, where protests turned into a mass movement and systemic threat toward incumbents, to Jordan, Algeria, and Morocco, where low-level protests were successfully contained by the authoritarian rulers.

It is tempting to employ a narrative that figures prominently in the media's coverage of the regional events, as well as in some immediate reactions of the academic community (see Chomiak and Entelis 2011; Dahi 2011): Socioeconomic factors and the lack of rights and liberties had triggered the people's revolt against the secretive regime of the 'pharaoh' Mubarak. In short, the argument goes, Mubarak had to fall because he was challenged by an impoverished, disenfranchised, and suppressed population. There is some empirical evidence that seems to support the 'economy argument.' Two decades of economic reforms following the recipe of the international financial institutions saw an ever-widening gap between a few rich and the poor masses of society (see Farah 2009; Soliman 2011). Fiscal austerity measures and the privatization of public enterprises led to macroeconomic stabilization, but they also affected the lower middle classes in particular as victims of economic reforms. At the outset of the uprising, the majority of the population had experienced a protracted decline in real wages; around 20 percent of the population were considered to fall below the poverty line and another 20 percent struggled on the verge of that line, while a few 'crony capitalists' had tightened their grip on both the economic fortunes of the country and political decision-making in the regime.

Economic developments in the second half of 2010 might contribute to an 'economic tipping point' explanation of the uprising. Since April of that year, the populace's tolerance for economic hardship was again put to the test by a significant increase in prices for food and mass consumer goods. Skyrocketing food prices on international markets could not be absorbed by state subsidies which, in 2010, had already reached around 25 percent of the annual budget. As a consequence, a few weeks before the month of Ramadan (late August 2010), the price of rice went up by 50 percent; wheat prices doubled in August; and meat and poultry prices rose by 40 percent and 25 percent, respectively. Rising prices for vegetables and cooking-gas cylinders also had a particularly significant impact for the household budgets of the lower middle classes and the poor. Inflation caused by rising food prices rose by 2.3 percent in July 2010 alone, up from 0.7 percent in June. To make matters worse, earlier in the year, consumers experienced an unprecedented number of immediate shortages of wheat, gas, and fuel.[2]

Economic hardship might have had an impact on an individual's decision to join anti-government protests, but such economic indicators do not suffice to explain sustained mass uprisings. Neither does an increasing awareness of the undemocratic and repressive nature of the state among the population. While this explanation—the poor and repressed revolt against the authoritarian 'pharaoh'—is seemingly plausible for the Egyptian case, a comparative perspective among the authoritarian regimes across the region demands a more nuanced approach. Table 12.1 below shows political and economic data on seven countries whose authoritarian regimes have, since late 2010, become the target of mass protests. Their common denominator is that, irrespective of the course and outcome of events, authoritarian incumbents faced a systemic threat which led to their ousting—as in Tunisia, Egypt, Yemen, and Libya—or the employment of immense coercive countermeasures—as in Bahrain, Syria, and Iran (after presidential elections in 2009). The data show the state of socioeconomic development as reflected by such measures as the UNDP's Human Development Index (HDI, country rank, and value), the Gross

National Income (GNI) per capita on purchasing power parity (PPP), and the Management Index of the Bertelsmann Transformation Index (BTI). The data also reflect the state of political reforms and the degree of liberties that authoritarian rulers granted to their populations, as in the Freedom House Index (FH) on political rights and liberties and the BTI Status Index, which measures political and economic transformation.[3]

Table 12.1: Mass uprisings in the MENA region, socioeconomic indicators for 2010

	HDI rank	*HDI value*	*GNI/capita (PPP 2008 $)*	*FH: rights*	*FH: liberties*	*BTI: Status*	*BTI: Management*
Bahrain	39	0.801	26,664	6	5	6.05	4.36
Libya	53	0.755	17,068	7	7	4.49	3.05
Iran	70	0.702	11,764	6	6	3.65	2.31
Tunisia	81	0.683	7,979	7	5	4.98	4.30
Egypt	101	0.620	5,889	6	5	4.82	4.30
Syria	111	0.589	4,760	7	6	3.88	2.77
Yemen	133	0.439	2,387	6	5	4.08	4.04
average	84	0.656	n.a.	6.43	5.6	4.56	3.59

(UNDP 2010; FH 2011; BS 2010)

At first sight, the data seem to support the argument: It is obvious that Egypt, and the other countries included here, are politically 'not free' (Freedom House 2011) as well as 'limited' or 'very limited' in their political and economic transformation (BS 2010). On the other hand, these countries show a significant degree of variance in the state of development, clearly detected in the difference in human development and economic strength between the 'more developed' countries Bahrain and Libya, on the one hand, and the 'less developed' countries Egypt, Syria, and Yemen. Like Iran, Tunisia falls somewhere in the medium range of development in that it has limited per-capita income, but one of the most advanced economies in the region. In short, mass protests can turn into a systemic challenge for authoritarian incumbents in both developed and less developed economies.

It would be equally inaccurate to invoke the people's thirst for democracy and political liberty as the major driving force for continued mass protests. Again, a comparative perspective challenges this assumption.

Table 12.2 identifies those countries that have not become the target of popular mass uprisings, at least not to the extent that protests turned into a systemic threat for incumbents.

Table 12.2: Countries with no mass uprisings in the MENA region: socioeconomic indicators for 2010

	HDI rank	HDI value	GNI/capita (PPP 2008 $)	FH: rights	FH: liberties	BTI: Status	BTI: Management
UAE	32	0.815	58,006	6	5	5.83	5.47
Oman*	n.a.	n.a.	n.a.	6	5	5.53	4.58
Qatar	38	0.803	79,426	6	5	6.06	5.59
Kuwait	47	0.771	55,719	4	5	5.91	4.30
Saudi Arabia	55	0.752	24,726	7	6	4.63	3.94
Jordan	82	0.681	5,956	6	5	5.15	4.46
Algeria	84	0.677	8,320	6	5	4.86	3.92
Morocco	114	0.567	4,628	5	4	4.47	4.02
average	65	0.724	n.a.	5.75	5	5.30	4.53

(UNDP 2010; FH 2011; BS 2010)
*Data on Oman in the Human Development Reports are included under the United Arab Emirates (UAE)

Again, a within-sample comparison of UNDP data shows that both rich/developed and poor/less developed countries have been able to avoid large-scale protest movements. Freedom House data show that more political rights and liberties are granted to the populations of these countries, but they also depict the respective regimes as 'not free' (with the exception of 'partly free' Kuwait and Morocco), and thus as authoritarian as the crisis-ridden states in table 12.1.

The most significant difference between states where mass protests took place and states where they did not can be detected in the BTI's Management Index (MI). The MI is a 'good governance indicator' of sorts and informs on the efficiency and governance capacities of political decision-makers. It measures the quality of the output of decisions on the basis of a 'level of difficulty' with which decision-makers have to cope. The MI serves as a viable indicator to test the people's satisfaction with their politicians, irrespective of the state of democratic transition, and thus the degree of political legitimacy that incumbents enjoy among their populations. It is interesting that, according to the MI, three of the most inefficient regimes—Iran, Syria, and Libya—witnessed the most defiant form of protracted popular mass protests despite serious coercive countermeasures initiated by the states' security forces. In contrast, the countries that triggered the recent wave of uprisings—Tunisia and Egypt—perform relatively well on the MI, similar to Kuwait and Jordan, and ahead of Morocco, Saudi Arabia, and Algeria. In summarizing this brief comparative outline, within-sample variance as much as cross-sample similarities show no clear pattern in the MENA region that allows for a generally applicable assumption that socioeconomic factors—poverty and economic development—or the degree of liberties and state efficiency can be easily employed to explain mass uprisings in Middle Eastern authoritarian regimes.

Hence, with respect to the Egyptian uprising, a good measure of caution is necessary when asking why protracted mass protests took place in that country, while demonstrations remained limited in states with similar levels of political and economic development, such as Jordan, Algeria, or Morocco. One possible way to account for these differences would be to look at specific dynamics during the events. This would include assessing whether the different crisis-management strategies of authoritarian incumbents were either successful in containing the protests or allowed for a dynamic to develop that increased protesters' defiance. While such a comparative study cannot be conducted in this chapter, an alternative explanation identifies a pattern that emerges clearly from the two samples collected above: the particular type of authoritarian regime.

Except for two deviant cases—Bahrain and Algeria—the above sample of Middle Eastern authoritarian regimes shows that presidential republics witnessed a moment of systemic crisis, whereas monarchies did not. Despite considerable differences in social formations, people's grievances, and levels of socioeconomic development, the republics have become vulnerable to popular mass uprisings (Anderson 2011). I argue that the republics in the Middle East lost legitimacy in the eyes of their people not mainly because of their intrinsic authoritarian nature—the relative stability of neighboring states with equally authoritarian rulers defies this assumption—but because of a common feature employed by presidential incumbents to arrange leadership change: the grooming of their sons as political successors. The current uprisings in the MENA region are indicative of a serious crisis of legitimacy into which presidential republics maneuvered themselves by applying a dynastic model of leadership change. Whereas the transfer of power in Syria from Hafez al-Assad to his son Bashar was made possible by elite consent (Stacher 2011), current events prove the general failure of this strategy. Instead of conducting a more substantial comparative analysis here, I will use Egypt as a case study.

Much has been written about the rise of Gamal Mubarak, the president's son, in politics since the early 2000s, and the uncertainty of a hereditary takeover of power that would necessitate the military's consent to the first 'civilian' president in Egypt's modern history (see, for instance, Abdel Aziz and Hussein 2001/2002; Abdelnasser 2004). Less emphasis, however, was put on the people's view of a 'hereditary republic,' not least because public opinion polls in general—and the succession question in particular—were regarded as highly sensitive by the regime's security establishment. Some singular incidents and indicators feed the assumption that there has always been hidden but widespread opposition to the idea of dynastic family rule in Egypt. In 2003, mass demonstrations were held to oppose the U.S.-led military invasion of Iraq. Entirely outside the context of international and regional politics, occasional calls of "Egypt is not a monarchy" were heard, indicating that demonstrators took the rare occasion of a permitted presence in the streets to voice their objections on the succession scenario. The Kefaya (Enough!) movement, established in 2004, raised not only the general demand of democratic change, but also the more specific demand that power not be transferred from one Mubarak to the other (see al-Sayyid 2009; El-Mahdi 2009b). Even at some workers' protests, which had gained momentum since 2006, calls were heard decrying Gamal's ambitions to follow his father into presidential office. Anecdotal evidence has it that many Egyptians, while they might have accepted Gamal's individual qualifications as a potential president, were deeply distressed by the apparent attempt of the political incumbency to create a dynasty. In the eyes of Egyptians, this would mimic traditional monarchical rule, perceived as backward, and thus lead to the erosion of the presumed achievements of the modern Egyptian state.

In conjunction with the smoldering popular distrust of the president's succession plans, people witnessed with equal suspicion the widening gap between their daily concerns and those of a small class of individuals consisting of old-guard party apparatchiks—caught in their security-dominated perspective on state–society relations—and younger cadres of 'crony-capitalists-turned-politicians.' This class lived a privileged life in gated communities, arranged to have urban highways blocked so that they could commute smoothly, consumed imported luxury goods, and dominated decision-making in politics and the economy, while deliberately distancing themselves from the lives of ordinary Egyptians. It was not just the degree of self-enrichment and corruption endemic in this relationship between ruler and ruled that led to the explosion of discontent on the Egyptian street. Rather, people were antagonized by the degree of patronizing arrogance and pretension with which this ruling class, which had made politics itself a 'gated community,' communicated to them that they were tedious subjects of the state, rather than its citizens.

The parliamentary elections in the fall of 2010 provide a telling example of the regime's arrogance toward its people (Albrecht and Kohstall 2010). Masterminded by Ahmed Ezz, one of the younger cadres who rose to power on Gamal Mubarak's coattails, the elections resulted in the ruling National Democratic Party (NDP) winning 94.7 percent of parliamentary seats. Whereas every Egyptian—whether a supporter or opponent of the regime—was aware that the process was flawed, the regime's bigwigs praised the NDP's successful efforts in a 'democratic' election.

Other indicators of the distance between rulers and ruled were the three speeches delivered by Hosni Mubarak in the course of the uprising, on 28 January and 1 and 10 February. It was obvious from the defiant reaction of the majority of protesters that Mubarak ultimately failed to address the people in a way that would help to contain the protests. His threats toward protesters provoked popular defiance among them, and his offers of limited concessions mainly aroused disappointment in a political leader who was more concerned with his historical role as a military-commander-turned-president than his people's grievances. "Down with Mubarak!" was the call behind which a critical mass of participants could unite, individual economic, political, and social demands could be set aside, and large-scale demonstrations could be sustained for more than two weeks. The social heterogeneity of crowds on Tahrir Square and other sites of protest across the country indicates that it was not specific social and economic grievances and interests that drove people to participate, but rather their conviction that Mubarak had to leave office—irrespective of future political and economic change which might work to the advantage of some protesters and the disadvantage of others. Demonstrations could only be sustained as a mass movement encompassing participants from virtually all strata of society because individual interests were put aside. Thus, the unfolding events saw the popular masses on iconic Tahrir Square engage the president in a struggle over the representation of the nation. Whereas people united under the battle cry "The people demand the fall of the regime," it was essentially an anti-Mubarak rally rather than a pro-democracy movement.

Why Did Mubarak Fall?

It remains to be seen whether Egypt experienced a fully fledged breakdown of authoritarianism, or whether the 25 January uprising merely indicated a significant crisis of authoritarian rule at a time of leadership change. Mubarak's fall and the substantial political opening in the months following the 25 January uprising are indicative of the first assumption; the continued presence of the military establishment that has established a junta regime is the most important indicator of the latter. Irrespective of possible future scenarios, the particular form of authoritarian regime change is intriguing: during the 25 January uprising, Egypt experienced a meltdown of political institutions and policing capacities, while the regime's core institution, the military apparatus, reemerged in a more prominent political role as a result.

The 25 January uprising, initiated by the calls of Facebook groups (see chapter 6), started as planned riots, on 25 and 28 January, with limited potential to initiate significant political and economic change. Mona El-Ghobashy argues that it "did not happen because Egyptians willed it into being. It happened because there was a sudden change in the balance of resources between rulers and ruled" (2011, 3). Several protesters who took to the streets at the very beginning of the uprising admitted that they would most likely have returned home if some limited demands had been met, such as the sacking of the minister of interior Habib al-Adli. The success of the 25 January uprising—that is, its continuation beyond the stage of politically motivated riots—was conditional upon the failure of authoritarian containment strategies, which consisted of both coercive measures and limited, and belated, political and economic concessions.

After fierce street battles on 28 January, the Central Security Forces (CSF), which were established to contain demonstrations, disappeared in the early evening of that same day. Whether this was the result of a physical defeat in the battles or—as suspected by many observers—orders given from above with the intention of creating chaos, the consequence was the same: the armed forces were deployed to protect strategically important sites in downtown Cairo. Beyond the disappearance of the CSF and the physical presence of the military, the events of 28 January had, as an immediate consequence, the 'militarization' of the political regime (Albrecht and Bishara 2011; chapter 9 of this volume). This is indicated by Mubarak's appearance in the company of military personnel instead of his regular political entourage: NDP bigwigs, cabinet members, and the bureaucracy's top brass. On 29 January, in a desperate attempt to appease the protesters, Mubarak appointed aides with a strong military background as vice president (former chief of intelligence Omar Suleiman) and as new prime minister (former minister of civil aviation Ahmed Shafik). This move and Mubarak's presence at meetings of the Supreme Council of the Armed Forces (SCAF), aired on state television, gave the impression that he ruled the country in his capacity as the army's commander-in-chief, rather than as the civilian president of the republic.

But it is not only this impressionistic view which suggests that the military—again, with Mubarak in his capacity of commander-in-chief—had taken over. Another immediate consequence of the events between 25 and 28 January was the implosion of the ruling NDP, evidenced by the torching and complete destruction of its headquarters in downtown Cairo. Those politicians who had engineered the day-to-day political affairs of the country—such as the NDP secretary general Safwat al-Sharif, interior minister Habib al-Adli, the president's chief of staff Zakariya Azmi, Gamal Mubarak's henchman Ahmed Ezz, and Gamal Mubarak himself—disappeared from the public scene (Shehata 2011, 31). The fact that the president's son and other individuals attempted to influence the course of events behind the scenes does not mitigate the demise of the NDP as a ruling party. Only hours after the CSF was stripped of its power to coerce, a number of prominent NDP members were identified at Cairo's international airport and prevented from leaving the country. These attempted escapes, in conjunction with the attempt by some NDP cadres to reconquer Tahrir Square by force on 2 February in what came to be known as the 'Battle of the Camel,' indicate that members of the political incumbency were no longer in a position to influence decision-making, which would henceforth be monopolized by the military junta.

Whereas the demonstrations in Tahrir Square and beyond resulted in the meltdown of political institutions and policing capacities, the question of Mubarak's fall must be raised independently of the extent of the popular uprising. Again, it is interesting to put this into a regional comparative perspective where mass protests triggered a violent response from the state's coercive apparatus. This led either to the suppression of protest movements, as in Iran in 2009 and, more recently, Bahrain and Syria, or to the ousting of incumbents through civil war, as in Libya and Yemen. On the other hand, Tunisia and Egypt experienced relatively peaceful regime change.

Looking at the wave of uprisings in the MENA region, a preliminary lesson is that autocrats do not politically survive mass uprisings of this kind without resorting to the use of force. Iran, Bahrain, and possibly Syria are telling examples. However, as the Libyan and Yemeni cases show, violent counterstrategies are not sufficient to avoid the collapse of the regime. The coercive and policing capacities of the state are nonetheless of paramount importance when it comes to increasing a regime's chances of survival, in particular when mass uprisings trounce the domestic security apparatus and when the military must step in to save the regime (Bellin 2012). Hence, the question should read: When and why does the military step in to contain mass uprisings and support an authoritarian incumbent? And when and why does the military choose not to?

The theoretical literature on the military's reactions to mass protest is not very informative, mainly due to the small number of empirical cases. Powell and Thyne recently found that only 3.4 percent of all military interventions from 1950 to 2010 were triggered by popular protests (2011, 253f). Terence Lee offers a game-theory model that assumes fissures within the military to be the decisive factor explaining military intervention (2009). His hypothesis—that militaries accept regime change when confronted by internal conflicts—is challenged, however, by the cases of Tunisia and Egypt, where homogeneous militaries turned against their respective incumbents. Looking at the current uprisings in the MENA region, another empirical pattern can be identified: It seems that the military's perception of the projected longevity of an incumbent's tenure determines its degree of loyalty. Militaries in authoritarian regimes challenged by mass-mobilizing societies support the 'young guns' and dump the 'lame ducks.' Henry Hale wrote in his analysis of the 'color revolutions' in post-Soviet Eurasia: "Massive street rallies are costly to suppress, and the more blood that will likely be shed in doing so, the more likely it is that the military will hesitate to engage in violence on behalf of a lame-duck leader or an unpopular would-be successor" (2005, 141).

Hale's observation on elite cohesion in the authoritarian regimes of the Caucasus and Central Asia can be used to describe the early days of the MENA uprisings. In fact, those states in which incumbents fell (Tunisia, Egypt) or parts of the military apparatus defected from the central command (Libya, Yemen) have had aging leaders in office with an average YIPPI Index ('Years-In-Power-Per-Incumbent') of 32.2 years (Perthes 2002, 103). In all these countries, incumbent presidents have groomed their sons or family members (the in-laws of Tunisia's Ben Ali, for instance) to succeed them—a negative scenario for the military once people took to the streets en masse to demonstrate against both the unpopular ruler and the principle of dynastic succession. By contrast, in Syria and Bahrain (which witnessed mass uprisings), and in Jordan and Morocco (where there were smaller-scale demonstrations), younger authoritarian rulers, with an average YIPPI Index of 11.7 years, have either relied on the loyalty of their armed forces, as in Syria and Bahrain, or prevented demonstrations from turning into popular mass uprisings, as in Jordan and Morocco.

Tarek Masoud speculates that "the military's refusal to back Mubarak was in part a function of its jealousy over the rise of the NDP and the latter's eclipse of the military as the fount of political authority" (2011, 23). The question remains, however, as to why the military was loyal to the political establishment in the 1980s, when the NDP rose to become the unquestioned center of power in the institutional texture of the state. In 1986, the suppression by the armed forces of the CSF uprising was a clear signal that they were loyal to Mubarak, who had acceded to office only five years earlier. Moreover, the NDP had—as a functioning ruling party— already virtually disappeared by 11 February, when Mubarak stepped down. Rather, it is the president's son Gamal who, in the eyes of the military, misappropriated the NDP for the purpose of his own rise in the political establishment and preparation for the presidency.

The coincidence of two factors has contributed to the success of popular uprisings in Egypt and elsewhere in the MENA region: the extent of mass protest, and the timing of imminent leadership change. Research on Syria shows that dynastic leadership change in republics necessitates the consent or profound reconfiguration of political elites (Stacher 2011). Najib Ghadbian opines that Bashar al-Assad's relatively smooth takeover was made possible by an earlier overhaul of the upper brass of the military and security apparatuses, engineered by the ailing Hafez (2001, 625f). Military support for an authoritarian incumbent is particularly important in times of social upheaval, when the coercive capacities of the armed forces prove vital to regime survival. The Egyptian military did not side with the protesters against the regime, of which it is part, but rather against the Mubaraks—father and son. They deposed the former in order to thwart the latter.

The Dawn of Mubarakism, or the Breakdown of Authoritarian Rule?

At the time of writing, it is premature to judge conclusively whether the 25 January uprising marked the beginning of a genuine transition to a more representative political order with consolidated democracy somewhere on the not-too-distant horizon or simply the final days of Mubarak's authoritarian regime. It is possible that a different, but similarly non-democratic, form of political order will rise from the ashes of the Mubarak era. A democratic transition cannot be ruled out, but it remains unlikely. While its result remains obscure, the process of political transformation itself is an intriguing case of political change under authoritarianism. Four interrelated factors inform the nature of the immediate post-Mubarak transformative period: the social dynamics of the uprising; the dominant political discourse; the internal stakes of the interim regime; and the formation of political organizations in the immediate aftermath of the uprising.

When addressing the prospects for Egypt's political future, one must take into account the nature of the popular uprising between 25 January and 11 February 2011. Demonstrators had a unified aim—namely Mubarak's resignation—but no program for political, economic, or social reforms. The fact that the message was limited to a single demand was advantageous at a crucial moment, because large-scale participation could only be sustained when partisan aims and demands were put aside. This has proved problematic in the transitional period, however, because after the pharaoh fell, the united Tahrir movement quickly disintegrated and gave way to the specific grievances of its diverse constituent groups. Sectarian divisions along religious, class-based, ideological, and generational lines are a common feature of a society as complex as Egypt. But the apparent unity of the people in Tahrir Square had fueled expectations that the country's problems could be solved in an equally unified way, and had masked for a few delirious weeks the often contradictory interests and aims that pit Islamists against liberals, rich against poor, workers against business people, young against old, and Muslims against Copts.

The honeymoon of national unity was as great as the disappointment when it ended, and people realized that national unity would not inspire Egyptian society at large except in a very specific revolutionary moment, or in public support of the national football team. The different groups and strata in Tahrir Square developed a strong sense of ownership of the revolution, which increased their stake in what that revolution would achieve. It became inconceivable to participants that their revolution would not usher in the change they desired, which has made consensus building in the ensuing political struggles increasingly difficult. In the months following the uprising, discussions evolved among political groups about the constitution and political institutions to be built, the framework for people's representation in parliament, and the nature of the polity between religion and liberalism. In light of these dynamic discourses and heated debates about the very nature of the state, decisions had to be made by the power brokers in the military that would inevitably—and independently of these decisions' inherent character—identify winners and losers. The losers, however, perceived themselves to be victims of 'counterrevolutionary' forces rather than having been defeated in regular political contestation. It is an ironic twist that the nature of the uprising—an event that created a strong sense of participation and ownership among distinct social groups—has itself undermined consensus-building and compromise as valuable currencies in the transition toward democracy, the form of political rule that requires both consensus *and* institutionalized contestation.

While consensus in the formative period of regime change was undermined by the people's empowerment in Tahrir Square, the idea of contestation—that is, the exchange of conflicting interests and ideas regulated by a commonly accepted legal framework or by informal understandings—has been undermined by nationalism as the dominant trait of political discourse in Egypt since 11 February. This is the second factor that proved detrimental to sustaining a democratic path in the transition period. Nationalist sentiments abound in Egyptian society at large; politicians and commentators have regularly played on them to hold the 'foreign hand' responsible for chaos, political turmoil, and mismanagement. The notion of national unity, however, was also employed in order to discredit specific demands and group interests in Egyptian society. Those were dubbed *fi'awi*, an Arabic term translating as 'sectoral' and implying the negative connotation of partisan interests as opposed to a common, national cause (Sallam 2011, 21). In the public debate, the term was increasingly employed by the military establishment, the government apparatus, and commentators to discredit the demands of a growing workers' movement. Workers had contributed to the 25 January uprising, but in its aftermath identified their own economic grievances as causes for continued protest (see chapter 5). Military officers and members of the government have repeatedly invoked the economic costs of the workers' strikes and activities during economically difficult times (cf. Sallam 2011). Members of opposition parties and civil society have also criticized *fi'awi* activities. Whereas this can be seen as symptomatic of these activists' frustrations with the overall course of the transition process, it ultimately neglects the fact that political cleavages—based on different and conflicting interests in society—constitute one of the core traits of a pluralist, democratic order. A transition period wherein efforts are made to establish a regulatory framework that can channel and resolve conflicting interests offers promise for the evolution of democracy; a political culture which neglects, or defies, conflicting splits and partisan interests does not.

This leads me to the third factor that suggests that the post–11 February period is a phase of authoritarian transformation, rather than a transition from authoritarianism: the internal stakes of the interim regime. While some institutions of the former authoritarian system have disappeared, its historical core—the military and the bureaucratic apparatus—remains intact and continues to dominate political decision-making (Shehata 2011, 31f). It is unlikely that the generals in the SCAF will fully relinquish power in the near future. Rather, they will—at the very least—strive to execute veto powers in political decision-making and enjoy autonomy from civilian political institutions in order to safeguard their economic privileges and their perceived role as guardians of the modern Egyptian state. While the military junta will likely step back once political institutions are reestablished, its management of political affairs in the interim period casts doubt on the military leadership's overall commitment to a pluralist political order.

Like large parts of society, military leaders have been inculcated with a strong sense of nationalism based on their own perception—and, again, wishful thinking—of society as an organic whole which should not break up along sectarian lines or class-based interests. Telling indicators of the military's unwillingness to accept the emergence of a pluralist society are the continued restrictive provisions in the law governing political parties. Similarly, a new law, issued on 23 March 2011, virtually prohibits strikes and thus poses a significant challenge to the creation of civil society pressure groups.

The national unity argument was repeatedly invoked by the military to threaten and prosecute political groups, primarily from the liberal and secular spectrum, that have increasingly criticized the military leadership for its continued human rights violations. For instance, the SCAF responded to the critique of the April 6 movement—famous for its active role in the Egyptian uprising—by accusing it, on 23 July, of inciting social unrest and causing divisions between the army and the Egyptian population. A similar attitude became apparent in the harsh three-year prison sentence handed down on 11 April by a military court to a young Internet activist, Maikel Nabil, who had criticized the armed forces on his blog. The military has shown a commitment to holding political incumbents more accountable to the public. It has not, however, proved itself able to distinguish between violent sectarian tensions, like those that broke out between Copts and Muslims on 7 May in Cairo's neighborhood of Imbaba (see Tadros 2011), and the legitimate formulation of partisan interests in a pluralist society.

A last major factor informing the current transformative period is the formation of political organizations. With the destruction of the authoritarian control mechanisms, civil society was presented with a major window of opportunity. Especially in March and April of 2011, optimism gained ground within the opposition establishment and civil society that the popular uprising could be transformed into a representative, pluralistic—and thus democratic—political order. A myriad of political parties and pressure groups proliferated onto the established landscape of political opposition groups and movements, like the Muslim Brotherhood, the leftist Tagammu' Party, the liberal al-Wafd Party and Democratic Front Party, and several other groups without legal party status, such as the liberal–Islamist Wasat and the socialist–nationalist Karama.

Within a few months after Mubarak's fall, around forty new parties were created, along with hundreds of youth groups and pressure groups. While this phenomenon in itself is indicative of the new opportunities available to an emerging civil society, the course and results of institution-building so far do not support a democratic transition. First, the emerging political organizations replicate some of the ills of the oppositional establishment in the *ancien régime* (see Stacher 2004; Albrecht 2005): Personal rivalries among individuals prevent the formation of strong groups with political leverage, leading instead to fragmentation and internal conflicts. Some of these new organizations seem therefore to serve primarily as political fiefdoms for their leaders and founders. A second problem, which affects the new parties and movements in the liberal–secular–leftist spectrum in particular, is programmatic arbitrariness and diffusion. This is the result of the short timeframe in which political organizations needed to be established if they wished to participate in the elections slated for the period between 28 November and 14 December 2011. Moreover, the aforementioned belief that political distinctions and partisan interests were largely negative—a feeling that is widespread in society and in the current political regime—inspired a party law inimical to programmatic distinction. As a consequence, the political messages of most of the new groups hover around broad concepts to which everyone can subscribe, like 'democracy,' 'human rights,' 'people's empowerment,' 'social justice,' and 'national unity,' without offering any clear ideas or concrete outlines for social, economic, and political reforms.

In the summer of 2011 the political establishment, both on the side of the state and in civil society, prepared to lay the groundwork for new political institutions through parliamentary and presidential elections and the drafting of a new constitution. At this time—when political battle lines were drawn between the military junta and the revolutionary society, Islamists and secularists, liberals and nationalists, and among groups within ideological camps—the new political bodies found themselves engaged in a battle on two fronts. On the one hand, new groups that emerged out of the 25 January uprising had to build their organizational capacity in order to extend their operations beyond Tahrir Square; established parties and movements had to consolidate in the face of increasing fragmentation. On the other hand, these same groups became increasingly engaged in political battles—with the military junta, the political–programmatic opponent, or with counterparts who challenged their bid to represent the constituency. The dilemma for Egyptian politics in the immediate post-Mubarak era was that the formation of a political society requires time, but the logic of transition demands that it be done quickly, to move away not only from the Mubarak era, but also from the military establishment consolidating its authoritarian control over society.

Conclusion

This chapter argued that it is necessary to treat with caution the apparently plausible explanations for the political uprisings in Egypt and other countries in the Middle East and North Africa. Variations in the ways in which these states were affected by and dealt with the recent unrest defy easy narratives which ascribe that unrest to poverty and economic under-development, or the lack of civil rights and political liberties. Internal dynamics within authoritarian regimes constitute a key variable in explaining the course and the result of political uprisings. Bureaucratic republican regimes ultimately lost legitimacy in the eyes of their people, whereas monarchies have remained relatively stable. It also appears that the attempt to establish hereditary succession is a key factor in the erosion of political legimacy; additional research exploring more case studies will be necessary to test this hypothesis in contemporary Middle East politics. This does not explain the specific timing of revolutionary uprisings, but it can elucidate the defiance of protesters who took to the streets with limited expectations, only to inspire and participate in sustained mass movements.

The duration of the tenure of an authoritarian president plays an important role in the decision of the military to support incumbents or to defect under the heavy pressure of popular discontent. Across the region, where developments are still unfolding, the military has so far decided to support presidential 'young guns.' On the other hand, military establishments have either abandoned 'lame duck' presidents or experienced large-scale defections of both rank-and-file soldiers and officers. Egypt is a particularly interesting case demonstrating the importance of the military's role both during the uprising and in the immediate post-Mubarak period. Its political takeover prevented the complete breakdown of the *ancien régime*. The dominance that the military continues to exert over the political process does not entirely preclude the chances of a democratic transition, but it makes a rapid shift to democracy highly unlikely. The military's strong instinct to preserve its privileges and autonomy will prove a stiff challenge to realigning civil–military relations in a way that is conducive to democracy.

The officers in the SCAF appear to support a political system with a greater degree of accountability by political incumbents; the reason for this support might be to avoid the crisis of legitimacy facing Egypt's power brokers during the late Mubarak years. The military is likely, however, to prevent the emergence of a competitive, pluralist political order that would legitimize social divisions. In short, the military will reinvent populism to avoid democracy. Political transformation in Egypt might therefore follow a path inspired by Turkey, with the military apparatus stepping out of the limelight of day-to-day political decision-making, but still enjoying autonomy and a veto over core developments in politics and the economy. Whereas the 'Turkish scenario' is among the most promising future prospects, a measure of caution is again necessary when considering this possible route to democracy. The current situation in Egypt does not mirror contemporary Turkish politics, but rather the 1961 coup—a period in Turkish history when liberal democracy was still some way off. Due to the weak party system and the personalization of politics during the Mubarak era, an alternative short-term scenario is more likely: rather than a parliamentary 'guided democracy,' a presidential system under the tutelage of the military is more likely to mirror the 'Algerian scenario' that unfolded with the reinvigoration of the presidency under Abdelaziz Bouteflika.

The coming months will be decisive in determining whether the empowerment of the people in Tahrir Square will translate into an empowerment of parliament or the rise of a strongman in the presidential office. It is not the election results that will determine Egypt's future, but the progression of political institution-building over the coming months and years.

Notes

1 I am grateful to Dina Bishara and the editors of this volume for their inspiring comments and critique. Karim Malak provided help in researching the topic. All errors and omissions are mine.

2 Data were compiled from several issues of *Al-Ahram Weekly*, online edition, nos. 985 (11–17 February 2010), 989 (11–17 March 2010), 1007 (15–21 July 2010), 1012 (19–25 August 2010), and 1018 (7–18 October 2010).

3 The HDI and BTI values read from a low number, indicating low levels of development, to higher numbers, indicating high levels of development. Freedom House ratings measure 'rights' and 'liberties' from 1 to 7, with the low number indicating a positive judgment. "Bertelsmann Transformation Index," Bertelsmann Stiftung (BS), 2010, www.bertelsmann-transformation-index.de/en/bti/ranking; "Freedom in the World Report 2011: The Authoritarian Challenge to Democracy," Freedom House (FH), 2011, www.freedomhouse.org; "Human Development Report 2010: The Real Wealth of Nations: Pathways to Human Development," United Nations Development Programme (UNDP), 2010, hdr.undp.org

13

Egypt and Beyond: The Arab Spring, the New Pan-Arabism, and the Challenges of Transition

Bahgat Korany

Egypt, a Microcosm?

Though focused on Egypt, the most central and populous country of the Arab world, this book also has a larger thematic focus. Raising the question as to why most of us were surprised by the 2011 mass protests attracts attention to a certain defectiveness in our conceptual lenses. Most of our analyses were obsessed with elite politics, 'authoritarian resilience,' or politics from above. Although decoding the top of the political pyramid is crucial to understanding state–society relations, it is still partial in both senses of the word: incomplete and biased. Egypt is thus studied here as an instance for correction—for balance—as a comparative case study.

As stated in the general introduction, while this book focuses on protest dynamics in Egypt, the analysis approaches these protests as part of a wider phenomenon. Egypt's 'politics from below' is seen as a microcosm. The term 'Arab Spring' is controversial for some people, mainly because this tsunami of protests has not—despite the protesters' cries of *"silmiya"*—been peaceful. In fact, not only in Libya and Syria, but also in Yemen, Bahrain, and even Egypt and Tunisia, it has been quite bloody, principally because the governments in power applied very literally their prerogative of 'monopoly in the use of violence.'

Moreover, the term could also be viewed as simplistic, as it gives the false impression of sameness—that is, that these protests and contexts, from

Yemen to Morocco, are exactly the same. They are not, because of either different patterns in state formation or recent socioeconomic contexts.

However, the term has been popularized by the regional/global media and by the protesters themselves. It basically denotes an urge for change and the beginning of a transition process—revolutionary or evolutionary. This process did start with the overthrow of aging and ailing government elites by a young, disgruntled, and alienated generation. The 'spring' image is thus justified by the presence of these young actors initiating this seismic change, but not by its destination. This destination is still unknown: full democracy, semi-democracy, or some form of soft authoritarianism. This transition process will certainly not be linear or even smooth. The lid of the political pressure cooker has been lifted, and the logical result is a spillover.

This is why, at present, one thing is certain. Political change is in process and some major authoritarian regimes have been overthrown. Furthermore, the regimes that continue to exist have been contested and even delegitimized. The clock cannot go backward and 'Arab exceptionalism'—the idea that, while the rest of world changes, especially politically, the Arab world does not—cannot be reinstituted. In fact, there were protests in the Middle East long before 2011, although they did not generate much interest at the time.

The first decade of the twenty-first century presents a different story: now Middle East protests are not only a national or regional phenomenon; they are at the center of world attention.[1] For instance, in its special annual issue published in December 2011, *Foreign Policy* magazine surveyed the hundred top global thinkers. They came from thirty-eight countries, but the lion's share were from the Arab world. The magazine's opening letter from its chief editor, Susan Glasser, is eloquent on the reason why:

A year ago, Nobel Peace Prize laureate and former International Atomic Energy Agency chief, Mohamed ElBaradei, ranked 20th on *Foreign Policy*'s list of top Global Thinkers as we saluted his audacity in returning to Egypt for the daunting task of bringing democracy to his homeland. 'I see a decaying temple, almost collapsing . . . it will fall sooner than later.' At the time few heralded his prediction, which seemed as much the wishful thinking of a determined activist as an actual guide of events to come.

But of course ElBaradei was right. And this year, we salute him and an extraordinary collection of brave men and women who helped make 2011 the year that democracy—haltingly, incompletely to be sure, but also dazzlingly and astonishingly quickly—came to broad swaths of the Middle East that had long languished under despotism and decay. (3)

The magazine goes on to introduce persons as diverse as Egyptians Alaa Al Aswany, Khairat el-Shatter, and Wael Ghoneim, the Yemeni Tawakul Karman (winner of the 2011 Nobel Peace Prize), and the Tunisian Rached El-Ghannouchi (for "working to reconcile Islamism and democracy"), and to the Saudis Iman al-Nafjan and Manal al-Sharif for "putting Saudi women in the driver's seat" (Glasser 2011, 3–42).

Similarly, *Time* magazine chose as 'person of the year' not a specific individual, but rather the phenomenon of the protester "from the Arab Spring to Athens, from Occupy Wall Street to Moscow" (Andersen 2011/2012, 28). As *Time* explains its choice:

No one could have known that when a Tunisian fruit vendor set himself on fire in a public square in a town barely on a map, he would spark protests that would bring down dictators in Tunisia, Egypt and Libya, and rattle regimes in Syria, Yemen and Bahrain. Or that that spirit of dissent would spur Mexicans to rise up against the terror of drug cartels, Greeks to march against unaccountable leaders, Americans to occupy public spaces to protest income inequality, and Russians to marshal themselves against a corrupt autocracy. (36)

The protesters believed that individual action can bring collective collossal change, and so they poured into the streets to translate this belief into political power. As *Time* notes: "Protests have now occurred in countries whose populations total at least three billion people and the word 'protest' has appeared in newspapers and on line exponentially more this past year than at any other time in history" (36).

The story featured forty-two individuals. Of these, three were from Syria, four from Tunisia, and fifteen from Egypt—twenty-two people from the Arab world, making up more than half of *Time*'s symbols of world protest. The opening article was accompanied by a big photograph of Muhammad Bouazizi, and a quotation from Mannubia Bouazizi, Muhammad's mother: "Muhammad suffered a lot. He worked hard but when he set fire to himself it wasn't about his scales being confiscated. It was about his dignity" (41).

Although issues such as poverty and unemployment were prime triggers, the protest phenomenon cannot be reduced to its economic dimension. In Egypt, in the region, and globally, those acting 'from below' share a different conception of the political, of state–society relations, and of the need for a new social contract:

> It is remarkable how much the protest vanguards share. Everywhere they are disproportionally young, middle class and educated. Almost all the protests this year began as independent affairs, without much encouragement from or endorsement by existing political parties or opposition bigwigs. All over the world, the protesters of 2011 share a belief that their countries' political systems and economies have grown dysfunctional and corrupt—sham democracies rigged to favor the rich and powerful and prevent significant change. They are fervent, small-*d* democrats. Two decades after the final failure and abandonment of communism, they believe they are experiencing the failure of hell-bent megascaled crony hypercapitalism and pine for some third way, a new social contract. (45)

This mass pressure for a new social contract emphasizes the timeliness of bringing in 'politics from below' to supplement rather than supplant 'politics from above,' in order to reduce the gap in state–society relations.

My content analysis of eighty-eight of the slogans most often repeated[2] in Cairo and other Egyptian governorates shows clearly that state and society do not communicate. For instance, while people proclaimed the "end of fear" from repression, the regime was still counting on police forces to disperse the protesters. In the face of the street's basic cry of "Dignity, freedom, and social justice," the regime was offering piecemeal measures, like Mubarak's willingness not to stand for the 2011 presidential elections. Confronted with the most widespread slogan—"Down with the regime!"—Mubarak offered to appoint his head of intelligence as vice president. This gap between elite and street political processes seems to be reflected in the gap between 'politics from above' and 'politics from below' and their divergent assumptions.

For the Arab world continues to be what media specialists dub 'newsworthy,' principally because of the rise of mass protests denting 'Arab exceptionalism' and initiating the 'Arab Spring.' Many of the slogans chanted in Tahrir Square broadened the context from the national to the regional, like the one that urged Mubarak to get on a plane and join Tunisia's ex-president Zin El Abidine Ben Ali in his Saudi exile. Already at this early stage of Egypt's protests, the contentious politics had spread region-wide.

This regional impact even reached such a fossilized regional organization as the League of Arab States (Korany 2012). Consistently respectful of traditional state sovereignty (in other words, exclusive domestic jurisdiction) and the regime policies of member states, the Arab League finally veered off on a different course, with regard first to Libya, then to Syria. In the case of Libya, it came down on the side of protesters and supported 'external intervention' for civilian protection. While much more cautious in its response on Syria, it joined in criticism of regime policies and established formal contacts with the opposition's transitional council. Whatever the motivation and results of such institutional policy restructuring, there does not seem to be a return to the pre-2011 status quo. Although the tide of transformation will not be linear and will have its setbacks and regression, perhaps even moving from one type of authoritarianism to a 'softer' one, 'Arab exceptionalism' seems to be dead.

This final chapter starts by reminding us of these present patterns of change at the national level, not only in Egypt but also in comparison with other Arab political systems (section 1). But since mass contentious politics spread in a domino effect from Tunisia to Yemen, the chapter also raises the question of the emergence of a new type of pan-Arabism (section 2). A short comparison is then made with the traditional state-based pan-Arabism 'from above' and the rhetoric that prevailed in the region with the establishment of the Arab League, Nasserism, and Ba'thism. While it is still too early to give definite answers at this regional level, questions should be raised about the regional spillover of the recent upsurge of politics from below to define the characteristics of this new pan-Arabism and identify its foundations.

Section 3 deals with the nagging issue of the future of the Arab Spring. If it is truly a consequential event, a milestone separating 'before' and 'after,' then what lies ahead? What does the current transition hold for the future? What does the massive literature on transition to democracy (transitology) say in this respect? More importantly, how can the experiences of previous similar transitions—especially in countries of sociopolitical conditions similar to those of Egypt and the Arab world— help in identifying the main transition challenges, and especially the 'best' ways to cope with them?

At the time of writing, change continues unabated at the national level, from Bahrain to Syria.[3] It is to be remembered that the book's introduction identified the following three patterns of contentious politics:

1. Regimes that have fallen, and even their governing elite are on trial or on the wanted list: Tunisia, Egypt, and Libya.
2. Regimes that are desperately trying to cling to power, even at the price of a bloody civil war: Syria, Yemen, and perhaps others will follow.
3. Regimes that have seen the 'writing on the wall.' They are trying to keep themselves in power by offering concessions (or bribes) to their people. These include generous financial offers, such as the $36 billion given to the Saudi people by their king upon his return from medical treatment in the United States. These concessions/bribes also include the suggestion that long-awaited constitutional changes will be implemented, for instance in Morocco, Jordan, and Algeria.

Whatever the pattern of protest, and whatever its immediate outcome, the process has not been easy. In fact it has been extremely costly, in both economic and human terms, as the following figures and tables show:

Table 13.1. Civil disturbances in countries of the Middle East 2011

Country and population	Type of upheaval	Outcome
Tunisia 10.6 million	Mostly peaceful sit-ins requesting greater political freedom, respect for human rights, an improvement in living conditions, and an end to the 50-year dictatorship	The "Jasmine Revolution"—the ousting of President Zin El Abidine Ben Ali
Egypt 82 million	Mostly nonviolent civil resistance calling for an improvement in living conditions, an end to police brutality and corruption, and requesting the fall of the Mubarak regime	Egyptian Revolution—the ousting of President Hosni Mubarak, who is now on trial
Yemen 24 million	Tribal fighting, protests, and riots originally against modifications to the country's constitution and for better living conditions, but which eventually turned into a call for President Ali Abdullah Saleh's resignation	Ongoing

Bahrain 1.2 million	Mostly peaceful protests against unemployment and corruption, originally seeking equal treatment between the ruling Sunni and majority Shi'a populations in addition to greater political freedom	The "Pearl Revolution"—crushed
Libya 6.6 million	Originally protests calling for better living conditions, which led to the occupation of entire cities by the opposition	Civil war
Syria 23 million	Civil resistance and mostly peaceful demonstrations calling for the resignation of the regime, better civil rights, and the lifting of the emergency law	Ongoing

Source: Now Lebanon, http://www.nowlebanon.com/NewsArticleDetails.aspx?ID=302711

As of April 2012, Qadhafi's regime in Libya had fallen, and Ali Saleh of Yemen had resigned in favor of his vice president al-Hady in exchange for amnesty from prosecution.

Figure 13.1. Estimated number of persons killed, as of mid-September 2011

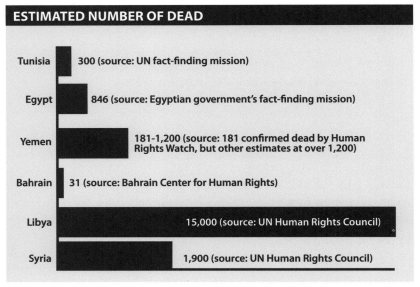

ESTIMATED NUMBER OF DEAD

Tunisia — 300 (source: UN fact-finding mission)

Egypt — 846 (source: Egyptian government's fact-finding mission)

Yemen — 181-1,200 (source: 181 confirmed dead by Human Rights Watch, but other estimates at over 1,200)

Bahrain — 31 (source: Bahrain Center for Human Rights)

Libya — 15,000 (source: UN Human Rights Council)

Syria — 1,900 (source: UN Human Rights Council)

Source: Now Lebanon, http://www.nowlebanon.com/NewsArticleDetails.aspx?ID=302711

As of April 2012, fatalities in Bahrain had reached 86; in Yemen, 2,000; in Syria, 9,000;[4] in Libya, an estimated 50,000.

Figure 13.2. Refugees created by uprisings, as of April 2012

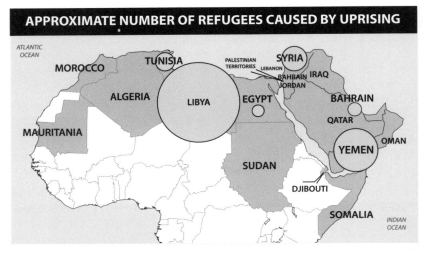

Tunisia: Some 4,000 to Italy (source: Al Jazeera)

Egypt: Minimal

Yemen: 100,000 displaced in Abyan Province (source: UNHCR) with many more undocumented

Bahrain: Minimal

Libya: Over half a million have fled to Egypt, Tunisia, and Italy (source: UNHCR)

Syria: 12,577 between Lebanon and Turkey (source: UNHCR)

Source: Now Lebanon, http://www.nowlebanon.com/NewsArticleDetails.aspx?ID=302711

According to the semi-official Anatolia news agency, there were 18,780 Syrian refugees in Turkey;[5] 10,000 in Lebanon,[6] and 5,000 registered refugees in Jordan;[7] the Jordanian government estimates an additional 80,000 unregistered Syrian refugees.[8]

Table 13.2. Overview of countries affected by civil disturbances

Country	Syria	Egypt	Tunisia	Yemen	Bahrain	Libya
Characteristics/ Type of upheaval	- Civil resistance and mostly peaceful demonstrations - Massive crackdown by the regime - Army defections - Insurgency led by the Syrian Free Army against government forces	Mostly nonviolent civil resistance	Mostly peaceful sit-ins	- Tribal fighting - Protests - Army defections	Mostly peaceful protests	Initial protests calling for better conditions turned violent as a result of the massive crackdown by the regime
Causes	- Dictatorship - Government corruption - Unemployment	- Police brutality - Rigged elections - Government corruption - Unemployment - Grooming of Mubarak's son as his successor - Low minimum wage	- Dictatorship - Government corruption - Unemployment	- Grooming of Saleh's son as his successor - Unemployment - Corruption	- Discrimination against Shi'a - Corruption - Slow pace of democratization	- Dictatorship - Government corruption
Goals	- Resignation of Bashar al-Assad - Democratic reforms - Regime change	Ousting of Mubarak and former ministers	- Ousting of Ben Ali	- Resignation of Saleh - New constitution - Dissolution of parliament	- Constitutional monarchy - Abdication of King Hamad - Equality for Shi'a	- Toppling of the Qadhafi regime - Recognition of the NTC as the legitimate government of Libya by the international community

continued

Table 13.2. continued

Country	Syria	Egypt	Tunisia	Yemen	Bahrain	Libya
Status	Ongoing revolution	Regime toppled	Regime toppled	Revolution has halted after Saleh resigned as president on 28 February 2012	Uprising crushed. However, there are some limited protests	- Regime toppled all over Libya (Qadhafi was killed in October 2011) - Weak control by the NTC over the militias - Secessionist tendencies by the oil-rich eastern region
Population, millions	20.4	81.8	10.5	24.1	1.3	6.6
Minimum number killed	9,000[9]	846[10]	300	2,000[11]	86[12]	30,000–50,000[13]
Deaths per million population	441.1	10.4	20.9	82.9	66.1	7,575.7
Period of unrest	March 2011–present	Jan–Feb 2011	Dec 2010–Jan 2011	Feb 2011–present	Feb–June 2011	Feb 2011–present
Approximate number of refugees caused by uprising	Syrian refugees in Turkey 18,780;[14] in Lebanon, 10,000;[15] in Jordan, 5,000 registered,[16] up to 80,000 unregistered[17]	Minimal	4,000	100,000	Minimal	Over 500,000

continued

Table 13.2. continued

Country	Syria	Egypt	Tunisia	Yemen	Bahrain	Libya
Economic loss	- Disruptions to industrial production, trade, worker remittances, foreign direct investment, and tourism - Estimated GDP growth of 1% in 2011[18]	- Disruptions to industrial production, trade, worker remittances, foreign direct investment, and tourism - Estimated GDP growth of 3–3.5% in 2011–12[19]	- Disruptions to industrial production, trade, worker remittances, foreign direct investment, and tourism, especially from Libyan tourists (18 percent of tourism revenue) - Youth unemployment 30 percent - Estimated GDP growth of 0–1% in 2011[20]	- Disruptions to industrial production, trade, worker remittances, foreign direct investment, and tourism - 200,000 lost jobs - Direct and indirect losses of $5–8 billion - Estimated GDP growth of 3% in 2011[21]	Disruption to tourism	Disruptions to oil production, trade, foreign direct investment. Oil production (95% of the economy) is not expected to return to normal capacity before 6-12 months[22]
Foreign/regional intervention	- Alleged military support from Hezbollah and Iran to the regime - Saudi and Qatari financial support to the protesters - Political and economic sanctions against the Syrian regime by the U.S. and the EU through the "Friends of Syria" conferences	- Threats by the U.S. to cut its $1.3 billion funding to the military - U.S. funding to pro-democracy NGOs - Alleged Gulf funding of NGOs[23] -Alleged Saudi funding to Salafis	French political backing of Ben Ali	Initial Saudi political backing of Saleh, then supporting the handing of power to his deputy al-Hady on medical grounds and in exchange for no legal prosecution	- Saudi political and military backing of the Bahraini king - Iranian and Hezbollah political backing of the Shiite protesters	- NATO political, military, and financial backing of the rebels - Emirati, Qatari, and Jordanian military support against Qadhafi - Serbian and African mercenaries fighting for Qadhafi

continued

Table 13.2. continued

Country	Syria	Egypt	Tunisia	Yemen	Bahrain	Libya
Regime adaptability/ Achieved so far	- Strong resistance to stepping down but promises of political reform - Referendum on a new constitution on 27 February 2012	- Mubarak stepped down after initial slow response to demands for reform; followed by his prime minister Ahmed Shafik - Armed forces assumed power - Suspension of constitution - Dissolution of parliament - Disbanding of the NDP and liquidation of its assets - Prosecution of Mubarak and his sons - Parliamentary elections - An elected constitutional panel - Opening the door for presidential elections	- Ben Ali stepped down after initial slow response to demands for reform; followed by his prime minister Rachid al-Ghannouchi - Disbanding of political police - Disbanding of RDC and liquidation of its assets - Elections held 23 October 2011	Despite an assassination attempt, Saleh strongly resisted stepping down before the end of his mandate. However, he resigned in exchange for amnesty from prosecution	- Strong resistance by King Hamad to Shi'a demands, but promises of reform - Establishment of the Bahrain Independent Commission of Inquiry and National Dialogue - Gift of 1,000 Bahraini dinars per family[24]	Qadhafi strongly resisted stepping down despite the fall of Tripoli to the rebels, but was killed at the end of October 2011

Wikipedia, "The Arab Spring," http://en.wikipedia.org/wiki/Arab_Spring

http://www.economist.com/blogs/dailychart/2011/03/unrest_middle_east

http://www.nowlebanon.com/NewsArticleDetails.aspx?ID=302711

http://blogs.worldbank.org/prospects/what-comes-after-the-arab-spring-prospective-developments-through-2013

Although this book has focused on tracing 'politics from below' in Egypt, it is clear from the above tables and figures that the whole region is in flux. Protests are the order of the day, but with different results. Why?

While a detailed answer to this basic question requires a book of its own, at least three factors can be succinctly mentioned to account for basic differences in results:

1. Although we lump Arab countries into a bloc, their types of social structure and pattern of state formation differ. These differences tend to determine both regime characteristics and opposition patterns. For instance, the presence of a sizable middle class in Tunisia or Egypt contrasts with Syria's sectarian divisions, Yemen's tribal politics, or Libya's institutional void.

2. Of much more immediate impact is the composition and position of the armed forces. The refusal of the armed forces of Tunisia or Egypt to fire on protesters played a key role in toppling the heads of those regimes.

3. Of equally immediate impact are the (financial) resources the governing regime controls and uses. This capacity to bolster army and police and co-opt opposition (both domestic and external) applies most clearly to the oil-producing countries of the Gulf Cooperation Council. Recent data show that the national combined domestic product of these rentier countries rose from $334 million in 2002 to $1.1 trillion in 2010, and is estimated to reach $1.35 trillion in 2011, a fourfold increase over nine years.[25] Bahrain's sectarian conflict notwithstanding, the continuing growth rate of these economies and their immediate cash flow allow them to meet some of the opposition's demands, at least for the time being. But even these financially rich countries have to find more durable means to cope with a regional spillover.

2

This regional spillover is leading to a new form of pan-Arabism, one that emerges 'from below.' We know that the ideal of pan-Arabism—in its different variations—was engendered 'from the top,' intellectually and/or politically. Thus its anti-Ottomanism after the first World War was the work par excellence of Arab intellectuals of the Levant, many of them influenced by western patterns of nationalism (Khalidi et al. 1993;

Tibi 1997). Politically, the Arab League adopted and paid lip service to pan-Arabism in the 1940s; this was the work of the most traditional and conservative Arab regimes, from Saudi Arabia to the monarchies of Jordan and Egypt. Even pan-Arab Ba'thism and charisma-based Nasserism in the 1950s and the 1960s came very much from the top, avowals to the contrary notwithstanding. These last models were obsessed— because of the primacy of the 'anti-imperialist' historical context—with direct control from above and did little to promote individual political participation or democratization.

This from-above bias in favor of direction and politics of command explains the easy decline of these last versions of pan-Arabism. Thus massive disillusionment with Nasserism followed the 1967 'setback.' Similarly, Ba'thist pan-Arabism vanished when it was taken over by the military establishment in Syria and Iraq. In fact the two wings of the party became trapped in an internecine war against each other (Kienle 1990). Egypt's 1978 signing of the Camp David agreement for a unilateral peace with the Arabs' arch-enemy, Israel, and Iraq's 1990 invasion of Kuwait confirmed the bankruptcy of this type of state-based pan-Arabism. An Arab feeling of togetherness continued, however, but as a cultural phenomenon amid a context of an Arab "balance of weakness and cognitive disarray" (Korany 2010, 34–42).

This cultural togetherness helped the region to continue to act as an overall 'sound system' where transnational interaction patterns reverberated across states' political borders (Noble 2008). Though still under-analyzed, this cultural version of pan-Arabism was reinforced from the 1970s onward with the rise of the Gulf region and petropolitics. This change stems from the massive increase in oil prices and accumulation of petrodollars in countries that needed to build almost everything, from government bureaucracy to roads. Since there was massive underemployment and ill-paid labor in countries such as Egypt, Palestine, Jordan, Syria, Lebanon, Morocco, and Sudan, a huge influx of Arab labor migrated to the Gulf. But this inter-Arab contact at the individual level was motivated by the economic exchange of 'wages for labor' rather than by feelings of pan-Arabism, especially in its political Nasserist/Ba'thist version. On the contrary, most Gulf countries based their political legitimacy on fighting pan-Arabism (for example, the Egyptian–Saudi War in Yemen 1962–67; the raging Arab cold war between 'revolutionary' and 'conservative' regimes from the late 1950s onward). Thus while political pan-Arabism was failing,

Arab feelings of togetherness or cultural pan-Arabism was surviving. In the 1990s, it got a valuable boost.

One phenomenon that built on cultural pan-Arabism and in fact reinforced it is related to communication technology: the rise and diffusion of twenty-four-hour news channels by means of satellites such as Al Jazeera or Al Arabiya. These have been called "one of the most important Arab political parties" (Abdullah 2010, 59–84). The last decade witnessed an explosion of Arab transnational broadcasting. In the five-year period from 2004 to 2009, the rate of increase reached 250 percent (UNDP, forthcoming). By July 2011, there were about 1,100 satellite channels, of which 600 were free. They reach 90 percent of households that have electricity, or about 250 million people, numbers that are bound to increase thanks to satellite program availability on cell phones (UNDP, forthcoming).

The present, post–January 2011 pan-Arabism, however, is different. It is not only much more politicized than the wage-oriented or satellite-based manifestations, but it is also especially proactive. It is not based on a temporary relationship of wage-for-labor exchange or a passive audience in front of television screens. The circulation of its slogans during mass protests against incumbent regimes — "Leave!" or "The people want to bring down the regime!" — indicate an 'agent' function: the people, and especially youth, are triggering the change.

We know that people under thirty years of age represent no less than 60 percent of the population in most of the countries of this region. This youth bulge (Korany 2010, 197–203) is both an influential mass and especially an active agent shaping the future (Kandil 2006; Mosaad 2000). It is thus logical that their action — building on earlier contentious politics by other groups — results in seismic change in state–society relations across the region. In a regional context where state authorities used to feel supreme, successful youth protests against police brutality ended by eliminating the barrier of fear. With the collapse of authoritarian regimes, their action also eliminated the powerlessness felt by civil society organizations (CSOs), too long co-opted, intimidated, or restricted by the regimes in power.

For CSOs are not a new phenomenon in the region. On the contrary, the last twenty years or so saw an explosion of these "overall voluntary, [supposedly] non-profit and autonomous organizations that fall between the family and the state" (as defined in Kandil 2010, 45). By 2007, their number ranged from 17 in Qatar to 24,600 in Egypt, 37,000 in Morocco, and as many as 70,000 in neighboring Algeria. In 2007 there were 161,787

CSOs across the Arab region, according to the official data of the relevant ministry in each country (49).

These official statistics may be inflated, for many of these CSOs were co-opted or even created by some governments, establishing what are sarcastically called 'GNGOs' (governmental non-governmental organizations). Some of these CSOs were family-based, acting to amass social prestige or interested in securing external funds, and many were not as effective as they would have liked to be or could have been (Abdelrahman 2004a). But they were there, and many were ready to act (Kandil 2011).

Youth activated many of these CSOs, especially young people suffering from restriction or intimidation. In Tunisia, Bouazizi's self-immolation acted as a spark; in Egypt, it was the actions of such groups as April 6, We Are All Khaled Said, lesser-known underground ones like the Revolutionary Socialists, some of the youth wings of the Muslim Brotherhood, Kefaya, and the ElBaradei campaign (Ghoneim 2012).

In other words, leadership in the Arab Spring came from new civil society organizations working outside the officially sanctioned and well-established mainstream. These new groups were primarily youth-based. Their 'youthfulness' explains why their tools of communication and networking were different, centering on the new media.[26]

These new media—including the Internet and interactive blogs—are becoming an "off-shore democracy" in the region (Abdullah 2010, 75) which escapes both hierarchy and governmental control. Their influence comes from their capacity to provide an unlimited supply of information almost as events happen. Although the number of Internet users in the Arab world is still modest (13 percent to 15 percent in 2008) and they are still hampered by illiteracy (computer and otherwise), their number is fast growing. It reached 57,425,046 in 2010 with a rate of increase for the period 2000–2009 of 1,642 percent (UNDP, forthcoming). As of 2011, 85 percent of the Arab press organizations have electronic sites (al-Ahram, al-Shuruq, Al-Masry Al-Youm, al-Sabei, al-Hayat), in addition to those that are solely electronic, like Elaph.

The impact of the new media is not only quantitative or limited to people who are electronically oriented. Many blogs, especially those stationed in areas of conflict where traditional media are not present (as during the protests in Syria or Libya), are used and diffused by opinion leaders through the printed media and transnational satellites such as The New York Times, CNN, or Al Jazeera. The Egyptian blogger Wael Abbas is an example of how widely the impact of new media is felt. He was selected in 2008 for the Knight International Journalism Award given by the International Center for Journalists. This was the first time a blogger, rather than a traditional journalist, had won this prestigious journalism award (Abdullah 2010, 77). And in fact one of the videos of police brutality that Abbas posted on his blog was used as evidence to convict the police officers involved.

Governments pursued these bloggers, of course, but with limited success. It is not a coincidence that, in the list of countries cited by Reporters Without Borders, Egypt, Tunisia, Saudi Arabia, and Syria figured prominently because of their pursuit of cyberdissidents.[27]

The use of new media as a youth-privileged tool of communication and networking continued to grow and reinforced the impact of 'politics from below.' According to Gamal Eid, executive director of the Arabic Network for Human Rights Information, by July 2010 there were 750,000 bloggers in the Arab world, 300,000 of whom were active. It is also estimated that 57 percent of Arab students aged thirteen to twenty-eight in the UAE and Jordan get their news from websites (Feuilherak 2011).

New media appear to provoke a snowball effect (Howard 2010). Because they have been successful in fueling the revolution, more and more people are turning to them. According to the executive chairman of Egypt's National Body of Communication, Amr Badawy, the number of Facebook users mushroomed from 4.4 million in October 2010 to 7.5 million in April 2011 and eight million in June 2011, bringing Egypt to rank twenty-second globally and first in the Arab world in Facebook membership. The increase in Internet use is even more impressive: according to an article in *Al-Masry Al-Youm* on 24 July 2011, it rose from 27 million in January 2011, two weeks before the uprising, to 47 million in March—the highest rate of increase in Egypt's history.

It is thus clear that a quiet revolution from below preceded the one that toppled the president. Alhough the new media did not cause the overthrow of the regime, they certainly fueled the Arab Spring.

3

The Arab Spring is a 'big bang' in political transformation (see Korany 2010 for an analysis of "big bangs" versus "incremental or gradual change," 11–20, 197–203). But the long-term impact of this tsunami of region-wide protests and flood of contentious politics will depend on what happens the 'day after,' notably the transition to a different—democratic—political regime.

In general, despite being widely studied, contentious politics is ignored in corresponding research on democratic transition.[28] Moreover, compared to Latin America, research on transition in the Arab world is still modest. Whereas the massive Latin American literature has gone from the analysis of democratic transition (or transitology) to democratic consolidation (or consolidology), similar analysis on the Arab world is still groping. As stated in the introduction, such transitology research in the Arab world has been diverted by the excessive attention given to authoritarian resilience/persistence and 'politics from above.' But that research did begin, in Arabic or English, without that overemphasis (see, for example, CAUS 1984; Al-Ahram Center for Political and Strategic Studies 1989, 285–312; 1991, 283–92; 1992, 233–267 [these volumes allow the progression of transitology research to be traced systematically]; the seven published volumes of Kawari and Maddy 2009; Brynen, Korany, and Noble 1995; Salame 1994; Anderson 1999; ARI 2010).[29]

In this transitology research, both Arab and foreign, the overall frame of reference has been Huntington's seminal periodization of the waves of democratization (Huntington 1991; Doorenspleet 2005). Despite some differences concerning the exact number of democratization waves and when they began, all agree that the rate of democratization has been accelerating worldwide. A concomitant to this finding—also emphasized by Arab researchers—is the Arab lag in this respect.

The success and primacy of the contentious politics of 2011 helped to overcome this lag, and consequently shifted interest and analysis back toward the challenges of transition. A whirlwind of panels and workshops ensued, to the extent that in a single week of June 2011, Cairo witnessed two simultaneous international conferences on the problems of transition.[30] Both conferences focused on (a) the impact the Arab Spring could have on the huge body of literature about transitology and the analyses and findings of that research; and (b) how this Arab Spring could profit from the experiences of those who had already experienced similar challenges, especially those countries from the Global South with sociopolitical conditions similar to those of the Arab world.

From the outcomes of these two conferences, we can tease out some findings concerning both the challenges of transition and how to face up to them. Three synthetic conclusions can be singled out:

1. One of the first challenges to appear frequently in both academic analysis and the narrative of political experiences is the widening gap between expectations and achievements, especially after the revolution. People in Tunisia, Egypt, or elsewhere, have waited for too long and believe that once old regimes have fallen, their demands—for employment, or improvement of heath or education services, for example—will be met almost immediately. Unfortunately, demands are soaring at a time when the capacity of the system to respond instantly is being constantly reduced. The danger of this gap continuing is that mass disillusionment could follow, and that a counterrevolution could even succeed. The situation in both Egypt and Tunisia may be even more problematic, since those who presently govern are not those who led the revolutions, and so miscommunication and mistrust could plague the transition process.

2. Another consensual finding is, of course, the dire need for immediate resources so that the transition can proceed smoothly, or at least successfully. Although economic resources can be marshaled to satisfy daily needs, the type of resources most needed are primarily political. Those in power must gain the trust of the governed, who are predictably mistrustful after a period of misrule, demagogy, and excessive corruption.[31] They must also—and especially—be able to negotiate differences and manage crises. For instance, the new governments in Egypt, Tunisia, or Libya have to tackle delicate issues such as constitutional reform and the conduct of elections. These are not only complex but can also be divisive, for they are often linked to issues such as the role of religion in society, civil–military relations, and the role of a private sector rife with corruption where the line between business and politics has been blurred. Political skill is a commodity very much in demand when facing up to the challenges and avoiding the breakdown of the transition.

3. Although meeting challenges successfully will prevent the collapse of the transition process, it will not guarantee the final result. Among the roadblocks is the fact that the transition to democracy is far from linear, and might even be reversed. A key to success, however, seems to be the establishment and maintenance of a unified front—a re-creation of the united national front that prevailed during the earlier period of the fight for independence from colonial powers. Indeed, some activists and analysts even go so far as to consider the present fight for democratic transition as equivalent to a second fight for independence.

In fact, activists and researchers from Latin America talk about 'pactos' or national pacts. Ali Al-Kawari and his team, after twenty years of directing the Arab project on democratization, talk about the prerequisite of constituting a 'historic bloc' to enable and protect the democratic transition (Kawari and Maddy 2009, 217–42). Admittedly, this consensus-building for the 'national pact' is not as easy as it sounds, and even involves parting ways with those comrades in government or civil society who do not share a commitment to the basic principles of democratization. It is also much more fixed on the short term, since it does not tackle structural problems such as the (tribal) basis of the state or the failure of (traditional) political parties. The 'national pact' can, however, still be a positive strategy for replacing exclusionary political culture with an inclusionary alternative. It is also a laboratory in which to educate all parties on ways to tolerate or negotiate differences and build compromises. These skills are necessary prerequisites for the democratic transition to avoid breakdown. Building national pacts is thus a means and a process by which opposing groups can learn to work together to formulate the kind of democracy they are building and to iron out its obstacles (Kawari and Maddy 2009, 31–94, 217–42).

National pact-building could also be a strategy of hope, an indication that things are working and that a new start is feasible. It thus has great value in the context of post-revolution flux, of group fragmentation and a rocky transition process. It can keep revolutionary momentum on track and steer it away from the unknown. Indeed, in the present Arab context, national pacts and historic blocs for democracy could help avoid the trap of Libya or Iraq; they could even indicate to those in Yemen or Syria that a workable alternative to despotic regimes—other than the collapse of authority or the failure of the state—is available and even attainable. Successful national pacts are a way out of a disempowering straitjacket that reduces choice to either autocracy or the unsettling and destructive uncertainty of a directionless or absent state.

In fact, the unexpected results of the survey by the Al-Ahram Center for Political and Strategic Studies in March and April 2012 cannot be explained except by this urge to save Egypt from the chaos of uncertainty. As many as 80 percent of those surveyed expressed their trust in the SCAF, followed by 60 percent for the justice system—two prominent institutions embodying state authority. Moreover, and as if to confirm their support for these symbols of state authority, 69 percent did not trust any of the existing political parties and as many as 85 percent would not vote for any of them to govern Egypt.[32]

Conclusion

As the book's title says, Egypt and the rest of the Arab world are in the midst of a wave of contentious politics and a revolutionary tide. Whatever its outcome, the events in Tahrir Square constitute a milestone in contemporary Arab history. These events are consequential, separating 'before' and 'after.' People feel empowered. All surveys confirm this datum.

Even in moderate 'autocracies' such as Mubarak's Egypt, only 25 percent felt that they had freedom of expression before the fall of the regime. After 25 January, the figure rose by 63 percent: now 88 percent of people surveyed feel unrestricted in expressing their views—all their views. Whereas some feel more insecure during the transition than they did before (64 percent compared to 25 percent), a huge majority—93 percent—are proud of what happened, and indeed of being Egyptian. More people are becoming interested in politics: 75 percent affirmed that they spend more time watching television news programs, and 39 percent spend more time reading the newspapers. Political programs have risen from fourth place to first in popularity, and the number of those watching films and soap operas has drastically declined. To confirm this rising politicization of the mass public, 85 percent of those surveyed said that they intend to vote in presidential elections and 80 percent in parliamentary elections. (Before the revolution, barely a fifth of eligible voters took part in national elections, and these official figures were contested). People now feel that their 'votes not only count, but can shape the future' (Shorouk newspaper survey, July 2011).

The future will tell us whether this revolutionary moment can be maintained (Teorell 2010), how the crucial transition will be managed, how long it will take to establish an alternative political system—and not a form of hybrid authoritarianism (Levitsky and Way 2010) or clientalistic politics (Kitschett and Wilkinson 2007). Will a successful transition allow the Arab Spring to have transformed Arab exceptionalism into a myth of the past?

Notes

1   The 'instant research' and abundance of books about the Arab Spring already in print and soon to be published indicate that Egypt's revolt is fast becoming a "global

case study," from the Koreas to Zimbabwe. Note what this fifty-three-year-old tutor in Yangon, Myanmar's biggest city, said: "Tears welled in my eyes when I watched the Egyptians overjoyed after Mubarak left. I want to tell them that your fight has paid off but we don't know where our future lies." The tutor spoke on condition of anonymity for fear of retribution from the authorities (Christopher Torchia, "Egypt Revolt Becomes Global Case Study," Associated Press, 19 February 2011).

Websites also proliferate. Not only do world media networks now treat events in Egypt as front-page news, but many have established special sections on their websites to allow their audience to follow the evolution of the Arab Spring almost hour by hour.

Ongoing coverage includes collected news and commentary by a number of news agencies and think tanks:

- "Unrest in the Arab World," Carnegie Endowment for International Peace
- "Issue Guide: Arab World Protests," Council on Foreign Relations
- "Arab Spring," *The Economist*
- "Middle East Protests," *The Financial Times*
- "Arab and Middle East Unrest," *The Guardian*
- "Rage on the Streets," *Hurriyet Daily News and Economic Review*
- "Middle East Unrest," *The National*
- "The Arab Revolution," Spiegel.de
- "The Middle East in Revolt," *Time*

Other resources include:

- "The Shoe Thrower's Index: An Index of Unrest in the Arab World," *The Economist*, 9 February 2011
- Interview with Tariq Ramadan: "We Need to Get a Better Sense of the Trends within Islamism," Qantara.de, 2 February 2011
- "Tracking the Wave of Protests with Statistics," RevolutionTrends.org
- "Arab Spring," Best of the Web Directory

Live blogs on the subject are also plentiful, among them:

- "Middle East," *Al Jazeera English*
- "Middle East Protests," *BBC News*
- "Arab and Middle East Protests Live Blog," *The Guardian*
- "Middle East Protests," "The Lede" blog at *The New York Times*
- "Middle East Protests Live," *Reuters*

Moreover, less than four months after Mubarak resigned, two French books were published in Paris, one by the two Cairo correspondents of *Le Figaro* and the second by Robert Solier, editor-in-chief of *Le Monde Diplomatique*.

Similarly, the six characteristics that Dina Shehata uses to describe protest movements in Egypt could apply equally well to other Arab countries: (1) the protests take place outside the framework of established political parties and other traditional organizations; (2) these new movements count on direct contention/ protest action; (3) the leaders of these new protest movements are in their thirties, born in the 1970s; (4) these new movements are based on trans-ideological pacts or solidarities; (5) they managed to attract and politicize a new generation of activists; (6) the new movements lack systematic coordination among themselves (Shehata 2010, 11–20).

2   It is time that Middle East scholars (even those bent on quantitative methodology) begin to content-analyze such unconventional research sources as slogans, graffiti,

and artistic symbols. These reflect more faithfully the 'mood' of the street and make the analysis of politics from below more rigorously reflective of its subject matter.

3   Not all Arabs are Muslims, and in fact the majority of Muslims are non-Arabs. Some research about Muslims, however, applies also to Arabs. Indeed, Arabs are perceived as the core of the Muslim world. The holiest Muslim sites are Arab, starting with Mecca, toward which the faithful among the 1.3 billion Muslims around the world turn five times a day. Consequently, recent research findings on lack of Muslim 'exceptionalism'—even in the field of religiosity—apply to the great majority of Arabs. According to M. Steven Fish:

> There does appear to be a difference in religiosity between Muslims and non-Muslims: Muslims are more religious. But the difference is modest and ranges between diminutive and non-existent. . . . The one instance in which we see a more dramatic difference is in mosque attendance among Muslim men. . . . Muslim men are more likely to attend religious services than are Christian men. But Muslim women are less likely to attend than are Christian women. (Fish 2011, 45)

4   UN High Commissioner for Human Rights, http://in.reuters.com/article/2012/03/27/syria-un-idINDEE82Q0I120120327

5   http://www.chinadaily.com.cn/world/2012-04/02/content_14972391.htm

6   http://www.guardian.co.uk/commentisfree/2012/mar/07/syria-refugees-tensions-lebanon?INTCMP=ILCNETTXT3487

7   http://www.news24.com/World/News/Syria-Refugees-brace-for-more-bloodshed-20120312

8   http://www.cbsnews.com/8301-501713_162-57396036/un-says-230000-people-have-fled-syria-violence/

9   UN High Commissioner for Human Rights, http://in.reuters.com/article/2012/03/27/syria-un-idINDEE82Q0I120120327

10 Egyptian government's fact-finding mission, www.thedailynewsegypt.com/human-a-civil-rights/fact-finding-mission-says-846-dead-and-6467-injured-in-egypts-uprising.html

11 http://www.google.com/hostednews/ap/article/ALeqM5h-RahixpQufEQj9Qg30UxpYourDA?docId=8bb4ea3a38954ebd9d1a25afd4c56278

12 http://en.wikipedia.org/wiki/Casualties_of_the_2011%E2%80%932012_Bahraini_uprising

13 Estimates are of thirty thousand dead and twenty thousand missing. Reuters, www.uk.reuters.com/article/2011/08/31/uk-libya-casualties-idUK-TRE77U17420110831. However, these figures were questioned by *The New York Times* on 17 September 2011 in its article, "Libya Counts More Martyrs Than Bodies," http://www.nytimes.com/2011/09/17/world/africa/skirmishes-flare-around-qaddafi-strongholds.html?_r=2&partner=rss&emc=rss&pagewanted=all

14 http://www.chinadaily.com.cn/world/2012-04/02/content_14972391.htm

15 http://www.guardian.co.uk/commentisfree/2012/mar/07/syria-refugees-tensions-lebanon?INTCMP=ILCNETTXT3487

16 http://www.news24.com/World/News/Syria-Refugees-brace-for-more-bloodshed-20120312

17 http://www.cbsnews.com/8301-501713_162-57396036/un-says-230000-people-have-fled-syria-violence/

18 al-Shorouq, http://www.shorouknews.com/ContentData.aspx?ID=536748

19 al-Shorouq, http://www.shorouknews.com/ContentData.aspx?ID=536748
20 al-Shorouq, http://www.shorouknews.com/ContentData.aspx?ID=536748
21 al-Shorouq, http://www.shorouknews.com/ContentData.aspx?ID=536748
22 al-Shorouq, http://www.shorouknews.com/ContentData.aspx?ID=536748
23 *al-Ahram*, http://www.ahram.org.eg/The-first/News/100560.aspx
24 Agence France-Presse, "Bahrain's King Gifts $3,000 to Every Family," www.
    france24.com/en/20110211-bahrains-king-gifts-3000-every-family
25 Naser Ben-Ibrahim, GCC Secretary General for Economic Affairs, interview with
    the author, Riyadh, 5 December 2011. See also http://www.deccanherald.com/
    content/123657/banner-300x250.swf
26 The most recent introduction to this under-researched but increasingly impor-
    tant aspect of the impact of new technology on politics is Philip N. Howard's
    2010 book, *The Digital Origins of Dictatorship and Democracy*. See especially "Revo-
    lution in the Middle East Will Be Digitized" and the analysis of "networked
    effervescence" (3–13).
27 Reporters Without Borders, "Press Freedom Index 2011/2012," http://en.rsf.org/
    press-freedom-index-2011-2012,1043.html
28 This literature is simply voluminous, an instant and prosperous industry. But
    most of it is flawed in being over-synchronic rather than longitudinal, neglecting
    specifics of state formation, evolution of (informal) institutions, characteristics of
    class, and societal processes (for example, the state of the middle class). A critical
    assessment of this literature is beyond the objectives of this chapter, and even of a
    book centered on contentious politics in the 'pre-transition stage.'
29 It is significant to note that one of the early Arab publications on democratization
    is the 1984 Center for Arab Unity Studies volume of almost a thousand pages. It
    consists of the papers presented at a conference that had brought together Arab
    researchers studying their countries. But when they tried to meet to present and dis-
    cuss their papers, no Arab country would receive them; they finally met in Cyprus.
        Notable also is Anderson's book (1999), which draws the reader's attention to
    a political science article published on the subject by Dunkwart Ruslow in 1970.
30 The first conference (4–6 June 2011), organized by the American University in
    Cairo, was primarily focused on academic research. It brought Arab researchers
    who were in Tahrir Square together with world scholars who had done research on
    problems of transitology, including Philip Schmitter and Alfred Stephan.
        The second conference was also held in Cairo, from 5–8 June 2011. It was orga-
    nized by UNDP and was much more centered on policy-making, inviting those
    who had actually led democratic transition, including the former presidents of
    Chile and Indonesia, the former foreign minister of Brazil, and an aide of South
    Africa's former president, Nelson Mandela.
31 Indeed, a positive response to popular demands to raise minimum wages, while
    long overdue, could generate a sociopolitical problem. If productivity does not
    increase at the same time as wages, prices could soon inflate, eroding purchasing
    power and thereby undoing any financial gain. The poor could feel cheated and be
    even more mistrustful of decisions coming from the top.
32 Significantly, when those surveyed were pressed to make a choice, they usually
    opted for new political parties: 9.1 percent selected the (Islamist) Freedom and Jus-
    tice Party; the Wafd Party came a distant second with 2.7 percent; and 1.5 percent
    opted for "Youth Movements" (Gamal Sultan survey, *al-Ahram*, 24 August 2011).

Appendices

Two appendices are included.

The first presents the most recent socioeconomic data about Egypt. This quantitative landscape fueled protests, not only in Egypt but in the region. Due to lack of space, Egypt is compared with only a few Arab countries with similar sociopolitical status on the development scale.

The second appendix presents two of Mubarak's speeches as well as the speech read by intelligence chief and then vice president Omar Suleiman to announce Mubarak's resignation. These now constitute significant historic documents.

As noted in the book's introduction and concluding chapter, these speeches indicate the gap between those political actors 'above' and those 'below,' between elite politics and street dynamics, between an aging/ailing mindset and a growing youth bulge. Consequently, these speeches—even if as short as the twenty-eight-second one announcing Mubarak's resignation—decode this very special moment in the country's society and politics, and point to its implications for the future.

Appendix 1

Human Development Report 2011

Sustainability and Equity:
A Better Future for All

Explanatory note on 2011 HDR composite indices

Egypt

HDI values and rank changes in the *2011 Human Development Report*

Introduction

The *2011 Human Development Report* presents 2011 Human Development Index (HDI) values and ranks for 187 countries and UN-recognized territories, along with the Inequality-adjusted HDI for 134 countries, the Gender Inequality Index for 146 countries, and the Multidimensional Poverty Index for 109 countries. Country rankings and values in the annual Human Development Index (HDI) are kept under strict embargo until the global launch and worldwide electronic release of the Human Development Report. The 2011 Report will be launched globally in November 2011.

It is misleading to compare values and rankings with those of previously published reports, because the underlying data and methods have changed, as well as the number of countries included in the HDI. The 187 countries ranked in the 2011 HDI represents a significant increase from the 169 countries included in the 2010 Index, when key indicators for many countries were unavailable.

Readers are advised in the Report to assess progress in HDI values by referring to Table 2 ('Human Development Index Trends') in the Statistical Annex of the report. Table 2 is based on consistent indicators, methodology and time-series data and thus shows <u>real changes</u> in values and ranks over time reflecting the actual progress countries have made.

For further details on how each index is calculated please refer to Technical Notes 1-4 in the 2011 Report and the associated background papers available on the Human Development Report website.

Human Development Index (HDI)

The HDI is a summary measure for assessing long-term progress in three basic dimensions of human development: a long and healthy life, access to knowledge and a decent standard of living. As in the 2010 HDR a long and healthy life is measured by life expectancy, access to knowledge is measured by: i) mean years of adult education, which is the average number of years of education received in a life-time by people aged 25 years and older; and ii) expected years of schooling for children of school-entrance age, which is the total number of years of schooling a child of school-entrance age can expect to receive if prevailing patterns of age-specific enrolment rates stay the same throughout the child's life. Standard of living is measured by Gross National Income (GNI) per capita expressed in constant 2005 PPP$.

To ensure as much cross-country comparability as possible, the HDI is based primarily on international data from the UN Population Division, the UNESCO Institute for Statistics (UIS) and the World Bank. As stated in the introduction, the HDI values and ranks in this year's report are not comparable to those in past reports (including the 2010 HDR) because of a number of revisions done to the component indicators by the mandated agencies. To allow for assessment of progress in HDIs, the 2011 report includes recalculated HDIs from 1980 to 2011.

Egypt's HDI value and rank

Egypt's HDI value for 2011 is 0.644—in the medium human development category—positioning the country at 113 out of 187 countries and territories. Between 1980 and 2011, Egypt's HDI value increased from 0.406 to 0.644, an increase of 59.0 per cent or average annual increase of about 1.5 per cent.

The rank of Egypt's HDI for 2010 based on data available in 2011 and methods used in 2011 is 112 out of 187 countries. In the 2010 HDR, Egypt was ranked 101 out of 169 countries. However, it is misleading to compare values and rankings with those of previously published reports, because the underlying data and methods have changed, as well as the number of countries included in the HDI.

Table A reviews Egypt's progress in each of the HDI indicators. Between 1980 and 2011, Egypt's life expectancy at birth increased by 17.1 years, mean years of schooling increased by 4.4 years and expected years of schooling increased by 3.5 years. Egypt's GNI per capita increased by about 130.0 per cent between 1980 and 2011.

Table A: Egypt's HDI trends based on consistent time series data, new component indicators and new methodology

	Life expectancy at birth	Expected years of schooling	Means years of schooling	GNI per capita (2005 PPP$)	HDI value
1980	56.2	7.5	2.0	2,288	0.406
1985	59.0	8.6	3.0	2,692	0.461
1990	62.0	9.1	3.5	3,132	0.497
1995	65.6	10.4	4.0	3,431	0.539
2000	69.1	11.4	4.7	4,051	0.585
2005	71.6	11.0	5.5	4,310	0.611
2010	73.0	11.0	6.4	5,321	0.644
2011	73.2	11.0	6.4	5,269	0.644

Figure 1 below shows the contribution of each component index to Egypt's HDI since 1980.

Figure 1: Trends in Egypt's HDI component indices 1980-2011

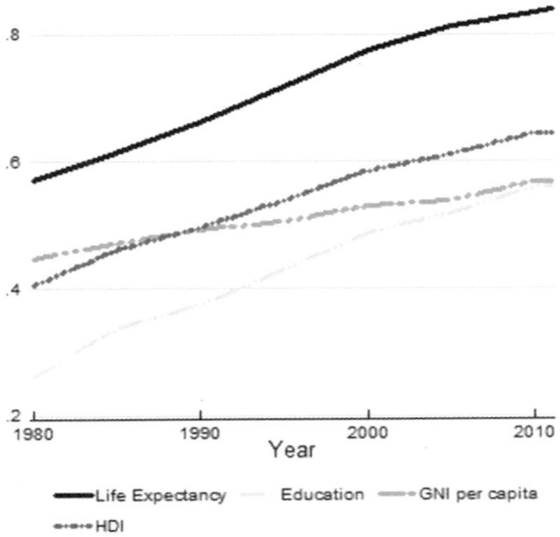

Assessing progress relative to other countries

Long-term progress can be usefully assessed relative to other countries—both in terms of geographical location and HDI value. For instance, during the period between 1980 and 2011 Egypt, Morocco and Tunisia experienced different degrees of progress toward increasing their HDIs (See Figure 2).

Figure 2: Trends in Egypt's HDI 1980-2011

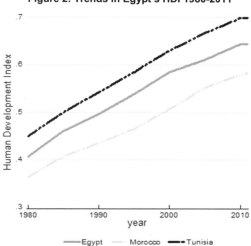

Egypt's 2011 HDI of 0.644 is above the average of 0.630 for countries in the medium human development group and above the average of 0.641 for countries in the Arab States. From the Arab States, countries which are close to Egypt in 2011 HDI rank and population size are Morocco and Syrian Arab Republic which have HDIs ranked 130 and 119 respectively (see Table B).

Table B: Egypt's HDI indicators for 2011 relative to selected countries and groups

	HDI value	HDI rank	Life expectancy at birth	Expected years of schooling	Mean years of schooling	GNI per capita (PPP US$)
Egypt	0.644	113	73.2	11.0	6.4	5,269
Morocco	0.582	130	72.2	10.3	4.4	4,196
Syrian Arab Republic	0.632	119	75.9	11.3	5.7	4,243
Arab States	0.641	—	70.5	10.2	5.9	8,554
Medium HDI	0.630	—	69.7	11.2	6.3	5,276

Inequality-adjusted HDI (IHDI)

The HDI is an average measure of basic human development achievements in a country. Like all averages, the HDI masks inequality in the distribution of human development across the population at the country level. The 2010 HDR introduced the 'inequality adjusted HDI (IHDI)', which takes into account inequality in all three dimensions of the HDI by 'discounting' each dimension's average value according to its level of inequality. The HDI can be viewed as an index of 'potential' human development and IHDI as an index of actual human development. The 'loss' in potential human development due to inequality is given by the difference between the HDI and the IHDI, and can be expressed as a percentage. (For more details see the technical note 2).

Egypt's HDI for 2011 is 0.644. However, when the value is discounted for inequality, the HDI falls to 0.489, a loss of 24.1 per cent due to inequality in the distribution of the dimension indices. Morocco and Syrian Arab Republic show losses due to inequality of 29.7 per cent and 20.4 per cent respectively. The average loss due to inequality for medium HDI countries is 23.7 per cent and for the Arab States it is 26.4 per cent.

Table C: Egypt's IHDI for 2011 relative to selected countries and groups

	IHDI value	Overall Loss (%)	Loss due to inequality in life expectancy at birth (%)	Loss due to inequality in education (%)	Loss due to inequality in income (%)
Egypt	0.489	24.1	13.9	40.9	14.2
Morocco	0.409	29.7	16.7	45.8	23.0
Syrian Arab Republic	0.503	20.4	10.0	31.5	18.3
Arab States	0.472	26.4	18.0	40.8	17.8
Medium HDI	0.480	23.7	19.2	29.4	22.3

Gender Inequality Index (GII)

The Gender Inequality Index (GII) reflects gender-based inequalities in three dimensions – reproductive health, empowerment, and economic activity. Reproductive health is measured by maternal mortality and adolescent fertility rates; empowerment is measured by the share of parliamentary seats held by each gender and attainment at secondary and higher education by each gender; and economic activity is measured by the labour market participation rate for each gender. The GII replaced the previous Gender related Development Index and Gender Empowerment Index. The GII shows the loss in human development due to inequality between female and male achievements in the three GII dimensions. (For more details on GII please see Technical note 3 in the Statistics Annex.) Due to a lack of relevant data the GII has not been calculated for this country.

Multidimensional Poverty Index (MPI)

The 2010 HDR introduced the Multidimensional Poverty Index (MPI), which identifies multiple deprivations in the same households in education, health and standard of living. The education and health dimensions are based on two indicators each while the standard of living dimension is based on six indicators. All of the indicators needed to construct the MPI for a household are taken from the same household survey. The indicators are weighted, and the deprivation scores are computed for each household in the survey. A cut-off of 33.3 percent, which is the equivalent of one-third of the weighted indicators, is used to distinguish between the poor and nonpoor. If the household deprivation score is 33.3 percent or greater, that household (and everyone in it) is multidimensionally poor. Households with a deprivation score greater than or equal to 20 percent but less than 33.3 percent are *vulnerable* to or at risk of becoming multidimensionally poor.

The most recent survey data that were publically available for Egypt's MPI estimation refer to 2008. In Egypt 6.0 per cent of the population suffer multiple deprivations while an additional 7.2 per cent are vulnerable to multiple deprivations. The breadth of deprivation (intensity) in Egypt, which is the average percentage of deprivation experienced by people in multidimensional poverty, is 40.7 per cent. The MPI which is the share of the population that is multi-dimensionally poor, adjusted by the intensity of the deprivations, is 0.024. Morocco and Syrian Arab Republic have MPIs of 0.048 and 0.021 respectively.

Table E compares income poverty, measured by the percentage of the population living below PPP US$1.25 per day, and multidimensional deprivations in Egypt. It shows that income poverty only tells part of the story. The multidimensional poverty headcount is 4.0 percentage points higher than income poverty. This implies that individuals living above the income poverty line may still suffer deprivations in education, health and other living conditions. Table E also shows the percentage of Egypt's population hat live in severe poverty (deprivation score is 50 per cent or more) and that are vulnerable to poverty deprivation score between 20 and 30 per cent). Figures for Morocco and Syrian Arab Republic are also shown in the table for comparison.

Table E: Egypt's MPI for 2011 relative to selected countries

	MPI value	Head count (%)	Intensity of deprivation (%)	Population vulnerable to poverty (%)	Population in severe poverty (%)	Population below income poverty line (%)
Egypt	0.024	6.0	40.7	7.2	1.0	2.0
Morocco	0.048	10.6	45.3	12.3	3.3	2.5
Syrian Arab Republic	0.021	5.5	37.5	7.1	0.5	1.7

International Human Development Indicators

Accessed: 10/31/2011,12:56 PM from: http://hdr.undp.org

Human Development Index

Year	Egypt	Medium human development	Arab States	World
2011	0.644	0.630	0.641	0.682
2010	0.644	0.625	0.639	0.679
2009	0.638	0.618	0.634	0.676
2008	0.633	0.612	0.629	0.674
2007	0.626	0.605	0.623	0.670
2006	0.618	0.595	0.617	0.664
2005	0.611	0.587	0.609	0.660
2000	0.585	0.548	0.578	0.634
1995	0.539	0.517	0.545	0.613
1990	0.497	0.480	0.516	0.594
1985	0.461	0.450	0.481	0.576
1980	0.406	0.420	0.444	0.558

Health

Indicator	Value	Notes
Expenditure on health, public (% of GDP) (%)	2.40	
Under-five mortality rate (per 1,000 live births)	21.00	
Life expectancy at birth (years)	73.20	
Health index	0.84	

Education

Indicator	Value	Notes
Public expenditure on education (% of GDP) (%)	3.80	
Expected Years of Schooling (of children) (years)	11.00	12
Adult literacy rate, both sexes (% aged 15 and above)	66.40	
Mean years of schooling (of adults) (years)	6.40	13
Education index	0.56	
Combined gross enrolment in education (both sexes) (%)	35.50	14

Income

Indicator	Value	Notes
GDP per capita in PPP terms (constant 2005 international $)	5151.00	
GNI per capita in PPP terms (constant 2005 international $) (Constant 2005 international $)	5269.00	
Income index	0.57	

Inequality

Indicator	Value	Notes
Income Gini coefficient	32.10	
Loss due to inequality in life expectancy (%)	13.90	
Loss due to inequality in education (%)	40.90	
Loss due to inequality in income (%)	14.20	
Inequality-adjusted education index	0.33	
Inequality-adjusted life expectancy index	0.72	
Inequality-adjusted income index	0.49	
Inequality-adjusted HDI value	0.49	

Poverty

Indicator	Value	Notes
MPI: Multidimensional poverty index (k greater than or equal to 3) (%)	0.02	15
MPI: Intensity of deprivation	40.70	16
MPI: Headcount (k greater than or equal to 3), percentage population in poverty (% of population)	6.00	17
MPI: Population living below $1.25 PPP per day (%)	2.00	

12: Data refer to 2011 or the most recent year available.
13: Data refer to 2011 or the most recent year available.
14: UNESCO Institute for Statistics estimate.
15: Published in 2011 using data from 2000-2010.
16: Published in 2011 using data from 2000-2010.
17: Published in 2011 using data from 2000-2010.

Gender

Indicator	Value	Notes
Population with at least secondary education, female/male ratio (Ratio of female to male rates)	0.73	
Adolescent fertility rate (women aged 15-19 years) (births per 1,000 women aged 15-19)	46.60	
Labour force participation rate, female-male ratio (Ratio of female to male shares)	0.30	
GII: Gender Inequality Index, value	0.60	
Shares in parliament, female-male ratio	0.04	
Maternal mortality ratio (deaths of women per100,000 live births)	82.00	

Sustainability

Indicator	Value	Notes
Endangered species (% of all species)	10.00	
Ecological footprint of consumption (global hectares per capita)	1.70	
Adjusted net savings (% of GNI)	3.10	18
Greenhouse gases per capita (tonnes of CO2 equivalent)	0.90	
Fresh water withdrawals (% of actual total renewable water resources)	n.a.	
Natural resource depletion (% of GNI)	7.30	
Carbon dioxide per capita emission (growth 1970-2008) (%)	3.90	
Forest area (thousand ha)	69.00	19
Change in forest area (%)	56.40	20
Impact of natural disasters: number of deaths (average per year/million) (average per year per million people)	0.00	
Impact of natural disasters: population affected (average per year/million) (average per year per million people)	5.00	
Environmental performance index (EPI)	62.00	
Forest area (% of total land area)	0.10	21
Carbon Dioxide Emissions per capita (tonnes)	2.60	

Demography

Indicator	Value	Notes
Population, total both sexes (thousands)	82536.80	
Population, urban (%) (% of population)	43.50	22
Population, female (thousands)	41095.04	
Population, male (thousands)	41441.73	

18: Data refer to the most recent year available during the period specified.
19: The Global Forest Resource Assessment 2010 (FRA 2010) is the main source of forest area data in FAOSTAT. Data were provided by countries for years 1990, 2000, 2005 and 2010. The data collected from official national sources through the questionnaire are supplemented with information from official secondary data sources. The secondary sources cover: official country data from websites of national ministries, national publications and related country data reported by various international organizations. Data for intermediate years were estimated for FAO using linear interpolation and tabulation.
20: The Change is over the period 1990-2008.
21: Less than 1 percent.
22: Because data are based on national definitions of what constitutes a city or metropolitan area, cross country comparison should be made with caution.

n.a.: Data not available

Appendix 2

Transcript of Speech by Hosni Mubarak, 1 February 2011

(http://www.nationalreview.com/blogs/print/258629;
transcript by Matthew Shaffer)
Delivered at 11:00 p.m., Cairo time

Fellow citizens, I speak to you in very difficult times—Egypt and people were tested and we were thrown into the unknown. The nation was put under hard tests beginning with youth and honorable citizens express-ing their demands and worries. Soon, though, chaos ensued and violence ensued and a breaking of constitution. . . . Some of the elements tried to express themselves freely but there were political forces pouring oil on the fire by creating havoc through looting, creating fires, taking state property, private property. . . .

We are living in difficult times, with the fear that overcame the major-ity of Egyptians and the hysteria around them, and their fear for their families and futures. The past few days have forced us as a nation and lead-ership to make choices between chaos and stability and the options are before us—we face a new changing reality and want the army and people to work with us to promote the best for Egypt and its children.

I have begun putting a new government with new priorities that respond to the youth's requests. And I put a vice president who will help lead the improvements democratically and constitutionally for the sake of making these changes and restoring order.

However, there are political parties that refused these requests to speak due to holding onto their private interests, forgoing the public good. And looking at this rejection to speak, an invitation that will not always be there, I will speak now directly to the people, to the farmers and workers, Muslims and Christians, sheikhs and youth, and to every Egyptian in city and rural on all its lands.

The people know the hard times I have taken responsibility in and what I offered the country in times of peace and war. I am a son of the armed services and not of the people who forgo responsibility. My first responsibility is providing security to the country to peacefully transition the power in a safe way for Egypt and give the country to those who Egypt chose in the coming elections.

I say this with all truth and independent of the current events—I will not run in new election. I have done enough at the service of Egypt and its people but want to close my service to the country in a good, safe way that keeps the constitution and ensures security.

I will say in clear ways what I will do in the coming months to ensure peaceful transition and fixing the constitution. Parliament will use articles 76 and 77 from the constitution, fixing the way that people are elected to president and imposing term limits. And the current parliament will debate these constitutional changes and what comes from it to the complete laws of the law—in an attempt to include opposition, I ask parliament to fix the errors from last election without any issues.

The parliament should work to improve the situation, to improve employment, decrease poverty and improve public good. The police will also be working for the people and protecting the citizen with honor and control and respect for their rights and freedoms and dignity.

I also ask the security services that they take care and find out the people who did this, and find those who did the bad things and protect the good people. This is my promise to the people in my coming few months, I hope that God gives me the strength.

My fellow citizens, Egypt will leave these hard times stronger than it was before. More confident and more stable. The people will exit knowing better what they want and more aware of controlling their destiny and future.

So Hosni Mubarak who speaks to you today, cares a lot for the people he has served for years. This great country is my country , the same way it is every Egyptian's country—I lived here, and waged war for it and fought for the people and I will die on its land and history will be the judge of me.

While the people may come and go the country will remain and its security is in the hands of its children, and God has protected this country generation after generation.

Transscription of Speech by Hosni Mubarak, 10 February 2011

Translated from Arabic by the Federal Document Clearing House (http://www.washingtonpost.com/wp-dyn/content/article/2011/02/10/AR2011021005290_pf.html)

In the name of Allah, the merciful, the compassionate, dear fellow citizens, my sons, the youth of Egypt, and daughters, I am addressing you tonight to the youth of Egypt in Tahrir Square, with all of its diversity.

I am addressing all of you from the heart, a speech from the father to his sons and daughters. I am telling you that I am very grateful and am so proud of you for being a symbolic generation that is calling for change to the better, that is dreaming for a better future, and is making the future.

I am telling you before anything, that the blood of the martyrs and the injured will not go in vain. And I would like to affirm, I will not hesitate to punish those who are responsible fiercely. I will hold those in charge who have violated the rights of our youth with the harshest punishment stipulated in the law.

I am telling families of the innocent victims that I have been so much in pain for their pain, and my heart ached for your heartache. I am telling you that my response to your demands and your messages and your requests is my commitment that I will never go back on to. I am determined to fulfill what I have promised you in all honesty, and I'm determined to execute and carry out what I have promised without going back to the past.

This commitment is out of my conviction of your honesty and your movement and that your demands are the demands—legitimate and just demands. Any regime could make mistakes in any country, but what is more important is to acknowledge these mistakes and reform and correct them in a timely manner, and to hold those responsible for it accountable.

I am telling you, as a president of the country, I do not find it a mistake to listen to you and to respond to your requests and demands. But it is shameful and I will not, nor will ever accept to hear foreign dictations, whatever the source might be or whatever the context it came in.

My sons and daughters, the youth of Egypt, dear fellow citizens, I have announced, without any doubt, that I will not run for the next presidential elections and have said that I have given the country and served the country for 60 years in public service, during wartime and during peacetime. I have told you my determination that I will hold steadfast to continue to take on my responsibility to protect the constitution and the rights of people until power is transferred to whomever the people choose during September, the upcoming September, and free and impartial elections that will be safeguarded by the freedom—the call for freedom.

This is the oath that I have taken before God and before you. And I will protect it and keep it until we reach—we take Egypt to the safety and security.

I have given you my vision to get out of this current situation, to accomplish what the youth and the people called for, within the respect for the legitimacy and the constitution in a way that will accomplish security, and security for our future and the demands of our people, and at the same time will guarantee a framework of peaceful transition of power.

Through a responsible dialogue between all factions in the society, with all honesty and transparency, I have given you this vision under commitment to take the country out of this current crisis, and I will continue to accomplish it. And I'm monitoring the situation hour by hour.

I'm looking forward to the support of all those who are careful about the security and want a secure Egypt, within a tangible time, with the harmony of the broad base of all Egyptians that will stay watchful to guard Egypt and under the command of its military forces.

We have started a national dialogue, a constructive one, that included the youth who have called for change and reform, and also with all the factions of opposition and of society. And this dialogue resulted in harmony, and preliminary harmony in opinions that has placed us on the beginning of the road to transfer to a better future that we have agreed on.

We also have agreed on a road map—a road map with a timetable. Day after day, we will continue the transition of power from now until September. This national dialogue has—has met and was formed under a constitutional committee that have looked into the constitution and what was required—and looked into what is required, and the constitution reforms that is demanded [inaudible].

We will also monitor the execution—the honest execution of what I have promised my people. I was careful that both committees that were formed—to be formed from Egyptians who are honorable and who are independent and impartial, and who are well-versed in law and constitution.

In addition to that, in reference to the loss of many Egyptians during these sad situations that have pained the hearts of all of us and have ached the conscience of all Egyptians. I have also requested to expedite investigations and to refer all investigations to the attorney general to take the necessary measures and steps—decisive steps.

I also received the first reports yesterday about the required constitutional reform—reforms that was suggested by the constitutional and law experts regarding the legislative reforms that were requested. I am also responding to what the committee has suggested. And based on the powers given to me according to the constitution, I have presented today a request asking the amendment of six constitutional articles, which is 76, 77, 88, 93 and 187, in addition to abolishing article number 79 in the constitution, with the affirmation and conviction that later on we can also amend the other articles that would be suggested by that constitutional committee, according to what it sees right.

Our priority now is to facilitate free election—free presidential elections and to stipulate a number of terms in the constitution and to guarantee a supervision of the upcoming elections to make sure it will be conducted in a free manner.

We—I have also looked into the provisions and the steps to look into the parliamentary elections, but those who have suggested to abolish article number 179 in the constitution will guarantee the balance between the constitution and between our security and the threat of terror, which will open the door to stopping the martial law, as soon as we regain stability and security and as soon as these circumstances—circumstances assure the stability.

Our priority now is to regain confidence between citizens among themselves and to regain confidence in the international arena and to regain confidence about the reforms that we have pledged.

Egypt is going through some difficult times, and it is not right to continue in this discourse because it has affected our economy and we have lost day after day, and it is in danger—it is putting Egypt through a situation where people who have called for reform will be the first ones to be affected by it.

This time is not about me. It's not about Hosni Mubarak. But the situation now is about Egypt and its present and the future of its citizens.

All Egyptians are in the same spot now, and we have to continue our national dialogue that we have started in the spirit of one team and away from disagreements and fighting so that we can take Egypt to the next step and to regain confidence in our economy and to let people feel secure and to stabilize the Egyptian street so that people can resume their daily life.

I was a young man, a youth just like all these youth, when I have learned the honor of the military system and to sacrifice for the country. I have spent my entire life defending its land and its sovereignty. I have witnessed and attended its wars with all its defeats and victories. I have lived during defeat and victory.

During the victory in 1973, my happiest days were when I lifted the Egyptian flag over Sinai. I have faced death several times when I was a pilot. I also faced it in Addis Ababa, Ethiopia and elsewhere. I did not submit nor yield to foreign dictations or others. I have kept the peace. I worked towards the Egyptian stability and security. I have worked to the revival in Egypt and the prosperity.

I did not seek authority. I trust that the majority—the vast majority of the Egyptian people know who is Hosni Mubarak, and it pains me to what I have—what I see today from some of my fellow citizens. And anyway, I am completely aware of the—what we are facing and I am convinced that Egypt is going through a historical—a historical moment that necessitates we should look into the higher and superior aspirations of the nation over any other goal or interest.

I have delegated to the vice president some of the power—the powers of the president according to the constitution. I am aware, fully aware, that Egypt will overcome the crisis and the resolve of its people will not be deflected and will [inaudible] again because of the—and will deflect the arrows of the enemies and those who [inaudible] against Egypt.

We will stand as Egyptians and we will prove our power and our resolve to overcome this through national dialogue. We will prove that we are not followers or puppets of anybody, nor we are receiving orders or dictations from anybody—any entity, and no one is making the decision for us except for the [inaudible] of the Egyptian [inaudible].

We will prove that with the spirit and the resolve of the Egyptian people, and with the unity and steadfastness of its people and with our resolve and to our glory and pride.

These are the main foundations of our civilization that have started over 7,000 years ago. That spirit will live in us as long as the Egyptian people—as long as the Egyptian people remain, that spirit will remain in us.

It will live amongst all of our people, farmers, intellectuals, workers. It will remain in the hearts of our senior citizens, our women, our children, Christians and Muslims alike, and in the hearts and minds of all those who are not born yet.

Let me say again that I have lived for this nation. I have kept my responsibilities. And Egypt will remain, above all, and above any individuals—Egypt will remain until I deliver and surrender its—it to others. This will be the land of my living and my death. It will remain a dear land to me. I will not leave it nor depart it until I am buried in the ground. Its people will remain in my heart, and it will remain—its people will remain upright and lifting up their heads.

May God keep Egypt secure and may God defend its people. And peace be upon you.

Speech by Omar Suleiman, 11 February 2011

(http://www.nytimes.com/2011/02/12/world/middleeast/12-suleiman-speech-text.html?_r=1&pagewanted=print)

In the name of God the merciful, the compassionate, citizens, during these very difficult circumstances Egypt is going through, President Hosni Mubarak has decided to step down from the office of president of the republic and has charged the high council of the armed forces to administer the affairs of the country. May God help everybody.

Bibliography

Abdalla, A. 2009. *The Student Movement and National Politics in Egypt.* Cairo: American University in Cairo Press.

Abdel Aziz, M., and Y. Hussein. 2001/2002. "The President, the Son, and the Military: The Question of Succession in Egypt." *Arab Studies Journal* 9/10:73–88.

Abdel Hay, A.T. 2001. "The Political Orientations of the New Generations." *al-Dimukratiya* 6 (April): 115–25.

Abdel-Malek, A. 1968. *Egypt: Military Society.* New York: Random House.

Abdelnasser, G. 2004. "Egypt: Succession Politics." In *Arab Elites: Negotiating the Politics of Change,* edited by V. Perthes, 117–40. Boulder, CO: Lynne Rienner.

Abdel Rahman, A. 2007. "al-Shabab wa-harakat al-taghyir." In *Harakat al-taghyir bayn al waqi' wa-l-tumuh,* edited by S. Fawzi, 177–96. Cairo: Cairo Institute for Human Rights Studies.

Abdelrahman, M. 2004a. *Civil Society Exposed: The Politics of NGOs in Egypt.* London: I.B. Tauris; New York: St. Martins Press.

———. 2004b. *Civil Society Exposed: The Politics of NGOs in Egypt.* Cairo: American University in Cairo Press.

Abdo, N. 2010. "Imperialism, the State, and NGOs: Middle Eastern Contexts and Contestations." *Comparative Studies of South Asia, Africa and the Middle East* 30 (2): 238–49.

Abdullah, R. 2010. "Arab Media over the Past Twenty Years." In Korany 2010, 59–84.

Abu al-Nur, A. 2001. *al-Haqiqa 'an thawrat 23 Yulyu.* Cairo: al-Hay'a al-Masriya al-'Amma li-l-Kitab.

Al-Agati, M. 2010. "al-Yasar wa-l-harakat al-ihtijajiya fi Misr: Ajij; al-lajna al-shabbiya li-da'm al-intifada, harakat 20 Maris." In Shehata 2010, 77–110.

Ahmed, S. 1984. *Public Finance in Egypt: Its Structure and Trends.* Washington, D.C.: World Bank.

Al-Ahram Center for Political and Strategic Studies. 1985–2010. *Markaz al-Dirasat al-Siyasiya wa-l-Istiratijiya: al-Taqrir al-istiratiji al-'Arabi.*

Albrecht, H. 2005. "How Can Opposition Support Authoritarianism? Lessons from Egypt." *Democratization* 12 (3): 378–97.

Albrecht, H., and D. Bishara. 2011. "Back on Horseback: The Military and Political Transformation in Egypt." *Middle East Law and Governance* 3:13–23.

Albrecht, H., and F. Kohstall. 2010. "Ägypten's letzte Wahl." *Informationsprojekt Naher und Mittlerer Osten* 64:39–43.

al-Ali, N. 2000. *Secularism, Gender, and the State in the Middle East: The Egyptian Women's Movement.* Cambridge Middle East Studies 14. Cambridge: Cambridge University Press.

Allison, G., and P. Zelikow. 1999. *Essence of Decision: Explaining the Cuban Missile Crisis.* 2nd ed. New York: Addison Wesley Longman, Inc.

Amin, Q. 1899. *Tahrir al-Mar'a.* Cairo.

Amin, M.M. 1980. *al-Awqaf wa-l-hayah al-ijtima'iya fi Misr 1250–1517.* Cairo: Dar al-Nahda al-'Arabiya.

Amin, S. 2007. "Political Islam in the Service of Imperialism." *Monthly Review* 59 (7): 1–20.

al-Anani, Khalil. 2010. "Limadha lam yuqif al-islahiyyun mahzalat intikhabat maktab al-irshad." *al-Dustur*, 1 January. http://www.dostor.org/weekly/reportage/09/december/29/1306

Anderson, K. 2011/2012. "Person of the Year 2011." *Time*, 26 December/2 January, 28, 36.

Anderson, L. 1995. "Democracy in the Arab World: A Critique of the Political Culture Approach." In Brynen, Korany, and Noble 1995, 77–92.

———, ed. 1999. *Transition to Democracy.* New York: Columbia University Press.

———. 2011. "Demystifying the Arab Spring: Parsing the Differences between Tunisia, Egypt, and Libya." *Foreign Affairs* 90 (3): 2–7.

Anderson, P. 1979. *Lineages of the Absolutist State.* London: Verso.

Arabic Network for Human Rights Information. www.anhri.net

Arab Reform Initiative (ARI). 2010. *Annual Report 2009*.

Assaad, R., and G. Barsoum. 2007. "Youth Exclusion in Egypt: In Search of Second Chances." *The Middle East Youth Initiative Working Paper* 2, September.

Assaad, R., and F. Roudi-Fahimi. 2007. *Youth in the Middle East and North Africa: Demographic Opportunity or Challenge*. Population Reference Bureau.

Al Aswany, A. 2011. *On the State of Egypt*. Cairo: American University in Cairo Press.

al-Awadi, H. 2004. *In Pursuit of Legitimacy: The Muslim Brothers and Mubarak*. New York: Tauris Academic Studies.

al-Awwa, M.S. 2006. *Thawrat Yulyu wa-l-Islam*. Cairo: Maktabat al-Shuruq al-Dawliya.

Ayubi, N. 1995. *Overstating the Arab State: Politics and Society in the Middle East*. London: I.B. Tauris.

Barnet, M.N. 1992. *Confronting the Cost of War: Military Power, State, and Society in Egypt and Israel*. Princeton, NJ: Princeton University Press.

Bayat, A. 1998. "Revolution without Movement, Movement without Revolution: Comparing Islamic Activism in Iran and Egypt." *Comparative Studies in Society and History* 40:136–69.

———. 2007. *Making Islam Democratic: Social Movements and the Post-Islamist Turn*. Stanford, CA: Stanford University Press.

———. 2009. *Life as Politics: How Ordinary People Change the Middle East*. Cairo: American University in Cairo Press.

Al-Bayoumi, M. 2001a. "al-Muthaqqafun wa-l-adab." *al-Azhar Magazine*, section 12 (March).

———. 2001b. *"Thaqafat al-du'ah al-judud." al-Azhar Magazine*, section 7 (October).

Baz, M. 2007. *al-Mushir: qissat su'ud wa-inhiyar Abu Ghazala*. Cairo: Kinuz li-l-Nashr wa-l-Tawzi'.

Beauvoir, S. de. 1949. *The Second Sex*. Translated 1952, reprinted 1968. New York: Vintage Books.

Beblawi, H., and G. Luciani, eds. 1987. *The Rentier State*. London and New York: Croom Helm.

Beinin, J. 2007. "The Egyptian Workers Movement in 2007." *Chroniques du CEDEJ (Centre d'Études et de Documentations économiques, juridiqes et sociales)*. http://www.cedej-eg.org/spip.php?rubrique35

Beinin, Joel. 2009a. "Workers' Struggles Under 'Socialism' and Neoliberalism." In El-Mahdi and Marfleet 2009a, 68–86.

Beinin, Joel. 2009b. "Workers' Struggles Under Socialism and Neoliberalism." In El-Mahdi and Marfleet 2009b, 69–86.

———. 2010. *The Struggle for Workers' Rights in Egypt*. Washington, D.C.: Solidarity Center, Afl-CIO. www.solidaritycenter.org/files/pubs_egypt_wr.pdf

Beinin, J., and Z. Lockman. 1984. *Workers on the Nile: Nationalism, Communism, Islam, and the Egyptian Working Class 1882–1954*. Princeton, NJ: Princeton University Press.

———. 1987. *Workers on the Nile: Nationalism, Communism, Islam, and the Egyptian Working Class 1882–1954*. Cairo: American University in Cairo Press.

Bellin, E. 2000. "Contingent Democrats: Industrialists, Labor, and Democratization in Late Developing Countries." *World Politics* 52 (2): 175–205.

———. 2012. "Reconsidering the Robustness of Authoritarianism in the Middle East: Lessons from the Arab Spring." *Comparative Politics* 44 (2): 127–49.

Ben Néfissa, S., and A. Arafat. 2005. *al-Intikhabat wa-l-zaba'niya al-siyasiya fi Misr*. Cairo: Cairo Center for Human Rights.

Bhatt, E.R. 2006. *We Are Poor but So Many: The Story of Self-employed Women in India*. Oxford: Oxford University Press.

Bianchi, R. 1986. "The Corporatization of the Egyptian Labor Market." *The Middle East Journal* 40 (3): 429–44.

al-Bishri, T. 2002. *al-Haraka al-siyasiya fi Misr, 1945–1953*. Cairo: Dar el Shorouk.

———. 2005. *al-Malamih al-'amma li-l-fikr al-siyasi al-islami fi-l-tarikh al-mu'asir*. Cairo: Dar el Shorouk.

Al-Boraie, A. 2011. Panel on labor issues in Egypt. American University in Cairo, 22 May.

Botman, S. 1988. *The Rise of Communism in Egypt*. Syracuse, N.Y.: Syracuse University Press.

Boutaleb, A. 2004. "The Parliamentary Elections of Year 2000 in Egypt: A Lesson in Political Participation." In "Elections in the Middle East: What Do They Mean?," edited by Iman A. Hamdy. *Cairo Papers in Social Science* 25 (1–2): 11–25.

Boyne, W.J. 2002. *The Two o'Clock War: The 1973 Yom Kippur Conflict and the Airlift that Saved Israel*. New York: Thomas Dunne Books, St. Martin Press.

Bradford, J. 2004. "The Indonesian Military as a Professional Organization: Criteria and Ramifications for Reform." *Explorations in South-East Asian Studies* 5. www.hawaii.edu/cseas/pubs/explore/bradford.html

Bradley, J.R. 2008. *Inside Egypt: The Land of the Pharaohs on the Brink of a Revolution.* New York: Palgrave MacMillan.

Brooks, R.A. 2008. *Shaping Strategy: The Civil–Military Politics of Strategic Assessment.* Princeton, NJ: Princeton University Press.

Brouwer, I. 2000. "US Civil-Society Assistance to the Arab World: The Cases of Egypt and Palestine." European University Institute Working Paper RSC no. 2000/5. Badia Fiesolana, San Domenico, Italy.

Brown, N. 2003. "Reinventing Themselves: Constitutional Development in the Arab World." *International Sociology* 33.

———. 2011. "Post-Revolutionary al-Azhar." *The Carnegie Papers: Middle East* (September): 1–25.

Brownlee, J. 2007a. *Authoritarianism in an Age of Democratization.* Cambridge: Cambridge University Press.

———. 2007b. "Hereditary Succession in Modern Autocracies." *World Politics* 59 (4): 595–628.

Brownlee, J., and J. Stacher. 2011. "Change of Leader, Continuity of System." *APSA Comparative Democratization Newsletter* 9 (2).

Brynen, R., B. Korany, and P. Noble, eds. 1995. *Political Liberalization and Democratization in the Arab World.* Boulder, CO: Lynne Rienner.

Bunte, M., and A. Ufen. 2009a. "The New Order and Its Legacy: Reflections on Democratization in Indonesia." In Bunte and Ufen 2009b.

———, eds. 2009b. *Democratization in Post-Suharto Indonesia.* London: Routledge.

Bush, R. 2005. "Mubarak's Legacy for Egypt's Rural Poor: Returning Land to the Landlords." ISS/UNDP Land, Poverty and Public Action Policy Paper No. 10 (August). The Hague: Institute of Social Studies. www.iss.nl/content/download/3830/37209/file/Egyptpercent2opaper.pdf

———. 2009. "The Land and the People." In El-Mahdi and Marfleet 2009a: 51–67.

Butler, J. 1997. *Excitable Speech: A Politics of the Performative.* New York: Routledge.

Cairo Institute for Human Rights Studies (CIHRS). 2010. "Parliamentary Elections: Egyptian Comedy against the Background of Abuses and Human Rights Violations." 15 December. http://www.cihrs.org

Carapico, S. 1998. *Civil Society in Yemen: The Political Economy of Activism in Modern Arabia*. London: Cambridge University Press.

———. 2002. "Foreign Aid for Promoting Democracy in the Arab World." *Middle East Journal* 56 (3): 379–95.

———. 2010. "Civil Society." In *Politics and Society in the Contemporary Middle East*, edited by M.P. Angrist, 91–110. Boulder, CO: Lynne Rienner Publishers.

———. 2011. "What al-Jazeera Shows and Doesn't Show." The Middle East Channel, Foreign Policy, 4 February. http://mideast.foreignpolicy. com/posts/2011/02/04/what_al_jazeera_shows_and_doesn_t_show

———. Forthcoming. *Promoting Arab Democratization: International Political Aid in Practice*. London: Cambridge University Press.

Carnegie, P.J. 2010. *The Road from Authoritarianism to Democratization in Indonesia*. New York: Palgrave Macmillan.

Cassandra. 1995. "Impending Crisis in Egypt." *Middle East Journal* 49 (1): 9–27.

Center for Applied Non-Violent Action and Strategies (CANVAS). 2004. "Canvas Core Curriculum." http://www.canvasopedia.org/legacy/content/special/core.htm

Center for Arab Unity Studies (CAUS). 1984. *Azmat al-dimuqratiya fi-l-watan al-'arabi*. Beirut: Markaz Dirasat al-Wihda al-'Arabiya.

Central Bank of Egypt. 1981–2000. *Annual Reports*.

Challand, B. 2010. *Palestinian Civil Society: Foreign Donors and the Power to Promote and Exclude*. London and New York: Routledge.

Chomiak, L., and J.P. Entelis. 2011. "The Making of North Africa's Intifadas." *Middle East Report* 259:8–15.

Clark, J. 1995. "Democratization and Social Islam: A Case Study of the Islamic Health Clinics in Cairo." In Brynen, Korany, and Noble 1995, 167–86.

Clément, F. 2009. "Worker Protests under Economic Liberalization in Egypt." In Hopkins 2009, 100–16.

Collier, R.B. 1999. *Paths toward Democracy: The Working Class and Elites in Western Europe and South America*. Cambridge: Cambridge University Press.

Collier, R.B., and J. Mahoney. 1997. "Adding Collective Actors to Collective Outcomes: Labor and Recent Democratization in South America and Southern Europe." *Comparative Politics* 29 (3): 285–303.

Cook, S.A. 2007. *Ruling but Not Governing: The Military and Political Development in Egypt, Algeria, and Turkey*. Baltimore: Johns Hopkins University Press.

Copeland, M. 1970. *The Game of Nations: The Amorality of Power Politics.* London: Weidenfeld and Nicolson.

Cordesman, A.H. 2006. *Arab–Israeli Military Forces in an Era of Asymmetric Wars.* Westport, CT: Praeger Security International.

Crouch, H. 2007. *The Army and Politics in Indonesia.* Jakarta and Kuala Lumpur: Equinox Publishing.

Dahi, O.S. 2011. "Understanding the Political Economy of the Arab Revolt." *Middle East Report* 259:2–6.

Darwish, S.A.H., ed. 2007. *A Latent Danger: Corruption in Egypt.* February. Cairo: Moltaka (Forum for Development and Human Rights Dialogue).

De Atkine, N. 1999. "Why Arabs Lose Wars." *Middle East Quarterly* 6 (4): 13–25.

Dekmejian, R.H. 1982. "Egypt and Turkey: The Military in the Background." In Kolkowicz and Korbonski 1982, 33–51.

Della Porta, D., and M. Diani. 2006. *Social Movements: An Introduction.* 2nd ed. Malden, MA: Blackwell Publishing.

Denis, E. 2006. "Cairo as Neoliberal Capital? From Walled City to Gated Communities." In Singerman and Amar 2006, 47–71.

De Veaux, A. 2004. *Warrior Poet: A Biography of Audre Lorde.* New York: W.W. Norton & Co.

Diab, M. 2010. "Signs of Trouble: Egypt's 2010 Media Crackdown." Global Integrity. http://www.globalintegrity.org/report/Egypt/2010/notebook.

Diamond, L. 2008. *The Spirit of Democracy: The Struggle to Build Free Societies Throughout the World.* New York: Times Books.

———. 2010. "Why Are There No Arab Democracies?" *Journal of Democracy* 21 (1): 93–104.

Dinh, H., and M. Guigale. 1991. *Inflation Tax and Deficit Financing in Egypt.* Working Paper 668. Washington, D.C.: World Bank.

Doorenspleet, R. 2005. *Democratic Transitions: Exploring the Structural Sources of the Fourth Wave.* Boulder, CO: Lynne Rienner Publishers.

Downing, B.M. 1992. *The Military Revolution and Political Change: Origins of Democracy and Autocracy in Early Modern Europe.* Princeton, NJ: Princeton University Press.

Droz-Vincent, P. 2007. "From Political to Economic Actors: The Changing Role of Middle Eastern Armies." In Schlumberger 2007, 195–214.

Ducros, J.-C. 1982. *Sociologie financière.* Paris: Presse Universitaire de France.

Egyptian Center for Housing Rights. www.echr.org.

"Egyptian Chronicles." Online blog. http://egyptianchronicles.blogspot.com

Egyptian Initiative for Personal Rights. www.eipr.org

Egyptian Organization for Human Rights. www.eohr.org

Elias, A. 2000. *Libéralisme et capitalisme d'état en Égypte: La privatisation impossible des banques publiques*. Paris: Harmattan.

Elmessiri, A. 2002. *al-'Ilmaniya al-juz'iya wa-l-'ilmaniya al-shamila*. Cairo: Dar el Shorouk.

Elson, R.E. 2006. "Indonesia and the West: An Ambivalent, Misunderstood Engagement." *Australian Journal of Politics and History* 52 (2): 261–71.

Emara, M. 2008. *Tayyarat al-fikr al-islami*. Cairo: Dar el Shorouk.

Encarnación, O.G. 2000. "Tocqueville's Missionaries: Civil Society Advocacy and the Promotion of Democracy." *World Policy Journal* 17 (1): 9–18.

———. 2003. "Beyond Civil Society: Promoting Democracy after September 11." *Orbis* 47 (4): 705–20.

Esposito, J.L., and D. Mogahed. 2007. *Who Speaks for Islam? What a Billion Muslims Really Think*. New York: Gallup Press.

Eytan, Z., and S. Gazit. 1991. *The Middle East Military Balance*. Jaffee Center for Strategic Studies (JCSS). Boulder, CO: Westview Press.

Eytan, Z., S. Gazit, and A. Gilbo. 1993. *The Middle East Military Balance*. JCSS. Boulder, CO: Westview Press.

Eytan, Z., and M.A. Heller. 1983. *The Middle East Military Balance*. JCSS. Jerusalem: Jerusalem Post Press.

Eytan, Z., M.A. Heller, and A. Levran. 1985. *The Middle East Military Balance*. JCSS. Boulder, CO: Westview Press.

Eytan, Z., M.A. Heller, and D. Tamari. 1984. *The Middle East Military Balance*. JCSS. Jerusalem: The Jerusalem Post Press.

Eytan, Z., and A. Levran. 1986. *The Middle East Military Balance*. JCSS. Boulder, CO: Westview Press.

Fadhel, K. 2008. *The Pains of the Egyptians*. Cairo: Fadhel Publications.

Fandy, M. 1994. "Egypt's Islamic Group: Regional Revenge?" *The Middle East Journal* 38 (4): 609–23.

Farah, N. 2009. *Egypt's Political Economy*. Cairo: American University in Cairo Press.

Fargues, P. 2001. "Demographic Islamization: Non-Muslims in Muslim Countries." *SAIS Review* 21 (2): 103–16.

Farouk, A. 2008. *Juzur al-fasad al-idari fi Misr: bi'at al-'amal wa siyasat al-ujur wa al-murattabat fi Misr*. Cairo: Dar el Shorouk.

Fattah, S. 2009. "al-Shari'a al-islamiya wa-l-muwatana: nahwa ta'sis al-jama'a al-wataniya." In Shobaky 2010, 31–72.

Fawzi, S. 2010. "Demand Movements and Political Movements: A Comparative Critical Reading." In Shehata 2010, 21–49.

Feuilherak, P. 2011. "Growing Appetite for News with the Boom of New Media." *Middle East Magazine* (January): 24–26.

Finer, S.E. 1962. *Men on Horseback: The Role of the Military in Politics*. London: Pall Mall Press.

Fish, S. 2011. *Are Muslims Distinctive? A Look at the Evidence*. Oxford: Oxford University Press.

Freedman, A.L. 2007. "Consolidation or Withering Away of Democracy? Political Changes in Thailand and Indonesia." *Asian Affairs* 33 (4): 195–216.

Friedan, B. 1963. *The Feminine Mystique*. New York: Norton Paperback.

Frisch, H. 2001. "Guns and Butter in the Egyptian Army." *Middle East Review of International Affairs* 5 (2): 1–14.

Gaffney, P.D. 1991. "The Changing Voices of Islam: Professional Preachers in Contemporary Egypt." *The Muslim World* 81 (1): 27–47.

al-Gamasy, M.A. 1993. *The October War: Memoirs of Field Marshal El-Gamasy of Egypt*. Cairo: American University in Cairo Press.

Gausse, G.F. 2011. "Why Middle East Studies Missed the Arab Spring." *Foreign Affairs* 90 (4): 81–91.

Ghadbian, N. 2001. "The New Asad: Dynamics of Continuity and Change in Syria." *Middle East Journal* 55 (4): 624–41.

Ghanem, I.E. 1998. *al-Awqaf wa-l-siyasa fi Misr*. Cairo: Dar el Shorouk.

Ghannam, F. 2002. *Remaking the Modern: Space, Relocation, and the Politics of Identity in Global Cairo*. Berkeley: University of California Press.

El-Ghobashy, M. 2011. "The Praxis of the Egyptian Revolution." *Middle East Report* 258:2–13.

Ghoneim, W. 2012. *Revolution 2.0*. Berkeley, CA: Houghton Mifflin Harcourt.

Glasser, S. 2011. "The FP Top 100 Global Thinkers." *Foreign Policy*, special issue, December.

Goetz, A. 2008. *Governing Women*. Routledge/UNRISD Research in Gender and Development, vol. 5. New York: Routledge.

Gomaa, A. 2008. *al-Tajruba al-misriya*. Cairo: Nahdet Misr.

Gramsci, A. 1971. *Selections from the Prison Notebooks*. New York: International Publishers.

Greer, G. 1970. *The Female Eunuch*. New York: Farrar Strauss and Giroux.

Guilhot, N. 2005. *The Democracy Makers: Human Rights and International Order*. New York: Columbia University Press.

Habermas, J. 1984. *Theory of Communicative Action*. Vol. 2. Translated by Thomas McCarthy. Boston: Beacon Press.

————. 1989. *The Structural Transformation of the Public Sphere: An Inquiry into a Category of Bourgeois Society*. Translated by Thomas Burger. Cambridge, MA: MIT Press.

Haenni, P. 2005. *L'Islam de marché: l'autre révolution conservatrice*. Paris: Seuil.

Haenni, P., and H. Tammam. 2003. "Egypt's Air Conditioned Islam." *Le Monde Diplomatique*, 3 September. http://mondediplo.com/2003/09/03egyptislam

Hafez, S. 2011. *An Islam of Her Own: Reconsidering Islam and Secularism in Women's Movements*. New York: New York University Press.

Haggard, S., and R. Kaufman. 1995. *The Political Economy of Democratic Transitions*. Princeton, NJ: Princeton University Press.

Hale, H.E. 2005. "Regime Cycles: Democracy, Autocracy, and Revolution in Post-Soviet Eurasia." *World Politics* 58 (1): 133–65.

Hamid, S. 2011. "The Struggle for Middle East Democracy." *Cairo Review of Global Affairs* 1:18–29.

Hammad, G. 2002. *al-Ma'arik al-harbiya 'ala al-gabha al-misriya*. Cairo: Dar el Shorouk.

————. 2010. *Asrar thawrat 23 Yulyu*. Vols. 1 and 2. Cairo: Dar al-'Ulum.

Hammad, M. 1990. "al-Mu'assasa al-'askariya wa-l-nizam al-siyasi al-misri." In *al-Jaysh wa-l-dimuqratiya fi Misr*, edited by A. Abdalla, 29–50. Cairo: Sina li-l-Nashr.

Hammami, R. 1995. "NGOs: The Professionalization of Politics." *Race and Class* 37 (2): 51–63.

Handoussa, H. 1990. "Fifteen Years of US Aid to Egypt: A Critical Review." In *The Political Economy of Contemporary Egypt*, edited by I.M. Oweiss, 109–24. Washington, D.C.: Center for Contemporary Arab Studies, Georgetown University.

————, ed. 2005. *Egypt: Human Development Report 2005*. Cairo: UN Development Programme and the Institute of National Planning.

Handy, H., et al. 1998. *Egypt beyond Stabilization*. Washington, D.C.: International Monetary Fund (IMF).

Hanley, C.J. 2011. "US Training Quietly Nurtured Young Arab Democrats." *Washington Post*, 12 March. http://www.washingtonpost.com/wp-dyn/content/article/2011/03/12/AR2011031202234.html

Hannigan, J.A. 1991. "Social Movement Theory and the Sociology of Religion." *Sociological Analysis* 52:311–31.

Hassabo, S. 2009. "Du rassemblement à l'effritement des jeunes pour le changement des Égyptiens: l'Expérience des générations qui ont vécu et vivent toujours sous la loi d'urgence." *Revue internationale de politique comparée* 16 (2): 241–61.

Hassan, H. 2003. *Christians versus Muslims in Modern Egypt: The Century-long Struggle for Coptic Equality.* Oxford: Oxford University Press.

Hatina, M. 2003. "Historical Legacy and the Challenge of Modernity in the Middle East: The Case of al-Azhar in Egypt." *The Muslim World* 93 (January): 51–68.

Haykel, B. 2009. "On the Nature of Salafi Thought and Action." In Meijer 2009b, 33–50.

Heikal, M.H. 1983. *Autumn of Fury: The Assassination of Sadat.* London: Andre Deutsch Limited.

Heller, M.A. 2010. *The Middle East Strategic Balance, 2009–2010.* Tel Aviv: The Institute for National Security Studies.

Henry, C., and R. Springborg. 2010. *Globalization and the Politics of Development in the Middle East.* 2nd ed. Cambridge: Cambridge University Press.

Herb, M. 2003. "Taxation and Representation." *Studies in Comparative International Development* 38 (3): 3–31.

Herrera, L. 2006. "Islamization and Education: Between Politics, Profit and Pluralism." In *Cultures of Arab Schooling: Ethnographies from Egypt*, edited by L. Herrera and C.A. Torres, 25–52. Albany: State University of New York Press.

———. 2011. "Egypt's Revolution 2.0: The Facebook Factor." *Jadaliyya*, 12 February. http://www.jadaliyya.com/pages/index/612/egypts-revolution-2.0_the-facebook-factor

Hintze, O. 1975. *The Historical Essays of Otto Hintze.* New York: Oxford University Press.

Hisham Mubarak Law Center. www.hmlc-egy.org

Hobsbawm, E.J. 2001. *Revolutionaries.* New York: The New Press.

Hole, J., and E. Levine. 1971. *Rebirth of Feminism.* New York: Quadrangle.

Honna, J. 2009. "From *dwifungsi* to NKRI: Regime Change and Political Activism of the Indonesian Military." In Bunte and Ufen 2009b.

Hopkins, N.S., ed. 2009. "Political and Social Protest in Egypt." *Cairo Papers in Social Science* 29 (2–3).

El Houdaiby, I. 2009. "Trends in Political Islam in Egypt." In *Islamist Radicalisation: The Challenge for Euro-Mediterranean Relations*, edited by M. Emerson, K. Kausch, and R. Youngs, 25–51. Brussels: Centre for European Policy Studies; Madrid: FRIDE.

Howard, M. 2003. *The Weakness of Civil Society in Post-Communist Europe.* Cambridge: Cambridge University Press.

Howard, P. 2010. *The Digital Origins of Dictatorship and Democracy.* Oxford: Oxford University Press.

Human Rights Watch (HRW). 1992. *Behind Closed Doors: Torture and Detention in Egypt.* www.hrw.org/legacy/reports/1992/07/01/behind-closed-doors

Huntington, S.P. 1957. *The Soldier and the State: The Theory and Politics of Civil–Military Relations.* Cambridge, MA: Harvard University Press.

———. 1968. *Political Order in Changing Societies.* New Haven, CT: Yale University Press.

———. 1991. *The Third Wave: Democratization in the Late Twentieth Century.* Norman: University of Oklahoma Press.

Huntington, S.P., and J.M. Nelson. 1976. *No Easy Choice: Political Participation in Developing Countries.* Cambridge: Cambridge University Press.

Imam, A. 1996. *Nasser wa Amir: al-sadaqa, al-hazima, al-intihar.* Cairo: Dar al-Khayal.

Inglehart, R. 1997. *Modernization and Post-modernization.* Princeton, NJ: Princeton University Press.

Insight Team of the London *Sunday Times.* 1974. *Yom Kippur War.* New York: Doubleday & Company.

International Federation for Human Rights (FIDH). 17 November 2001. www.fidh.org

International Monetary Fund. 1991. *Government Finance Statistics Yearbook.*

Jad, I. 2004. "The NGO-ization of Arab Women's Movements." *IDS Bulletin* 35:24–42.

———. 2007. "NGOs: Between Buzzwords and Social Movements." *Development in Practice–Oxford* 17 (4–5): 622–29.

Jamal, A.A. *Barriers to Democracy: The Other Side of Social Capital in Palestine and the Arab World.* Princeton, NJ: Princeton University Press, 2007.

Janowitz, M. 1960. *The Professional Soldier: A Social and Political Portrait.* New York: Free Press.

———. 1967. "The Military in the Political Development of New Nations." In *Garrisons and Government: Politics and the Military in New*

States, edited by Wilson C. McWilliams, 67–79. San Francisco: Chandler Publishing Company.

Jefferis, J.L. 2009. *Religion and Political Violence: Sacred Protest in the Modern World*. London and New York: Routledge.

Kabeer, N. 2001. "Reflections on the Measurement of Women's Empowerment." In *Discussing Women's Empowerment: Theory and Practice*. Swedish International Development Cooperation Agency.

———. 2004. "Globalisation, Labour Standards and Women's Rights: Dilemmas of Collective (In)action in an Interdependent World." *Feminist Economics* 10 (1): 3–35.

Kam, E., and Y. Shapir. 2003. *The Middle East Strategic Balance, 2002–2003*. JCSS. Tel Aviv: Kedem Printing.

Kamat, S. 2003. "NGOs and the New Democracy: The False Saviors of International Development." *Harvard International Review* 25 (1): 65–69.

Kandil, A. 2006. "al-Shabab fi munazzamat al-mujtama' al-madani." *Annual Report 2006*. Cairo: Munazzamat al-Jam'iyat al-Ahliya.

———. 2010. "An Attempt to Evaluate the Development of Arab Civil Society." In Korany 2010: 43–58.

———. 2011. *What Role for Civil Society?* Cairo: Network of Arab Civil Society Organizations.

Kassem, M. 2004. *Egyptian Politics: The Dynamics of Authoritarian Rule*. Boulder, CO: Lynne Rienner Publishers.

Kato, A. 2011. "al-Malamih al-asasiya li-idarat al-azma wa i'adat al-amn fi rubu' Sinai." *al-Nasr* 867:12–15.

Kawari, A., and A. Maddy, eds. 2009. *Why Others Transited to Democracy and the Arabs Lagged: A Comparative Analysis*. Beirut: CAUS.

Kechichian, J., and J. Nazimek. 1997. "Challenges to the Military in Egypt." *Middle East Policy* 5 (3): 125–39.

Khalidi, R. 2004. *Resurrecting Empire: Western Footprints and America's Perilous Path in the Middle East*. Boston: Beacon Press.

Khalidi, R., et al., eds. 1993. *The Origins of Arab Nationalism*. New York: Columbia University Press.

Kheir, A. 2011. *Biblioghrafiya al-harakaat al-ijtima'iya*. Cairo: Merit Publishers.

Kienle, E. 1990. *Ba'th vs. Ba'th: The Conflict between Syria and Iraq, 1968–1989*. London and New York: I.B. Tauris.

———. 2001. *A Grand Delusion: Democracy and Economic Reform in Egypt*. London: I.B. Taurus.

Kissinger, H. 1994. *Diplomacy*. New York: Simon & Schuster.

Kitschett, H., and S. Wilkinson, eds. 2007. *Patrons, Clients and Policies: Patterns of Democratic Accountability and Political Competition.* Cambridge: Cambridge University Press.

Kolkowicz, R., and A. Korbonski, eds. 1982. *Soldiers, Peasants, and Bureaucrats: Civil-Military Relations in Communist and Modernizing Societies.* Boston: George Allen & Unwin.

Konsouah, S. 2006. "Evaluation of NCW for UNDP." Unpublished manuscript.

Korany, B. 2008. "Patterns of Democratic Deficit: Is It Islam?" In *Reform in the Middle East Oil Monarchies*, edited by A. Ehteshami and S. Wright, 61–78. Reading: Ithaca.

———, ed. 2010. *The Changing Middle East: A New Look at Regional Dynamics.* Cairo: American University in Cairo Press.

———. 2012. "Middle East Regionalisms." In *The Ashgate Reference Companion to Regionalisms*, edited by T. Shaw, J.A. Grant, and S. Cornelissen, 273–94. London: Ashgate.

Kriesi, H. 1998. "Social Movements in Western Europe: An Analysis of Major Recent Trends." In *Dynamics of State Formation: India and Europe Compared*, edited by M. Doornbos and S. Kaviraj, 333–58. New Delhi: Sage.

Kristeva, J. 1995. *New Maladies of the Soul.* New York: Columbia University Press.

Land Center for Human Rights (LCHR). 2001. "Impact of Law no. 96 of 1992 on the Educational Condition in the Egyptian Rural Areas." Land and Farmer series no. 11.

———. 2004. "Women, Land and Violence in Rural Egypt." Land and Farmer series no. 29.

———. 2007. "Elhorya Village between the Lack of Services, Unemployment and the Absence of Justice." Land and Farmer series no. 42.

Lee, T. 2009. "The Armed Forces and Transitions from Authoritarian Rule: Explaining the Role of the Military in 1986 Philippines and 1998 Indonesia." *Comparative Political Studies* 42 (5): 640–69.

Lesch, A.M. 1989. "Democracy in Doses: Mubarak Launches His Second Term as President." *Arab Studies Quarterly* 11 (4): 87–107.

———. 2004. "Politics in Egypt." In *Comparative Politics Today*, edited by Gabriel A. Almond et al., 580–632. 8th ed. New York: Pearson Longman.

Levitsky, S., and L. Way. 2010. *Competitive Authoritarianism.* Cambridge: Cambridge University Press.

Lockman, Z. 2005. *Contending Visions of the Middle East: The History and Politics of Orientalism.* Cambridge: Cambridge University Press.

Lofgren, H. 1993. "Economic Policy in Egypt: A Breakdown in Reform Resistance?" *International Journal of Middle East Studies* 25 (3): 407–21.

Lotfy, W. 2005. *Dawlat al-du'ah al-judud*. Cairo: Dar al-Khayaal.

Luciani, G. 1995. "Resources, Revenues, and Authoritarianism in the Arab World: Beyond the Rentier State." In Brynen, Korany, and Noble 1995, 211–28.

———. 2009. "Oil and Political Economy in the International Relations of the Middle East." In *International Relations of the Middle East*, edited by L. Fawcett, 81–103. Oxford: Oxford University Press.

Lust-Okar, E. 2005. *Structuring Conflict in the Middle East: Incumbents, Opponents and Institutions*. Cambridge: Cambridge University Press.

El-Mahdi, R. 2009a. "The Democracy Movement: Cycles of Protest." In *Egypt, Moment of Change*, edited by R. El-Mahdi and P. Marfleet, 87–102. Cairo: American University in Cairo Press.

———. 2009b. "Enough! Egypt's Quest for Democracy." *Comparative Political Studies* 42 (3): 1011–39.

———. 2010a. "'Ummal al-Mahalla: zuhur haraka 'ummaliya jadida." In Shehata 2010, 171–212.

———. 2010b. "The Workers of Mahala: The Emergence of a New Labor Movement." In Shehata 2010, 143–70.

El-Mahdi, R., and P. Marfleet, eds. 2009a. *Egypt: Moment of Change*. Cairo: American University in Cairo Press.

———. 2009b. *Egypt: Moment of Change*. London: Zed Press.

Mahmoud, S. 2004. *The Politics of Piety: The Islamic Revival and the Feminist Subject*. Princeton, NJ: Princeton University Press.

Mahoney, J., and R. Snyder. 1999. "Rethinking Agency and Structure in the Study of Regime Change." *Studies in Comparative International Development* 34 (2): 3–32.

Mann, M. 1986. *The Sources of Social Power*. Vol. 1: *A History of Power from the Beginning to A.D. 1760*. New York: Cambridge University Press.

Marfleet, P. 2009. "State and Society." In El-Mahdi and Marfleet 2009a, 14–33.

Martin, J. 1998. *Gramsci's Political Analysis: A Critical Introduction*. London: Macmillan Press Ltd.

Marx, K. [1852] 1963. *The Eighteenth Brumaire of Louis Bonaparte*. New York: International Publishers.

al-Mashat, A. 1986. "al-'Awamil al-kharijiya wa-l-tatawwur al-dimuqrati fi Misr." In *al-Tatawwur al-dimuqrati fi Misr: qadaya wa munaqashat*, edited by A. Helal, 53–78. Cairo: Maktabat Nahdat al-Sharq.

Masoud, T. 2011. "The Road to (and from) Liberation Square." *Journal of Democracy* 22 (3): 20–34.

Al Masry, S. 2008. "Egyptian Blogs: A New Social Space." *IDSC Information Report* 2 (17).

McAdam, D., S. Tarrow, and C. Tilly. 2001. *Dynamics of Contention*. Cambridge: Cambridge University Press.

McDermott, A. 1988. *Egypt from Nasser to Mubarak: A Flawed Revolution*. London: Croom Helm.

Meijer, R. 2009a. "Introduction." In Meijer 2009b, 1–31.

———, ed. 2009b. *Global Salafism: Islam's New Religious Movement*. London: Hurt and Company.

Melucci, A. 1980. "The New Social Movements: A Theoretical Approach." *Social Science Information* 19:199–226.

Migdal, J.S. 1988. *Strong Societies and Weak States: State–Society Relations and State Capabilities in the Third World*. Princeton, NJ: Princeton University Press.

Mill, J.S. 1869. *The Subjection of Women*. Republished 2008 by Forgotten Books.

Millett, K. 1970. *Sexual Politics*. Urbana: University of Illinois Press.

Ministry of Economy. 1982–2000. *Monthly Economic Bulletin*.

Ministry of Finance. 1981–2003. *Closing Account of the Budget*.

———. 2008. *The Financial Monthly Report* (June).

———. 2010a. *The Financial Monthly Report* (March).

———. 2010b. *The Financial Monthly Report* (May).

———. n.d. *General Features of the New Income Tax Law*.

Ministry of Justice. 2001. *Justice Yearly Book*.

Mir-Hosseini, Z. 2006. "Muslim Women's Quest for Equality: Between Islamic Law and Feminism." *Critical Inquiry* 32 (4): 629–45.

Mitchell, T. 1991. *Colonising Egypt*. Berkeley: University of California Press.

Mohammed, R.S. 1997. "al-Dara'ib bayna al-fikr al-mali wa al-qada' al-dusturi: dirasa tahliliya li-aham al-ahkam bi-'adam al-dusturiya wa-athariha." PhD diss., Faculty of Law, University of Helwan, Cairo.

Mohanty, C. 2003. *Feminism without Borders: Decolonizing Theory, Practicing Solidarity*. Durham, NC: Duke University Press

Moll, Y. 2010. "Islamic Televangelism: Religion, Media and Visuality in Contemporary Egypt." *Arab Media and Society* 10:1–27.

Moore, B. 1966. *Social Origins of Dictatorship and Democracy: Lord and Peasant in the Making of the Modern World*. Harmondsworth: Penguin Books.

Morcos, S. 2009. "al-'Uqubat wa-l-shari'a bayn dustur al-haraka al-wataniya wa dustur walyy al-amr." In *al-Muwatana fi muwajahat al-ta'ifiya*, edited by A. Shobaky, 73–92. Cairo: Al-Ahram Center for Political and Strategic Studies.

Mosaad, N., ed. 2000. *Idrak al-shabab al-'arabi li-l-'awlama*. Cairo: Ma'had al-Dirasat al-'Arabiya.

Mostafa, Y. 2011. *'Ala hamish al-tahrir: al-mugtama' al-madani wa-l-muwatana wa huquq al-mar'a*. Cairo: United Nations Democracy Fund.

Moustafa, T. 2000. "Conflict and Cooperation between the State and Religious Institutions in Contemporary Egypt." *International Journal of Middle East Studies* 32 (1): 3–22.

Mubarak, G. 2009. "We Need Audacious Leaders." *Middle East Quarterly* 16 (1); translated from *Politique Internationale*, 10 July 2008. www.meforum.org/meq/issues/20901

Mujani, S., and W.R. Liddle. 2009. "Muslim Indonesia's Secular Democracy." *Asian Survey* 49 (4): 575–90.

Mukhopadhyay, M., and S. Meer. *Gender, Rights and Development: A Global Sourcebook*. The Netherlands: Royal Tropical Institute.

El-Naggar, A.E. 2009. "Economic Policy: From State Control to Decay and Corruption." In El-Mahdi and Marfleet 2009a, 34–50.

———. n.d. Interview. Frontline World, PBS TV. www.pbs.org/frontlineworld/stories/egypt804/interview/extended2.html

Naguib, M. 1984. *Kunt ra'isan li-Masr*. Cairo: al-Maktab al-Masri al-Hadith.

Needler, M.C. 1975. "Military Motivations in the Seizure of Power." *Latin American Research Review* 10 (3): 63–79.

Noble, P. 2008. "From Arab System to Middle Eastern System? Regional Pressures and Constraints." In *The Foreign Policies of Arab States: The Challenge of Globalization*, edited by B. Korany and A.E. Hilal Dessouki, 67–166. Cairo: American University in Cairo Press.

Nordlinger, E.A. 1977. *Soldiers in Politics: Military Coups and Governments*. Englewood Cliffs, NJ: Prentice-Hall, Inc.

O'Donnell, G., and P. Schmitter. 1986. *Transitions from Authoritarian Rule: Tentative Conclusions about Uncertain Democracies*. Baltimore: Johns Hopkins University Press.

Offe, C. 1990. "Reflections on the Institutional Self of Movement Politics: A Tentative Stage Model." In *Challenging the Political Order: New Social and Political Movements in Western Democracies*, edited by R.J. Dalton and M. Kuechler, 232–50. New York: Oxford University Press.

Oliver, P.E., J. Cadena-Roa, and K.D. Strawn. 2003. "Emerging Trends in the Study of Protest and Social Movements." In *Research in Political*

Sociology, vol. 12, edited by T. Buzell, L. Waldner, and B. Dobratz, 213–44. Amsterdam and Boston: JAI Press.

Organisation for Economic Co-operation and Development (OECD). 2010. *Business Climate Development Strategy. Egypt. Tax Policy*. December.

Pateman, C. 1988. *The Sexual Contract*. Stanford, CA: Stanford University Press.

Perlmutter, A. 1974. *Egypt: The Praetorian State*. New York: Transaction Publishers.

Perthes, V. 2002. *Geheime Gärten: Die neue arabische Welt*. Berlin: Siedler.

Petras, J. 1999. "NGOs: In the Service of Imperialism." *Journal of Contemporary Asia* 29 (4): 429–40.

Poggi, G. 2001. *Forms of Power*. Cambridge: Polity Press.

Population Council. 2010. "Survey of Young People in Egypt, Preliminary Report." February.

Posusney, M.P. 1997. *Labor and the State in Egypt: Workers, Unions, and Economic Restructuring*. New York: Columbia University Press.

Powell, J., and C. Thyne. 2011. "Global Instances of Coups from 1950 to 2010: A New Dataset." *Journal of Peace Research* 48 (2): 249–59.

Pratt, N. 2006. "Human Rights NGOs and the 'Foreign Funding Debate' in Egypt." In *Human Rights in the Arab World: Independent Voices*, edited by A. Chase and A. Hamzawy, 114–26. Philadelphia: University of Pennsylvania Press.

Przeworski, A. 1986. *Democracy and the Market*. Cambridge: Cambridge University Press.

Pye, L.W. 1962. "Armies in the Process of Political Modernization." In *The Role of the Military in Underdeveloped Countries*, edited by J.J. Johnson, 85–100. Princeton, NJ: Princeton University Press.

Quandt, W. 1981. *Saudi Arabia in the 1980s: Foreign Policy, Security, and Oil*. Washington, D.C.: The Brookings Institution.

Rabi', A.H. 2011. *Watha'iq 100 yawm 'ala thawrat 25 Yanayir*. Cairo: Al-Ahram Center for Political and Strategic Studies.

Rabie, M.A.S. 1992. *al-Dawr al-siyasi li-l-Azhar: 1952–1981*. Cairo: Center for Political Research and Studies.

Rapoport, D. 1982. "The Praetorian Army: Insecurity, Venality, and Impotence." In Kolkowicz and Korbonski 1982, 252–80.

Richards, A., and J. Waterbury. 1990. *A Political Economy of the Middle East: State, Class, and Economic Development*. Boulder, CO: Westview Press.

———. 1996. *A Political Economy of the Middle East*. 2nd ed. Boulder, CO: Westview Press.

Richter, T. 2007. "The Political Economy of Regime Maintenance in Egypt: Linking External Resources and Domestic Legitimation." In Schlumberger 2007, 177–94.

Ricks, T.E. 1998. *Making the Corps*. New York: Simon & Schuster.

Robinson, W.I. 1996. "Globalization, the World System, and 'Democracy Promotion' in U.S. Foreign Policy." *Theory and Society* 25 (5): 615–65.

Rueschemeyer, D., E.H. Stephens, and J.D. Stephens. 1992. *Capitalist Development and Democracy*. Chicago: University of Chicago Press.

Ruslow, D. 1970. "Transition to Democracy." *Comparative Politics* 2/3:337–63. Cited in Anderson 1999.

Rutherford, B. 2008. *Egypt after Mubarak*. Princeton, NJ: Princeton University Press.

Sadiki, L. 2000. "Popular Uprisings and Arab Democratization." *International Journal of Middle East Studies* 32 (1): 71–95.

———. 2007. *al-Bahth 'an dimuqratiya 'arabiya*. Beirut: Center for Arab Unity Studies.

Sadowski, Y.M. 1993. *Scuds or Butter: The Political Economy of Arms Control in the Middle East*. Washington, D.C.: The Brookings Institution.

Said, E. 1978. *Orientalism*. London: Pantheon Books.

Salame, G., ed. 1994. *Démocracies sans démocrats*. Paris: Fayard.

Salehi-Isfahani, D., and N. Dhillon. 2008. "Stalled Youth Transitions in the Middle East: A Framework for Policy Reform." The Middle East Youth Initiative Working Paper 8. October.

Sallam, H. 2011. "Striking Back at Egyptian Workers." *Middle East Report* 259:20–25.

al-Sayyid, M.K. 2009. "Kefaya at a Turning Point." In Hopkins 2009, 45–59.

Schlumberger, O. 2000. "Arab Political Economy and the European Union's Mediterranean Policy: What Prospects for Development?" *New Political Economy* 5 (2): 247–68.

———, ed. 2007. *Debating Arab Authoritarianism: Dynamics and Durability in Nondemocratic Regimes*. Stanford, CA: Stanford University Press.

Schmitter, P.C. 1974. "Still the Century of Corporatism?" *Review of Politics* 36 (1): 85–131.

———. 2011. "Retrospective Wisdom from Twenty-five Years of Reflection on Transitions from and Consolidation of Democracy." Preliminary paper submitted to the conference "Transitions and the Egyptian Revolution," Cairo, 4–7 June.

Scott, J. 2009. *The Attack on the* Liberty: *The Untold Story of Israel's Deadly 1967 Assault on a U.S. Spy Ship.* New York: Simon & Schuster.

Seligman, A.B. 1992. *The Idea of Civil Society.* Princeton, NJ: Princeton University Press.

Shaaban, A.B.E. 2006. *Kifaya: Past and Future.* Cairo: Kifaya Publications.

Sharmani, M. 2011. "Pathways of Women's Empowerment." Unpublished analysis of personal status laws in Egypt.

Sharp, G. 2010. *From Dictatorship to Democracy: A Conceptual Framework for Liberation.* 4th U.S. ed. East Boston, MA: The Albert Einstein Institution.

Shatz, A. 2010. "Mubarak's Last Breath." *London Review of Books* 32 (10): 6–10.

Shawqi, B., and S. Soliman. 1998. "Tashrih iqtisadi ijtima'i li-l-tabaqa al-wusta al-misriya." *Ahwal misriya* 1 (1): 35–57.

Shehata, D. 2009. "Islamists and Non-Islamists in the Egyptian Opposition." In *Conflict, Identity, and Reform in the Muslim World: Challenges for U.S. Engagement,* edited by D. Brumberg and D. Shehata, pp. 309–26. Washington, D.C.: U.S. Institute of Peace Press.

———, ed. 2010. *'Awdat al-siyasa: al-harakat al-ihtijajiya fi Misr.* Cairo: Al-Ahram Center for Political and Strategic Studies.

———. 2011. "The Fall of the Pharaoh." *Foreign Affairs* 90 (3): 26–32.

Shobaky, A., ed. 2009. *al-Muwatana fi muwajahat al-ta'ifiya.* Cairo: Al-Ahram Center for Political and Strategic Studies.

Shobaky, A. 2010. "Protests of Real Estate Tax Civil Servants." In Shehata 2010, 171–212.

Sholkamy, H. 2008. "State and CSO Partnerships in Poverty Alleviation." *Egypt Human Development Report.* Cairo: UNDP.

———. 2009. "Gender and Population." In *Population Status in Egypt: International Conference on Population and Development (ICDP)@15 Report,* edited by H. Zaky, 22–36. Cairo: Egyptian Cabinet Information and Decision Support, Evidence-Based Population Policy and UNFPA.

———. 2010. "No Path to Power: Civil Society, State Services and the Poverty of City Women." *IDS Bulletin* 41 (2).

al-Shorbagy, M. 2010. "The Kefaya Movement: Redefining Politics in Egypt." In Shehata 2010, 111–42.

Shtauber, Z., and Y.S. Shapir. 2005. *The Middle East Military Balance, 2004–2005.* JCSS. Brighton: Sussex Academic Press.

Sims, D. 2010. *Understanding Cairo: The Logic of a City Out of Control.* Cairo: American University in Cairo Press.

Singerman, D., and P. Amar, eds. 2006. *Cairo Cosmopolitan: Politics, Culture, and Urban Space in the New Globalized Middle East.* Cairo: American University in Cairo Press.

Singh, B. 2000. "Civil–Military Relations in Democratizing Indonesia: Change Amidst Continuity." *Armed Forces & Society* 26 (4): 607–33.

Sirrs, O.L. 2010. *A History of the Egyptian Intelligence Service: A History of the Mukhabarat, 1910–2009.* New York: Routledge.

Siyyam, E. 2006. "Kifaya Movement." Unpublished paper.

Skocpol, T. 1979. *States and Social Revolutions.* Cambridge: Cambridge University Press.

Smith, R., ed. 1974. *Southeast Asia: Documents of Political Development and Change.* Ithaca, NY: Cornell University Press.

Snow, D., and R. Benford. 1992. "Master Frames and Cycles of Protest." In *Frontiers of Social Movements Theory,* edited by A. Morris and C. Mueller, 117–34. New Haven and London: Yale University Press.

Soliman, S. 1998. "State and Industrial Capitalism in Egypt." *Cairo Papers in Social Science* 21 (2).

———. 2006. *al-Musharaka al-siyasiya fi-l-intikhabat al-niyabiya 2005: al-'awa'iq wa-l-mutatallabat.* Cairo: The Egyptian Society for the Promotion of Social Participation, EU Commission.

———. 2011. *The Autumn of Dictatorship: Fiscal Crisis and Political Change in Egypt under Mubarak.* Stanford, CA: Stanford University Press.

Springborg, R. 1989. *Mubarak's Egypt: Fragmentation of the Political Order.* Boulder, CO: Westview Press.

Stacher, J. 2004. "Parties Over: The Demise of Egypt's Opposition Parties." *British Journal of Middle Eastern Studies* 31 (2): 215–33.

———. 2011. "Reinterpreting Authoritarian Power: Syria's Hereditary Succession." *Middle East Journal* 65 (2): 197–212.

State Information Service (SIS). www.sis.gov.eg/en

Sullivan, D., and K. Jones. 2007. *Egypt: Country Report.* Washington, D.C.: Freedom House. www.freedomhouse.org/uploads/ccr/country-7170-8.pdf

Tadros, M. 2009. "Vicissitudes in the Entente between the Coptic Orthodox Church and the State in Egypt (1952–2007)." *International Journal of Middle East Studies* 41:269–87.

———. 2010. "Between the Elusive and the Illusionary: Donors' Empowerment Agendas in the Middle East in Perspective." *Comparative Studies of South Asia, Africa and the Middle East* 30 (2): 224–37.

———. 2011. "Sectarianism and Its Discontents in Post-Mubarak Egypt." *Middle East Report* 259:26–31.

Tarrow, S. 1996a. "Social Movements and Contention Politics: A Review Article." *American Political Science Review* 90:312–26.

———. 1996b. "States and Opportunities: The Political Structuring of Social Movements." In *Comparative Perspectives on Social Movements: Political Opportunities, Mobilizing Structures, and Cultural Framings*, edited by D. McAdam, J.D. McCarthy, and M.N. Zald, 41–61. Cambridge: Cambridge University Press.

———. 1998. *Power in Movement: Social Movements, Collective Action, and Politics*. Cambridge: Cambridge University Press.

El-Tawila, S., et al. 2000. *The School Environment in Egypt: A Situation Analysis of Public Preparatory Schools*. Cairo: The Population Council (New York) and the American University in Cairo Social Research Center.

al-Tayyib, T. 1968. *al-Hall al-islami ma ba'd al-nakbatayn*. Cairo: al-Mukhtar al-Islami.

Teorell, J. 2010. *Determinants of Democratization: Explaining Regime Change in the World, 1972–2000*. Cambridge: Cambridge University Press.

Therborn, G. 1997. "The Rule of Capital and the Rise of Democracy." *New Left Review* 103:8–17.

Thompson, W.R. 1975. "Regime Vulnerability and the Military Coup." *Comparative Politics* 7 (4): 459–87.

Tibi, B. 1997. *Arab Nationalism: Between Islam and the Nation-State*. Houndmills: Palgrave Macmillan.

———. 1998. *The Challenge of Fundamentalism: Political Islam and the New World Disorder*. Berkeley: University of California Press.

Tilly, C. 1978. *From Mobilization to Revolution*. Reading, MA: Addison-Wesley.

———. 1990. *Coercion, Capital, and the European State, AD 990–1990*. New York: Basil.

———. 2007. *Democracy*. Cambridge: Cambridge University Press.

Tilly, C., L. Tilly, and R. Tilly. 1975. *The Rebellious Century*. Cambridge, MA: Harvard University Press.

Trager, E. 2011. "The Unbreakable Muslim Brotherhood: Grim Prospects for a Liberal Egypt." *Foreign Affairs* 90 (5): 114–26.

Trimberger, E.K. 1978. *Revolutions from Above: Military Bureaucrats and Development in Japan, Turkey, Egypt, and Peru*. Brunswick, NJ: Transaction Books.

Tucker, K. 1991. "How New Are the Social Movements?" *Theory, Culture & Society* 8 (2): 75–98.

Tugal, C. 2004. *Passive Revolution: Absorbing the Islamic Challenge to Capitalism.* Stanford: Stanford University Press.

Turner, V. 1969. *The Ritual Process: Structure and Anti-structure.* New Brunswick, NJ: Rutgers University Press.

———. 1974. *Dramas, Fields, and Metaphors: Symbolic Action in Human Society.* Ithaca, NY: Cornell University Press.

United Nations Development Programme (UNDP). 2010. *Arab Human Development Report 2009: Challenges to Security.* New York: UNDP.

———. 2010. *Egypt's Progress towards Achieving the MDGs.*

———. Forthcoming. *Arab Empowerment.* Tenth Anniversary special volume of the Arab Human Development Report. New York: UNDP.

Vagts, A. 1959. *A History of Militarism: Civilian and Military.* New York: Meridian Books.

Van Gennep, A. 1960. *The Rites of Passage.* Reprinted 2004. London: Routledge.

Vatikiotis, P.J. 1978. *Nasser and His Generation.* London: Croom Helm.

Vignal, L., and E. Denis. 2006. "Cairo as Regional/Global Economic Capital?" In Singerman and Amar 2006, 99–151.

Wahid, L. 2009. *Military Expenditure and Economic Growth in the Middle East.* New York: Palgrave Macmillan.

Webber, D. 2010. "A Consolidated Patrimonial Democracy? Democratization in Post-Suharto Indonesia." *Democratization* 17 (6).

Weiss, D., and U. Wurzel. 1998. *The Economics and Politics of Transition to an Open Market Economy.* Paris: Development Center at the OECD.

Wickham, C.R. 2002. *Mobilizing Islam: Religion, Activism and Political Change in Egypt.* New York: Columbia University Press.

Wiktorowicz, Q. 2000. "The Salafi Movement in Jordan." *International Journal of Middle East Studies* 32 (2): 219.

———, ed. 2004. *Islamic Activism: A Social Movement Theory Approach.* Bloomington: Indiana University Press.

Wollestonecraft, M. 1792. *A Vindication of the Rights of Women.* Online edition 1999: bartleby.com

Wolman, D. 2011. "The Techie Dissidents Who Showed Egyptians How to Organize." *The Atlantic,* 3 February. www.theatlantic.com/technology/archive2011/02

World Bank (WB). 1991. *Report and Recommendation of the President of the International Bank for Reconstruction and Development to the Executive Directors on a Proposed Structural Adjustment Loan to Egypt.* Washington, D.C.: World Bank.

Youssef, M.S. 1994. *Dawr al-mutasawiffa fi tarikh Misr fi-l-'asr al-'uthmani (1517–1798)*. Belbeis: Dar al-Taqwa li-l-Nashr wa-l-Tawzi'.

Zaghal, M. 1999. "Al-Azhar and Radical Islam." *International Journal of Middle East Studies* 31 (2): 371–99.

Zaki, R. 1997. *Wada'an li-l-tabaqa al-wusta: ta'ammulat fi-l-thawra al-sina'iya al-thaniya wa-l-libiraliya al-jadida*. Cairo: Dar al-Mustaqbal al-'Arabi.

Zayed, A. 2007. *Suwar min al-khitab al-dini al-mu'asir*. Cairo: al-'Ayn.

Zegart, A.B. 1999. *Flawed by Design: The Evolution of the CIA, JSC, and NSC*. Stanford, CA: Stanford University Press.

Zirakzadeh, C.E. 2006. *Social Movements in Politics: A Comparative Study*. Gordonsville, VA: Palgrave Macmillan.

Index

succession 257, 258, 263; economic issues 45, 61, 236–37; mass protests 254; military 186, 187, 262–64, 269; monarchy 257, 269; neoliberal authoritarianism 58; persistency 8, 251; religion 64, 78; rentier revenues 55; resilient authoritarianism 2, 3, 7, 8, 232, 271, 288; *see also* Indonesia; republic

autocracy 167, 187, 231, 235, 246, 290, 291

al-Azhar University 65–68, 79–80, 126, 128–29, 143, 146; 25 January Revolution 137–38, 146; al-Azhar Document 79; Gomaa, Ali 143; legitimacy 141; *Majalet al-Azhar* 70–71; modernization 65–66; NDP 67; state/Church/al-Azhar/Islamist movements interaction 3, 64, 68, 70, 78, 80; state control over 65–66, 70, 128–29, 150; state, role and nature 142, 144, 151; women, 172; *see also* Islam; Islamist movements

B

Bahrain 1, 236, 255, 257, 262, 263, 271, 283

Ba'thism 275, 284

Battle of the Camel 88, 216, 261; *see also* 25 January Revolution

Bayat, Asef 10, 13, 67, 135

al-Bayoumi, M. 70–71

Bishara, Dina 3, 83–103

Boutros Ghali, Youssef 21, 50, 54

bread riots 2, 32, 110

C

Camp David Accord 194, 230, 284

Carapico, Sheila 4, 199–22

Center for Applied Non-Violent Action and Strategies (CANVAS) 200, 210–11

Center for Trade Union and Workers' Services (CTUWS) 87, 94, 99

civil society 4, 9–10, 32, 64, 199–222, 267, 286; civil society promotion 199–201, 202, 205–209, 220, 221; concept 203–205, 220; contentious politics 202; democracy promotion 4, 199; 'donor-driven' civil society 201–202, 205–208, 220; framing 12, 201–202, 220; gender issues 156, 157, 166, 167, 170, 173; 'home-grown/organic' revolution 4, 220–21; nonviolent resistance 209–11, 214; 'people-centered' civil society 202, 217; 'professionalization' 202; western support 199–209, 218; *see also* 25 January Revolution; civil society organizations; Middle East Partnership Initiative; non-governmental organizations

civil society organizations (CSOs) 4, 201, 206–208, 285–86; 'GNGOs' 286; *see also* civil society

collective action 10, 12, 39, 92, 99, 165, 166, 174; communication action 12

Committee of Wise Men, 120

Constitution: 1882 Constitution 227; 1923 Constitution 227; 1956 Constitution 227; 1958 Constitution 227; 1963 Constitution 227; 1971 Constitution 162, 228, 231; constitutionalism 225, 226, 228, 232, 240, 241; Provisional Constitution of the Arab Republic of Egypt 240; *see also* constitutional reform

O

Olson, Mancur 10

opposition 32–38, 39, 61, 119, 252, 267; elections 22, 23, 24; exclusion 22, 24, 38–39, 135; *see also* Muslim Brotherhood

P

Palestine 201, 205–206

Palestinian Intifada 9, 14, 32, 105, 109, 133; Egyptian Popular Committee for the Support of the Palestinian Intifada (EPCSPI) 109–10, 111, 117, 118

Pan-Arabism 275, 283–85; Ba'thism 275, 284; cultural togetherness 284–85; League of Arab States 284; Nasserism 275, 284; New Pan-Arabism 275, 284; state-based pan-Arabism 275, 284

People's Assembly 18, 50, 98; elections 21, 23, 30, 57; *see also* political system

police: corruption 19–20, 56; inflation 56; Military Police 181; torture 20, 37; violence 11, 18, 19–20, 24, 32, 37–38, 56, 119, 181, 203, 212, 216, 285; *see also* security forces

political economy 3, 8–9, 43–62, 253; economic planning 43–44; from semi-rentier state to tax state 43, 47, 54–55, 61; national deficit 45, 46; public debt 48–49, 50, 52; 'state revenues/political character of state' relationship 8–9, 55, 61; *see also* economic issues; tax system

political system 18, 57, 78, 290–91; businessmen in politics 20–21, 57–58, 62, 258–59; concentrated power 18–19, 21, 22–23, 38, 50; corruption 18, 20–21, 28–29, 38, 259, 274; nepotism 20–21, 36, 38, 73, 76, 223, 238, 257, 258, 263; political alternatives 36; *see also* elections; government; National Democratic Party; People's Assembly

politicization 291, 292; military 38, 177–79, 228, 230, 263; military, depoliticization 224, 244, 248; Salafi movement 78, 126, 130, 140; Sufi orders 142

'politics from above' 8, 9, 14, 271, 274, 288

'politics from below' 2, 8, 9, 156, 271, 274, 283, 287, 293

Populist Unionist Party (PUP) 114

post-revolution period 268; 19 March referendum 122; al-Azhar Document 79; democracy 62; divisions between political activists 121–22, 123, 264–66, 267–68; gender issues 168–71, 173–74; Islamist movements 126, 136, 142–47; labor mobilization 98, 101; new parties 267–68, 294; social movements 77–78, 79; tax system 62; youth movements 121–23, 285; *see also* military transition period

poverty 27–28, 223, 254, 274; impoverishment 46, 253; rich/poor divide 30–32, 253; women, 165, 172; *see also* wealth

protest movement 1, 2, 9, 75, 76, 153, 253, 262, 272, 273, 292; characteristics 292; economic issues 253–56; fear to protest 32, 33, 115, 285; results 283; street protests 32–33; suppression by government 26,

tax 47–48, 52; Real Estate Tax
Authority 94–96; sales tax 47, 50–52;
tax collectors' demonstration 35, 86,
94; tax evasion 53–54; tax on workers
abroad 51–52; taxpayer 56; *see also*
economic issues; political economy
terrorism 130
torture 20, 25, 37, 112, 130
trade unions 35, 60, 84, 86, 88, 89,
94, 101; Center for Trade Union
and Workers' Services 87, 94, 99;
Egyptian Federation of Independent Trade Unions 95; Independent
Union of the Real Estate Tax
Authority 94–96; *see also* Egyptian
Trade Unions Federation
transition period, challenges 5, 275,
288–91; *see also* military transition
period
transitology 201, 212, 220, 275, 288, 294
Tunisia 119, 211, 255, 257, 262, 271; Ben
Ali, Zine El Abidine 1, 38, 130, 135,
137, 223, 263, 275; Bouazizi, Muhammad 107, 136, 211, 273
Turkey 269–70, 278
Turner, V. 154–55

U
Ultras 11
unemployment 31, 38, 58, 223, 274, 284;
youth 31, 73, 107–108
United States 230, 239; Indonesia
234–35, 239; invasion of Iraq 32,
75, 109, 110, 133, 258, 284; military
188–90, 197, 201, 224, 230, 246;
non-governmental organizations
199–200, 232; Obama, Barack 224,
239; USAID 200, 208, 209

universities 25, 33, 38, 118; 9 March
movement 32, 33, 77; freedom of
faculty and students 33, 77, 117, 118

V
Van Gennep, A. 154
violence 271; against journalists 24,
34; authoritarianism 252, 254,
260, 262, 264; Indonesia 4, 224,
234; military 181, 195, 248; *see also*
police; security force

W
al-Wafd Party 22, 23, 24, 114, 120, 267
Wahhabism 129, 132, 150
wealth 27–28, 235; concentration of
27–30, 76; corruption 21, 28–30;
redistribution of 203, 221; rich/poor
divide 30–32, 253; *see also* corruption; poverty
'We Are All Khaled Said' 37–38, 105,
109, 116–17, 119, 212, 286; Said,
Khaled 37, 116, 212–13
women 4, 153–74; 25 January Revolution 153–54, 167–68; blogging
167–68; Convention on the
Elimination of All Forms of
Discrimination against Women
160, 164; education 107, 172; Islam
72, 73, 161–62, 293; labor mobilization 166–67; old regime agenda
4, 156; political exclusion 72, 125;
poverty 165, 172; sexual harassment
of 32, 167, 168; UN Women 160,
169; women's empowerment 158,
160, 162, 170; *see also* feminism;
gender issues; National Council of
Women; women's rights